*Women in Ancient America*

# Women in Ancient America

Karen Olsen Bruhns and Karen E. Stothert

UNIVERSITY OF OKLAHOMA PRESS : NORMAN

**Library of Congress Cataloging-in-Publication Data**

Bruhns, Karen Olsen.
    Women in ancient America    /    Karen Olsen Bruhns and Karen E.
Stothert.
        p.    cm.
    Includes bibliographical references and index.
    ISBN 0-8061-3169-1 (cloth)
    1. Indian women.    2. America—Antiquities.    3. Sex role—America.
I. Stothert, Karen E.    II. Title.
E59.W8B78    1999
305.48'897073—dc21                                                            99-16368
                                                                                        CIP

Text design by Gail Carter.

To TW and NM

and to the memory of Olaf Holm and Presley Norton

# Contents

# Figures

# *Preface*

The goal of archaeology is to describe and understand prehistoric peoples and their cultures. Those of us who are teachers want to feel confident that the ancient cultures and societies we discuss in class have been reconstructed responsibly from the existing evidence. We aspire to present interpretations that are well balanced and free from obvious biases. These goals are probably shared by most archaeologists practicing and teaching today, yet the authors, like most students of our generation, were taught archaeology as part of an anthropology that was shaped by an androcentric model of the universe.

Many of us began to question these models during graduate school in the 1960s and 1970s. Questions of gender were not among the important intellectual concerns of that time, but our questions have initiated a degendering of the past, and scholars are now beginning to look at female roles in human and nonhuman societies in the past and in the present. In American archaeology, this approach has been carried out most successfully in cases where there are historic documents, especially in studies of peoples whose cultures were affected by contact with European cultures during the early centuries of foreign domination. However, it has begun to spread into prehistoric studies and the interpretation of the archaeological record.

We began to teach engendered archaeology in the 1990s because of personal convictions that any science that built its norms on the behavior or physical characteristics of only one segment of society (men) was scientifically and morally irresponsible. We began to teach the archaeology of gender as a response to what Margaret Ehrenberg, in her preface to *Women in Prehistory*, calls the "ignorant and undiscriminating use of archaeological evidence" as seen daily in the entertainment media and in textbooks. Yet most archaeologists are also chagrined by the misuse of the past in women's studies literature and in programs that pretend to train feminists. For example, the Goddess Movement and its paraphernalia testify to a recently created myth of the human past that is as dubious as any androcentric one. Sadly, the Goddess Movement has the potential to damage women's aspirations as it further trivializes women and women's endeavors in the perception of many. Far from empowering women, as it claims, it may marginalize them. Although archaeological sites and ancient American deities have been appropriated by the Goddess Movement and other cults, archaeological remains can be used in other ways to responsibly serve the needs of our students, our society, and ourselves.

As we both began to select appropriate materials for teaching engendered courses, we found useful articles in mainstream archaeological publications and edited volumes, but we saw the need for synthetic works outlining the problems and presenting some of the research that has been done on those problems.

Our book is an introduction to the study of women in the American past. Because American peoples were separated from those of Eurasia and Africa between the Upper Paleolithic and the end of the fifteenth century, their cultures developed in different ways. Many of the interpretations made on the basis of Eurasian cultures do not apply in the Americas. The order of cultural development in the Old World was not repeated in many places in the New World where metal was worked before pottery was invented, where civilization developed without urban settlements, and where conquest states were possible without draft animals, wheeled vehicles, or writing. In the two worlds, people developed social and theological systems separately. Thus it is not surprising that the relations between women and men and the ideologies that validate those relations were somewhat different as well.

Most standard treatments of the prehistory of the Americas have neglected aspects of human activity that, since the feminist revolution, are receiving more attention. These areas include childbearing and child rearing, family and household structure, food processing and other domestic technologies, and gender relations in all areas, including religion, art, politics, and economics. It is clear that in order to understand the lives of individuals, the dynamics of groups, the nature of societies, the functioning of cultural and ecological systems, and the trajectory of history, one needs to take into account the dimension of gender. Gender has been an important dynamic in human life since earliest times, and despite the androcentric inclinations of academics, it is now our responsibility to consider the activities of both women and men in any archaeological, anthropological, or historical study.

In the following pages we reverse the normal tone of archaeological reconstruction, which has been to emphasize and to value the activities of men above those of women, in the hope of providing a means of viewing American societies more equitably. We have tried to describe a wide variety of indigenous American societies. Although we have done some engendering and revisionist interpretation from original site reports, in practical terms we have been restricted to a consideration of those cultures for which engendered archaeological investigations have been undertaken and reported by our colleagues. In addition, we have interpreted in some depth societies with representational art styles and others for which we have historical data. Our work focuses upon well-studied culture areas, such as Mesoamerica and the Andean region, and upon the more complex societies of North America. We also favor the late prehistoric and early historic societies because of the existence of native and European documents concerning aspects of these cultures that are difficult to infer from the archaeological record. Despite the biases and deficiencies of such documents, they remain invaluable tools for engendering the Conquest-period societies and interpreting some late prehistoric cultures. The recent decipherment of the precolumbian Maya writing system has provided valuable information, giving us the first real voices from deep prehistory.

A synthesis of prehistory can be only as good and complete as the research and interpretation upon which it draws. Women still do not figure in most interpretations of the archaeological record, but there is a growing number of gender-conscious studies of Native American societies: the authors of these studies help us to see ancient societies as composed of human beings engaged in human activities. We extend our deepest thanks to all of our colleagues who are undertaking fieldwork to answer questions involving gender and who are reevaluating their data and building societal models that include both females and males as actors. Their work is cited in our bibliography.

We would like to thank especially the following people who generously contributed advice, information, illustrations, and encouragement to this project: John Drayton; Tom Weller, computer expert, illustrator, and inspiration; Neil Maurer, computer artist, photographer, and helpmate; Barbara Stark and the Committee on the Status of Women of the Society for American Archaeology; Jim Burton and the COSWA-list colleagues; the late Olaf Holm; and the following people who helped with illustrations and/or information: Wes Christensen; Tom Cummins; Jonathan Damp; Jane Day; Tom Dillehay; Christopher Donnan; Virginia Fields; Ana Maritza Freire; Anne Galloway; David Grove; Margaret A. Hoyt; the late Wesley Hurt; Todd Howell; Alice Kehoe; Jane Kelley; Patricia J. Lyon; Jorge Marcos; Geoffrey and Sharisse McCafferty; Donna McClelland; Roberta McGregor; Richard McReynolds; Dorothy Menzel; Virginia E. Miller; Chuck Maurer (Command P); Raphael X. Reichert; Mario Rivera; John H. Rowe; Payson D. Sheets; Helaine Silverman; Arelyn Simon; David Starbuck; Theresa Lange Topic; John Topic; the late Adan Treganza; Sue Turner; Dwight Wallace; Yoshiko Yamamoto; and James Zeidler. Thanks are also due to the Bancroft Library, University of California, Berkeley; the British Museum; the Field Museum of Natural History, Chicago; the Los Angeles County Museum of Art; the Los Angeles County Museum of Natural History, La Brea Tar Pits; the Museum of Western Colorado; the National Museum of Natural History, Smithsonian Institution; the Treganza Museum of Anthropology, San Francisco State University; the University Museum, University of Pennsylvania; and the Witte Museum, San Antonio, Texas.

*Women in Ancient America*

# CHAPTER ONE

# *Women and Gender*

Archaeology is the means by which we understand the human past. While the concept of humanity embodies both women and men, women rarely appear in accounts of human history. Because our society uses the results of archaeological studies to validate its myths of origin, it is unacceptable to write histories that omit women and their perspectives. They must be included because women and girls constitute half of humanity, and their participation in and contributions to the course of history were distinct from those of men and boys.

Human societies are made up of females and males in approximately equal numbers, and women and men of the same population overlap with respect to height and weight unless one sex is seriously underfed or otherwise stressed because of cultural practices. Moreover, observing human biological patterns leads biologists to expect similarities in women's and men's strategies in feeding and other social activities. For instance, with respect to mating strategies, Sarah Blaffer Hrdy has observed that sexual dimorphism among humans indicates that both females and males are likely to maximize reproductive success through multiple mates: they are both mildly polygamous. This lack of difference between males and females is frequently obscured by the multiplicity of values and cultural stratagems that different societies overlay onto these basic biological aspects of humanity—that is to say, gender.

Gender is a social script designed arbitrarily on the basis of a biological fact. While a person may feel that the gender system she grew up with is completely natural and universal, the arbitrariness of such systems is demonstrated by the fact that they change through time, often even in a lifetime, and are variable across space. Recently anthropologists have begun to investigate cultural constructs of gender, discovering how gender affects every individual's participation in society. Scholarly research has begun to reflect the fact that gender is a crucial factor in all social life and in history. Engendering the past involves placing the missing half of humanity back into those scientific studies and andro-centric narratives, which so often have omitted women and ignored those aspects of life associated with them.

In the last decade, feminists have raised our consciousness about gender and history by drawing attention to the persistent pattern of exclusion of women from many highly valued areas of social life. This pattern is noted within the fields of anthropology and archaeology, where studies of the activities of men have been emphasized routinely and valued above those of women. Male behavior has defined the norm. Today many inadequate narratives that pretend to describe universal human patterns are presented as science but are really our own just-so stories. We should all be aware that other societies, past and present, have fostered different values and different stories, ones in which women's and men's roles are surprising to us, and that the historical narratives generated by other cultures are different from those of the Euro-american–Western Asian religious and cultural tradition.

Ethnographic studies of groups unaffected by European influences show that many of our common-sense ideas about the "natural and universal" division of labor are not present. For instance, hunting, defined in our society as a quintessential male activity, figures prominently in our scientific myths of origin. We are surprised to find that among the Agta of the Philippines, it is natural for women to hunt. Indeed, cross-cultural studies reveal many examples of female hunters: aboriginal women hunt kangaroos with dogs in Australia, and indigenous women hunt coop-eratively with their husbands in South America. A Mimbres woman (fig. 1.1), great with child and bearing an antelope, may be a hunter.

Ethnographic and archaeological evidence demonstrates that patterns of human behavior are tremendously variable and often run against both Western folk wisdom and our common-sense interpretations of human nature. Sifting through the data concerning women in the corpus of male-focused scientific studies, we begin to see that many of our assump-tions concerning normal behaviors are ethnocentric and untenable.

Because gender has always been a key dynamic of human life, scholars must consider the activities of both women and men if they hope to

---

FIGURE 1.1. ■ The painted image on this Mimbres bowl, which portrays a woman great with child and transporting an antelope, celebrates the hunting prowess of a real or a mythical woman.

understand history. Looking at Murdock's 1950 classic *Outline of Cultural Materials*, a list of over 800 aspects of culture studied by anthropologists, one can appreciate how behavior varies by gender as well as by time, mode of economic production, and social organization. For example, Topic 27, "Drink, Drugs, and Indulgence," has the following subheadings: water and thirst; nonalcoholic beverages; alcoholic beverages; beverage industries; drinking establishments; narcotics and stimulants; tobacco; and pharmaceuticals.

How do women and men participate in these aspects of culture? Who owns the water? Fetches it? Drinks it? What is the meaning of consumption? There are as many answers as there are groups of human beings, and in each case, women may differ from men of the same community with respect to ideas and practices related to the drinking of water. Similarly, ask, "Who brews the beer?" In the Andean region of South America, brewing has historically been women's sacred/ceremonial work. In the adjacent Amazon lowlands, some men brew, and women and men both drink. Who grows the tobacco? Who uses it and when, and for what reasons? Tobacco is part of a complex of sacred, medicinal, and ceremonial practices in some societies; in others, it is a secular, personal indulgence. In some societies, both women and men smoke, in others only men, and among others this has changed in knowable history. Who is the expert in the preparation and use of medicines? In Colonial North America, it was women. Later men dominated medicine and pharmacy and forced women out, while today many women have reentered those fields. Examining each aspect of culture with curiosity concerning women's and men's roles and ideologies is the key to creating a more dynamic and detailed understanding of humankind.

## What Do Archaeologists Do?

Archaeologists use scientific methods to recover, analyze, and interpret archaeological evidence. The goal is to reconstruct social life in the past. Archaeological interpretation depends both upon scientific technologies and the theories and ideologies that affect social description and history. Archaeologists control an immense arsenal of techniques for excavating and analyzing the remains of human activity. Today, archaeological materials are dated by a large number of means, soils are analyzed to give evidence of plants once used in the ancient context, artifacts are analyzed to reveal the point of origin of the primary material, multivariate analysis and DNA studies of the remains of human bodies reveal origins of the group and kinship patterns within it, and even feces are tested to show the diet and the sex of the person who defecated. The amount of data that can result from an archaeological analysis of evidence is astounding in its quantity and variety. However, the usefulness of these raw data is determined by the body of theory that guides scientific interpretation.

## The Role of Theory in Engendering the Past

All scientific research is governed by theory and by the specific historic and social circumstances that dictate what is useful and desirable to investigate—which data should be gathered, which interpreted, and which ignored. Theory links archaeology to the wider fields of scientific endeavor, social thought, and history, and makes archaeology subject to the waves of fashion in the broader community of scholars. Archaeology has utilized evolutionary theory, ecological theory, structuralist and functionalist thought, Marxist models, and, most recently, postmodern and feminist theories.

In practice, Americanist archaeology employs an eclectic theoretical framework, but it always depends heavily upon historical and ethnographic analogies for constructing models and making interpretations. Almost all archaeological models are formulated on the basis of the variations of human societies in history or in the ethnographic present. If there is evidence of a continuity between a prehistoric people and the historic ones in a region, then the direct historical approach may serve the archaeologist, although the reconstruction of the prehistoric past using models drawn from the historic period may be flawed by the fact that cultures are subject to dramatic change in conquest and colonial situations.

General analogical thinking is the basis for archaeological imagining, but this thinking is limited because, even taken together, the known historical cases and the entire body of ethnographic description do not cover the entire range of human cultural potential. Another problem with thinking analogically when doing engendered interpretations of the past is that archaeologists, despite their best intentions, project their under-standing of their own society onto other cultural contexts. For example, during the nineteenth and twentieth centuries, social scientists have tended to view women's and men's spheres as distinct, and women's sphere as intrinsically of lesser value. Writers in the materialist science tradition of the industrial age have viewed women as having fewer and less interesting economic opportunities. Similarly, the social scientists who carried out the ethnographic observations upon which archaeologists base their thinking frequently omitted women as sources of information, neglected to observe what women actually did, and failed to consider women as significant actors in public affairs. Anthropological research has perpetuated stereo-types concerning women's motivations, creativity, organizational capa-cities, political interests, and economic activities. The credible reconstruc-tion of past societies is hampered by the uncritical use of anthropological research that ignores the female half of humankind.

Feminism appeared in anthropological fieldwork only about two decades ago and has not yet affected significantly the androcentric data base utilized by archaeologists. Many archaeologists continue to labor with a distorted understanding of human societies, which developed because researchers focused upon social institutions outside the household in which males often predominate. Archaeologists and ethnographers frequently show more interest in the extra-household activities of the elite sectors of past societies, studying the organization of public institutions and generating an overly masculinized view of society. Anthropologists and archaeologists inadvertently have defined women as nonparticipants. If only certain institutions are taken as the measure of employment and leadership, then female activities and groups with female participants are trivialized. This dichotomy between the formal and public, on the one hand, and the informal and private, on the other, may be an artifact of the field investigator's predisposition, not an accurate reflection of social reality.

While many societies in the recent past and present were/are characterized by gender-based hierarchies in which males seem to dominate in many areas of human activity, other types of societies, which demonstrate greater parity between women and men, predominated earlier in history. In reality, the relationships between women and men in past and present societies are as variable across cultures as any other aspects of human behavior.

There is no single ethnographic model of the future society to which feminists aspire, but it is useful to imagine and work toward a community life in which there is sexual equality and a division of labor without an ideology that stereotypes the social, political, and economic activities of one sex as important and those of the other sex as trivial. The aspirations of modern women do find support in anthropological evidence. Ethnographic studies show social contexts in which women form work groups and alliances that operate independently of men, and they show economic networks managed by women that control materials, create opportunities, achieve political goals, and meet challenges.

For people of Western cultural heritage or those converted to the cultural and religious ideologies of the West, it is often difficult to imagine women in any of these ways. Nevertheless, in the past there were societies in which women's economic contributions were valued and celebrated by the society at large. Before colonization, in many parts of the world there were institutions that fostered women's economic networks outside the household. Women in such societies engaged in reciprocal exchanges and mutual assistance outside their immediate family groups. Because such societies are present in recent times, it behooves archaeologists to consider the proposition that similar organizations may have existed in ancient contexts and that material remains could well reflect gynocentric organizations.

Anthropology and ethnographic models provide archaeologists with grounds for making interpretations that differ fundamentally from those based on the western Asian–European ideological system. It is imperative that archaeologists consider alternative models of sex roles and relations rather than relying on what has been termed the "direct ethnocentric approach." Thus, in the reconstruction of past societies, archaeologists might draw upon appropriate models from among historical and contemporary non-Western societies in which there is a greater parity between the sexes than that existing in the public sector of Euroamerican society. One model of parity can be derived from ethnographic studies of foragers among whom there is only minimal divisions of labor along sexual lines, and among whom sexual hierarchy is not very important because no individual systematically makes decisions for anyone else. Such models need to be considered as the archaeologist interprets the remains of past foraging societies and imagines how these societies became more complex.

Another model of parity can be seen among the Iroquois and Huron, groups in which sex roles were clearly marked and differentiated, but not obviously ranked. In such societies, women and men are believed to be very different, but both make key economic contributions, both have equally valued roles, and both exercise power. Women and men in such societies control their own sexuality and labor, and both have strategies for achieving their self-defined goals. They both participate in decision making, allocation of resources, and negotiating social values. Interdependence between the sexes in these societies is high.

The study of these societies presents us with alternatives to androcentric interpretations. In order to write a responsible prehistory of America, it is imperative to adopt an engendered viewpoint, putting women and men alike into the narratives of the past. To understand social dynamics and social evolution we must model how the two sexes divided labor, created serviceable ideologies, negotiated leadership, and managed change. What women and men did in any particular past cultural context cannot be assumed because women's and men's roles are not fixed, but vary with time, space, and culture. The activities and roles of women and men should be assessed case by case as the archaeological record is interpreted. Even when the evidence of such reconstruction is thin, scholars may still productively and responsibly imagine the lives and values of female and male people if they reject androcentric stereotypes.

## Studying Women and Men Archaeologically

If men are knowable in the archaeological record, women must be knowable as well. Finding women and men in the archaeological record depends on the skill and imagination of archaeologists, but they can be identified with greatest confidence by the study of human physical remains and the analysis of art. Human skeletons reveal what ancient individuals were like, and they enable anthropologists to ascertain ancient diet, activities, and health histories. The investigation of relationships between skeletons and tomb offerings and other cultural contexts results in hypotheses about gender roles, kin patterns, and other aspects of culture. While the excavation and analysis of human remains has been interdicted in North America because of the beliefs of some Native American groups, such research is welcomed by people in most Latin American countries. In another approach to the identification of women and men, the study of art helps archaeologists to flesh out a picture of the past because artistic representations of people communicate ideas about their economic, political, and religious activities.

## The Interpretation of Physical Remains

Human remains are best preserved by extreme aridity or constant cold or wet conditions, situations that are rare. At most sites, only bones and teeth are preserved for archaeologists, and their recovery is impeded by decomposition, vandalism, scavenging activities, and cultural practices associated with the disposal of the dead.

Given a fairly well-preserved skeleton, researchers can tell the sex of the deceased, and they can address questions about the health and mortality of women, men, and young people, or members of particular social groups. The proper excavation of human skeletons involves the measurement of the bones while they are still in their original positions, the identification of the osteological materials by a specialist, the sampling of soil from around the body for pollen and phytolith analysis, and fine screening of burial soils to recover small bones, fragments, and fetal remains.

Because humans are sexually dimorphic, skeletal remains may be identified by sex. Female pelves are wider and more bowl shaped than those of males, and the sciatic notch is relatively open in females and closed in males. Similarly, the preauricular sulcus in most female skeletons is marked by a pronounced groove. Finally, the proportion of the ischium to the pubis is distinct in males and females. With respect to each of these features, the difference between males and females is a matter of degree, so one can be confident of an identification only by evaluating several features. Females tend to be more gracile (slighter) and males more robust, although there can be considerable variation in individual size within a population. Female skulls and mandibles normally are smaller, their orbits more rounded, the supra orbital ridge less marked, the mastoid process less massive, and the nuchal crest unmarked by heavy muscle attachments. Again, these are matters of degree within a given population, and one cannot use any one feature to tell sex with certainty.

It is difficult to tell females and males apart on osteological evidence alone until individuals reach sexual maturity between ages twelve and fourteen. Various approaches, including DNA methodologies, have been suggested to sex the remains of young children, but these have not generated much confidence and are not available to all researchers.

Archaeologists also study physical remains to determine individuals' age at death. This is the first step toward answering questions about whether men and women had different mortality profiles. Aging children's skeletons is relatively easy because the eruption rates of teeth are fairly standard across our species. One can determine the age of the child at death by observing which teeth had developed. Aging adult skeletons depends upon the wear and general state of the teeth, the closure of cranial sutures, the amount of ossification in the long bones, and wear and tear on the skeleton. This allows adults to be sorted into age categories with some confidence.

Many factors impinge upon human life expectancy, including genetic propensities that affect survivorship, the prevalence of parasites and disease, the quality of diet, and other cultural practices (such as warfare). Gender is often a significant factor in determining the life expectancy of individuals in particular societies because females and males have different life experiences.

In studying ancient skeletal populations, researchers identify certain bioindicators of stress that can be useful in the reconstruction of women's and men's lives in a particular time and culture. Malnutrition and episodes of severe illness will leave clear skeletal indications. Common osteological indicators of stress are porotic hyperostosis and cribra orbitalia. Both cause lesions of the cranium. Affected persons probably suffered from one of several anemias. Studies of prehistoric populations in Mexico and Central America have shown that this condition occurred among agricultural peoples whose staple crop was maize and whose diet did not include much animal protein. Maize-dependent populations may be characterized by a high incidence of porotic hyperostosis among children three to five years old. The first period of great risk for the new generation is just after birth; the second is at weaning, when anemia may contribute directly to ill health and inhibit the digestive system from absorbing nutrients precisely when the weanling is being exposed to parasites and microbes in the food and water. Children from past societies who evidence severe porotic hyperostosis often show lesions of the bone, indicating the presence of infection, as well. In traditional societies throughout the world where both anemia and infections are common, weanling death rates are high.

Harris lines and enamel hypoplasia are other common indications of episodic stress, including a number of nutritional problems and diseases. Harris lines are traverse marks that can be seen in X-ray photographs of the growing ends of human long bones, and enamel hypoplasia produces visible, horizontal grooves or lines on the teeth. Both types of lines are caused by growth resuming after a period in which development was slowed or stopped because of disease, malnutrition, or physical restriction.

Because bone is a dynamic system and is constantly affected by remodeling through growth, its condition is an indicator of health. Cortical thickness increases through childhood in a healthy individual then remains relatively stable until the fourth decade of life, when bone mass decreases. Caloric and protein malnutrition can affect cortical thickness and cause premature aging of the bones. Young women who are chronically underfed will lose cortical thickness dramatically due to pregnancy and lactation. Skeletal evidence from Teotihuacán (see chapter 5) shows little infant growth in the last months of gestation, evidence that the health and nutritional status of the mothers was so poor that fetal bone development was retarded.

These and other indicators can be used to show differential stress on a population. Specific signs of aging and other skeletal modifications caused by work habits also show on bones and teeth, and these can be studied as indicators of the tasks performed by women and men. Evidence of trauma, such as broken bones and accelerated arthritis, is also useful in assessing a population. The high rate of physical trauma in the skeletons of children and male adults sacrificed in the Sacred Well of Chichén Itzá show that they were probably slaves who were expendable because of infirmity.

Pregnancy and rape may also cause indications of trauma that are specific to women. It has been suggested that certain scars on a female pelvis may correlate with the number of pregnancies experienced by the woman, but these scars have little diagnostic value because pregnancy does not always result in scars. Moreover, such scars can be can be caused by pelvic inflammatory disease and other conditions.

Forcible rape has not often been reported from archaeological contexts, although it is often practiced by soldiers, bandits, and others in a variety of social settings. If death occurs within a relatively short time after a violent rape, distinctive physical traumas can be observed on the skeleton. The presence of this uncommon trauma could provide evidence of social customs or ideologies that involved violence against women.

Physical anthropology supplies excellent tools for the study of human remains, but osteological analysis and interpretation requires expert knowledge. Regrettably, sexing frequently is done by untrained excavators who ignore the skeleton and base their identification upon cultural associations or unfounded assumptions. In the following case, despite professional identification of the ancient skeleton, some scholars were loath to recognize a high-ranking Maya woman.

## The Lady of Altar de Sacrificios

The archaeological site known as Altar de Sacrificios is located on the Pasión River in the jungle of Guatemala. Excavations there in the 1960s were notable in that the team included Frank Saul, a specialist in the analysis of human skeletal remains. Among the palaces, plazas, and temples of Altar were found 136 burials containing the remains of 144 people. Of the 69 skeletons that could be sexed, only 38 were associated with grave offerings, mainly pottery and other nonperishable artifacts. In the published analysis of the excavations, the excavators noted that 61 of the vessels were found in male graves and 37 in female graves. Of 21 sexed burials in which pottery vessels protected the head of the skeleton, 11 were male and 10 female and 4 males and 3 females had jade in their mouths. Ten females and 10 males had cranial deformation, and 9 males and 10 females had decorated teeth, both cosmetic alterations that were signs of high social status among the Maya.

From all of these data, Richard Adams and his colleagues concluded that in Maya society, men were valued more highly than women. Does the evidence really lead to this conclusion? The sample of burials is small, and in most cases neither females nor males have ceramic offerings. At Altar, 33 of the ceramic vessels come from two graves. In Burial 88, the simple interment of a middle-aged male, 18 plain ceramic vessels had been placed in the tomb, and archaeologists also recovered the remains of a ceramic and shell necklace, several green stone and shell beads, a bone pin, an obsidian bladelet, a rotted wooden object, and a mass of red pigment near the head. This was the second most elaborate burial found at Altar. In any ranking of burials in the Maya region, this would be considered the burial of an elite person, although probably not a ruler.

The other important tomb contained two female bodies. Burial 128, a woman in her early forties, was overlain by Burial 96, a woman in her late twenties. Burial 128 was placed in a specially constructed rectangular tomb within an existing temple platform. Tombs such as this were built only for the most important people in Maya society. The lady herself shows evidence of an upper-class upbringing: her head was modified artificially, and her upper teeth were inlaid with jade. The lady's offerings were far more lavish than those of any other person buried at Altar de Sacrificios. Many of the associated ceramics were elaborately decorated. The body had been laid out on a mat. A jade bead was placed in her mouth, and a *Spondylus* shell lay over that orifice. Covering her head and face were fragments of a fine red painted cloth under a tripod plate. She was buried with three necklaces: one of *Spondylus* beads, another of jadeite beads, and a third of green stuccoed ceramic beads, disks, and pendants. This last set had matching ear flares. She had another pair of jadeite ear flares and some mother of pearl beads. The lady was also buried with her carved and painted slate-back mirror (the reflecting surface was made of pyrite mosaic) and a small pottery mask. In addition there was a group of broken stingray spines, 4 with carved hieroglyphs on them, which may have been contained in a bag that hung from her belt. Excavators found another group of 17 stingray spines by her right knee. Three obsidian blades and a core were also placed with her, and some 900 flint chips were found scattered in the tomb.

The Lady of Altar did not go to the underworld alone. Above her in a separate cyst tomb was another woman, Burial 96, an apparent sacrifice. This young woman also enjoyed elite status, judging from her artificially deformed skull and her decorated teeth. She was laid on her back and accompanied by one ceramic vessel covering her face, three other vessels, two green stone beads, and a flint knife placed near her right shoulder.

It is surmised that this young woman was sacrificed during the funeral ceremonies, as illustrated by one of the accompanying vessels. This poly-chrome cylinder vase has a hieroglyphic inscription that dates it to A.D. 754. On the vase, the figure of a young woman, painted and decorated with symbols of sacrifice and death, is poised to cut off her own head with a knife like the one by the body (fig. 1.2). Autosacrifice of this sort is known from other Maya funerary vase paintings and was, apparently, the most prestigious sort of sacrifice among the Maya.

The lavish offerings with Burial 128 and the human sacrifice made to accompany her are well-known signs of royal burial among the Maya. Had there been no physical anthropologist on the project, it is quite likely that the Lady of Altar would have been identified as the "Lord of Altar," a ruler of the eighth century A.D. Although the specialist identified Burial 128 as a female, several art historians later claimed that she had to be a male because of the stingray spines, which were used by the Maya to draw blood in self-sacrifice on important occasions. At Yaxchilán there are monuments showing male rulers piercing their genitals with these implements. In their fervor to see only male rulers among the Maya, scholars have forgotten that ancient Maya noblewomen pierced their tongues and earlobes in the same act of blood offering and with the same instruments of bloodletting.

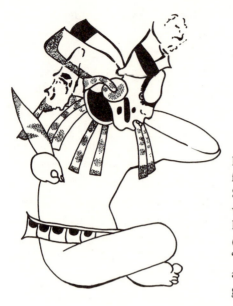

FIGURE 1.2. ■ A painted vase found with Burial 96 at Altar de Sacrificios shows a young Maya woman cutting off her own head. Her face paint, blood-spotted (paper?) ornaments, and belt with "death eyes" all indicate her status as a self-sacrifice, the most prestigious type of Maya sacrifice.

Burial 128 and its accompanying sacrifice were not given much attention in the original publication of the Altar de Sacrificios excavations. In the thirty years since the discovery of the polychrome vase buried with the sacrificed lady-in-waiting, it has become possible to read Maya hieroglyphs. Yet, apart from a preliminary study by Richard Adams, no further translation of the texts has been published despite the fact that this is one of the few vases from an excavated context with good historical associations.

## The Interpretation of Art

Ancient art is the other major source of information concerning gender in prehistory. In order to study gender roles, women and men must be identified. The only sure way of telling the two sexes apart is by identifying realistic representations of genitalia. After the preliminary identification of female and male, it is possible to see how secondary sexual characteristics may be represented and how features such as hairstyle, ornamentation of the skin or body, and clothing differ by sex. Many, perhaps most, human cultures do distinguish female from male in hairstyle, ornamentation, and clothing, but this must be demonstrated, not taken for granted.

Gender roles in an ancient culture may be inferred from art works that show females and males interacting. From these it is often possible to delineate what the members of this culture thought of as gender-appropriate roles or activities. However, both ancient and modern art is limited in subject matter. Maya relief sculpture, for example, deals almost exclusively with formal activities of the ruling caste: their accession, marriage, wars, and dynastic ceremonies. The Moche artists of ancient Peru modeled and painted ceramics to represent a limited number of rituals, myths, and legends. Moreover, in many cases archaeologists and art historians lack the information necessary to translate the symbolism of ancient representations. Frequently, because much of ancient art arrives in museums as the result of unscientific looting, the ancient art objects must be interpreted without the benefit of archaeological context (see chapter 7). All of these factors limit what can be understood about gender roles from art. However, the existence of representational art stimulates and supports many interpretations of ancient cultural practices and ideologies. When the analysis of art is combined with other archaeological data, it is often possible to test hypotheses about ancient gender relations.

## Finding Ancient Maya Women

The Mayan-speaking peoples of southern Mexico and northwestern Central America have constituted a distinctive cultural grouping from the earliest Preclassic (ca. 1800 B.C.) until the present day. Since the European discovery of Maya centers in the nineteenth century, scholars have been entranced with their elaborate architectural sculpture and freestanding monuments, their realistic clay figurines and polychrome pottery, and their hieroglyphic writing system (the only indigenous writing system in ancient America).

The Europeans who began to study the prehistoric archaeology of Mexico and Central America created a series of myths concerning Maya culture. Art historians and archaeologists portrayed the Maya as a simple two-class society ruled by priests and priest-kings obsessed with time and astronomy. This elite was supported by peasants who lived in the jungle, practiced slash-and-burn agriculture, and sustained the ceremonial centers with their labor and devotion. This scenario, upheld by the fact that until the 1980s only the calendric and astronomical parts of Maya inscriptions could be read, was fostered by the identification of the figures shown in the art as priests and gods. Scholars did not identify any of the Maya figures as female despite the fact that Colonial sources refer to goddesses and priestesses.

In the 1960s, the work of Tatiana Proskouriakoff began to transform these erroneous perceptions of Maya culture. She was able to show that the stone monuments at the site of Piedras Negras were political in nature, erected by historic rulers to celebrate the events of their reigns. At the same time, excavations and looting in the Maya area, especially on Jaina Island, off the Yucatán Peninsula, brought to light many realistic clay figurines showing people in what appeared to be poses from daily life. Among these figurines were representations of partly nude females and males. From these it was possible to recognize gender-specific clothing, and Proskouriakoff noted that some of the figurines wore garb similar to that of contemporary Maya women (fig. 1.3). Even though no one could read Mayan writing, Proskouriakoff correctly identified a female head glyph ("Ix" or "Lady," a feminine honorific), a sign that introduced a female personage in the inscriptions on the stone monuments. Further examination of these public works revealed that certain robed figures shared not only costumes and title glyphs, but had a consistent set of associations vis-à-vis other figures and certain inscriptions, now known to be expressions concerning royal accessions. Proskouriakoff's interpretation of these figures as women was supported with information from Colonial documents.

More recent work with Maya iconography by Karen Bruhns has involved the analysis of costumes as a way of investigating gender roles. This study showed that women and men shared an elaborate garment made of netting that was associated only with events such as coronation and royal marriage. Because these highly distinctive robes were restricted to rulers, it is reasonable to assume that women who wore them were equal in status to the males similarly dressed. Females and males also shared elaborate versions of ordinary clothing and ornaments, which appear in monuments that commemorate less transcendental events. Similarity in dress supports the idea that women and men shared many roles in public life. Rosemary Joyce has analyzed figurines and poly-chrome vessels with the goal of documenting the interaction of females

FIGURE 1.3. ■ Lady Xoc of Yaxchilán. Her elaborate costume, jewelry, and high-backed sandals show that she was a woman of the highest rank, while the decorative spirals on her face perhaps refer to the ceremony, in which she presents a feline helmet and a shield to a male ruler.

and males. She too discovered a much wider range of activities for Classic-Period Maya women than had been assumed. Thus, analysis of depictions of women and men executed by Maya artists themselves shows the modern viewer a reality that is different from the stereotype of ancient Maya women as chattels and kitchen furniture.

## The Moche of Northern Peru

The identification of women in Maya dynastic monuments was accomplished because of Proskouriakoff's deep knowledge of Maya history, art, and archaeology, and her observations of the clothing worn by contemporary indigenous women. Lamentably, in much of western South America indigenous clothing has been replaced by garments of European origin, making the attribution of sex on the basis of ancient costume a dubious activity. But a few prehistoric cultures produced sufficiently detailed artistic representations of humans that gender roles can be appraised.

The Moche culture of northern Peru is famous for its modeled and painted ceramics featuring lively scenes of people, animals, plants, structures, and supernatural beings. These scenes are currently interpreted as representations of rituals, myths, and folklore. Vessels illustrating human sexual activity generally show the male clothed, his loose, diaperlike loincloth pulled aside to expose his penis, and the woman nude or partly clothed. The headgear, ornaments, and hairstyles of females and males are as indicative of gender as are genitals. Moche women wear their hair in two twisted tresses and generally have straight-cut bangs (fig. 1.4). Males wear their hair cut straight across the forehead as well, but the rest of their hair is worn pulled behind the ears and hanging to the shoulders.

Because of these distinctions, it has proven easy to differentiate female from male clothing and confidently identify the sex of players in various scenes. This opens the way for the description of Moche gender roles. In the Moche ceramic world, if not in their social world, women appear as sexual partners with men and on their own in many other scenes. At least one woman is commemorated in a portrait vessel thought to represent Moche rulers. One character, a woman with a child peeking from behind her back, may be a specific personage from folklore or legend. Women are shown in a series of vessels depicting childbirth, in which the mother

FIGURE 1.4. ■ A ceramic figurine shows a Moche woman with pigtails carrying a baby on her back.

a

FIGURES 1.5a and 1.5b. ■ New World sites and cultures mentioned in the text.

is aided by an Owl Woman midwife, who also appears alone or as a curer in other scenes of magico-religious practices. Several "burial theme" vessels show a female being devoured by vultures. Colonial documents referring to northern Peru say that a doctor who lost a patient through malpractice was punished in this manner. The documents also refer to female deities and at least one example of a series of obviously powerful priestesses.

The ability to distinguish females and males in the ceramic art of the Moche makes further engendering of Moche prehistory possible, although some scholars have behaved as if they knew more about Moche culture than the ancient Moche artists. For example, there is a Moche

Kogi
SINÚ
• Tequendama Rock Shelter
Quimbaya
ANDEAN
Jama Valley,
San Isidro
CANELOS QUECHUA
Salango, Las Vegas, Valdivia,
Real Alto, Loma Alta
Amazon River
TUPINAMBÁ
Lambayeque
Valley
• Moche, Chan Chan, Huaca Prieta
• Chavín de Huantar, Kuntur Wasi, Recuay
CULTURES
Pachacamac,
La Paloma
• Cuzco
Nazca
CHINCHORRO
0     1000
KILOMETERS
Monte
Verde

**b**

bowl with a scene of a weaving workshop painted on it. Although the weavers have male clothing and male haircuts, they are virtually always identified as women because scholars believe that women were weavers in the Andean culture area. This belief was so compelling that when the *National Geographic* published an article on the ancient Peruvian city of Chan Chan, women were depicted weaving in the workshops even though the illustration was based on the famous bowl. Braids were painted onto the figures despite the objections of a (female) specialist consultant. Engendering the scholarly interpretation of the past depends upon respecting the evidence and using it responsibly to create a picture that includes both female and male actors.

## The Past Informs the Present

Theory causes scholars to ask questions, and directs them toward answers. Researchers armed with older theoretical models did not approach the archaeological record with the idea of discovering gender patterning in it. Only recently has new theory inspired new research goals. Postmodern and feminist theory focuses on and accepts gender as an important dynamic, insisting that both women and men are actors and innovators, and that women as well as men have activities important in culture and history. This body of theory causes archaeologists to take gender into account and write a more well-balanced history by including both women and men.

Prehistoric narratives often begin with a critique of androcentric archaeology, but engendering the past also requires positive approaches, such as developing interpretations involving gender and proposing alternative interpretations even when there may be insufficient evidence for choosing among the alternatives. Because anthropologists recognize the infinite variability in human social and cultural behavior, they are prepared to create alternative interpretations of the past and imagine different scenarios for the future of our own society.

Engendering the past is thus a service to the present. Not engendering the past would allow ignorant models to persist in our minds and in public images. An engendered past replaces the inaccurate fictions that are sometimes used in our society to validate myths about gender relations.

The following chapters describe research that explores the diverse social and cultural experiences of ancient American people, a story about how both women and men participated in populating the Americas and developing and managing social, economic, political, and religious systems. Examples are drawn from North America, Central America, and South America (figs. 1.5a and 1.5b) and from all periods of American history (fig. 1.6).

Eastern United States

| | |
|---|---|
| Paleoindian | 12,000 BC (?)–7,000 BC |
| Archaic | 7,000 BC–1,000 BC |
| Woodland | 1,000 BC–AD 900 |
| Mississippian | AD 900–AD 1600 |
| Historic | AD 1600–present |

Southwestern United States

| | |
|---|---|
| Paleoindian | 12,000 BC–7,000 BC |
| Archaic | 7,000 BC–100 BC |
| Basketmaker & Anasazi, Hohokam, Mogollon & Mimbres | 100 BC–AD 1540 |

Mesoamerica

| | |
|---|---|
| Preceramic Archaic | 8500 BC–1800 BC |
| Formative or Preclassic | 1800 BC–AD 150 |
| Classic | AD 150–AD 900 |
| Postclassic | AD 900–1521 |
| Colonial | AD 1521–1822 |

Colombia

| | |
|---|---|
| Preceramic | BC 8000–3000 |
| Formative | BC 3000–AD 1 |
| Chiefdoms/Regional Development | AD 1–1527 |

Coastal Ecuador

| | |
|---|---|
| Preceramic | 8,500 BC–4,700 BC |
| Formative | 3,500 BC–300 BC |
| Regional Development | 300 BC–AD 800 |
| Integration | AD 1150–1531 |
| Colonial | AD 1531–1820 |

Peru

| | |
|---|---|
| Preceramic | 9500 BC–1800 BC |
| Initial | 1800 BC–900 BC |
| Early Horizon | 900 BC–200 BC |
| Early Intermediate | 200 BC–AD 600 |
| Middle Horizon | AD 600–1000 |
| Late Intermediate | AD 1000–1476 |
| Late Horizon | AD 1476–1534 |
| Colonial | AD 1534–1822 |

FIGURE 1.6. ■ List of named periods commonly recognized in American archaeology and mentioned in the text

# CHAPTER TWO

# *The First Women in America*

Modern archaeological studies of the sites inhabited between 15,000 and 8,000 years ago have enabled archaeologists to expand their understanding of the earliest Americans, called Paleoindians. New archaeological evidence has resulted in a shift away from the traditional emphasis on stone tools and hunting in the description of Paleoindian lifeways. New, engendered interpretation permits scholars and the public to see the female members of Paleoindian society, not just the male hunters (fig. 2.1).

FIGURE 2.1. ■ "Man the Hunter." An artist's conception of Paleoindian hunting perpetuates a stereotype of the earliest male inhabitants of America.

Evidence from Siberia and the Americas indicates that Paleoindian women, men, and children made their momentous migration into the New World from Asia around 15,000 years ago. These first Americans were fully modern humans, *Homo sapiens sapiens*, who walked across the Bering Land Bridge or the winter ice pack, bringing with them a very flexible and successful cultural adaptation that enabled them to thrive in severe climates. The far northern environment was rich in resources: large terrestrial herbivores, fish and birds, animals that provided food and the primary materials for clothing, tools, and shelter. Although Paleoindian sites often are poorly preserved, archaeologists have recovered stone and bone tools, some food remains, an occasional burial, and vestiges of shelters. By inferring from this evidence and developing models based on ethnographic analogues between Paleoindians and cold-adapted hunters and gatherers who lived in America and Asia in the historic period, archaeologists have challenged the older interpretations of early American life.

## Deconstructing the Old Model

The idea that Paleoindian life was dominated by male hunters and their stone projectile points has been popular for a long time. The people who entered America at the end of the Ice Age were first recognized because their distinctive stone tools were found in primary association with the bones of extinct Pleistocene mammals. Before radiocarbon dating was available, archaeologists concentrated their efforts upon these kill sites rather than on habitation sites because the ancient bones were irrefutable evidence that the site was very old. These kill sites then became the basis of the popular view that the first inhabitants of the Americas were exclusively hunters. More recently it has been shown that habitation sites of equal antiquity reveal evidence of a much broader range of activities than was known from kill sites alone, thus offering excellent opportunities to deconstruct the old model and build an engendered view of early American life.

Because of the kill site focus, Paleoindians were stereotyped as big game hunters who subsisted on late Ice Age mammoths, giant bison, horses, and similar species. One of the best known scenarios for the rapid peopling of the Americas is that these "efficient" hunters attacked unwary herds of animals that had never seen humans, drastically reduced the available population, and then moved onward to repeat the slaughter. This view, focused upon males aggressively performing the human-defining hunting behavior, was based on evidence from kill sites with diagnostic projectile points located primarily in the ancient grasslands of the North American West. This spectacular evidence militated against any study of the "nondiagnostic" flake tools also found in the kill sites and meant for cutting tasks. Researchers were discouraged from looking for variations in the archaeological record and modeling other aspects of daily life, including women's activities. Logically, finding tools in association with animal bones does not necessarily indicate men hunting. These remains could indicate people of either sex butchering after a communal hunt or even a scavenging event.

Early Paleoindian studies mimic the narratives about early human ancestors in Africa and Asia, where the concept of "Man the Hunter" dominated scholarly thinking about the distant past. Hunting, an upper-class activity in Europe, has figured as a hyper-masculine activity in explorers' tales and other manly fantasies. In its simplest form, the Man the Hunter myth holds that all human progress was due to men hunting animals with the stone tools they themselves had made. Because scholars accepted hunting tools as both the cause and the evidence of human progress, scientific emphasis was placed upon the study of projectile points thought to be designed to pierce the hides of large animals.

This line of thinking was fostered by anthropological studies of Eskimo (Inuit) and Cree hunters, historic peoples who lived full time or seasonally in tundra and boreal forests. These people were erroneously held to be "living fossils," providing evidence of how the earliest Americans had survived in a similar environment. Anthropological studies, done by men and focused on male activities, then provided a model for Paleoindian studies in which men hunted and women processed food. Other activities of women were largely ignored, and women and their work were devalued by anthropologists. In reality, these northern peoples may not be good analogues of Paleolithic people because they became specialized in harvesting animals to sell skins to Europeans. Contact with Europeans caused women to lose status and roles because many traditional social institutions disappeared as the population was decimated by disease, and because interaction with missionaries and traders caused groups such as the

Chippewayan, Inuit, Cree, and other boreal hunters to adopt misogynistic attitudes along with new technologies.

New research on living hunters/gatherers has begun to change the earlier androcentric views by including women and their activities as objects of study. These studies have highlighted the importance of resources other than large mammals in the subsistence systems of foraging peoples. For example, aquatic resources were important to all Arctic and Subarctic groups and were almost certainly important to the earliest Americans. River, lake, and ocean fishing, and gathering shellfish, beached whales, kelp, and other sea vegetables probably were important subsistence activities in the past as in more modern times. Bird trapping and egg collecting in the summer, as well as the gathering of berries, mosses, and edible ferns, were crucial to the economies of the northern peoples and would have been important to the first immigrants into unglaciated central Alaska.

In many hunting societies, women are responsible for much of the exploitation of water and land resources, including the traps and snares set for the small mammals that are an important everyday source of food. The classic compilation of ethnological studies, *Man the Hunter*, demonstrated that the bulk of the food consumed by modern subsistence hunters is gathered, not hunted, and the authors of this book concluded that almost everywhere below the Arctic Circle, people gather for a living. This idea has finally begun to infiltrate contemporary Paleoindian studies.

Fourteen years after *Man the Hunter*, *Woman the Gatherer* was published. In this book, anthropologists reassessed women's activities among historic and modern foraging groups and applied those assessments to stories about early hominids. This engendering of the early human record is important to American archaeologists not only because of the feminist critique of the previous model, but also because it offered the opportunity of including real people and social dynamics (including gender relations) in the interpretation of early prehistory. It is now possible to reject the limited view of the past that focused on men, large beasts, and projectile points.

Recent studies of sites in diverse environments have proven that the Paleoindians, most of whom lived *below* the Arctic Circle, ate a varied diet and enjoyed a richer material culture than previously thought. New research, informed by contemporary ethnographic studies and developing feminist perspectives, presents a broader picture of the past, featuring more actors and more activities.

## Early Women in Ethnographic Perspective

The first people who moved into the Americas were a cold-adapted people who depended upon the efforts of both women and men to survive. Everyone's labor was needed to meet the challenges of the long, cold northern winter and satisfy the need for food, clothing, shelter, and food storage. Although we should not project our division of labor upon this group, a gender-based division of labor may have been found among early Americans. Social scripts vary, but in most context females and males are encouraged to take on certain tasks assigned by sex, and people then cajole and coerce their kin (mothers, sisters, fathers, brothers, spouses) into doing the work that is expected of them.

Ethnographic data from recent cold-adapted peoples suggest that men benefit when women make clothing for them. This is a grueling and time-consuming process that begins with preparing the animal skins and results in a wide variety of protective garments for heads, hands, feet, and bodies. Garment production requires specialized labor, meaning that the women receive lengthy training.

Similarly, women find it advantageous to have men bring home the raw materials and produce some of the primary tools they require in their work. Men undertake the economically and personally risky business of hunting animals, while women convert meat into food for immediate consumption and storage against the barren seasons. Women also transform hides into clothing, bedding, containers, and tents. Together, women and men manage social and biological reproduction, integrating their respective contributions in creative and flexible ways.

Ethnography suggest to archaeologists some of what cannot be seen in the archaeological record and illustrates dramatically that it is impossible to infer exactly what ancient life was like because human behavior is variable and people are only "set in their ways" for the short run. They have the potential to change as new challenges arise. As the first Americans entered the continents and occupied new environments, the particular activities of women and men were negotiated on a continuing basis in response to new situations.

Archaeologists think that the first Americans lived in small kin-based groups, and thus there was no need for political leaders. Within families, decisions can be made by consensus. Lacking evidence such as artistic representations of human beings, we have no idea how the Paleoindians negotiated roles or leadership or how these early peoples thought about femininity and masculinity. In later times, North American Indian societies showed flexibility in their construction of gender categories. It seems safe to assume that some tasks at least were divided along sex lines and that others were divided by age and personal preference. It also seems likely that the tasks necessary for subsistence were assigned in a complementary fashion within family groups. Gender complementarity is deeply rooted in surviving Native American societies. Native Americans often created gender differences within a social system that featured complementarity and interdependence. That many nonegalitarian variations on this theme developed later does not negate it as a basic organizing principle in Native American societies.

## Ingalik Gender and Material Culture

The artifacts and other remains found in Paleoindian sites were used by women and men, adults and children. But archaeologists want to know more specifically who made them, who owned them, and what customs and ideologies governed their use. Cross-cultural comparisons demonstrate the complexities of artifact systems, so it is not always clear how to interpret archaeological remains. Paleoindian behavior can be modeled on the basis of historic cold-adapted peoples such as the Ingalik (Deg Hit'an, an Athabascan people of Alaska). They, like other peoples used as sources of models, were modern peoples, documented by ethnographers early in the twentieth century. They are not fossilized remnants of the Paleoindians and are as unrelated to the ancient peoples as any other twentieth-century group. Nevertheless, some of the features of Ingalik cultural adaptation may be similar to those inferred for the Paleoindians and, as such, are of interest in trying to flesh out the meager remains of the ancient peoples. For example, their primary foods and sources of materials for artifacts were all wild species, and their manufactures involved hand labor and individual skills applied to locally available raw materials. Because Ingalik manufactures were embedded in a complex system involving gender, it is tempting to infer similar gender ideas for the Paleoindians.

Ingalik material culture, meticulously documented by Cornelius Osgood, carried a nonmaterial ideological element, as does material culture everywhere. This can be shown by the traditional Ingalik artifacts listed in figure 2.2. These artifacts were made by men and women for themselves, by women for men, by men for women, by adults for children, and even by children for other children. These items, as well as a smaller number of things made by women for other women and girls, demonstrate the depth of engendered relationships within Ingalik society. Artifacts serve not just as aids to material living, but as means to achieve social cooperation and interdependence.

Although this list shows that men make more things, women's manufactures often involved a greater investment of time and skill. Compare an awl, made by a man for a woman, to a parka, made by a woman for a

| | USED BY MEN | USED BY WOMEN | USED BY CHILDREN OR ANYONE | TOTAL |
|---|---|---|---|---|
| Made by Women (33%)* | 14 (15%) | 40 (43%) | 39 (42%) | 93 (100%) |
| Made by Men (62%) | 98 (57%) | 56 (35%) | 19** (8%) | 173 (100%) |
| Made by Men & Women Together (5%) | 2 (14%) | 1 (7%) | 11 (79%) | 14 (100%) |
| Total Items | 114 | 97 | 69 | 280 |

* Of the 280 items in the sample, this percentage was produced by the maker or makers indicated.
** Seven of these items are made by men exclusively for boys.

Figure 2.2. ■ Analysis of 280 items of Ingalik material culture showing the artifacts made by women and men, and used, respectively, by women, men, and children. Based on Cornelius Osgood's descriptions of artifacts.

man. Men make more things, with which women make more complex things. Women make more items for children as well.

The loci of production of male and female manufactures were also different. Men worked out of doors or in a men's ceremonial house, whereas women worked in their smokehouse in the summer or in winter houses with other women. This traditional spatial separation was linked to the idea that an individual of one sex might contaminate or be damaged by specific items associated with the other sex. The two sexes were differentiated in myriad ways, including the production of cordage. Because women and men specialized in making lines from distinct materials, it was necessary for both to seek out members of the opposite sex to acquire the kind of line they themselves did not make. The system required and reinforced dependence between women and men.

Gender distinctions also characterized Ingalik ceremonial regalia and acts: women were associated with dentalium shell and men with ocher. Women's and men's ritual activities were largely separate, expressing the idea of the distinctness as well as the interconnectedness of the two sexes, much as in the more mundane material culture. Separation also afforded individuals of both sexes control over their own activities.

The Ingalik show us one way even "simple" societies work out complex systems in which their members participate in the business of living. The differentiation of tasks and the artifacts that are associated with these tasks is accompanied by a model of integration. All societies create cultural scripts that bind people and their activities together in ways that work to solve the basic problems of subsistence, mental and physical survival, and personal satisfaction. The Paleoindians certainly organized their social lives in a variety of ways to meet local challenges. We cannot claim that any Paleoindian band was organized exactly like the Ingalik, but this case serves to remind us of the potential complexity of ancient lifeways, including the importance of gender dynamics, in those systems. With this awareness we can approach the archaeological record in a less simplistic manner and arrive at a better understanding of what the surviving material culture really represents.

## Deconstructing Clovis Hunters

The quintessential hunting Paleoindians were the ancient Clovis people of the Western Plains, first identified on the basis of their distinctive stone projectile points, which were sometimes found in direct association with the carcasses of now-extinct elephants. Clovis points have inspired hyperbole. George C. Frison believes, "It may not be too strong a statement to say that the Clovis projectile point is the first piece of flaked stone weaponry in the world that was well-designed enough to allow a single hunter a dependable and predictable means of pursuing and killing a large mammal such as a mammoth or a bison on a one-to-one basis." This scenario is a romantic fantasy. It is unrealistic that a lone individual would willingly take on an elephant or any other large beast. In contrast, some scholars have suggested that the Clovis peoples were scavengers. Reality may lie in the middle. For example, Jean Auel in her novel *The Mammoth Hunters* envisions men, women, and children cooperating in the woolly mammoth hunt (although she makes men the directors of the enterprise).

Surely the hunt was important to Paleoindians, and hunting stories, embellished with derring-do and great feats, doubtless were told around campfires at night, but these tales may have celebrated cooperative labor and not the prowess of individual males. In real life, hunting is often done by a team of specialists or by large organized groups of adults, including children as lookouts. The goal, of course, is to provide a living for the group.

Recent studies have redefined Clovis people as diversified foragers, living in small groups and creating large sites only by multiple reoccupations across the centuries. While meat was surely important to them, they had strategies for harvesting many wild animal and plant species. These sites were slow to be recognized as Clovis by archaeologists because they lacked the diagnostic extinct megafauna and specific types of projectile points. Advances in dating technologies and the input of archaeologists trained to look beyond male hunters has changed Clovis archaeology. Archaeologists working in lower latitudes, such as the southern Great Plains, have interpreted the Paleoindians as generalists who lived in a wide variety of environments during a period characterized by rapid environmental changes at the end of the Ice Age. Remains of plants and small animals are evidence that the first North Americans processed resources other than Pleistocene elephants and giant bison. The highly variable stone tool kits, only occasionally including diagnostic projectile points, show us that Paleoindians everywhere harvested and processed a wide variety of plants, extracting from them fibers for containers, clothing, and tools.

Based on analogies with recent temperate foragers, one can imagine women managing these plant processing technologies. This alerts us to the idea that Paleoindian women would have been as independent, skillful, and self-directed as their later Native American sisters.

According to recent scholarship, Clovis people chose to situate their camps, and to move them seasonally, in order to satisfy many criteria. Hunting was only one of several factors considered in determining settlement location. In southern Mexico, the ancient people of the Tehuacan Valley expressed their desire for company by locating their spring sites near immensely productive stands of prickly pear fruits and mesquite beans. The sites of the historic western Mono of the Sierra Nevada of California were pegged to the requirements of women's subsistence activities, particularly acorn procurement, processing, and storage. According to Thomas Jackson, settlements and their locations were determined by the work of the women who built the storage silos and who created and owned the stone mortars used to grind the staple nut. This emphasis on women's work is remarkable because it departs from the old models, in which hunting was the master behavior that explained most aspects of culture. Recent interpretations place women back into Paleoindian cultures as active participants in the negotiation of the way of life of the group. Women's work in some environments was probably the reliable economic strategy that underwrote the more risky activities often associated with men.

Paleoindian archaeology has been dominated by attention to big game hunting weapons—projectile points—their morphology, technology, and distribution. Rethinking projectile points is part of the process of balancing the androcentric view of the earliest Americans. Some scholars now believe that many projectile points were hafted as cutting tools and that they functioned in a variety of ways, thus making it more likely that they were used by women as well as men. The notion that the long, slender, and fragile Paiján-style points were employed for fishing by Paleoindians in Peru also separates them from the Man the Hunter myth.

It is also possible that Clovis and other elaborate points had ideological functions. It has even been suggested that Clovis technology was spread as an emblem of male identity associated with an ancient men's cult. This scenario imagines men producing these fancy bifaces as a way of celebrating their societal role, and perhaps as a means of drumming up enthusiasm for a risky activity. In this case, women may have avoided contact with these artifacts, fearing that female power might interfere with the functioning of the points. Still, if the Clovis points also functioned as knives, an equally reasonable interpretation of their ideological value is that they were symbolic tools first presented to a girl, say, on the occasion of her first menses or some similar important coming-of-age event. Ideology does not need to be androcentric.

This positing of an ideological function for stone tools reflects the still-strong focus of researchers upon stone tools. Yet it is unlikely that stone tools occupied as central a place in Paleoindian life as archaeologists imagine. Now scholars are paying more attention to the diverse artifacts manufactured by Paleoindians and to the sites that were oriented to many different kinds of resources. Attention to these other aspects of Paleo-indian production has provoked the deconstruction of Man the Hunter as the focus of early American history.

## Engendering Stone Tools

Human adaptability is founded upon stone tools, and the humble, unretouched stone flake, easily manufactured by anybody, even a young child, is the most abundant and earliest evidence of ancient Americans. Because male archaeologists dominate in the study, interpretation, and replication of lithic artifacts, and due to our modern gender prejudices about tools, many scholars believe that lithic technology was a male domain going back to Adam. Despite this prejudice, Joan Gero has reinterpreted stone tools in a more balanced gender perspective, taking us beyond "Man the Toolmaker."

Because it is known that women make and use stone tools in living cultures, and because biological strength is not a constraining factor in their manufacture, it would have been "inefficient" for ancient women to have relied upon men for the production of adequate cutting edges. Although Gero concedes that exactly who made what, where, when, and why is subject to great variation across time and space, she engenders lithic artifacts by assuming that the remains of women's activities will be found "on house floors, at base camps and in village sites" where women gathered and worked.

The most common artifact in these contexts is the technologically simple, utilized flake, a preeminently expedient tool, easily manufactured and used for many chores. These flakes normally are devalued by archaeologists, perhaps because of their technical simplicity, but possibly because they are associated with women and housework, which is devalued by our society. There should be, of course, no stigma attached to making and using cheap and efficient technology, and Gero argues that "there is no reason to believe that women did not produce elaborate worked stone tools" as well. After all, women produced high-status objects in many ethnographic cultures in the New World. Because gender systems are very complex and respond to many factors, we expect variation in the past. Neither stone nor metal has been identified exclusively with a particular sex.

Stone projectile points dominate the written archaeological record of the preceramic period, but most tools in the Paleoindian tool kit were not fluted bifacial points, but scrapers, knives, choppers, and humble utilized flakes. These, as Joan Gero has demonstrated, are the backbone of any stone tool kit. In the new, holistic picture of Paleoindian life, based on understanding the total tool kit, the wide range of food sources, and the locations of sites, Man the Hunter does not appear alone.

## Paleoindian Living Sites

Many Paleoindian living sites have now been investigated, proving that from the very beginning of the human occupation of the Americas, there was variation from locality to locality in the exploitation of plant and animal species. Themes of diversity and variability have begun to replace simple hunting models. For instance, archaeologists now infer variable economic, technological, social, and ritual roles for Paleoindian women and men, and they expect great variation in the social construction of gender roles in each ancient group because they appreciate how female and male activities respond to the exigencies of regional and local conditions. The following early sites have been chosen for review because they clearly demonstrate these variations in economic and social adaptations.

## Paleoindians of Southernmost South America

The earliest known Paleoindian site today is Monte Verde, dated to about 12,000 B.C. and located in the cold forests of southern Chile. This site is

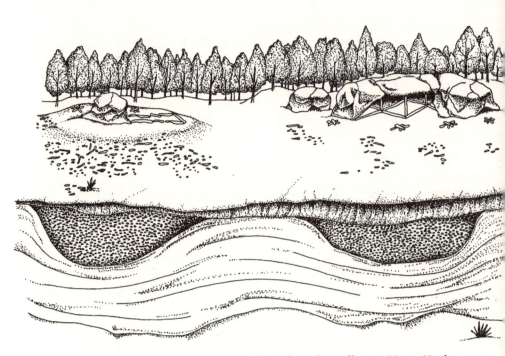

FIGURE 2.3. ■ Reconstruction of the Paleoindian village at Monte Verde in southern Chile. Excellent preservation of houses made of skin and wood and other organic remains enlarges our view of Paleoindian life.

especially important because excellent organic preservation and thorough reporting make it possible for us to imagine the activities of women and men at the site. Like the bodies in the Danish bogs, organic material was preserved by waterlogged peat along the creek where the ancient inhabitants built a village of some twelve wood, skin, and sod houses and a larger communal structure (fig. 2.3). Several houses have small clay-lined pits for fires inside, but large, presumably communal, hearths for cooking or conviviality were located outside the line of houses and adjacent to the large structure.

Evidence of woodworking and skin-working in the vicinity of the houses was preserved by the peat, and activities such as cooking and eating were indicated by remains in the houses and around the communal hearths. The animal bone recovered in the debris of the hearths and in the midden included the remains of seven mastodons, killed elsewhere and transported back home in pieces. Plant remains were abundant: seeds, fruits, berries, various leaf vegetables, and tubers and rhizomes, among which were wild potatoes. The variety of plants suggests that Monte Verde was a permanent settlement, not a seasonal one. Wooden mortars and grinding stones indicate that plant processing was important. There are also many nonedible plants, including leaves and seeds of several species still important in native pharmacopoeia. Interestingly, there are no projectile points among the relatively abundant tool remains. Stone weights were found, hinting that bolas were used for hunting small and medium-sized animals. Presumably the mastodons were "hunted" by the tried and true method of driving them into the bog, where, mired and immobilized, they were killed. Butchering, involving entire families, may have depended upon the use of hafted flake tools, several of which were preserved in the habitation site. These show that unprepossessing flakes were important cutting tools in a location where both men and women worked.

## Comparative Data from Warmer Regions

To the north, in the warm and semiarid Tehuacan and Oaxaca Valleys of southern Mexico, a series of regional surveys have yielded detailed information on ancient society and economy. For thousands of years, the ancient inhabitants of this region moved seasonally through a series of different ecozones. Their movement and the size of the group at any given time of the year were tied to the availability of key plant staples, which formed the major portion of their diet. They hunted medium- to small-sized animals, including deer, tortoises, mollusks, insects, and cotton-tail rabbits. The fact that projectile points are rare in these sites supports the idea that ancient procurement strategies included trapping, clubbing, and communal drives in addition to hunting with spears. Coxcatlán Cave (Tehuacan) and Cueva Blanca (Oaxaca) preserve the remains of many gophers, tortoises, cotton-tail rabbits, jackrabbits, wood rats, a few white-tailed deer, and foxes. These last serve some people as food, and fox pelts are often highly valued for clothing (Inuit women used to make their underdrawers out of this fur). In the Paleoindian period, mammoths lived along the shores of the swampy lakes that filled the Valley of Mexico, but it seems that the people living there apprehended few of them, subsisting most of the time on small prey in the manner of their cousins in Tehuacan and Oaxaca. The bagging of a very large animal must have been a cause for celebration.

Because their diet was not dominated by meat, the yearly foraging schedule of these early Mexicans probably was not dictated by male hunting. In the spring, when the huge stands of prickly pear cactus bore quantities of fruit and the mesquite bushes along the river course were heavy with sweet bean pods, people would gather together in multifamily groups to consume the food and trap a few rabbits with the snares that have been found in their sites. In Oaxaca one of the earliest known structures in America, a dance floor, is evidence that families socialized and enjoyed performing ritual activities in their spring camps.

In early summer this community would break up into smaller family groups, moving into the higher valleys to forage among the wild grasses and other seed-bearing plants, including the ancestors of now domestic maize and amaranth, and to gather the ripening fruits from scattered avocado and zapote trees, which bear abundantly in good years. By September, however, these resources would have begun to play out, and groups split up further to move into the higher hills, where they gathered acorns and hunted the white-tailed deer. Within a few months, as the cold dry season advanced, resources supported only nuclear or small extended families. In this meager season, people survived by consuming the hearts of agave (the so-called "century plant," which requires lengthy cooking in an earth oven) and eating whatever birds, insects, or plants they could find until spring came once more. Under such conditions everyone's labor is valuable, and the survival of the group depends upon the expertise of every forager.

## Paleoindians of Temperate Regions

Indian Creek, a deeply stratified Paleoindian site in south central Montana, was occupied from late winter through early spring. It was utilized for some thousands of years, people coming back each season much as they did to the Mexican sites. The largest animal hunted at Indian Creek was the bison, but far more common in numbers and contribution to the diet were small animals: yellow-bellied marmots, prairie dogs, voles, and jackrabbits. The excavators suggest that preferentially collecting fat-bearing small animals was an adaptation to the hard times of late winter. Indian Creek has preserved evidence of numerous domestic activities as well as abundant refuse from stone-working. Although the excavators identify the stone refuse as the result of males making and maintaining stone tools, more than 85 percent of the total stone tool inventory consisted of scrapers and knives, which they admit is evidence of women working at the site as well.

Other Montana sites reflect similar foraging activities focused on small animals, while sites with good organic preservation show that plants formed an important part of the diet. Barton Gulch, to the southwest of Indian Creek, has the remains of earth ovens, evidence of one technique of transforming plants and animals into food. Barton Gulch has also yielded bone needles and other bone implements, grinding and pounding tools, scrapers, knives, and many utilized flakes. All of these implements suggest that a great many different activities were being undertaken by the women and men at this site.

In the northeast United States, sites vary considerably in size, and some of the better preserved indicate that people were living in small portable or quickly constructed shelters, perhaps like the wigwams or teepees of later peoples. The only well-published site with substantial plant preservation is Shawnee-Minisink, in the upper Delaware Valley of Pennsylvania. During the Paleoindian period, this area was a transitional zone between the boreal pine forest and the preboreal spruce and fir forest. Shawnee-Minisink is apparently a late summer–early fall camp to which two families returned year after year. They worked outside around the fireplace and probably used their shelters for sleeping and storage. Most tools are scrapers of various sorts, knives, spokeshaves, hammerstones, cores, and debitage. A single Clovis point/knife was also found.

Plant remains around the shelters included amaranth, chenopods, smartweed (*Polygonum* sp.), wintercress, and a host of fruits, including blackberries, hackberries, grapes, and hawthorn plums, all rich in vitamin C. Judging from the fish remains found in their refuse, the Paleoindians of Shawnee-Minisink must have caught salmon, an important seasonal food of foragers in many colder zones. Hunting seems often to have been a secondary activity in much of the eastern woodlands, where many peoples were forest gatherers, supplementing their plant diet with fish, birds, rabbits, and an occasional deer or mastodon. That the Shawnee-Minisink people also hunted caribou is suggested by the site location, not by actual bone remains.

## *Family Structure, Gender, and Work*

The archaeological evidence summarized above suggests that the basic unit of Paleoindian social life was the small family group in which wife-husband and parent-child ties were the most important. For the people of Tehuacan and Oaxaca, the nuclear family was the basic subsistence group, especially in the hardest parts of the year. Thus, strong affective ties and cooperation between the members of this minimal human social group would have been crucial in assuring the survival of all. Shawnee-Minisink shows two families living side by side at one season of the year. If Monte Verde was a permanent village, as the excavators suggest, then the possibility exists for greater separation of activities, perhaps along some lines similar to the Ingalik model, where material culture was strongly engendered to promote cooperation and mutual dependence among women and men, young and old.

A gender-based division of labor is a social script that is not inevitable or fixed but is a flexible model designed by people to meet their current needs. The archaeological record makes it difficult to identify female and male activities, so archaeologists have to make serious efforts to avoid ethnocentric interpretations of evidence and eschew the old stereotypes of women's work and men's work. Because hunting is romantic in the minds of European scholars, it has been given elevated importance in interpretations of Paleoindian life, devaluing other activities that were fundamental to prehistoric cultural systems. This perspective is changing with the realization that the conversion of animals and plants into food and the consumption of food are crucial and ideologically charged activities in all sociocultural systems. Who did the cooking? Hearths, burned bones, and vegetable remains show that meals were prepared and consumed. People invested skill, knowledge, and hours of time to produce meals that were nutritious, satisfying, even enjoyable. Meals then, as now, symbolized and reinforced the basic structures of social life in the minds of individuals.

Who did the snaring? The assignment of activities may have varied with the group and the context. The Paleoindian evidence does not indicate that women and men were set against each other in antagonistic interest groups of the kind found in some historic societies. It seems likely that cooperative and flexible family interactions characterized their lives, and we can be sure that labor of women as well as men is reflected in the archaeological record at Paleoindian sites. Not all Paleoindians were hunters.

The women who operated in the Paleoindian habitation sites surely made clothing—at least it is known that in modern times, skin-working frequently is women's work. The transformation of raw animal skins into processed hides that are soft and supple enough to wrap around the body requires laborious cleaning and scraping, and the stretched skin probably requires treatment with urine or other substances. In temperate and Arctic climates, skin-working was essential to the survival of the group because skins were the basic material of both clothing and shelter. Only at Monte Verde do skin shelters survive, but we can imagine that similar shelters were an essential part of the equipment of many peoples moving through North and South America.

When the archaeological record preserves remains from a wide range of activities, these usually include the manufacture of items from skin, wood, and plant fiber: clothing, carrying equipment, netting, cordage, and basketry. Small impressions in clay of fragments of twined netting and, perhaps, cloth have been found at 27,000-year-old Dolni Vestonice in Czechoslovakia. Rope was found in somewhat later contexts at Lascaux in France. In the New World, fragments of twined sandals or bags have been found in terminal Paleoindian contexts on San Miguel Island off Santa Barbara, California, and coiled basketry was being made by the inhabitants of Huachocana Cave in Argentina around 7000 B.C. Paleoindian tool kits include many bone skin-working and twining and coiling tools that must have been used frequently by women.

Because of the success of the Paleoindians in surviving and multiplying in this harsh environment, they must have had adequate clothing, shelter, and equipment. There could have been no migration across the Bering Land Bridge without adequate garments. It would have been mandatory for Paleoindians living in the tundra and the taiga to cover their bodies because they faced life-threatening cold much of the year and masses of biting flies and mosquitoes in the short summer season. There could have been no hunting in Maine, or the Great Plains, or Chile without clothing. The artists' cavemen clad only in crude skins covering their genitals are unrealistic.

No substantial pieces of clothing have yet been found in Paleoindian contexts. Excavations at the Russian site of Sungir, north of Moscow, have provided evidence of ancient garments, reconstructable because of their beaded decoration. One suspects that "waders" like those worn by a Sungir male or leggings and moccasins with some sort of shirt or parkalike garment were worn by all the late Ice Age peoples of northern Eurasia. Many Native American groups preserved vestiges of this sort of skillfully made clothing into the historic period.

Art and ritual were probably important in Paleoindian life, but aside from a few scratches on stone and bone, there are no figurines, no engraved plaques, no decorated tools from American sites. The box turtle shells reported by Albert Redder and John Fox from the tomb of a Paleo-indian adult at the Horn site in Texas might have been rattles used in dances and ceremonies, but the only known Paleoindian artwork is the sacrum of an extinct camelid found in the Valley of Mexico, carved into the form of an animal when the bone was fresh. Although evidence of personal orna-ments is uncommon, it seems likely that Paleoindians wore bone toggles, buttons, or other sewn-on ornaments like those common in the European Paleolithic. The discovery of steatite pendants and beads at several north-eastern North American sites show us that such adornments existed, although they may have more commonly been of perishable materials such as seeds and wood. It is sure that the women and men who walked out of Siberia into America brought with them the mythology, music, dance, and religious practices of their original homeland.

In the Americas, hallucinatory states were achieved through rhythmic drumming and chanting, but one characteristic of many historic and contemporary Native American religious practices, and one that seems to have great time depth, is the use of psychoactive substances of plant origin. Peter Furst has summarized the evidence of mescal beans (the psychoactive red seeds of the Texas mountain laurel, *Sophora secundiflora*) in Archaic and Paleoindian contexts in caves of the Southwest and in northern Mexico, and snuffs containing *dimyethyltriptamine* (DMT) have been found in Archaic contexts in northern Chile. The late prehistoric people contributed magical tobacco to the Old World at the end of the fifteenth century.

The religious use of mind-altering substances may well have come from Siberia with the first peoples. Later, many Native American groups devel-oped detailed knowledge of the chemical properties of medical, hallu-cinogenic, and poisonous plants as they explored each new environment

           WOMEN IN ANCIENT AMERICA

of the New World. Curiosity and self-interest were probably important motivators. Paleoindian women who, like recent foraging women, may have been specialists in plants and plant collecting probably took up the challenge of discovering useful plants as the family moved into a new region.

In America female participation in rituals using hallucinogens today is quite restricted, but contemporary Huichol women on pilgrimages chew hallucinogenic cactus buds. Evidence from the archaeological record includes ceramic figurines from West Mexican tombs dating to between 500 B.C. and A.D. 300 that depict females, perhaps shamans, in trances or preparing peyote (*Lophophora williamsii*, a small cactus whose buds contain mescaline). In the past, throughout the Americas, women have taken magical healing roles and often engaged in divination, two important focuses of hallucinogenic drug use. Because women are often knowledgeable about plants and their uses, they likely participated in the ubiquitous rituals involving psychotropic plants, even if they did not ingest concoctions themselves.

## At Home in the Tequendama Rock Shelter

The rock shelters of Tequendama yield abundant evidence of the activities of the earliest inhabitants of the Sabana de Bogotá, a swampy plain at high altitudes in the mountains of Colombia. The drier parts of the plain and hills around the Sabana were forested, and the swamps provided valuable resources, including fish, mollusks, and turtles. Excavations in one rock shelter revealed a number of superimposed living floors out of the cold wind and rain, where people prepared food and carried out other productive activities.

There were two hearths in the earliest excavated levels and more in later ones. The fires were built in a well-lighted portion of the rock shelter, where they served as the center of activity. The pattern of remains shown in figure 2.4 indicates that the kitchen wastes of the earliest occupants of the rock shelter accumulated a little way from the hearths, mixed with the debris from a variety of tasks performed there. Little plant material was preserved, but the excavators, led by Gonzalo Correal and Thomas van der Hammen, carefully documented the distribution of animal bone and artifacts on the old cave floors. Stone tools were manu-

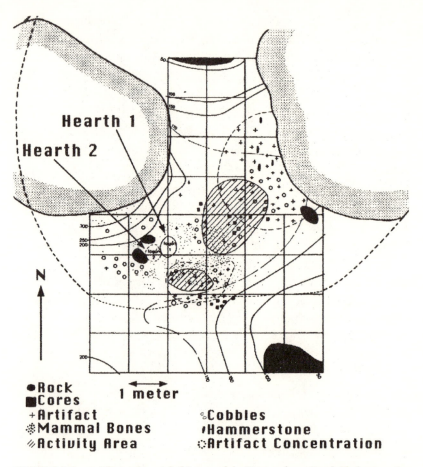

**Hearth 1**

**Hearth 2**

N

● **Rock**
■ **Cores**
+ **Artifact**       ⸰ **Cobbles**
※ **Mammal Bones**   ⸀ **Hammerstone**
⸮ **Activity Area**  ⸜ **Artifact Concentration**

← 1 meter →

FIGURE 2.4. ■ The earliest inhabitants of the Tequendama Rock Shelter on the Sabana de Bogotá, Colombia, occupied a protected living area beneath a rock overhang (marked by a broken line) and between rock walls (stippled). The remains of hearths and workshop areas (large circles) show where activities took place between 9000 and 8000 B.C.

factured just two meters east and southeast of the hearths, where cores were found, and where hide-working and other tasks were performed beneath the rocky overhang.

The people of Tequendama brought food, water, and fuel from outside to be processed, cooked, and consumed in the cave, where they also manufactured and repaired wooden tools, worked skins and fibers, and assembled clothing. Members of a family carried out the work necessary for subsistence and comfort, but we can not specify who performed each task. Perhaps women engaged in stone-working and made the bone tools they themselves used. The majority of the tools recovered are knives and scrapers, including abundant unretouched flakes, which might have been used by anybody. Bone tools and perforators are evidence of the manufacture of clothing, bags, cordage, and baskets. Grinding tools indicate that seeds and other plants were important in the diet. Most of the animals represented in the midden are small, such as species of cotton rat, rabbit, armadillo, guinea pig (first hunted and later domesticated at the site), hog-nosed skunk, and two kinds of deer. The proportion of small to large animals suggests that the people were collectors who snared and netted as often as they hunted. Stone projectile points were not used by these Paleoindians.

Although the excavators identified Tequendama as the home of specialized deer hunters, the occupants of the cave performed many different activities and consumed a wide variety of food. The map of the spatial arrangement of artifacts and food and other debris on the cave floor helps us to envision the human group that produced the archaeological record. They were not all men, and we need not conjure a cartoon version of men hunting. Extrapolating from historic and contemporary hunting and foraging peoples, we speculate that women provided the bulk of the food consumed. Because the labor pool was small, women (like men) flexibly undertook whatever work needed to be done.

One can imagine older women and men by the fire working and chatting, while vigorous adults tote heavy loads up the slope, and children and infants help or play. During the day the adult women collect food, using their profound knowledge of the plant and animal species in their environment. Later, everyone processes the foodstuffs contributed by women and men. Women, with the help of girls, invest long hours in other productive activities that require years of training and the skilled use of tools and materials. Female as well as male people engage in solving problems such as healing sick and injured family members, developing plans for a ceremony, and finding mates for maturing offspring. In this reconstruction of the deep past, when people return to the cave at evening for food and the company of their kin, women and girls appear in the center of the scene, not as the shadowy, peripheral figures of artists' reconstructions.

## Engendering the Deep Past

The archaeological record affords neither art nor burial assemblages from which archaeologists can argue about gender roles in Paleoindian societies, and yet we know that both women and men participated in the peopling of America. By analogical argument, an interpretation of Paleoindian women that is consistent with the evidence can be made using ethnography, imagination, and a critical perspective on the archaeological record. Because stone tools dominate the corpus of remains, their interpretation led to androcentric reconstructions of the past, but this is changing. Scholars like Joan Gero and Kenneth Sassaman have demonstrated that both women and men made and used those stone tools. Even if the fluted bifacial points of the Paleoindian period were super weapons, emblems of male gender identity and paraphernalia used in male hunting cults, most of the tool kit found in Paleoindian base camps and kill sites is not composed of the elegant points but of scrapers, knives, choppers, and humble utilized flakes—evidence of the economic activity that made life possible in ancient America. In the new, holistic picture of Paleoindian life, based on understanding the total tool kit, the wide range of productive activities and food sources, and the location of habitation sites, Man the Hunter does not appear alone.

# CHAPTER THREE

# *Women in the Archaic*

In America the Paleoindian period was followed by a span of time during which people progressively intensified their foraging activities, focusing on a wide range of resources in reduced territories. The dates of this Archaic way of life are not fixed because in local areas it developed at different times and persisted variably: for 8,000 years in some parts of North America, for only a few millennia in other regions. Most Archaic cultures are thought to have lacked permanent architecture, ceramics, and food production, although some eastern North American Archaic sites show an early development of these characteristics. Based on analogy with recent foragers, Archaic societies are believed to have been characterized by low population densities and small egalitarian social groups in which status was achieved, not ascribed.

The Archaic peoples descended from Paleoindians, but they differed culturally from their ancestors, who may have depended more heavily on hunting as they moved like pioneers through the Americas. No Paleoindian groups, however, depended solely on male hunting for survival, and in any scenario, women's knowledge and contributions to subsistence were important. It is likely that the skill and knowledge accumulated by Paleoindian women became the foundation of the way of life of the less mobile Archaic peoples. Some anthropological studies have suggested that males are predominant in situations of migration, but that parity is established with sedentism. The broad-spectrum foraging of many Archaic peoples may have been a good cultural setting for women, and some scholars believe that women may have negotiated equal social power under these conditions. It seems likely that as Archaic people settled down into areas where an array of resources was harvested, women would have continued to exercise control over their own working conditions and the distribution of the food they produced, a situation that meant greater economic power. Under some circumstances, this foraging adaptation culminated in women creating new food-producing systems based on the cultivation of plants.

The transition from mobile hunting to more sedentary, broad-spectrum foraging in the eastern forests of North America involved changes in lithic technology that may reflect evolution in the division of labor between women and men. According to Kenneth Sassaman, the archeological record reflects the progressive reduction of high-risk hunting activities in favor of more reliable subsistence activities, including the exploitation of plant resources and other nonmobile resources such as fish and small animals. This shift correlates with a reduction in the production of specialized hunting equipment and an increase in the production of more expedient tools. Archaic sites are characterized by large quantities of technologically simple flakes, produced easily and used by sedentary Archaic people, especially women, who processed foods and produced an expanding inventory of material culture. Sassaman demonstrates that women became much more visible in the archaeological record because of their increased activity in the production and use of stone tools, and later, pottery.

Later in the Archaic, as people in the eastern United States grew more sedentary, formal tools were produced with less and less frequency. Fancy bifacial projectile points lost their prominence, although in late prehistory men continued to perform rituals involving these tools. According to Sassaman, this suggests a kind of male resistance to technological change.

## Engendering Archaic Burials

Some of the strongest engendered interpretations in New World prehistory come from the study of burials. While it is often difficult to distinguish the remains of male activities from those of female activities in the archaeological record, we can distinguish male from female skeletons with some confidence.

Some of the Archaic people who were relatively sedentary buried their dead in cemeteries, and human remains and their mortuary contexts allow for the reconstruction of some aspects of prehistoric gender behaviors. While many archaeologists remain conflicted about the ethics of disinterring the ancient dead, the scientific study of cemeteries is a very productive method for reconstructing the past.

## Status among Foragers

Status refers to the relative position of individuals in society. In our society this means ranking on a socioeconomic scale and involves distinctions between high-status individuals and low-status ones, over whom others hold power. In contrast, under egalitarian conditions there is relatively little exercise of authority over others, although there is social differentiation and several statuses. The old and the young may differ with respect to role, emblems, and access to goods, just as women will differ from men. Talented people may be assigned leadership roles in limited contexts, and elders can be expected to be more central in decision making, but hierarchy is not a necessary dimension of social organization in all cases. Women's status is variable among hunters and gatherers, although some scholars have asserted that women universally have high status in foraging societies.

Brian Hayden and his colleagues have defined several indicators of female status that vary greatly among societies and are difficult to identify in the archaeological record. Some of the indicators of high status for women include female voice in domestic decisions, female control of children, female control of food they have procured, female ownership or control of the dwelling, female voice in interband affairs, and the possibility of female leaders. Status is interpreted as low if females are frequently beaten or poorly treated, if they are excluded from ritual activity, if (in hunting societies) their participation in hunting is limited by taboos, if there are myths of former female control of males, and if there is a belief in the inferiority of females with respect to males.

This research on ethnographic foragers has shown that the status of women of childbearing years in both the domestic and the political spheres is strongly related to the frequency and severity of environmental crises. Hayden and his colleagues conclude that in groups under high stress, men force heavier work loads upon females. This may alleviate local stress because the women act to control their fertility by resorting to infanticide. Women's status increases, according to Hayden, and their work loads ease, only after menopause. This cultural pattern, observed in many foraging societies, suggests that adaptation is achieved at great cost to women. However, Hayden has shown that women's status in ritual domains is variable and not controlled by techno-environmental factors. Furthermore, women's status may be high in the absence of adverse conditions. The presence of warfare may reduce women's status, but if the men travel great distances and leave women in charge, the reverse may be true.

It is important to emphasize that female status has been observed to be high in some situations and low in other techno-environmental conditions. As circumstances change, so do social patterns. It is unwise to generalize any interpretation: women's and men's statuses change and vary. In the archaeological record we expect to confront diversity and uniqueness.

In the ancient Americas, the assessment of comparative status of women and men in society is difficult because they frequently do not participate in the same activities. Women and men may not compete for the same things as they do in modern Euroamerican society. It is unproductive to define high status only in terms of the spheres open to men. In some societies, sexual segregation means that women and men have different spheres. In their own sphere, women may have considerable autonomy, make their own decisions, and achieve respect via competent performance. After death women will be interred with things important and relevant to them, whereas men may be buried with other things having divergent meanings that are not comparable to female things.

### The Chinchorro Archaic Tradition in Chile

Along the desert coast of northern Chile and southernmost Peru, the Chinchorro people exploited cold-water marine and adjacent terrestrial environments, eating sea mammals, fish, shellfish, seaweed, and terrestrial plants and animals from 9,000 to 2,000 years ago. Good preservation in their coastal habitation sites and cemeteries facilitates our interpretation of the roles of women and men.

The following partial list of their material culture helps one imagine the productive activities of both women and men about 4,000 years ago. They possessed many wooden artifacts, including spears, spear throwers (atlatls), and needles; bone items such as compound fishhooks, *chopes* (sea lion ribs with one end sharpened and the other covered with a soft hide, used to process shellfish), and decorated flutes; vegetable-fiber bags and pubic covers; reed mats and baskets; camelid hair loincloths and bags; seabird, sea lion, and camelid hides prepared as leather and made into garments; stone net weights, mortars, and knives; seeds used in rattles; cactus thorns used in fishhooks; human-hair cords; feather headbands; sea lion teeth; unfired clay figurines; discoid shell artifacts; and red, white, and green paint.

A group of Chinchorro foragers studied by Sonia Guillén and Marvin Allison were generally healthier than the later agricultural people in the same area. Their skeletal remains show that women and men had a good life expectancy for that period in history. If they survived childhood, their average life expectancy was twenty-five years, although some individuals lived to be fifty or more. Guillén's study of the Chinchorro cemeteries found little evidence of pathology in the skeletons, the normal pattern for foragers living in small groups and eating well. The high number of auditory exostoses in males has been suggested as an indication of a sexual division of labor in which men spent more time diving in cold waters, were more subject to ear infections, and hence developed the auditory condition. However, modern studies of professional swimmers have shown that women, even when they are diving deep in cold waters as frequently as men, do not form exostoses with the same frequency as males. This makes it difficult to say for certain whether women as well as men were diving among the Chinchorro. However, 18 percent of the male skeletons showed fractures in their lower back regions, evidence of frequent diving accidents in the rough, rocky waters.

Allison's work revealed that female skeletons had highly developed facets on their ankle bones, a condition caused by the habitual bent or squatting position of women cleaning shellfish, further evidence of an ancient division of labor. Women were also affected by spinal arthritis, found in a third of all their skeletons, and one in five women suffered from compression fractures in their spines, due to osteoporosis, perhaps aggravated by multiple pregnancies. Forty percent of all people suffered from severe infections in their legs that actually damaged their bones.

Another study of fifty-one Chinchorro individuals from about 2000 B.C. shows some deterioration in health. Here, 86.4 percent of the adults had Harris lines (4.8 lines per individual), evidence of nutritional stress. Eighty-six percent of the children had lines (about 6.1 lines per individual),

---

and women showed 50 percent more lines than males (in a small sample of twelve individuals). These figures may not reflect accurately the differential health status of women and men, but simply the fact that Harris lines more often disappear from men's bones because they are heavier than women's and more likely to be remodeled in their lifetimes. Nevertheless, women are often subject to greater nutritional and disease problems during pregnancy, and the poor health of mothers can cause prenatal lines in the tibiae of their children. One study of the Chinchorro population at the Morro 1 site concluded that most health problems occurred when children were between seven and sixteen years old and among young women who would have had greater nutritional requirements due to pregnancy, parturition, and nursing infants. Generally, however, there is a pattern of good dental health and no evidence that either women or children were systematically prejudiced by social or cultural practices of the sort that become common later in history.

Chinchorro ritual life focused on artificial mummification. The bodies of men, women, and children were defleshed and eviscerated, then they were reassembled using artificial supports of wood, stuffed with plants, coated with clay, tar, and paint, and festooned with ornaments and wigs (fig. 3.1). The elaborate preparation of mummies was a way of preserving and venerating the dead, and mortuary ceremonialism probably had multiple social functions. For instance, in societies in which there is little differentiation between the public and domestic spheres, ceremonialism makes possible the integration of kin groups. During burial ceremonies among some South American Indians today, people strive to achieve ethnic and family solidarity, which facilitates decision making by consensus, thus avoiding the need for political hierarchy or central leadership. Anthropologists suggest that the communal disposal of the dead may be part of a group's strategy for buttressing its territorial claims in conditions of competition over local resources.

A single 4,000-year-old cemetery in Morro de Arica contained seventeen Chinchorro individuals who were evidently part of a single kin group. Sixteen artificially mummified bodies were interred along with a male body that had been naturally preserved by the arid environment. The investigators did not record the order of the burials. Each was dressed with a loincloth made of wool cords or reed fiber, and most were wrapped with leather cloaks made from the hides of camelid, sea lion, or seabirds.

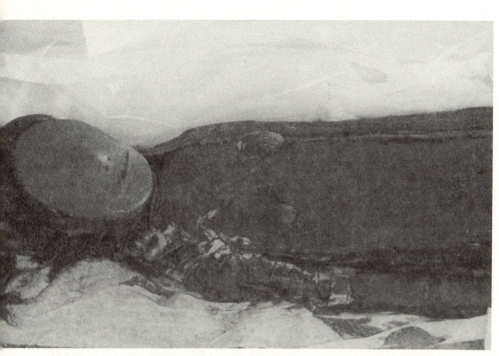

FIGURE 3.1. ■ A mummy from the El Morro I site in northern Chile illustrates how the body of a woman of the Chinchorro culture was prepared with clay facial features, modeled breasts, and a wig.

There were no food offerings. Both male and female mummies were lacking crania, the heads having been removed before burial. Guillén analyzed the grave goods by sex and says that most artifacts aside from clothing were related to the extraction and processing of marine resources. Six mummies had net bags used to hold fishing gear, two of which were associated with a male, one with a female, and three with individuals of undetermined sex. Cactus fishhooks and a compound fishhook were found with two male children and one fetus of undetermined sex. Other fishing gear elements were lines, weights, *chopes*, and a knife, associated with three male children and three mummies of undetermined sex. None of the female mummies had such tools, although some of the unidentified mummies could be female. The available information suggests that offerings of fishing gear were suitable for males. However, in another study Allison reports that in northern Chile women were buried with harpoons, fishhooks, and lines, as well as with elaborate turbans, and he suggests a sexually undifferentiated society. Artifacts associated with both male and female skeletons included reed brushes decorated with transverse red bands; bags containing colored clays, such as red ocher and copper oxide, probably used for body decoration; and tiny stones individually wrapped in skin.

The development of cemeteries in the Archaic period has been explained on the grounds that people were more sedentary and that they were concerned with controlling territories and access to particular resources. People lived on the slopes of Morro de Arica for a long time and made elaborate mummies for almost 3,000 years. They clearly prepared the mummies to be viewed and kept around for a period of time. Later the bodies were deposited in communal graves not far from residential areas. Guillén does not see this as ancestor worship, since the more elaborate mummies are those of children. This could reflect an ancestor cult in which the larger the group of mummies displayed was, the stronger the claim of the family to territory and nearby resources. Periodically, groups of mummies were interred without offerings or food, their function apparently complete. Women and men may have innovated this solution because they were in competition with other groups and made this symbolic effort to protect their claim to traditional marine resources near the Morro site. Only later, as the local people became agricultural, did they adopt funerary practices that involved the disposal of individuals in personal tombs.

In another interpretation, Mario Rivera suggests that competitive, individually oriented Chinchorro bands achieved better social integration among themselves by practicing group-oriented mortuary rituals. By communally preparing selected female and male Chinchorro dead, the Chinchorro people counterbalanced individualistic or family economic activities and reduced competition. This kin-based religious activity, while ritualizing themes of communication with ancestors and, perhaps, fertility, would have permitted the recognition of part-time leaders and created a focus of community identity.

A belief in the importance of the dead as continuing participants in community life explains the Chinchorro mummies. The function of ancestor worship among ancient peoples is well documented in the ethnohistoric and ethnographic literature. The Chinchorro people may have worshipped both female and male ancestors to ensure growth and fertility:

WOMEN IN ANCIENT AMERICA

the ancestors received homage because they were thought to protect the welfare of the community. In many nonmodern groups, communication with the dead and other mortuary rituals are widely seen as validating the territorial claims of the living. In Archaic contexts in Chile, women and men, living and dead, participated in these important social activities.

## La Paloma in Desert Peru

La Paloma is a site on the desert coast of Peru with excellent preservation of habitation remains and burial features. People lived there from 7,000 to 4,500 years ago. The Palomans were gatherers and fishers who exploited the resources of the coast and the nearby hills, which, bathed by fog, supported lush vegetation and animal populations. Palomans in the later periods cultivated plants such as squash, beans, and gourds, and collected vegetable foods. A decrease in the stem diameter of firewood through time may indicate that the environment was being degraded through over-exploitation.

Palomans lived in reed houses, and they were usually buried flexed, wrapped in mats and with a few simple offerings, below the floors of the houses, although there seem to have been a few special group mortuary facilities, including an infant burial house. However, all burials were recovered in or near houses, probably showing the importance of the household in the social organization. This kind of small kin organization is favorable to women and men because when decision making takes place at the level of the family, everyone's personal concerns can be taken into consideration. The burial of a twenty-five-year-old male and a twenty-four-year-old female (Burials 51 and 52) in the earliest levels of the Paloma site shows the equality of the sexes. The two people had similar wrappings. He was buried with several cut-shell amulets; she had twenty-five bone beads.

With respect to gender relations in the late phases of the occupation of Paloma, Jeffrey Quilter observed that female burials had fewer grave goods and that males appear to have had higher status than females. Furthermore, Quilter suggests that sedentary life results in the limiting of women's autonomy and influence. It is possible, however, to interpret the evidence in a different way. The Paloma burial data show gender parity, and they suggest that age was a more important factor than sex in accounting for variation among burials. Quilter's cluster analysis identified three major groups of burials, but there was no significant clustering in any of the three on the basis of gender. Of the seventy-six burials studied, the most elaborate were those of infants and small children.

An alternative interpretation suggests that the burial goods associated with adult female and male burials from the latest levels at Paloma are similar. It is difficult to see how the small differences between the number of artifacts found in male and female burials could translate into difference in status. A simple tally of associated items (counting each as one, without respect to size or quality) indicates that males have a higher average number of offerings only if you omit the beads and amulets associated with the woman and man mentioned above. It seems risky to assert an overall superordination of men over women when there is so little variability among the graves.

Difference in status between males and females also cannot be inferred from evidence such as Burial 159, the most elaborate burial at Paloma. A seventeen-year-old male lay under a cane structure, covered with several mats, accompanied by many funerary offerings. His death had been horrific. His left leg was missing, and cut marks on the pelvis suggest that a shark had removed it. This grave is special not because it contains a male skeleton, but because of the manner of death. Some out-of-the-ordinary graves contained all males, but at least one had two females and two males, and at a closely related site nearby, five females were found in a unique tomb.

There is very little expression of special status in the Paloma remains. Although a few exotic items such as monkey bone, tropical seashells, and obsidian were acquired, the Palomans did not accumulate or manufacture any obvious luxury goods, and even beads seem to decrease in frequency through time. These people may not have invested surplus production in elaborate ceremonial activities, and the site was abandoned before the coastal people intensified their fishing and cotton-growing activities and embarked upon the course of social and cultural intensification that led to the construction of monumental architecture and other dramatic social, ideological, and technological changes.

An analysis of 200 skeletons demonstrates that the ancient people were healthy by preceramic standards, but they suffered from tuberculosis and carcinomas, as well as frequently broken foot bones, osteoarthritis of the spine, and back problems. Apparently, everyone performed hard physical labor. Studies of the hair found in some Paloma graves showed sharp differences in mineral composition, suggesting seasonal variation in diet.

The excavators see population increase through time at Paloma, and they believe that people were healthier, taller, and better-adapted later in history at the site. According to Robert Benfer, life expectancy increased through time, and the incidence of tooth wear, Harris lines, and cribra orbitalia decreased, although hypoplastic lesions were fairly common in all periods. The relative numbers of fetal and infant burials decreased over time, perhaps indicating an improvement in living conditions.

There are some curious patterns in the burial evidence from Paloma. Almost twice as many adult females died in their thirties than in their twenties. This contrasts with the expected pattern of premodern societies, in which high female mortality occurs among women in their twenties due to pregnancy and childbirth. If the sexing of very young skeletons from Paloma is accurate, the data indicate more female infants were interred than males. The data show that older, noninfant male skeletons occurred twice as frequently as female ones. Benfer has suggested that this might be evidence of a social strategy: in an effort to control population size and growth, the ancient people may have postponed marriage and practiced female infanticide. It is not surprising that the Palomans tried to control their population using strategies often used in history, but it is hard to believe that there were twice as many men as women, so we expect that there are other explanations for the recovery of more male skeletons. One wonders also if polyandry was practiced at Paloma.

Benfer has made an effort to show that division of labor by sex was dynamic at Paloma. He noted that sexual dimorphism in musculature was marked in the early Paloma skeletal population, suggesting that males and females did very different activities, and that men were very robust. Later, women increased their muscle mass by more vigorous and prolonged activity, while men showed reduced amounts, probably reflecting reduced mobility and less hard work. The major changes in the shape of both men's and women's upper arm bones may reflect more intensive maritime tasks such as netting fish or intensified gardening and food processing.

Trace element analysis has revealed a convergence in male and female diets from the early to late occupations of La Paloma. In the early period men and women exploited, and apparently consumed, different foods. Later there was a decrease in the availability of wild plants and fur-bearing animals and, with increased sedentism, the investigators infer an increased emphasis on fishing and cultivating plants. In this later period, men, helped by women and children, may have fished and hunted marine animals, while women processed products of the sea and worked gardens with the help of children and men.

A glimpse of the ancient gender roles of the Palomans comes from an analysis of the burials. Females were more frequently interred on their right sides and males on their left than might be expected in a random distribution. Quilter hypothesizes that projectile points, flakes, and miscellaneous tools were associated with male activities and that grinding stones were associated with preparing foods at home, but he found only a weak statistical association between males, hunting, and small processing tools, and between females and grinding stones. Points and flakes were associated mostly with men, but both men and women had grinding tools interred with them.

In actuality, all adult burials had very similar ranges of artifacts. In making gender activity attributions, one must remember that in small communities women and men cannot afford to be inflexible about who does what. Five female skeletons and four males were associated with bone tools of the kind commonly used, even in the present, in the manufacture of nets, cordage, and textiles. Quilter speculates that men used these artifacts to repair fishing nets and tackle and that women made house mats and clothing, although, as he notes, gifts to the dead may not reflect the activities of the deceased person. Twined junco reed mats were very common at Paloma, and there were also fine twined textiles of maguey-like plant fiber that served as clothing and head coverings. The Palomans also made knotted netting bags, fish nets, and twined baskets. Making and repairing fishing gear must have required a great amount of energy and care. Net and hook manufacture was time-consuming, although we have no real evidence concerning who did what tasks.

During the long occupation of Paloma, change occurred throughout the social-cultural system. Sarah MacAnulty, working with Quilter at Paloma, has shown that animal fur and hides decrease in quantity through time, while textiles increase. This may reflect degradation of animal resources and changes in labor allocation. A shift from hunting to more focused fishing for males, resulting in a shortage of hides, might have necessitated the investment of more effort in plant-fiber collecting and processing, and increased investment in textile production. Such a change would have had a gender component: if the processing of animal hides and the production of plant-fiber textiles were both women's work, then female workload might have been altered. Did women press for this change because they found textile production more convenient? Or did they resist the change because it required increased effort on their parts? Later in prehistory, in much of Peru, weaving was practically and symbolically associated with women. It seems possible that the women of Paloma undertook the manufacture of textiles because, compared to skin garments, textiles were more expressive of women's skill and pride. Did the development of textile production offer women more independence, an area of productivity in which they were relatively autonomous and creative? Was it more efficient for women to harvest reeds and century plant fiber to increase their productivity than to intensify snaring seabirds and trapping rabbits? Were men happy that women no longer demanded a steady input of skins? Ultimately these speculative questions may be pointless if men as well as women made textiles, as was sometimes the case later in Andean history.

## The Archaic Las Vegas People of Ecuador

The preceramic Las Vegas people, who inhabited the southwest coast of Ecuador between 8000 and 4600 B.C., were broad-spectrum hunters, fishers, and gatherers adapted to an ecologically complex tropical coastal environment with a high biotic potential. They added plant cultivation to their subsistence system around 5000 B.C. The largest Las Vegas site may have been occupied permanently or revisited seasonally. It also served as a preferred burial place in the later Las Vegas period.

Study of the skeletal population shows that the Las Vegas people were typical preintensive agriculture peoples with none of the degenerative diseases associated with agricultural groups. Life expectancy was over thirty years, somewhat greater than the later agricultural populations of coastal Ecuador.

A study of the remains of 192 individuals from the main Las Vegas site shows clear gender-related practices in disposal of the dead. Males were buried in a flexed position, generally on their right sides and with their heads toward the west or southwest—toward the setting sun or the open

---

sea. Often a pillow of shell was placed under the head, and offerings of some stone flakes, a cobble tool, or a conch shell were common.

Adult women were buried in a similar way, but their heads were oriented in every direction, with a slight preference for the northeast. Women's grave furniture included shell dishes, stone flakes (knives), and cobble tools. Regrettably, the fibers and gourds, surely used for shrouds, clothing, and containers, were not preserved. Age differences in burial practices are reflected in the relatively shallower graves of subadults, who were buried flexed on their left sides with their heads to the east or southeast.

Among the primary burials there were no significant differences in the distribution of grave goods by sex or age. However, females (74 percent of 19 burials) and subadults (78 percent of 9 burials) were more likely to have durable offerings than males (only 56 percent of 9 burials). Secondary burials, evidence that mortuary ritual continued long after the death of an individual, were common. Small bundles contained the reburied bones of 8 men, 7 women, and 6 children. Often only a few body parts, or selected bones of several individuals, were included in these burial bundles. The bones of the dead evidently had special meaning for the ancient people.

In three massive secondary burials (large, circular ossuaries), adult males and females were about equally represented, and there were subadults as well. Among the communal offerings in one of these ossuaries was a cache of 26 selected, polished pebbles, interpreted as a shaman's charm stones representing all the individuals in the burial.

Douglas Ubelaker identified the sex of 118 adult Vegas skeletons: 53 percent were female and 47 percent male. In contrast to this general parity, among the 26 adults of known sex recovered in primary burials, only 31 percent were male, and 66 percent were female. This sexual imbalance in the primary burials indicates that females apparently received or remained in primary burials more frequently than males. Males may have been exhumed and kept elsewhere more often than females. It is clear that the remains of women and men were manipulated differently, evidence of different statuses or contrasting roles for female and male ancestors vis-à-vis their living descendants.

Of some importance is that the single individual found buried under the threshold of an early Las Vegas shelter was a female over forty-five years old. This suggests the importance of female ancestors or lineage heads.

The most provocative Vegas burial is that of a twenty-year-old female, buried in normal flexed posture, embraced in the tomb by a twenty-year-old male arranged in an amorous posture (fig. 3.2). Their deaths may have been extraordinary. They apparently died together or within a short time of each other. Their relatives arranged them in the tomb and placed several large stones over the bodies, perhaps to keep them from returning in search of their loved ones, or as a gesture of magical protection.

There is evidence that in late Vegas times, the people increased their dependence on fishing, began taking a broader range of shellfish species, and added domesticated plants to the resources they exploited. The Vegans probably found that gardening increased the productivity of the river bottoms and expanded the variety of resources they relied upon. One could speculate that the men expanded the hours invested in fishing while the women intensified food collecting and invested progressively more labor in gardening.

Evidence of bottle gourd, squash, and primitive maize were found in La Vegas soil samples dated to the phase when burial ceremonialism was at its height. Because in many hunting-gathering societies, women are associated with plants, it seems logical that they were the ones tending experimental species, intervening in the reproduction of the species that later became domesticated. New evidence suggests that squash was domesticated on the coast of Ecuador, and Vegas women may have been the ones who reserved the seeds from the tastiest fruits for replanting and who weeded and watered them. Their careful attention and selection then produced the genetically engineered species so important in the diets of their descendants.

Perhaps the Vegas people intensified both the cultivation of plants and fishing as responses to population growth, or because of drier conditions or changes in the coastline around 5000 B.C. Alternatively, women and men may have adopted new economic strategies because of escalating social needs: participation in burial ceremonialism and trade requires surplus production. A polished stone ax found in pristine condition in the tomb of a Las Vegas woman, buried between 6000 and 5000 B.C., is evidence of long-distance exchange. No other axes have been found in Las Vegas sites, so the burial artifact was not a Vegas manufacture, but it is

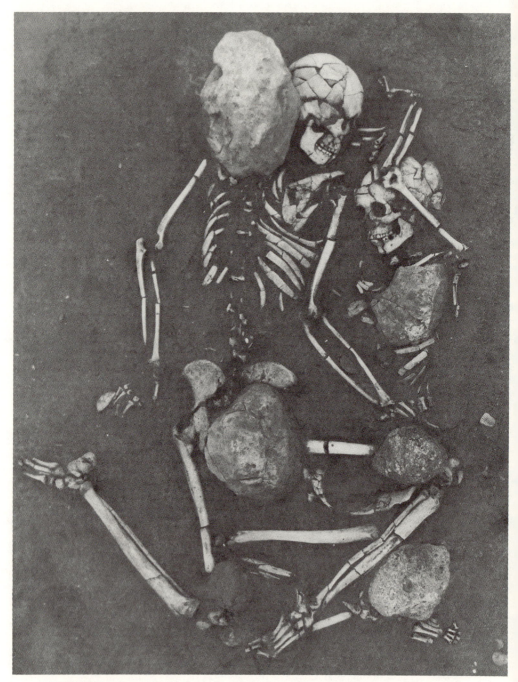

FIGURE 3.2. ■ The bodies of a young man (left) and a young woman, both twenty years old at death, were interred together about 5000 BC in southwestern Ecuador. Because of the position of the bodies, they are known as the Lovers of Sumpa and have been popularized as the preceramic Adam and Eve.

very similar to axes manufactured and found in abundance in preceramic sites near Talara in northern Peru. The mature woman buried with the ax may have traveled to Talara, or received the ax from a trading partner, or acquired it in some other form of exchange. The lack of use-wear indicates that it functioned as a token or talisman, and not as a cutting tool.

Regardless of what motivated change in Vegas society, the founding of the cemetery at Site 80 may have had the practical effect of facilitating social connectedness. The creation of a body of mortuary rituals and other commemorative and magical activities could have provided opportunities for cooperative labor and might have increased the size of the functional kin group, making it more capable of defending its territory. As this group organized to carry out rituals, it may have developed more elaborate social mechanisms, which conferred economic benefits by permitting larger task groups or supporting economic specialization by sex, domestic unit, or family group. Change and attendant social adjustment would have affected the lives of both women and men.

We see the archaic Las Vegas people through a veil, because the majority of their material culture has not been preserved. But the evidence shows us healthy, enduring, egalitarian people in benign ecological conditions. Life may have been good for both women and men as they invented new technologies (plant cultivation) and new social mechanisms (burial cere-monialism) to meet changing needs.

## Change in the Archaic

Culture change involves people making choices that in turn create conflicts in all areas of their lives. New activities have to be accommodated. Often, sex roles and, ultimately, gender ideologies change as individuals undertake new tasks. At the same time, changes in production will result in changing symbolic value and meaning of particular products; social arrangements will be reorganized to handle new activities or in response to the loss of old ones; diets will be modified, as well as tools, cooking, and so forth. Many little related changes may add up to a major historical trend. History is made by women and men making small adjustments that result in the evolution of sociocultural systems. This is an aspect researchers need to consider as they seek possible explanations of change.

Recent studies in North American Archaic cultures show us some situations in which the causes of cultural change can be inferred.

## Archaic Adaptations in California

Hunter/gatherers thrived in the Central Valley of California from early in prehistory until the time of European contact. Archaeological data from about 2500 B.C. until A.D. 1450 show a pattern of subsistence change as acorn consumption increased and salmon fishing replaced deer hunting. This was accompanied by an accelerating rate of population growth, and skeletal remains indicate a decline in longevity. Women and men show little difference in basic health, but gender played a crucial role in their life experiences as women's and men's activities changed dramatically through time.

David Dickel and his colleagues have suggested that as acorn-based economies developed, birth spacing decreased and local populations grew. This change must have radically altered the lives of women. At the same time, adult mortality increased. Although Dickel and coauthors do not show evidence of differences in female and male mortality, they hypothesize that young adult females were dying at a higher rate due to the risks of more frequent childbirth. There is evidence of heavier mortality in later Archaic periods for unweaned children aged 0–2 years, which Dickel attributes to the loss of their mothers. Dickel's interpretation of the paleodemographic information, based on aging and sexing skeletons from Central Valley Archaic cemeteries, indicates that, overall, subadult survivorship increased through time, while adult survivorship decreased.

The changes observed in the Archaic reflect the choices of generalized foragers who were sparsely settled in the Central Valley in the Early Archaic period. Progressively they redefined their subsistence strategies, eliminating old subsistence activities and focusing on a reduced number of plant and animal species. By the Late Archaic, these foragers were emphasizing acorns and salmon and were living in more stable settlements. They had increased their population size and density, and they adopted various kinds of cultural activities that anthropologists normally associate with early agricultural peoples.

This shift, like many other important changes in history, was linked to changing material conditions resulting from women having more babies.

The culture changes in the Central Valley probably involved greater emphasis on gendered labor. Assigning labor by sex is one form of specialization, one way to achieve greater output. Among the historic California Indians, acorn processing and storage was women's work. Women may have resisted the shift to acorn processing because it committed them to the heavy, tedious labor of detoxifying acorns. On the other hand, they might have been willing to undertake the processing and storing chores because the labor could be carried out in company with other women, because the new subsistence strategy solved some perceived problems with food shortage, and because it relieved them of the burden of moving camp so often. One wonders also if men were happy with an intensified focus on salmon. Was this an activity of choice, or were they pressured by women and children to forgo deer hunting because fishing was especially reliable and productive?

Dickel suggests that the subsistence shift toward specialization may have resulted from a series of prolonged and stressful dry periods. Under these conditions, people may have perceived that acorns were productive and reliable, so they increased their exploitation of this food source. Focusing on acorns then resulted in a more sedentary lifestyle to facilitate the processing and storage of the nuts. This innovation may be linked to population increase caused by reduced birth spacing, a situation often seen when mobile people become sedentary. Dickel also suggests that the ancient people chose to exploit resources that involved heavy labor investment because of demographic stress in their circumscribed valley.

A study of skeletal pathologies indicates considerable biological stress among the Central Valley Archaic people. Subsistence change did *not* result in better health for the people. In fact, data from Early, Middle, and Late Archaic skeletons show that although acute stress decreased, chronic stress increased, presumably due to inadequate nutrition and disease. This pattern of change in health that accompanied the development of specialized collecting in Central California is analogous to the changes seen in the shift from foraging to agriculture in other regions. Dickel explains that the Archaic people may have been creating a new system in response to perceived health problems. They worked out a system to decrease the seasonal lack of food (acute stress) that may have been perceived as a cause of morbidity. They achieved resource stabilization but may not have perceived the costs of increased infant and maternal death, and overall higher mortality due to increased population density and disease.

One of the most important aspects of the female role in history is each woman's potential to reproduce. This is sometimes under the control of women themselves, but sometimes it is under the control of male relatives (or even the state). In addition, societies develop a variety of conscious and unconscious mechanisms to control the fertility of women. This area of choice and policy is not only of personal concern but one of the major dynamics of human history. Babies may translate into population growth, demographic pressure, competition for resources, conflict, techno-economic change, and sociopolitical evolution. In the California Archaic, individual women must have made decisions that resulted in a greater number of pregnancies. They decided to have sex sooner after a birth because they were more sedentary and no longer worried about carrying more than one small child; they chose to wean sooner onto acorn gruel, thereby increasing the probability of ovulation and pregnancy; they opted to keep a baby that more mobile families might have let die. When mobility is decreased, energy demands on adult women decrease, which may allow them to keep up their fat levels, thus increasing fertility. More children may have been desirable to help with the labor-intensive activities of acorn and salmon processing. Relatively sedentary people often slacken the onerous controls on fertility normally practiced by mobile foragers. In this way, the decisions made by individual women or families had revolutionary consequences for history: higher fertility meant progressive subsistence change and contributed to persistent stress. High mortality in the later Archaic periods, however, may not have been obvious to the people because it was not directly tied to lack of food.

Culture change in the Archaic period surely involved negotiations between women and men as they chose new strategies that required innovative commitments of time, labor, and technology. We know from ethnographic descriptions that entire families cooperated in harvesting acorns in one season, that women took responsibility for processing acorns and building and managing storage facilities for that staple, and that men invested energy and time in salmon fishing. One underlying concern was settlement location, which evolved with changing subsistence strategies. Women's interests and voices were surely heard because settlements and their locations had to be tailored to acorn processing and storage, as well as to hunting and fishing.

Recent interpretations of Archaic peoples in California have drawn attention to the importance of women's work in food production (not just reproduction) and to the role of women as actors in ancient cultures. In the Sierra Nevada, the Late Archaic acorn-eating people studied by Thomas Jackson were interpreted by analogy with the ethnographically known Western Mono and other acorn-dependent Indians. Jackson showed that women's food-production activity was the key factor in community decisions about subsistence behavior, social and economic relations, and settlement location. The late prehistoric Indians were characterized by a settlement system involving the creation of bedrock mortars and storage silos that facilitated women's labor and production (fig. 3.3). Jackson suggests that the archaeological distribution of sites responded to women's social and resource needs. Within the big winter camp sites, Jackson identifies groups of mortars around the houses and main midden area, where both men and women worked and left debris, and other mortars 50 meters away, interpreted as women's areas. This exclusive space may have been balanced by men's sweat lodges, which in the historic period were a little distance from the main camp. In the summer, women may have dominated the small, high-altitude sites, where men may have spent less time. In these camps there were no isolated mortar facilities.

Jackson points out that in the historic period, the Western Mono people were matrilineal, a kind of social organization that often confers benefits upon women: they inherit rights and have substantial authority within their families. That granaries for acorn storage were the personal property of women in the historic period is evidence of their status and potential power, although men were in charge of exchange and intergroup relations and had access to surpluses generated by women.

Acorn-pounding facilities similar to the prehistoric ones were built by women in the historic period, and some have sacred and ceremonial connotations. By analogy it can be inferred that prehistoric groups of women spent long hours pounding acorns at sites near water sources and stationary acorn-storage facilities. These sites were very likely occupied during extended periods by matrifocal families where men lived with their wives and their wives' relatives. In the historic period, women

FIGURE 3.3. ■ The association of bedrock mortars for pounding acorns and petroglyphs at this Archaic site near Volcano, California, indicates a connection between women's work and prehistoric ritual practice.

claimed rights not only to bedrock mortars and granaries, but also to certain trees and seed plots.

This recent interpretation of Archaic people draws attention to the importance of women's work, including pounding acorns, which produced the storable staple that sustained life for many ancient Californians. Jackson believes that the settlement system of the late prehistoric people, and perhaps their social organization, was determined by the requirements of women and their labor in acorn processing. This is a refreshing interpretation, since in most discussions of prehistoric groups, men's hunting activities have been given central importance. The development of new hunting technology (the bow and arrow replacing the spear thrower) was an important event in Archaic history, but so was the innovation of acorn-processing technologies, including the manufacture of bedrock mortars and the restructuring of settlement patterns.

## The Shell Mound Archaic of Southeastern North America

In her study of the end of the Shell Mound Archaic way of life, Cheryl Claassen asked why shell fishing intensified during the Archaic period and then disappeared. Her response focused on the activities of women and men and the meaning of those activities.

The Shell Mound Archaic is a cultural phenomenon restricted to tributaries of the Mississippi in the states of Alabama, Kentucky, Tennessee, West Virginia, and Illinois. Between 3500 and 1000 B.C., Archaic people, who left no evidence of permanent housing, created huge mounds of shell, presumably having used the mollusks as food. They buried humans and dogs within the mounds, which suggests to archaeologists that the mounds had a sacred function. The study of human remains from the mounds showed no significant difference in health between the sexes, and while men, women, and children all had good-quality burial offerings, it is of special interest that more women than men were sprinkled with red ocher, and that ceremonial items such as medicine bags, turtle shell rattles, and flutes were found with both women and men. Only men and children were accompanied by artifacts belonging to several categories, which some archaeologists think is indicative of high status.

Why did people build shell mounds in one period, and then cease to do this? Did shell fishing intensify during one historical period, and then decline? Perhaps the weakest explanations are environmental, viewing the human group as simply responsive to external change. Claassen claims that the environmental explanations deny human choice.

Claassen's understanding of the shell mounds grew out of a consideration of gender and a study of modern ethnographic cases. She argues that the elderly, infirm, and children make significant contributions to their own and their family's diet by shell fishing, although shell fishing may also be undertaken by men for fishing bait. In ethnographic cases, shell fishing may or may not generate highly valued food, and mollusks may play a greater or a lesser role in diet.

According to Claassen's hypothesis, Archaic women allotted time for shell fishing by season or as part of their weekly or monthly schedules. She also guesses that the activity had some additional ideological or social significance. While some theorists imagine that people undertake activities such as shell fishing to maximize the effectiveness of their time and effort in the production of consumable energy, real people may engage in an activity because of its prestige value, because it provides social enjoyment, because it fits with child rearing, or because it allows one to realize spiritual goals.

The challenge for archaeologists is to explain the intentional creation of dense shell heaps along the tributaries of some rivers in the Midwest. One can imagine how the onset of warmer conditions and the relative sedentism of Archaic communities created a circumstance in which people, by repeated activity on the same spot, might erect mounds and create burial grounds in their traditional territories, but Claassen believes that this scenario accounts for the mounding effect only in part. Because the mounds contained high percentages of paired valves, the mollusks probably were steamed open, the meats removed, and the shells dumped on the mound. Claassen suggests that the women were harvesting mussels and drying the shellfish flesh for consumption in winter and spring. But the mounds were more than functional refuse heaps: they were thought of as ceremonial structures. This interpretation is supported by the fact that in some of the mounds there was more than one burial per cubic meter and that the majority of the ocher-sprinkled burials were of women. Claassen argues that the shell mound was the center of a ceremonial site, visited by large groups seasonally and preferred as a burial spot for specific group members, especially women. She notes that shell is commonly associated with ceremonialism and funerary ritual throughout the Americas and that the shell itself may have been a valued substance used to create special burial contexts for women shell fishers, the providers of storable protein, and perhaps religious specialists by virtue of an ideological system that associated shell with value, procreation, and death. Those buried were individuals active in reproductive and economic affairs of the aggregate social group, while others were interred in non-shell mound sites.

In this interpretation, shell fishing and shell-mounding were both economic and religious activities important in women's lives. But by the end of the period, the construction of shell mounds ceased, and environmental change is not an adequate explanation for the change in custom.

Some scholars hypothesize that dried shellfish meat, a storable resource, lost importance around 1000 B.C. because it was replaced by domesticated crops harvested in late summer and fall. Although starchy seed horticulture, featuring chenopods, maygrass, marsh elder, and sun-flower, was increasing in importance at this time, the growing population continued to gather shellfish even in the subsequent period, when changes in ideology may have rendered shell-mounding a less symbolically charged activity. Claassen postulates that the old religious metaphors were mooted by new ideas associated with the cycle of planting, growing, and har-vesting, and that the gourd replaced the shell as the most provocative fertility symbol. The daughters of important woman religious specialists who had carried out symbolically important shell fishing and who were buried with red ocher in the mounds in the Archaic period created metaphors more suitable to horticulture as the latter grew in importance. Claassen hypothesizes that the cause of the end of the Shell Mound Archaic may have been ideological. People decided to abandon the custom of mounding shell because the symbolism and metaphors no longer worked for them. Layers of dirt, instead of shell, were intentionally heaped on top of these mounds as they continued to serve as the residential and ritual foci of communities. People may have continued to eat mussels, but the shells were dumped in the river and lost.

This highly speculative interpretation merits consideration because it models a complex social process and makes women and men active parti-cipants in culture change.

## Women's Diverse Roles

Evidence from the Archaic leads to a rejection of the stereotype that women have always done the same thing. There was remarkable variation in women's and men's roles from the earliest epochs, as early foragers occupied every possible American environment from the Arctic to the tropical forest, including marine beaches and desert oases. The evidence indicates that all adults worked very hard and suffered frequently from physical exertion, trauma, disease, and food shortages. Adults, including women, were skilled in crafts and had detailed knowledge of their natural environments, as do modern foragers. Archaic women and men, such as those of the Lower Pecos of Texas, produced spectacular cave paintings, employed stone and clay figurines, and performed ceremonial activities whose meanings can sometimes be inferred from the archaeological record.

At Huaca Prieta, a site in Peru, an extraordinary female burial suggests that older women had important social roles. In a situation in which very few people had any offerings at all, this woman held in her mouth the slightly chewed remains of plant material, including a flower still used in traditional healing to soothe toothache. She also had two pouches. One, of worn cattail fiber, contained a gourd bottle, a gourd stem, two gourd seeds, willow leaves, more of the flowers, and two pieces of reed tuber (a common foodstuff at this site). The other pouch enclosed two gourd containers with carefully cut lids and pyroengraved decoration. No similar gourds were found in the other burials or elsewhere at Huaca Prieta. The patterns engraved on the gourds are not found in preceramic Peruvian art but are similar to pottery designs executed by Valdivia people in coastal Ecuador during the same period. It is possible that these gourds came from the Valdivia region, perhaps brought by the woman herself or received as a gift. The materials buried with this elderly woman seem to indicate special status achieved by virtue of her age, her talents in healing, or her origin.

The Archaic way of life was enduring and admirable precisely because people were behaviorally flexible and innovative. A well-preserved archaeological record reveals that in every local history there was significant change as women and men separately and together sought to improve their conditions, minimize risk, compensate for exogenous factors, create new opportunities, or achieve a less rigorous lifestyle.

Evidence from the Archaic period also indicates relatively egalitarian conditions compared to later times. There is little concrete evidence of differentially ranked status among women and men, but surely female and male roles varied widely from group to group. The material culture of the Archaic is proof of the knowledge and skills of those ancient Americans, both women and men. In the Archaic, women produced admirable works, were buried with special offerings, and were valued members of their families and communities. Postmenopausal women were often honored in death by the members of their communities.

Some scholars think that with growing sedentism, female status may decline, or that with resource stress, female status is low, but this is not a necessary pattern. In almost any context, women may negotiate for themselves spheres of control, such as in burial ceremonialism or ancestor worship; or they may take advantage of family structures to call attention to their important roles and facilitate their exercise of authority; or they may take on innovative productive activities and economic functions that give them influence. The rise of food production is an example of such an activity.

# CHAPTER FOUR

# *Women and Food Production*

The development of food production in America is really many stories. The usual narrative features American foragers who, early in prehistory, sought and harvested resources produced by nature. Their descendants became farmers, or food producers, who invested time, labor, and technology in controlling the reproduction of cultivated plants and domestic animals in managed environments.

Not all Native Americans adopted food-producing strategies, but in many regions south of the Arctic, agriculture eventually became the foundation of prehistoric life. According to the archaeological record, diverse groups of foragers in the postglacial period, after about 10,000 years ago, began to change their interaction with other species. They harvested certain wild plants and animals more intensely than others and engaged in experiments designed to encourage the growth of favored species. Humans in many places managed their environments (by burning, for example). The intentional cultivation of some plants, including storing and sowing their seeds, produced changes favorable to human beings in the biological makeup of several plant populations. In some American regions, as human intervention in the reproduction of plants and some animal species increased in importance, new economic systems emerged, systems characterized by both foraging and food production.

Archaeology now has techniques to trace the development of the wide variety of Native American subsistence systems and to document the domestication of plants and animals. Archaeologists also investigate the changing patterns of health and disease among prehistoric cultivators and evaluate demographic trends. The lengthy process of change that resulted in agricultural economies is often seen as revolutionary because human groups experienced unprecedented economic diversification, proliferation of material culture, and social elaboration. In many cases these emerging agricultural societies were also characterized by dramatically transfigured roles and statuses for both women and men. Some communities experienced tremendous population growth and developed social hierarchies that further altered gender roles and relations.

There is no single cause of the food-production "revolutions." Surely people perceived that there were advantages in intensifying particular economic activities and adopting more complex social arrangements, but they could not have predicted that, in some places, these behaviors would give rise to a new way of life based on agriculture. The period of development of this way of life, called the Neolithic in the Old World and the Formative in the New World, is characterized by intensification of plant cultivation and animal husbandry, the development of crafts such as pottery making and weaving, and the creation of permanent settlements, larger trading networks, and complex social organizations.

People had many reasons for rescheduling their gathering and hunting activities and increasing their labor investment in plant cultivation and animal husbandry. Some may have striven to increase the carrying capacity of the environment to cope with population growth or environmental degradation; others probably tried to minimize risk and even out seasonal scarcity of desirable foods, or to increase production of storable food. Perhaps some women and men hoped to reduce group mobility or increase the availability of food and raw materials (such as fiber) that could be used in trade, while still others wanted to produce surpluses that could be invested in social activities that improved individual and group viability, integration, or competitiveness. No matter what the motivations, the process of change would have involved both women and men working out solutions to technical and social problems.

The adoption of cultivation had a variety of social consequences and a great impact on human health. As people chose to dwell in nucleated settlements, where they could take advantage of the high potential productivity of arable land, community health declined. Where there was high population density, the incidence of disease increased dramatically. Diarrheal and other infectious vectors and parasites, including tapeworms and pinworms, which have been found in ancient coprolites from many groups, caused debilitation and prevented absorption of food, leading to malnutrition, anemia, and death. In the Southwest, dental and oral diseases

were common among prehistoric agricultural people, evidence of malnutrition affecting especially children and women during their childbearing
years. People in ancient America who performed certain activities habitually, like grinding maize, were affected by tendinitis and permanent
skeletal modifications, including damage to their toes and ankles caused
by long hours of work in a squatting position.

## Developing Food Production

Food production was developed or adopted in some places in response
to localized problems in the foraging way of life. Researchers working in
Mexico suggest that ancient people may have wished to stay together in
larger social groups for longer periods each year. In order to support the
enlarged group, people deliberately increased their emphasis upon fewer
gathered species and encouraged the proliferation of those species in
convenient locations. Such activities would have destabilized the social
and economic system with differing consequences among different
peoples. While some mixed foraging and horticultural systems lasted for
millennia, others lost stability, and more intensive agricultural systems
developed. As women reduced their mobility, they produced larger numbers of offspring, who had to be fed. Some local groups grew and became
land hungry, and their sociopolitical systems changed to cope with the
management of social relations and economic tasks.

In some locales, whole communities shifted from being foragers
dependent on wild resources to food producers who took responsibility
for controlling the reproduction of plant and animal species, modifying
the environment, and even generating new species through selective
breeding. The type of food production called horticulture usually involves
people using simple technology and hand labor to cultivate root and tuber
crops. The more labor-intensive form of food production, called agriculture, normally is based upon staple grain crops. People may invest in
elaborate technologies, including irrigation and engineered landscapes,
for both types of food production.

By 5,000 years ago, native peoples in eastern North America autonomously developed food production based on gourds and native plants
found in that region, including goosefoot, marsh elder, sunflower, and
some of the squashes that we still consume today. The early agricultural

systems of the highlands of Mexico were based on maize; beans; squash (the "winter squashes," that is, those with hard rinds); fruits, including avocados; and domestic dogs. In the Andean highlands, early people depended upon potatoes and other tubers and roots, grains such as quinoa and amaranth, summer squashes, beans, fruits, domestic dogs, guinea pigs, and camelids (llamas). In the moist tropics, the early domesticates included manioc, maize, beans, and fruits. Later in prehistory, domesticates such as tropical maize were dispersed outside the region or regions in which they were originally domesticated and were progressively modified by humans to thrive in a wide variety of habitats and climates. Despite the differences among the indigenous American food-producing systems, all differed from those of Eurasia in that domesticated animals were of less importance. Except in the Andes, where llamas were bred as pack-bearing animals and alpacas were developed for their hair, there were few wild animal species appropriate for domestication. Virtually all people had dogs for food and other purposes, but other animal food was fished, gathered, or hunted, and most burdens were transported on the backs of humans or by watercraft.

## Female Autonomy and Status

Feminist archaeology is interested in the proposition that women may have lost status as the Formative way of life evolved. It has been observed that in Africa, !Kung San women lost status when they became less mobile. This was probably not the case in ancient America, because women's roles as providers would not have diminished with sedentism. The !Kung San may not be an appropriate analogue for modeling change in early America (or elsewhere) because those San who settled down entered systems dominated by other cultures. In these systems there was no place for traditional !Kung subsistence activities. Thus, women lost control of production and became dependent upon men. Moreover, Christian missionaries, government bureaucrats, and non-San farmers were governed by religious and legal ideologies concerning the proper place of women and their activities that were damaging to !Kung San women, ideologies that were nonexistent in ancient America.

An impediment to understanding female status in early agricultural societies is our tendency not to recognize that women in horticultural societies frequently have spheres of activity in which they are considered fully adult, exercise autonomy and control, and can achieve high status via competent performance in positions of leadership. High female status in the prehistoric record may be difficult for scholars to recognize because modern. Western people are culturally programmed to value only male activities and symbols of male status, but in many cultures, an individual can attain high status through female roles, not solely through roles open to men. Furthermore, people who share in the Euroamerican cultural adaptation have become so accustomed to stratification and hierarchy that they imagine it is natural to the human condition. They habitually make dualistic, ranked categories. But there are more than two possibilities in the real world. While there are many cases of domination by fathers, husbands, and brothers, it is also true that men are not always necessarily dominant or predominant. Many societies are successfully structured around differentiated roles that are conceived as equal, contrasting, and complementary. The scholarly discussion of the comparative status of women and men in ancient American society may be unproductive because women and men did not necessarily participate in the same activities or compete for the same positions. In modern times, some feminists struggle for women to be just like men, but it is inappropriate to think that that was the case in the past. In many ancient Native American societies, the interdependence of women and men was fostered, gender complementarity was promoted by ideologies, and collaboration was enforced by special division of labor. There existed many societies in which women did have the ability to achieve health, acquire wealth and privilege, and wield power.

The slow transition from foraging to food production in many parts of America ultimately involved radical changes in all parts of society. All of those changes involved the activities and relations of women and men. One of the processes of social transformation was specialization. Economic specialization in many ancient systems developed in tandem with new food-producing strategies and other productive activities as well as with human concentration in large settlements. The specialization of tasks in human groups means that goods and other services are produced by one individual or family and exchanged for goods and services produced by other units. Among known foraging peoples, specialization by sex and age within the family is common. People create culturally gendered behavior and age grades, each with its appropriate and assigned activities. In this way, women and men embrace different strategies and functions as specialists integrated at the family level.

The Formative way of life was characterized by developing specialization based on gender, age, and other social dimensions, resulting in a more complex division of labor that became a prominent feature of economic organization in late prehistory. Formative cemeteries demonstrate social complexity and dimensions of social differences unknown in earlier times. The location of graves, the form of graves, the treatment of the bodies, and the burial furniture indicate that individuals were differentiated by sex, age, occupation, rank, and membership in other groups, including kin groups.

Specialization and the greater size of some local groups in the Formative created problems of organization and integration. For all the disparate elements of complex societies to work together, people tried many kinds of governing mechanisms: some people formed egalitarian organizations, others hierarchical governments, but most others developed organizations with a mix of features—heterarchy. Social complexity developed as women and men created new opportunities for themselves.

## Farmers in Eastern North America

The history of food production in the eastern woodlands of North America has been traced through several Archaic phases, followed by the Early, Middle, and Late Woodland periods, which were characterized by ceramics and by change in most aspects of sociocultural adaptation. According to Bruce D. Smith, native North American cultivation began with crops that flourish in the rich, disturbed soils around human habitations. Weedy domesticates provided containers and food and, combined with the wild resources of wetlands, made the stable occupation of base camps possible. In these camps women could shorten birth intervals, thus provoking population growth.

Some researchers have suggested that domestication happened opportunistically ("naturally") as plants, animals, and humans became accustomed to each other. The weakness of this scenario is that it eliminates the need for innovators and maintains the presumed passivity of females. Patty Jo Watson and Mary Kennedy have developed a model that builds upon the association of Native American women and plants and rejects the scholarly bias that associates women with passivity and males with activity. In their model, adult women specialized in harvesting of wild plants. Because they possessed extensive botanical knowledge, they intentionally worked to improve seed size and increase the availability of desirable plants outside the area of their natural distribution. Late Archaic sites supply abundant evidence, including coprolites preserved in caves, that people were increasingly sedentary and consumed larger quantities of plants, cultivated and intensively gathered from preferred habitats near settlements—weedy plants such as goosefoot and sunflower, as well gourds and squashes.

For thousands of years, Archaic peoples in this region lived by mixed hunting and gathering, emphasizing nut harvesting, riverine resources, and deer, with minor cultivation of oily and starchy seeds, squash, and gourds. This subsistence system was adequate to support some ceremonial activity. In the Middle Archaic period, along the Illinois River, people built bluff-crest earthen structures, apparently as foci for community celebrations. Claire Cassidy describes what life was like based on burials associated with the earthen platforms. Both female and male skeletons exhibited evidence of stress due to heavy work, and they showed similar pathologies, including the telltale signs of periodic hunger. Despite this apparent similarity in experience, females exhibited lower life expectancies than males at every age. By the end of the Archaic, more clearly differentiated gender roles are reflected in osteological evidence. Men spent more time hunting deer, and women apparently spent less time gathering in the forest and dedicated more energy to tending their gardens. When pottery was integrated into social life, its manufacture, if we can judge from historic peoples, was women's work.

In the Early and Middle Woodland periods in the Ohio and Illinois Valleys, people who lived in autonomous hamlets had wide trading networks and buried some individuals in log tombs under earthen mounds. This community activity, which produced the decorated artifacts diagnostic of the Adena and Hopewell mortuary cults, is evidence of growing social complexity. Adena people developed elaborate mortuary rituals and committed significant seasonal labor to building tombs and moving tons of earth to form platforms. Children were favored with more burial goods, indicative of special status, but in a departure from previously egalitarian burial practices, Adena communities often buried males in central positions in the platforms, some with log tomb chambers, suggesting their roles as leaders. Adena and Hopewell art and burials indicate religious practices in which men evidently were prominent actors.

Cassidy reports that in the Ohio Valley of Kentucky, males were buried in artificial platforms and women and children in caves, showing a more pronounced differentiation of social roles than in the preceding Archaic period. If this were the only evidence taken into consideration, one might conclude that men dominated in these communities, but such an interpretation rests on our evaluation of the two styles of burial. Cave burial may have been desirable for women for symbolic reasons. Archaeologists often find caches of precious seeds from domesticated plants stored in caves by the ancient people. The burial data indicate that female health was slightly better than that of males, and there were many healthy adults over thirty. The fact that people were mobile, occupying villages only seasonally, may have contributed to their good health.

The ceramics that marked the beginning of the Woodland period signaled new customs in food processing, eating, and feasting. By the Middle Woodland period, 150 B.C. to A.D. 400, Hopewellian people were living in small, isolated homesteads and maintained themselves by hunting, collecting, and cultivating crops. A number of important indigenous plants were added to their subsistence at this time. Bruce Smith mentions knotweed, maygrass, and little barley, noting that while tropical maize was present in the Hopewell plant inventory, it was not an important cultigen. Ceramic vessels and festive meals apparently were part of the increasingly elaborate mortuary ceremonialism of the Hopewellians. If these pots were made and decorated by women, then they constitute evidence of female participation in the activity that integrated Woodland society.

In the eastern woodlands, the Adena and Hopewell mortuary complexes are examples of cultural elaboration involving wide trading networks and extraordinary art and crafts. In all areas, males were buried in or under earthen platforms more frequently than females, and, where comparative data exist, the males in platform burials tend to be larger than males buried in other contexts. But there is no clear picture of female subordination. Women from presumed high-status tombs showed little difference in health profiles from other women, and, in one case, a young woman and man were buried together under a platform at the Hopewell site, with a tremendously rich array of exotic and precious items, including copper ear-spools.

The Adena and Hopewell mortuary behavior, like that of the Chinchorro people, may have had many social functions. In one interpretation of charnel house rituals, Mark Seeman suggested that when the Hopewell people feasted with the dead, they stimulated hunting activity and achieved a wider distribution of foodstuff, particularly meat supplied by male hunters. Women must have supported and encouraged this ceremonialism because it benefited themselves and their children.

This interpretation is supported by the analysis of strontium in human bones, which shows little difference in male and female diets. Evidence of increasing warfare in the Woodland phases and some worsening of childhood health suggests that the people were competing for scarce resources, so perhaps potential warriors and war leaders were defined as especially important members of the society, and they received exotic burial offerings that archaeologists interpret as valuables. In some regions, this burial focus on high-status males disappeared between A.D. 400 and 500.

Endemic syphilis appeared by the Middle Woodland period, affecting women as well as men. The overall prevalence of syphilis was about 50 percent in the Middle Woodland, considerably greater than in Archaic times, and must have affected health and fertility substantially. With the expansion of long-distance travel and trade, diseases such as syphilis were spread by traders of either sex.

Exchange may have been an integral part of family economic activity, so that family members had roles in both production and trade. In historic times in lowland South America, women and men developed part-time craft specialization to participate in exchange relationships. Some women may have been traders themselves or joined male family members on expeditions, as in ancient Mesoamerica. While in ethnographic cases it is usually males who participate in ceremonial exchange that benefits the whole group by creating economic and social networks, women often engage in utilitarian exchange of domestic surpluses, adding an important flexibility to family economy. It is an open question which was more important: ceremonial exchange, which stimulates people to participate, or utilitarian trade, which may satisfy practical needs.

Despite the Victorian folk belief that ladies should not sweat, most human societies assign grueling labor tasks to both sexes. In many places women are thought to be as appropriate as men for carrying large loads short or long distances, and some female skulls show grooved foreheads

FIGURE 4.1. ■ A Moche vessel demonstrates how prehistoric women used a tumpline to bear a burden basket.

from habitual use of a tumpline to move heavy loads (fig. 4.1). In fact, burdening women with hard physical labor may be an excellent birth control strategy, more effective than advocating moral restraint.

During Middle Woodland times in the Lower Illinois Valley people showed gains in nutrition and health compared to Late Archaic people, and there was no significant difference in bone strontium between females and males, suggesting that their diets were similar. By Late Woodland times, male and female activities had changed. Males were eating more meat, perhaps because organ meat was consumed from animals killed away from home or perhaps due to ideologies about appropriate food for making men warriors. Competition for deer-hunting territories is likely since the faunal evidence shows a decline in deer consumption and a relative increase in the use of fish and mussels. At the same time, women began to show more robust bones and muscles, a trend that continued into Mississippian times. However, women were increasingly shorter than males. This has been taken to indicate an ever greater participation of women in cultivation and suggests that they were fed poorly in their growing years. By the time of first European contact, virtually all agriculture was done by Native American women. Men hunted, made war, and traded. Women farmed, thus facilitating, and indeed underwriting, all the rest.

Although maize was present in the eastern woodlands by 2,000 years ago, it did not become a significant dietary staple until much later. Watson and Kennedy believe that indigenous female horticulturists developed the Northern Flint variety, the ancestor of modern hybrid corn, from a tropical variety originally domesticated in Mexico. In the eastern woodlands, this revolutionary species (Northern Flint) was the result of purposeful investment of skill and knowledge in agricultural experimentation and selective breeding. The new cultigen, adopted widely after A.D. 800 in the Late Woodland and Mississippian phases, became progressively more important in local diets. In the archaeological record, the cultivation of increased quantities of maize is associated with rapid cultural change and growth in many settlements. After A.D. 1100 this productive crop became the staff of life for Indians all over the East, and it was the basis for the development of complex chiefdoms along the Mississippi.

That women were farmers is shown in their skeletons, which present more arthritis of the left arm and spine than do those of earlier Woodland females. Maize farming necessitates much more hoeing and other hard labor than did cultivation of the indigenous plants. The maize-based diet brought worsening childhood health, although this effect was surely not due to the food, but to the less healthy environment of villages. The result of the progressive development of agricultural systems was that the late Mississippian people did not suffer from nutritional diseases or seasonal stress, but Della Collins Cook argues that disease load, the result of infections common when people congregate without adequate sanitation, affected them adversely. Human crowding and competition is indicated by evidence of Late Woodland and Mississippian warfare.

The founding of Cahokia, the only major urban center in North America, brought a large population together, and crowded and unsanitary conditions fostered disease. Cahokia's population may have been greater than 25,000 by A.D. 1200, when it was a great trading center. Without clean drinking water and controlled sewage removal, even well-fed people were vulnerable to disease. Perhaps the major health problem of Mississippian times, and one exported directly along Cahokia's trade routes into interior America, was tuberculosis.

Female body size and nutritional status fluctuated in later prehistory. Along the Georgia coast, where neither agriculture nor foraging was physically demanding, the late prehistoric skeletal population showed a reduction in body size, robusticity, and mechanical stress. But in many regions, females exhibit a progressive increase in development of the deltoid tuberosity from Middle Woodland through Mississippian time. Patricia Bridges found that this increased strength in Mississippian women's arms and legs was due to increased workloads, including agricultural work, and other chores such as pounding corn, carrying water, and making pottery. Males showed little change in activity since the Archaic.

Jane Buikstra and her coauthors point out that as human groups proliferated and grew in size, emphasis was placed on resources that were dependable, easily stored, and available nearby. The Mississippian subsistence strategy at some sites focused on riverine bounty and agriculture and deemphasized deer and nut crops. At great cost to female maize farmers, the community sought to avoid seasonal shortages, but health was compromised as dental disease increased due to a sticky carbohydrate staple and as people coped with the infections and epidemic diseases of village life.

What explains the increasing investment of labor on the part of women farmers, the exaggeration of the gender-based division of labor, and the dramatic differential health status among Mississippian people? There was pressure for people to work to feed a larger population and contribute to expensive sociopolitical activities, such as supporting elites, importing elite symbols, and building giant earthen platform complexes for the temples characteristic of Mississippian sites. Renewed contact with Mesoamerica and new ideas concerning ceremonialism and tribute may have been a part of this major shift in agricultural emphasis. Communities were seeking ways to compete with their neighbors for what must have been perceived as limited resources, and women and men were rendering portions of the production to the elite while producing surplus to negotiate alliances, marriages, and peace accords.

The advantage of food production is that, compared to gathering, it can be more effectively expanded through technological innovation and increased labor investment. One can imagine serious-faced elder women in villages and towns making the decision to commit more labor to the production of larger surpluses of food. They discuss the importance of supporting men in their travels and trade, which bring the benefits of foreign alliances; they speak of the necessity of engaging in warfare and undertaking religious activities to ensure community welfare. The women making decisions about food production would have been aware of the costs to themselves, but they probably did not have much choice because of the needs of their extended families and the tribute payments owed to elites in chiefly centers.

The decision to intensify maize production 1,000 years ago had a tremendous effect on women's work and women's health (fig. 4.2). It also may have affected women's status, which, by the time of first European contact, was definitely subordinate to that of males in most of the horti-cultural societies of the eastern United States. Nevertheless, women's efforts in domestication and improving maize varieties made possible the development of complex societies characterized by hierarchy, urban settlements, long-distance trade, ceremonialism, many social statuses, and warfare. In some regions these developments affected the average, overworked, poorly nourished woman negatively. Nevertheless, these stresses were nonfatal, and populations grew, at least in part as the result of decisions made by women.

Hardin Village, a Mississippian site in the Fort Ancient area along the Ohio River, shows that increased commitment to maize may have meant an unbalanced diet that could have affected women. Skeletal evidence demonstrates that osteoporosis and cribra orbitalia were highest in children under the age of six and in women in their thirties. This is a sign of iron deficiency anemia, the result of weaning children onto iron-poor gruel. In adult women it is caused by insufficient nutrients. Women who got their calories from carbohydrates and consumed less protein than men showed growing rates of dental caries, thus affording them more oppor-tunity to encounter infectious organisms. At the Averbuch site in Tennessee, tuberculosis and anemia may have resulted in elevated mortality among young adults of both sexes. Life expectancies of females at birth were only about fifteen years, and about 17 for males. The early loss of important

FIGURE 4.2. ■ A sixteenth-century woodcut shows Native American women processing maize. One grinds with a metate, another prepares tortillas on a griddle, and a third wraps tamales in leaves.

working and reproducing segments of the population would have compromised the defense, agricultural productivity, and reproduction of the group.

An interesting aspect of women's health in late prehistoric Georgia is that females show a growing incidence of periosteal reactions in the bone, indicative of major, but nonfatal, infections. Earlier in prehistory, such lesions had a roughly equal occurrence in females and males and were observed on various parts of the body. Here, however, the lesions were concentrated on the lower limbs of adult women. In horticultural activities, the lower legs are prone to injury. In a situation where women were doing most of the farming, and especially if they were fertilizing the fields with night soil, they would have been exposed to more accidents to the lower limbs and a greater variety of pathogens than people whose exposure to human feces was more limited.

Another growing aspect of ill health that increased women's discomfort and lessened their capacity for labor was osteoarthritis. In much of the southeastern United States, the incidence of this wear-related disease increased among women, but not among men, again suggesting an increase in time spent in laborious chores in late prehistory. Nevertheless, the data from Fort Ancient show that just before European contact, the life expectancy of females was higher than that of males, due to high male mortality in warfare.

The intensification of maize agriculture had considerable effects on women's lives. Female skeletons from the East show a progressive change in pathologies, especially arthritis, suggesting that in late prehistory women increased their investment of labor in cultivation, food preparation, and food transport. In contrast, from the Archaic to the late prehistoric in the East, male roles changed less, and their skeletons record less variation from period to period, although the bow and arrow replaced the spear thrower in Mississippian times, causing increased arthritis in the left elbow.

### Farmers of the North American Southwest

In the arid southwestern region of North America, the Archaic people showed a diversified pattern of gathering and hunting, but some groups manipulated wild plant populations through burning, pruning, and other interventions normally associated with cultivation. According to Paul Minnis, the people of the Southwest and northern Mexico added domesticated species to their subsistence programs in the second millennium B.C. as they adopted what is called "casual agriculture." Mixing foraging and horticulture was a low-effort way to subsist while maintaining their traditional seasonal movements and other ecological and social relationships.

In the ethnographic literature of the Southwest, women are associated with agriculture, and here too, it is very likely they were involved in the initial decision to undertake cultivation. Stress may have been among the factors that motivated their efforts: local populations were competing for the wild food, or wild food resources had decreased due to environmental causes. Alternatively, the early people may not have experienced great want but may have seen an opportunity to control the timing of food collection and increase yields, predictability, and storability. Imagine overhearing ancient kinswomen discussing the relative merits of foraging wild species and experimenting with the domesticated species (already used by Mesoamericans in the South). Some women from families with many potential workers may have favored the investment of labor in planting, tending, harvesting, and storing because it meant more security and flexibility for their families. As some individuals or families tried out the new technology, their modest successes were observed by kin who repeated the experiment if they recognized a good return for labor invested, or appreciated the value of an additional storable surplus for the winter season or for exchange.

The first experiments probably gave minor advantages to families who also continued traditional activities. In the wake of these early experiments, male family members may have been willing to alter their seasonal movements because of the potential to underwrite trade, feasts, and ceremonial activities. The new cultivation efforts may have appeared desirable to older people who were stressed by changing camps, and they may have been attractive to women who sought to produce more palatable food or seeds that could be stored against the season of scarcity, which is so hard on small children. Cultivation did not result in decreasing workloads.

The casual cultivation of crops of Mesoamerican origin such as maize, squash, and beans in the first millennium B.C. fit into the production system because people already manipulated wild plant resources. They already were familiar with cooking and eating wild grasses (maize), legumes (beans), and wild native squashes. Ethnographic evidence shows that small-scale plant cultivation does not alter patterns of mobility common among foragers. Gardens may have been planted in the spring and tended for a while and then left until harvest time, a pattern seen among the historic Western Apache. Men could have been drawn into agriculture because of the need for labor at the time of field preparation and planting and again at harvest time.

Women and men surely negotiated the investment of labor, the timing of work, and the amount of labor required. The need for labor at planting time corresponded well to a period when exploiting wild resources would not demand much effort. Harvest times were also flexible: the cultivated plants waited in the fields until wild resources were garnered, if there was any conflict. Mobile families may have assigned a few less mobile individuals the task of remaining to guard the fields.

Women endured heavy workloads at the end of the Archaic and in early Basketmaker (Formative) times. Ethnographic analogy and archaeological evidence suggest that women gathered wild plants, did hoe farming, prepared food, gathered fuel and water, cared for children, manufactured clothing, baskets, mats, and bags, worked hides, laundered, and did other household maintenance activities. In the first centuries A.D., people living in stable, autonomous pithouse villages adopted pottery making and more food-processing chores.

It is almost certain that the spectacular pottery of the ancient Southwest was made by women. In a recent interpretation, Patricia Crown and W. H. Wills argue that women were motivated to undertake ceramic manufacture in the Southwest when, with greater dependence on cultigens, the scheduling conflicts between foraging, horticulture, and food processing increased. One way women cope with workload conflicts is early weaning. Worldwide, women who contribute to subsistence by cultivating plants introduce solid foods to their infants early. Grinding cultivated seeds and boiling them in water in ceramic vessels permitted early weaning. Giving an infant gruel for lunch allows a woman greater mobility and relieves the stress of producing milk. Because ovulation resumes when nursing lessens, early weaning has the unintended consequence of shortening the average birth interval and spurring demographic growth.

Women's activities, technologies, and choices have far-reaching cultural consequences. For example, undertaking ceramic production itself produced new opportunities. Women in food-producing societies frequently make pottery not just for cooking and containers, but as a vehicle of religious and social expression that can figure in gender negotiations.

Crown and Wills also hypothesize that as women began making pottery in the Southwest, a new race of maize, more productive and more suitable for grinding, was adopted, further encouraging cooking innovations. Dry, mature corn seeds store well and make nutritious stews and soups. The use of large pots for cooking maize may reflect changes in the way food was distributed in the extended family group. It may have favored a more equitable distribution of meat, giving women and children access to stews containing a variety of ingredients. Boiling animal bones as a soup base may have made more fats available to the entire family.

The transition to greater maize dependency was delayed in the Mogollon highlands, where people continued to be relatively mobile foragers and horticulturists until after A.D. 650, the date of the adoption of a new, highly productive race of corn. In Michael Diehl's interpretation, Mogollon people consumed increasing amounts of this maize even though it required more time to process and probably created scheduling conflicts. Because of time constraints for women, new grinding technology was adopted in the form of the Mexican trough metate with a two-handed mano. These artifacts were not only costly to make, they required greater energy expenditure and caused more fatigue for women who could not shift the position of their arms and bodies to reduce muscle stress. Nevertheless, they were more efficient grinding tools than those previously used in the Southwest, and scholars argue that, despite the drawbacks, women adopted the mano and metate to save time while maintaining nutritional yields. Diehl argues that as a result of the adoption of this technology, maize consumption increased in the Mogollon area, and this change correlated with innovative family organization, new kinds of settlements and land use, and increased trade.

Initially, food production and the new cuisine moderated seasonal scarcity in the food supply, then cultivation gradually provided increased storable surpluses and better yields. The fact that maize became so highly integrated into the religions of later southwestern peoples, with the development of Corn Mothers and other female spirits functioning as land-givers and mediators of fertility and regeneration, is evidence of the prehistoric perception that maize was critical in assuring community well-being in later prehistory.

After hundreds of years of mixed economy and casual horticulture, labor-intensive agriculture became the mainstay of many peoples in the Southwest. By A.D. 1000, women's contribution to subsistence had increased, populations increased, and more cooking technologies were developed (griddles and stones for baking piki bread). Female skeletons show kneeling facets on their bones caused by hours of grinding. They also show evidence of habitual hyperextension of the neck from the use of a tumpline across the forehead to support heavy burdens. Male bones show left arm degeneration at the elbow, probably related to bow and arrow use.

Despite the pronounced division of labor and the adoption of intensive agriculture, people continued to suffer from nutritional stress. Paul Minnis's analysis indicates that human skeletons in the Southwest show persistent evidence of malnutrition, although recent modeling has suggested that disease load caused by crowding in nucleated settlements may be as important a factor as actual protein-calorie malnutrition. Women, children, and the elderly people who spent more time at home and who had less access to meat were at greater risk than males.

The extreme emphasis on corn in the Southwest in later prehistory had other implications for prehistoric women. Corn processing in this region was women's specialty, as shown by the modifications observed on female skeletons. The location of grinding bins is an important setting for understanding women's lives because these areas were used by women at least three hours a day, in sickness and health, throughout life. Katherine Spielmann argues that through time there were changes in the location of bins. Data show that in the early phases of intensive agriculture, groups of bins were located in interior household settings, whereas after A.D. 1300, single bins were moved to outdoor locations in plazas and on rooftops. This shift came at the same time that grinding bins disappeared from ritual locations in kivas. Male loom-weaving was characteristic of the later kivas, suggesting that men had appropriated the communal ritual space. Women may have responded by moving their work into more public areas to maintain visual and auditory contact with neighbors and access to news in the pueblo.

In Arizona the Hohokam were intensive agriculturists who developed an elaborate material culture, traded, and built earthen ceremonial platforms. Randall McGuire's analyses of early Hohokam burials (mostly cremations) at the village of La Ciudad shows that there was considerable diversity and inequality among the grave lots: households within the kin group varied in size and were probably ranked. If the burial offerings were made by the people gathered for the funeral ceremonies, one can understand why adult males were associated with more artifacts than adult women: the number of offerings may be indicative of the wider social contacts of men. Curiously, teenagers attracted the most offerings, perhaps reflecting their special status and, probably, the importance of young adult labor. McGuire identified household leaders as those individuals having hairpins, turquoise, and turtle shell in their cremations. These leaders were predominantly male, but one cremated individual with a hairpin was a female, suggesting that women were also household heads, as they sometimes are in ethnographic cases.

A study of 132 later burials from two Classic-period Hohokam village cemeteries by Douglas Mitchell showed that people were buried together with their kin in extended family groups or local lineage segments. Most Hohokam people lived in villages organized and regulated by kinship, but the whole village was integrated into a hierarchical political system. Thus, the full range of ranks and statuses would be apparent only in studying all the constituent settlements and cemeteries, but even among the people in the villages were a few specialists and traders who evidently participated in a variety of task groups in secular and nonsecular activities.

Some individual roles appear to be shown by the grave goods. In Mitchell's study of mortuary offerings, burial associations were taken to indicate each person's functional role and social status, including their power and wealth. Some individuals showed greater social position in the sense that they may have had more duties and rights with respect to a wider number of people during their lives, resulting in the acquisition of material items. At the Grand Canal site, both adult men and women were buried in family plots. Subadults had fewer grave goods on the whole, and adults commonly were associated with sex-specific items. The adult females were accompanied by an average of 4.8 vessels, subadults had an average of 4.1 vessels, and males had an average of 3.4 vessels. Only women were buried with more than 10 vessels each, and female burials were more likely to contain jars (42 percent, compared to 26 percent for males). There was no significant difference in the occurrence of ornaments between adult females and males (46 percent of the males versus 36 percent of the females), but males had a greater number of ornaments, including marine shell and stone pendants, and subadults at Grand Canal were more likely to have ornaments than adults. It is regrettable that poor preservation has prevented an evaluation of the quantity and quality of textiles associated with women. In this case, relatively egalitarian gender relations are implied. Neither the large number of vessels associated with women nor the great number of ornaments associated with men can be construed as evidence of ranked statuses in this family context.

At the Casa Buena site, 70 percent of the adult male tombs contained ornaments, compared to only 47 percent of the female burials, and several categories of ornaments, shell artifacts, stone pendants, and bone hairpins were almost exclusively associated with adult males. Males also got more of what the excavators decided were "ritual artifacts." Males were commonly associated with arrow points, axes, and abraders, while spindle whorls and food-processing tools such as manos and pestles were associated with adult women. It is wrong to assume that these items are not themselves ritually significant, since spindles appear in the costumes of Mesoamerican female deities, and grinding stones were often used in ceremonial contexts and elevated as art tools. In the communities of food-producing people, women and men were identified with their separate work. The "ritual items" identified in tombs demonstrate that gender was important in both mundane and ritual activities. The difference in offerings by sex indicates an ideology of gender complementarity at the level of food and craft production. It is reflected also in the pairing of female and male images on some ceremonial bowls made by the ancient Hohokam.

The funerary rituals reconstructed at these two villages appeared egalitarian, but the contents of the tombs suggest both gender complementarity and significant social differentiation and inequality. At some Hohokam sites studied by Mitchell, privileged individuals were buried in special areas, sometimes near platforms. At other sites, highly ranked individuals were observed in only a few family plots, suggesting that economic and social wealth was concentrated in some kin groups and not others. A few unusual burial assemblages probably corresponded to village headmen who had prominent social positions in ritual and secular contexts within and beyond the village. Most of the burials containing exotic items, including polychrome pottery, were those of males. This indicates that at least some of the best products of women's work were circulated to men for use in public ceremonies. Overall, the Hohokam burial patterns show that although the standard of living was high for almost everyone, an individual's experience in society would have varied depending on the rank of her family.

Other southwestern indigenous people had a much harder life, and paleopathological studies often show people struggling with a difficult environment and escalating cultural and physical stress. At Grasshopper Pueblo, an autonomous Mogollon village occupied from A.D. 1275 to 1400, women and men had different experiences in society as stress increased. These people apparently tried various strategies to maintain their standard of living and health, all of which failed. Grasshopper Pueblo was abandoned as the environment deteriorated.

According to Joseph Ezzo's interpretations, men ate mainly meat and maize in the early phase of the settlement of Grasshopper, while women consumed more wild plants. Men's access to meat and maize has been interpreted as a marker of high status and this is supported by evidence that the men who died early in the history of the settlement were afforded more elaborate grave goods than women.

As time passed, male diet changed little, but female diet shifted dramatically to maize, although there was considerable variability among individual women. Everyone ate fewer wild foods. A study of kin groups within the village showed that families consumed agricultural products and wild plants in different proportions, so that women's activities would have varied from household to household. Skeletal analysis revealed that later in time, everyone in the village experienced reduced meat intake, probably reflecting environmental degradation and overhunting.

Ezzo's information from Grasshopper indicates a pattern of high infant and child mortality, a high load of pathology in teeth and postcranial bones, high rates of deficiency disease, and low life expectancy with increasing food/subsistence stress through time. Although some archaeologists suggest that males enjoyed preferred status at Grasshopper, the data show a life expectancy of about thirty-eight years for both for females and males. One intriguing fact about Grasshopper is that female skeletons are disproportionately represented in the remains. Where were the men buried? At remote sacred locations? It is possible that women maintained their domiciles in the pueblo, while men spent a considerable portion of the year away from Grasshopper, returning during the ceremonial round. This is a known pattern in the Southwest.

Because Grasshopper was an autonomous village, problem solving was probably undertaken at the local level, and frequently by households. Among the responses to stress were a reduction in household size, a decrease in expenditure in burial furniture, and a progressive loss of differences in burials between males and females. Household autonomy might have given women a degree of flexibility and explain why some kin groups did more foraging for wild species than others. One persistent question is whether poor female health was due to their lack of power in a system biased against them or to other circumstances. Scholars believe that poor health was due to stress caused by crowding, the rapid transmission of infectious diseases, and resource depletion and protein-calorie malnutrition, all combining to reduce the life span of the people of Grass-hopper Pueblo and cause high infant mortality rates. Cultural practices, such as male traveling and absence help to account for the disparate sex ratios in village cemeteries. This was probably a strategy that reduced male demands on limited carbohydrate foods stored in pueblos. Male absence also meant that women and children did not benefit as much from hunted food, although females probably had direct access to rodent meat.

At Grasshopper these combined strategies adopted by women and men to confront the obvious problems failed. Conditions became intolerable, and all over the region settlements were abandoned in the late prehistoric period as some families sought new places to do agriculture, while others became more mobile and less intensely agricultural.

### Early Farmers in Coastal Ecuador

The development of food production took a different path in coastal Ecuador, where the Las Vegas preceramic people were followed by the Early Formative Valdivia people (ca. 3000–1500 B.C.). The Valdivians lived in permanent villages and made some of the earliest ceramics in the Americas. They allocated more labor to food production and specialized fishing than the preceramic people. Although there is little hard evidence of the ancient division of labor, historical and ethnographic materials suggest that Valdivia women tended fields, hauled water and wood, col-lected shellfish, helped men fish, stored and processed foods, and pro-duced cotton textiles and ceramics for daily and ceremonial use. In coastal villages, men may have fished and produced equipment such as cotton nets while also using surplus production to create alliances and participate in exchange networks for salt and a few valuables. Men living in inland villages may have hunted, collected forest products, cooperated in agri-cultural activities, maintained exchange networks, and manufactured artifacts of wood, stone, and shell for ceremonial use. Women and men participated in religious activities.

There may have been a small degree of specialization by household or by village. Every family grew its own food and harvested wild resources, but some villages may have specialized in fishing, exchanging their catch for agricultural products, raw materials, or craft items. Other villages may have invested additional labor in producing squash, beans, root crops,

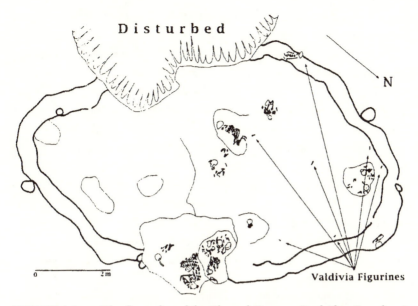

FIGURE 4.3. ■ The floor plan of the Charnel House at Real Alto, Ecuador. A mature women was buried fully articulated under the threshold in a tomb lined with broken grinding stones.

peppers, fruits, maize, and cotton or salt for exchange. There is evidence that some households may have produced pottery, shell ornaments, and textiles in excess of domestic needs.

In later Valdivia times, some people lived in dispersed settlements, but they practiced rituals that took place at village centers on platforms designed for communal activities. This is evidence that people were actively involved in a complex web of responsibilities and privileges took developed along with a differentiated economic system and intensified production.

The site of Real Alto has two ceremonial structures on earthen platforms. One, the Fiesta House, gets its name from the broken vessels found there, perhaps the remains of celebrations involving beer drinking. The other, the Charnel House, is characterized by unusual burials and ceramic figurines representing females (fig. 4.3).

The Charnel House contained burials from Valdivia Phase 3 (2800–2600 B.C.). A female about thirty-five years old was buried beneath the portal in a tomb lined with grinding stones. Nearby were found the remains of two adult males and six subadults of various ages. They may have composed a family group or, as one excavator suggested, sequential sacrifices to the original female burial. Regardless of which of the many interpretations ones chooses, the pattern of burials at Real Alto suggests some adults and children merited burial in a special central structure, while others were buried in and around their houses. The woman in the portal tomb was surrounded by unusual offerings, indicating that she was a special person whose role was associated with grinding, cooking, or brewing. Alternatively, she may have been a sacrifice buried there when the building was erected and later joined by the partial remains of captives whose flesh had been consumed during postraid feasting.

The adoption of village life and the development of dependence on horticulture had important consequences for the health of the Valdivia people. One hundred and one skeletons from Real Alto have yielded valuable data. Life expectancy at birth was 24 years, lower than in the Las Vegas preceramic period, but higher than that calculated for later peoples. The Valdivia life expectancy at the age of 15 (after childhood risk was passed) was the lowest of all Ecuadorian populations that have been studied. Valdivia adults died young: the mean age at death for males was 38.7 years; for women, 32.3 years. Compared to earlier people from the same region, Valdivia skeletons showed higher incidences of infection and trauma, including cases of interpersonal violence. Valdivia teeth show higher frequencies of dental hypoplasia, caries, and abscesses than Las Vegas teeth, suggesting an increase in dependence on maize. Females lost more teeth than males, but they had no severe anemias.

Douglas Ubelaker, who analyzed the Valdivia skeletal sample, says that the remains show the expected effects of incipient food production. Valdivia populations were expanding, but the skeletons do not show the high incidence of diseases and growth disruptions characteristic of later, more intensively agricultural populations living in nucleated settlements. The Valdivia pattern of disease and health, compared to that of the Las Vegas people, does mirror increased sedentism, greater population density, changing diet, and even warfare. The signs of interpersonal violence among the Valdivians may be evidence of intergroup conflict over territory or intracommunity or domestic violence. The data do not show that men and women had very different life experiences of the kind often attributed to discrimination or stratification. Warfare evidentially had not escalated to the point of compromising female access to community resources.

The archaeological evidence from Las Vegas and Valdivia sites supports an hypothesis of change, including an evolution of gender roles. The Formative Valdivia way of life was characterized by the development of crafts and food-producing technologies, which must have been accompanied by changes in activities, scheduling, sex roles, and thought habits—all of which evolved together. Women and men domesticated themselves as they became task-oriented, disciplined farmers and fishers who manufactured ever-increasing numbers and types of structures and artifacts. The size of Valdivia houses increased through time at Real Alto (see chapter 5), indicating that larger cooperative units were developing. In order to cooperate in larger groups, the people must have developed new kinds of social relations.

## Food Production, Society, and History

Native American agricultural systems evolved in a variety of ways, and women were frequently the farmers at the center of the stage. The archaeology of gender alerts us to variability in the ancient evidence. Food producers have lived in many kinds of settlements and in communities organized along variable lines, with mutable definitions of families and their activities. Women may have controlled the products of their labor in some cases, but not in others. Food producers have experienced an ever-changing division of labor with concomitant changes in the definitions of the roles of girls, boys, women, and men of all ages. They have had variable concepts of religion and of leadership.

For better or worse, humans construct social order and structure. Gender roles represent one response to the problem of order took has been highly successful. What is interesting is that the roles associated with any particular gender vary from case to case and may not correlate with the biological sex of individuals in a fixed way.

Plants, gathering, horticulture, and food processing and storage are frequently interpreted as female areas of expertise. These cultural specializations are routinely gendered female not because of any biological imperative but were selected for in many cultures because under conditions of simple technology, women who are responsible for childbearing and child nurturing prefer to reduce their mobility to alleviate their workload and lower the risk to young children. By performing activities such as gathering, cultivation with hand labor, food processing, and domestic crafts, women increase the predictability of the food supply for themselves and their children.

The early American farmers and their husbands seem to have been successful in that their communities grew and people lived in progressively larger, sedentary settlements where they became progressively more productive cultivators. They solved some of the problems associated with foraging, such as seasonal shortfalls. From another perspective, they progressively destabilized their hunting and gathering systems, forcing additional changes designed to compensate for economic/demographic stress. In late prehistory, endemic warfare was probably a consequence of competition among burgeoning agricultural populations.

Paleopathologists have shown us the down side of the transition to agriculture. In many places, human skeletal populations show that early gatherers/hunters in America had enamel hypoplasias and Harris lines, evidence of periodic stress related to seasonal shortages of food. Food production changed some of this, but early agricultural peoples still suffered severe and chronic stress and higher mortality rates caused by changing diet combined with the heavy impact of pathogens associated with sedentary lifestyles.

The effect of agriculture on human groups is variable, and the evidence of biological stress varies by age, sex, and social class in time and space. Mark Cohen points out that life expectancy often declined with the adoption of farming. The problem may not have been food shortages, but rather the combined effects of sedentism, poor sanitation, and lower-quality food combined with reduced dietary variety. This did not impede population growth, which gives us the impression that the ancient people adapted successfully. The expansion of agricultural populations, both in size and geographic extant, was only sometimes associated with improved standard of living for individuals. While some may have enjoyed improved life expectancies, many had shorter life spans or more episodes of disease. Moreover, inadvertent population growth and other factors destabilized some of the early agricultural systems, leading to new social and economic arrangements.

# CHAPTER FIVE

# Women in Households

History and archaeology traditionally have focused upon the public lives of elites and the temples, tombs, and art associated with them. Because of this bias, the family lives of both our elite and our non-elite ancestors have been ignored. Moreover, archaeologists have given little attention to ancient kinship because of their personal experiences in postindustrial society, where a major school of anthropology held, erroneously, that kinship is no longer a salient factor in social life. Yet family life and kin relations are as recoverable in the archaeological record as any other abstract social dimension. Because the patterns and processes of history are generated by the activities of all members of a society in the course of their daily lives, many archaeologists today seek to give those individuals faces by exploring family contexts.

Family is important to all people at some stages of their life cycles, and throughout most of human history the household has been the basic unit of interpersonal interaction and productive labor. The household is a group of people that shares a residence or domestic context, such as a house, which becomes the focus of parental, sibling, and other kin ties; the site of procreation and socialization of children, assuring the transmission of culture; and the locus of economic activity, especially production and consumption. Women and men participate as members of households. In less complex societies, the household is often the dominant social unit. In very simple societies, it is the sole focus of social, economic, and religious activities.

There is no necessary identity between family and household. Households usually are composed of people tied to each other by bonds of kinship and marriage, but a large extended family may be organized in several households, or a single household may well embrace members of several different families as well as nonkin. The ethnology of the Americas shows that families and households were and are variously constituted to carry out productive, reproductive, and other social activities. These units are important to study because the lives of women and men are shaped by the kinds of families and households in which they participate. Within families and households, different cultural ideologies may be enacted: some peoples emphasize harmony or complementarity, others institutionalize conflict and its mediation. Within families and households, women and men may take divergent or similar roles, and they may be characterized by radically different or convergent statuses. Societies create different definitions of motherly and wifely roles.

In Native American societies that are known ethnographically, some families are organized matrilineally, some patrilineally, some bilaterally or with mixed characteristics. It seems likely that in ancient America, some households were constituted as patrilocal and some as matrilocal and that marriage patterns varied across space and time. Some groups practiced monogamy and others polygyny. Polyandry is largely restricted to fraternal forms in the Americas, although in the past it may have been a preferred marriage form, as it is in some societies in the Old World. Some households were autonomous; others were integrated into polities such as chiefdoms and states in which the household lost exclusive control over its labor, personnel, and products.

Flexibility is one of the key features of both family and household organizations. These social units are responsive to change because they are small. Through the agreement and behavior of just a few people, the organization can alter its structure and function and evolve to meet the needs of its members and changing circumstances. Part of the function of families/households, in both stratified and unstratified systems, has been to engage in relations with other households forming larger communities or networks of economic, ritual, or defensive interaction. In some settings the important links are forged by marriages, so that gender relations are crucial in the social relations of the primary building blocks of society. Men may be the links between matrilineal and uxorilocal families; or, more commonly, women may serve as links between patrilineal groups. Both women and men can gain political and economic advantage for themselves and their kin by marrying particular individuals and linking their two families.

Households in ancient America ran the gamut of known domestic arrangements. Some were the sole locus of decision making and the fundamental unit of production and reproduction in society. In these units women were active participants at the center of the household, where people negotiated all important decisions and processes of production, biological reproduction, and the creation and communication of social and religious ideologies. Religious life, economic life, and political life were one fabric with many intertwined threads. Although labor may have been divided, both women and men were close to the functioning of all systems and would have been expected to participate in them all. In more complex societies, chiefdoms and early states, families and households were subordinated in complex systems. Political structures such as the state can have profound effects on all domestic relations, including gender relations.

## Reconstructing Family and Marriage Patterns

It is relatively easy for archaeologists to identify some of the activities performed by members of ancient households, but more difficult to reconstruct the family's social form. Archaeologists can sometimes reconstruct family relations using art and epigraphy, by extrapolating from the ethnographic and historic record, or by arguing from archaeological data using general ethnographic analogies. In addition, burial data, including DNA studies and multivariate analyses of skeletal populations excavated in residential contexts, can help determine who was related to whom. For example, the ancient people of Hawikki, an ancestral Zuni village in New Mexico, buried their dead in at least ten discrete cemeteries surrounding their village between A.D. 1300 and 1630 (fig. 5.1). Todd Howell and Keith Kintigh studied the human remains and other mortuary data belonging mainly to the latest prehistoric phase (a.d. 1375–1630) before significant European contact. They were able to find evidence that each cemetery was used by a distinct biological group (of kin). In this case, the distribution of bodies in space was interpreted as a manifestation of kinship, an interpretation supported by the biological evidence. By focusing on aspects of dental morphology that reflect genetic affinity, the researchers concluded that kin (individuals who shared physical traits indicating their close biological relationship) were buried together in formal, spatially discrete mortuary facilities. This burial pattern reinforces the view that

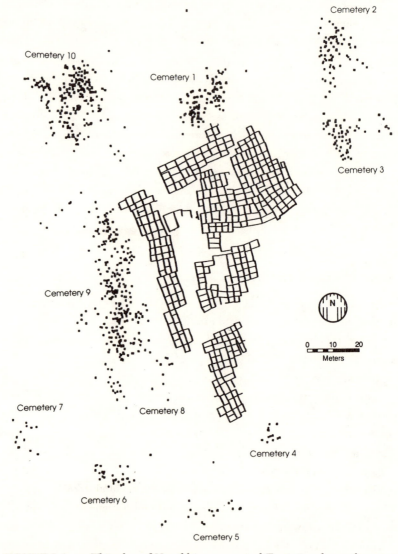

FIGURE 5.1. ■ This plan of Hawikki, an ancestral Zuni site, shows the room blocks flanked by ten discrete family or lineage cemeteries. Each dot represents a burial made between A.D. 1300 and 1630.

family life dominated the experience of individuals. The people who were buried together probably viewed themselves as members of the corporate family. Surely their principal responsibilities would have been toward other members of this kin group, and they derived benefits (or disadvantages) from membership. Surely they worked together and played together, and, through time, some families were able to achieve greater access to power and control of goods.

In archaeology, the skill and creativity of the archaeologist are the main factors that determine what will be learned, and new approaches are always possible. For example, a recent study of pit houses in British Columbia by Brian Hayden, Edward Bakewell, and Rob Gargett illustrates how the careful analysis of archaeological materials resulted in the identification of what the researchers claim to be the "world's longest-lived corporate group" (i.e., a family). At the Keatley Creek site, each of several pit houses had a distinctive pattern of cherts and chalcedonies, raw materials for the manufacture of stone tools, and this pattern remained consistent in each house for over 1,000 years. The archaeological inference was that the occupants of each large pit house foraged in an exclusive territory that belonged to the members of the household (called "residential corporate group"). These kin groups apparently maintained both their residence and family integrity (including economic rights) for an extremely lengthy period.

## The Archaeological Study of Households

The archaeological study of households and families, pioneered by Kent Flannery and Marcus Winter in Mexico, has been based on the excavation of the places where people actually lived: rock shelters, open camp sites, and the living spaces within the confines of buildings. Ethnoarchaeologists believe that the entire space utilized by a household, called the household cluster, must be investigated, because many important activities take place outside the actual dwelling in and around the tombs, outbuildings such as storage facilities, menstrual huts, sweat lodges, pits, household garden, and activity areas associated with the habitations. These are important indications of the structure of the family and its activities. Because women as well as men make contributions to reproduction and production, archaeological remains of household contexts must necessarily reveal the presence of women in the archaeological record.

## Early Ecuadorian Life

Useful archaeological evidence of family life comes from the early agricultural villages of the Ecuadorian coast. Here, between 3000 and 1500 B.C., people of the Valdivia culture lived in hamlets adjacent to patches of river bottomland or along the tropical seacoast near the mouths of rivers. Early villages were about a day's walk apart, but as populations grew, other communities filled the spaces between them wherever there were areas suitable for gardening.

Much is known about Valdivia economy from the analysis of ancient tools and plant, animal, and human remains, but the organization of family labor is open to speculation. Judging from ethnohistoric accounts by the early Spanish explorers in the region, we might imagine that women worked in the river-bottom fields, collecting wild cotton and bringing manioc, maize, achira (the bulb of species of canna lily), squash, and beans back to the village. In some seasons the women would have done most of the work themselves, planting, weeding, and calling on men for labor seasonally to cut down the forest to make new gardens. Historically the women also prepared food, storing it in pits they dug with the help of the rest of the family. People also kept small kitchen gardens with herbs and fruits near the house. Women may have had their favorite places in the mangrove swamp, where they fished and collected shellfish with their children. Young and old people walked away from the village in small groups to look for firewood, collect fruits and nuts, and draw water from pits dug along the river. In their houses, women would be found stirring pots over the fire or grinding seeds near the house doors. Some people might be seen manufacturing artifacts of shell, bone, or fiber, others spinning or pyroengraving gourds, and, in some communities, pottery was manufactured, perhaps by women in collaboration with their families.

In this scenario men spent time fishing in the estuaries and the bay or worked in groups on the beach or in lean-tos alongside the houses making craft items and repairing hunting and fishing equipment. When not engaged in fishing or clearing gardens, men might work with others in building a new house or repairing an old one (although building shelters is commonly women's work), or in securing raw materials for crafts and construction from the hills. In the dry season, some groups of men set off to hunt and trap in the forested hills. Larger groups composed of a whole extended family or several related nuclear families may have made forays to more distant locales to collect salt, harvest shellfish for dying cotton thread purple, mine good-quality chert for making stone tools, and obtain red ocher for painting.

The lives of the ancient Valdivia women can be reconstructed from their houses. At many sites the remains of residential structures and midden form a large circular or horseshoe-shaped mound around a central area. At Real Alto, seven houses were identified by tracing patterns of postholes in the sterile clay below the refuse layers. The excavation of the floors of these abandoned structures showed that they had walls of wood, cane, and other perishable materials. Pieces of sun-dried clay suggest that the houses were covered with a mixture of mud and grass to make them draft free. Doors were oriented downwind for the same reason. The postholes show that Early Valdivia–phase houses were small, circular huts about 3 to 5 meters in diameter (fig. 5.2). This small size shows that a house would not have held many people. Most likely, each was the home of a single nuclear family—a woman, her husband and children and, perhaps, another relative or so. These little houses would have been used mainly for sleeping and protection of people and belongings in the rain. Most activities would have taken place out of doors.

Around the edges of the houses were concentrations of shell and other refuse, including charred beans, wood charcoal, fish and deer bones, broken pottery, and tools, accumulated in a toss zone extending about 1.5 meters from the house. Inside, the dirt floors were kept relatively clean by sweeping. Each house had an inside pit for storage, and a grinding stone was stored near a wall. In one house, several stone figurines were found. Other pits near the walls contained broken grinding stones or fragmentary human bone. At Real Alto, charred beans were found associated with grinding stones outside a house in a food-preparation area.

A household cluster from Loma Alta, described in detail by the excavators, offers a glimpse of family activities (fig. 5.2). The hut itself is tiny, only about 3.1 by 2.3 meters. Within its walls Jonathan Damp recognized an area that may have been used for sleeping because a space about the size of two adults was free of any debris and characterized by a distinctive soil feature that might be the remains of a mat that decayed on the ground there. In the activity areas around the hut, excavators found a hearth associated with a scatter of fire-broken rock and stone tools, including a

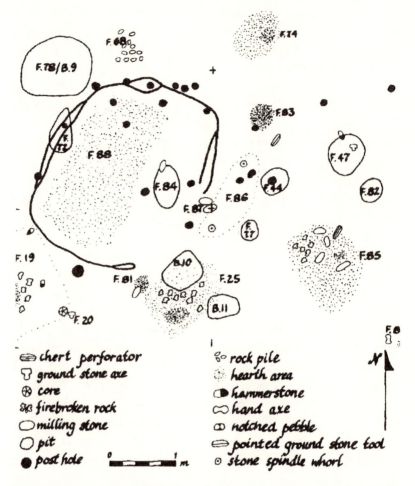

Key:

- ⊜ chert perforator
- ♉ ground stone axe
- ⊗ core
- ⊠ firebroken rock
- ◯ milling stone
- ◯ pit
- ● post hole

- ℅ rock pile
- ⋯ hearth area
- ◖ hammerstone
- ∞ hand axe
- ⊂⊃ notched pebble
- ⊜ pointed ground stone tool
- ⊙ stone spindle whorl

0 ▬▬▬▬ 1 m

N

FIGURE 5.2. ■ An Early Valdivia household unit, Structure 4, from Loma Alta. The shelter, about 3 m in diameter, may have been used by a small family for sleeping. Other activities would have taken place outside: F. 86 is a possible spinning area; F. 84 and 72 are two of may refuse pits; cooking areas are at F. 25, 81, 83, and 85; F. 19 is a lithic workshop; and B. 9, 10, and 11 are human burials.

broken stone ax. Axes like this were probably used to clear riverbottom forest for slash-and-burn agriculture. Near the door of the house was another hearth, again with fire-broken rock, grinding stone fragments, and pot sherds. Spindle whorls nearby may indicate that women sat here, watching the cooking and the kids and spinning. The household area also included a variety of pits utilized for refuse, human burial, and setting wooden posts that might have supported a roof for shade. Just outside the door were two human burials. Articulated skeletons normally are associated with early Valdivia houses and probably are the remains of family members.

Investigations at early Real Alto and Loma Alta suggest that the basic building block of Early Valdivia society was the nuclear family. This group was the main unit of production, reproduction, and consumption. Rituals involving stone and clay figurines may have been performed in the domestic setting. Similarly, the disposal of the dead was a family activity: the deceased were put to rest where they had worked and played in life. Among the houses in the earliest Valdivia villages there is no evidence of differentiation in size or function, leading us to believe that there was little difference from household to household.

The early Valdivia villages probably contained 150–200 people at any one time. The individual nuclear families living in their little round houses may have been relatively independent economic units, but one imagines a robust exchange of labor, food, and tools among relatives who interacted socially on a daily basis. Related people in villages maintain close connections with their siblings, parents, and other relatives throughout their entire lives, adding new responsibilities, ties, and privileges when they form new relationships by marrying.

The structure of Valdivia family relations is open to question. It is not known whether villages were endogamous or exogamous, or whether households were matrilineal and matrilocal or had some other form. In one possible scenario, women stayed in the villages of their birth, if that is where they had access to agricultural land, while their brothers sought wives in other villages and joined a new household. Certainly there must have been some mechanism for linking all the Valdivia villages across southern Ecuador because they exhibit both coordinated changes and regional variation in their ceramics through the centuries.

The Early Valdivia–phase villages were not static entities. Within a few centuries, the site of Real Alto grew considerably in size, ceremonial earthen platforms were constructed, and the space between the former tiny hamlets was filled with new villages, showing population growth on a regional level. Houses changed as well, growing from an average floor area of 14.4 square meters in Early Valdivia to 49.1 square meters in Middle Valdivia. This suggests that extended family households had replaced nuclear families as the principal social and economic unit, a situation that could have facilitated more complex productive activities. Perhaps the autonomous nuclear families found making a living more difficult as good agricultural land became scarcer, so that young people stayed under their parents' umbrella at marriage. Alternatively, perhaps some families had an economic or social advantage that made affiliation with that family attractive to relatives. Perhaps factional competition between groups forced the creation of large, more competitive units.

Anthropologists have observed that when land is abundant, the independent nuclear family is a viable unit of production. When there is a scarcity of land, pooling efforts and centralized control may offer competitive advantage. In extended family groups, the more numerous producers are often organized under household heads, who can function as managers. Such households may undertake larger projects involving more labor: agricultural intensification can result in increased production per unit of land, and fishing and craft productivity may be improved. Extended families can also support some people in activities other than primary production, thus moving the group toward greater specialization and stimulating technological change. However, the price may be a loss in personal autonomy to family members.

Based on ethnoarchaeological studies of the modern Shuar people, who now occupy southeastern Ecuador, James Zeidler has interpreted the use of space in the large Middle Valdivia houses. Traditional Shuar houses, like those of many tropical forest peoples, are occupied by extended families, and the interior space is differentiated into female and male areas. This differentiation is both conceptual and functional because the sexes maintain spatial separation as they go about their daily activities. This kind of spatial separation of female and male gives both sexes considerable freedom of action. Zeidler has noted that Shuar men, when they are not out hunting or clearing forest for agricultural plots, congregate at the front of the house, where they chat, make and repair craft items, receive male guests, eat, and, if unmarried, sleep. Male belongings are generally stored in this part of the house as well. Women spend most of their time at the other end of the house when not gardening or foraging. Here they tend their children, gossip, and cook for their individual or extended families, and here married couples and their young children sleep. Zeidler also noted multipurpose areas used by all adults. The area where corn beer

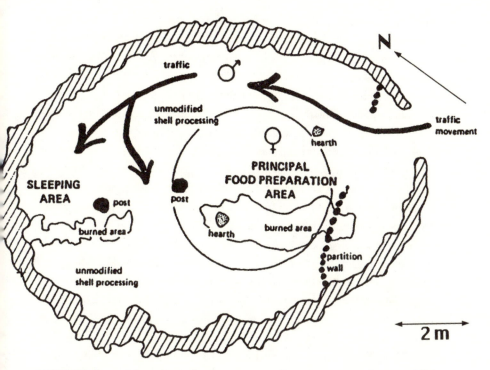

FIGURE 5.3. ■ A hypothetical reconstruction of activity areas in a large Middle Valdivia house, Structure One, probably occupied by an extended family at Real Alto about 2700 B.C.

was stored was used by all the women of the household, as was the maize-grinding area. Men all used a given spot for blowgun manufacture, and everyone used the areas where machetes were habitually sharpened and where beer was consumed.

Zeidler then compared this known spatial division of areas occupied to the floors of two excavated Middle Valdivia houses to see whether the artifact distribution reflected anything similar (fig. 5.3). In one house he found fragments of anthropomorphic figurines concentrated around a burned area, where broken ceramics, carbonized seeds, wood charcoal, and bone refuse indicated that foods had been prepared. Zeidler identified this and a similar area by the door of this large house as female space. Because chipped stone debris was found all over the place, he concluded that everyone chipped stone tools. The remains of shell ornament making, concentrations of stone tools, and unworked shell found around the periphery were identified as evidence of male craft areas. The remains of fancy ceramic vessels along the right wall he identified with a food and drink consumption area used by men and guests. Analysis of a second, smaller house revealed areas with no artifacts, which were identified as sleeping spaces and female multipurpose spaces.

This kind of ethnoarchaeological study focuses attention on the fact that females and males in indigenous South America often lead parallel lives, but it is doubtful that the modern Shuar are appropriate models for interpreting the ancient Valdivia people. We should be alert, as we engender activity areas, that our interpretations often rest upon the restatement of our own cultural prejudices. The conventional picture of women cooking and grinding often is recreated. Similarly, we need to be cautious because archaeological remains are only rarely preserved by some unexpected cataclysm, such as the volcanic eruptions that buried Pompeii, and the distribution of artifacts in the Middle Valdivia house may represent disturbances that occurred after the house was abandoned. Even if the remains accurately reflect ancient activities in the house, they may not represent clear distinctions between the activities of females and males. Susan Kent's ethnoarchaeological studies of Navaho hogans and their yards in the North American Southwest have shown clearly that in groups with relatively few belongings and living in a single space, virtually all tools and spaces are multiuse and multigendered. For ritual reasons, the paterfamilias had his sheepskin bed on the east side of the hogan, but she found that this was the only truly gendered use of space among traditional Navaho. Nevertheless, studies such as Zeidler's draw attention to the house as a locus of human activity and the fact that people do allocate space and tasks along gender lines and for other reasons.

Each large Middle Valdivia house probably was occupied by an extended family, and this kin group may have been the main social and economic unit. The Middle Valdivia settlement pattern reflects the use of garden land along the rivers, although marine and forest resources were important to the ancient people as well. Deborah Pearsall's archaeobotanical studies at Real Alto have led her to suggest that the major agricultural tasks, such as planting, weeding, and harvesting, were carried out by women and their older daughters, while males took care of field clearing and irrigation as well as hunting and fishing. A division of subsistence tasks in this broadly diversified economy would have required

scheduling, especially for agricultural activities. Based on the anthropological observation that scheduling problems in agricultural societies can
be solved by an extended family household organization, and noting the
evidence of larger houses and spatially distinct clusters of some sorts of
activity debris in Middle Valdivia sites, Zeidler has suggested that Middle
Valdivia people organized a large coresident labor force that could then
undertake spatially diverse subsistence activities. Within the household
some adults may have watched the children and cooked, others invested
more time in cultivation, and others banded together to leave the village
for net fishing or hunting. These sorts of activities can increase the productive capacity of the group with benefits to all, permitting the local
group to be relatively self-sufficient.

The nature of social organization in the Middle Valdivia community is
speculative, but many ethnographic communities in the tropical forest
regions of South America are characterized by localized lineages or even
clans. At Real Alto the members of the household may have belonged to
a particular clan, members of which all lived in the same area of the
village. Women may play significant roles in decision making in clan and
lineage organizations.

Neither burials nor art suggest that the social system was dominated
by males. Zeidler interprets the change in household size and composition
and the variability in household size (as indicated by larger and smaller
houses) as indicative of a strategy of competition among households in
which the differential accumulation of wealth led to the emergence of
social ranking. Feasting in a special structure such as the Fiesta House at
Real Alto could be understood as a communal activity that served to
integrate local households, but feasting can also be a mechanism of competition in which some families attempt to gain prestige and dominance
over others. Burial in the special Charnel House may be the ultimate
indication of ranking, special treatment in death being the prerogative of
individuals of a highly ranked extended family or lineage. That rank was
hereditary is indicated by the fact that infants were found in the same
burial context as a middle-aged woman and other adults in the Charnel
House at Real Alto. However, there is no real evidence of conspicuous
consumption by elites at Real Alto and no other real indications of social
hierarchy in life or death. There is, for example, no evidence of exchange
of luxury goods, no sumptuous burials, and little evidence of storage

---

facilities. Only a few figurines, all female, show ritual practitioners seated on stools, a traditional sign of ritual power or authority. It is unclear whether there was ranking within the community of Real Alto or among the Middle Valdivia communities. We do not know whether Valdivia social organization was favorable to women, to men, or to both as they moved through their separate tasks within the extended household context.

Reconstructing family and household dynamics from the 5,000-year-old remains excavated in Valdivia sites is difficult because archaeological contexts are blurred by postdeposition processes, and because the Valdivia people have no closely related historical descendants whose culture can be used to suggest interpretations. Luckily, as shown in the following example, there are some rare archaeological cases in which the archaeologists may benefit from excellent preservation of household contexts and use ethnographic analogy with confidence.

## The Village of Ceren in El Salvador

The tiny Maya village of Ceren was buried as the result of a volcanic eruption that occurred one summer's evening about A.D. 600. Because of the extraordinary preservation of remains under the ash fall, many details of ancient life can be recovered. More than eleven structures have now been excavated, including a civic structure for multifamily gatherings or male beer drinking, a ritual steam bath, and a number of household clusters. The latter are very like traditional lowland Maya households of the present. The buildings, made of wattle and daub on low earthen platforms, form clusters of small, separate structures that served as sleeping quarters, storage facilities, and kitchens (fig. 5.4).

At the Ceren site, plants have been identified from the impressions they left in solidified ash, and archaeologists have described an ancient household garden for the first time. In these kitchen gardens, ancient Maya women cultivated manioc as well as medicinal plants, and right near the house they had agave plants from whose leaves people extracted fiber for textiles. In the habitation area, the remains of three kinds of beans, maize, squash, chiles, avocados, and chocolate were found. *Ristras* (garlands or plaits) of chiles hung from the ceiling of a house, and the storage houses were full of stored beans and other seeds, as well as tools not in daily use and supplies such as colored paints for religious use. The villagers

FIGURE 5.4. ■ A reconstruction of the group of buildings, including a round kitchen, storehouse, main house, and small roofed workshop, which formed Household One at Ceren, El Salvador.

also consumed considerable quantities of deer, dog, and other animals. One victim of the eruption was a duck, tied to the stand of a metate! The remains show that the people of Ceren ate better than many of their descendants.

Metates in the kitchen area were mounted on *horquetas*, forked-branch stands very like those in use today, evidence that the women who did the grinding were not very tall. The big metates were used for processing maize and other foods, while miniature metates, apparently utilized for preparing cosmetics and paint, were found stored in ceramic vessels along with colored pigments contained in tiny vessels and seashells. Wall niches in the houses and the rafters were used to store tools, and apparently, parents stored their sharp obsidian tools in the thatched roof, where the children could not find them.

Food apparently was prepared in the kitchen but brought out and consumed in individual servings by people sitting on the benches in the houses or perhaps along the porch in the cool evening air. On the porch of one house, some woman or man flaked obsidian to make useful cutting tools. Another special craft area was found within Household One, where the housewife was making ceramic vessels at the time of the eruption. Archaeologists were surprised to find how many vessels each family had in use at one time. One small household had seventy vessels, including locally made cooking and storage vessels and many imported, painted vessels used to serve food and drink. The people of Ceren also had many gourds, used, as they are today, for drinking, food preparation, and storage. Some of these gourds were painted with designs like those on the pottery.

In an area that may have been used by the women of Household One for spinning and other domestic production, a crude miniature vessel and twenty sherds perhaps indicate the play area of a child who was learning to count in the base-twenty system used by all Mesoamericans.

Because life in these quarters was halted early in the evening, archaeologists have not discovered who slept where, but they did find sleeping mats rolled up and stored along the tops of the walls in an opening left for light and ventilation just below the roof.

The household clusters indicate a social organization involving groups of nuclear families related by blood and marriage, demonstrating clear continuities with modern Mayan peoples. These nonroyal families were probably monogamous, and like the later Maya, they may have reckoned kinship bilaterally, although with a slight patrilineal bias. They may have practiced patrilocal or neolocal residence after marriage. One can imagine two women grinding side by side in the patio, one of them laughing as the children tease the captive duck destined for a special dinner. Another puts aside her spinning as the men come in from the field, leaning their digging sticks against the side of the house. An elder is sitting on the porch fixing a deer-skull headdress that will be used in a ritual planned for after the harvest. A woman hands her adolescent son a painted bowl full of *atole*, which he is drinking as fast as he can, wiping out the gourd with his fingers in an attempt to satisfy his hunger. Then, without warning, the Laguna Caldera eruption began, just as the sun was setting, and people fled, leaving their houses and their artifacts exactly where they used them, to be covered with ash for 1,400 years.

This evidence, combined with ethnographic descriptions of modern Maya households, makes it easy to imagine women working and interacting in ancient domestic contexts. It is perhaps more difficult to create an image of women in the wider village context. Archaeologists working at Ceren have described another, larger building with niches, columns, and a window that contained a set of artifacts unlike the assemblages found in other household contexts. This building has been interpreted as the residence of the village curer and religious practitioner. Payson Sheets believes that this person may have been female, as is common today in El Salvador, where few villages lack a traditional wisewoman healer and fortune-teller. Presumably, the sweat bath, used all over Mexico and Central America for purification before religious rites, was built and maintained by the villagers together, but as in the rest of Mesoamerica, a woman may have been in charge of the steam bath, used also for the treatment of physical and nervous ills and by the midwife in the care of young mothers.

Another building with larger rooms and benches has a wide doorjamb with the handles from broken storage jars set into the sides to hold a curtain or mat. Inside there are big vessels for beer, all of which suggest that this was a meeting house for the men of the village. Simple graffiti on the back wall seem to be the result of children doodling in fresh clay plaster.

The Ceren villagers were part of a larger polity with its capital at San Andrés, a few kilometers to the west. Presumably, the villagers paid tribute in the form of produce and were required to labor for the rulers, who reciprocated by sponsoring exciting multicommunity rituals and civic events. San Andrés, as the political and economic center of the region, also had markets where people could acquire elaborate painted ceramics, obsidian, jade brought from Guatemala, and seashells. The Ceren community, composed of various families, was probably autonomous for most practical purposes, although it formed part of a larger polity, described as a chiefdom. Many of the tropical and temperate forest peoples of the Americas formed chiefdoms, political organizations with hereditary leaders and ranked lineages. A chiefdom has the potential of more roles and statuses for women and men because of surpluses generated by the group and collected by the leader. In situations such as that at Ceren, surpluses were transferred to the regional capitol, but the local village elders surely reserved some surplus to support community rituals and festivities. In the local context, it is likely that women and men participated together in producing surplus and deciding how it was expended.

The houses of Ceren demonstrate that the nuclear family has been the basic unit of production and social interaction among Maya people for more than 1,000 years. The Ceren site also shows that engendering tools and activity areas can be done with confidence when archaeologists rely on historic and ethnographic material from related peoples. Archaeologists assert with security that the women of Ceren engaged in grinding corn, cooking, and weaving because adult females among the later Maya do these activities. That the curer was female, as Payson Sheets has claimed, is a matter of speculation.

## Families in Ancient Colombia

The late prehistoric Tairona were successful tropical horticulturists living in a mountain environment of northern Colombia. They are famous for their lapidary art and gold working, and they exhibited their impressive architectural and engineering skills in their drainage and irrigation works, terraced fields, roadways, plazas, and temples arrayed along the steep slopes of the Sierra Nevada de Santa Marta. Some historic data on the Tairona indicate that they had a complex stratified society with secular chieftains and war captains, a class of priests, and many types of artists and artisans.

Excavations at Buriticá 200, described by Carlos Castaño Uribe, have uncovered various kinds of domestic structures, the residences of families, some of which required more labor to build than others. Some circular structures greater than 4 meters in diameter have been interpreted as houses, based on analogy with the putative descendants of the Tairona, the modern Kogi Indians. Archaeologists have inferred that the ancient Tairona houses had conical thatched roofs, not unlike those of the Kogi. Excavation of ancient houses often reveals, under the threshold, a pot containing a number of pebbles that, according to Kogi custom, represent and magically protect the occupants. The floor plan of one of these ancient houses shows a probable woman's area to the right of the entrance. Here are water jars, cooking pots, grinding stones, small axes and scrapers, and the fireplace. On the other, male, side are axes, hammerstones, perforating tools, fishhooks, nondomestic ceramics, whistles, and other ceremonial gear and tools and debris from working gold and semiprecious stones. Male gear also included batwing pendants (worn for dances) and stools. This distribution of goods gives archaeologists the impression that the houses were divided, with men performing stereotypical activities along one side and women cooking along the other. This interpretation rests, of course, on the presumed association of women with one set of remains and not the other.

An alternative interpretation of the way humans lived in one of these houses, generated from Kogi ethnography, indicates that the entire contents of the house belonged to either a woman or a man. Tom Zuidema has found among the Kogi a version of an Andean kinship and inheritance pattern in which the women are organized in lineages featuring descent from mother to daughter; similarly, men are organized in male lineages figured from father to son. After marriage, Kogi couples occupy their own houses, located opposite each other, and meals are served and consumed in the space between the houses. In this scenario the house with remains of cooking might belong to a wife who, with her immature children, owned and used the items in both the right and left activity areas. These activities would include manufacturing and using ceremonial items and nondomestic pottery. Because of the unusual social patterns that people can work out for themselves, engendering the archaeological record can be a risky business. In this instance, if we look at the Tairona's descendants, ceremonial pottery is made by male priests. Men also do all the weaving.

In addition to residences, Castaño Uribe describes other structures at Buriticá. Closely associated with what are almost certainly domestic structures are buildings that lack fireplaces. These appear to be where craft activities, such as gold working, lapidary production, weaving, or woodworking took place. Storage structures associated with the houses contained enormous quantities of ceramic jars and stone tools. Household clusters seem to have been the loci of storage of food and manufactured items.

Burials also are associated with these architectural groups, reinforcing the idea of the central importance of the family. Because bone was poorly preserved, there is no independent evidence of the sex of the interments, but researchers have interpreted some division in the offerings as indicative of two genders. Some burials have stone axes, celts, and hoes, decorated staffs, and anthropomorphic figurines of semiprecious stone. The excavator thinks these are male, whereas the burials containing smaller axes, polishing stones, stone beads, and shale figurines are female. The interpretation that houses were divided along gender lines is not supported by burial evidence, since burials of both sorts are made under both sides of the house, in the patio areas, and in nearby refuse dumps. Apparently the location of the burial and the kind and depth of the tomb are reflections of social rank more than gender.

The Tairona family was organized to carry out the fundamental economic activities of the society. Some families may have been more successful because of their size and access to labor. In such ranked societies, people surely sought to arrange beneficial marriages that might enhance family fortunes. Polygyny among the higher-ranking families may have helped households to grow and prosper. Despite the impressive architecture and sophisticated crafts of the Tairona, there is no evidence of specialized production apart from the family setting, nor is there evidence that a public arena existed apart from the sphere dominated by families.

Archaeological investigations in northern Colombia also illustrate the variability of family composition and organization through time and space. According to Castaño Uribe, around A.D. 100 in the Río de la Miel region, the Colorado-phase people lived in dispersed settlements in defensible locations away from the big rivers. Families occupied oval *malocas* with floor areas of 60–70 square meters. Houses this size known ethnographically are the residences of single extended families of no more than fifteen people. The dead were buried in urns in nucleated cemeteries near the villages; the burials showed little social differentiation. However, the next phase, Butantán, showed major changes in family structure. Villages now consisted of several huge malocas along the river's edge. These houses had three to four times the floor space of the earlier ones, indicating growth in the size of the household unit. One of these large houses could hold 80 to 100 people. Butantán people were much more involved in commerce and specialized crafts such as gold working than their ancestors had been. This more complex economic structure is reflected in the social structure. Aside from the fact that larger family groups were coresident, burial offerings expressed greater emphasis on rank.

Life in a Butantán village must have been much altered from earlier times. Living in a larger settlement, in a house with many more people, more expressed ranking of individuals, numerous ties to the outside, and increased possibilities for the acquisition of goods must have changed the very tenor of life. The larger villages were apparently organized for defense as well as production and trade. Leaders took a prominent part in decisions, and perhaps polygyny was introduced for some as a means of optimizing production. These changes must have meant busier and more active lives for everyone but also increased stress caused by more people and the threats of neighbors.

Detailed information concerning the evolution of family structure in northern Colombia are lacking, but house size, burial patterns, and an altered artifact inventory all show that there were major changes. Family

WOMEN IN ANCIENT AMERICA

organization did not alter randomly but was surely the result of behavioral changes adopted consciously by people, including women and girls, in the course of their lives.

## An Early Iroquois Migration

In an example of adaptive change, the ancestors of the late prehistoric Iroquois of the northeastern United States may have adopted matrilineal organization to increase their adaptability in a period of migration. The Owasco people, who were the ancestors of the modern Iroquois nations, migrated out of central Pennsylvania and into what is now New York around A.D. 900, displacing the Algonquian groups who were living there. The early Owasco people described by Dean Snow were organized into bigger family groups than those of their Algonquian neighbors, and they had the economic advantage of a mixed economy, based in part on the cultivation of squash, beans, and maize. Because of the large size of the Owasco cooking pots, archaeologists have hypothesized that the number of people being fed in a single unit was large. An increase in the size of cooking pots is often accompanied by a growth in house size in the archaeological record, reflecting how prehistoric people organized to undertake warfare, trade, or large building projects. Owasco houses were large, although not quite so large as those of some of their descendants, who lived in multifamily dwellings known as longhouses.

Using the conventional wisdom of anthropological theory to understand the Owasco people, Snow has hypothesized that the Owasco adopted a matrilocal residence pattern that facilitated their aggressive expansion into the thinly populated northern regions. In this system, when a woman married, her husband joined her household and lived with his wife, her parents, and her sisters and their husbands. Matrilineal family organization has several advantages for migrating people. If their tribal organization is egalitarian, then the matrilineal segments can successfully occupy a new region without intergroup competition because hostility can be repressed and focused on an external enemy, such as the Algonquian hunters and gatherers. In this kind of organization, men from various families marrying into and taking up residence with their wives' families become brothers-in-law to men from various lineages. This breaks up groups of potentially aggressive men related along the patriline, who, in a patrilineally organized system, frequently engage in violent competition among themselves. It would be unlikely for these men to conspire against other Iroquois families because they themselves come from those families (including their own maternal family and the families where their brothers live with their own wives and children). In this way, feuding and internal warfare between Iroquois families and lineages might have been averted and aggression and violence focused outside of the community.

The Iroquois, in the course of sporadic warfare, may have abducted, enslaved, and married women from the Algonquian populations they were displacing. This process would account for some of the unusual ceramic assemblages (found mixed in pits in archaeological sites): the captive women continued to make and use their own styles of ceramics as they lived alongside women making Owasco pottery.

The late prehistoric and historic Iroquois longhouses were up to 100 meters long, and the people were organized in villages of as many as 500 people (fig. 5.5). When the Europeans came they observed six to ten nuclear families per longhouse, living in pairs, facing each other across a hearth. The nuclear families were formed around women who belonged to the same matrilineal clan segment. Women worked in family units in fields cleared by their clan brothers (who lived nearby). The heaviest cutting and clearing was done by the men, but the rest of the horticultural work was done by women: planting, hoeing, and harvesting, along with collecting roots, sap for maple syrup, greens, nuts, berries, and small animals. Much of this was communal work supervised by clan matrons.

The longhouses were expandable at the ends, where storage areas were rather lightly built. Men married outside their lineage but usually within the village or a neighboring village. Men were also frequently absent from home, especially as intertribal warfare increased in later prehistory. Both the structure of the family and the absence of men gave women autonomy: the villages were the domain of women, while men were said to own the forest. Social life was characterized by separate spheres for women and men, by reciprocal obligations between the sexes, and by gender roles that were nonhierarchical.

In Iroquois society, daughters may have been preferred over sons since a daughter helped to increase the size and power of the household. Snow has suggested that women exercised control over family size by using

FIGURE 5.5. ■ An artist's view of the interior of an Iroquois longhouse. Matrilineally related families occupied compartments along the walls, sharing hearths with relatives across the center aisle.

herbal medicines and by selective abortion. Abortion medicines were common in traditional Iroquois pharmacopoeia.

Gender behavior can be inferred through the analysis of Iroquois pottery, traditionally manufactured by the women. Archaeologists observe that Iroquois pottery was made and discarded locally, whereas pipes, made and used by men, were spread widely over Iroquois territory. In this case, historical data tell us that men traveled widely to exchange gifts, trade, and engage in diplomacy and warfare. They required the contribution of resources controlled by women to undertake these activities.

Historic studies and more recent ethnographic accounts of the Iroquois show that women participated widely in religious activity, including the performance of sacred dances in seasonal ceremonies. In each village, women formed societies to maintain these traditional ceremonies. They also formed mutual aid societies to cultivate private (nonclan) plots.

Iroquois mythology illustrates the division of labor by gender: women were always farmers, and men hunters and warriors. When the famous Iroquois league was formed, female delegates from the dominant clan segments in each of the constituent nations named the League chiefs (*sachems*). The women also replaced the *sachems* and removed them from office when necessary. In later history, when large belts of wampum became important ritual symbols, matrons spoke through belts to the war chiefs, which demonstrates women's access to symbols of authority. These female elders were not, however, matriarchs. Both female and male authority was clearly defined in this kin-organized society. Women's role as food producers was in part the basis of their authority, but it was the extension of the kinship system into political life that benefited Iroquois women. In contrast, in Europe the patriarchal structure of family life did not work to the advantage of women when it was extended into the public sphere.

## Grasshopper Pueblo Families

The study of Grasshopper Pueblo in New Mexico has resulted in a good understanding of ancient households and community organization. The burial data from Grasshopper, occupied by Mogollon Tradition peoples between A.D. 1300 and 1400, also show that gender greatly affected individual experience in that ancient community. Grasshopper consisted of three major room blocks and several outlying groups of houses. J. J. Reid and S. M. Whittlesey studied rooms with different functions, as determined by the artifacts left on the floors when the pueblo was abandoned, and identified separate households. While all households participated in the same range of activities, each carried out activities in different proportions and in different spatial contexts. Variation among the household units and change through time demonstrate that there was no fixed female or male experience in prehistoric societies. A woman's experience at Grasshopper would have been different from a man's, but any individual born into a large, well-established household would have had a very different daily life and life trajectory from that of a same-sex person born into a smaller household.

Some family groups occupied multiroom houses in the main room blocks. Here, several women probably worked in a main room and used additional storage and manufacturing rooms. In single-room houses, presumably a smaller group of women or a single woman labored in that one space, which combined habitation, storage, and manufacturing functions. Studying the room blocks occupied by discrete kin groups in the center of the pueblo, researchers found that female equipment dominated in some contexts, male items in others, and that markers of women and men were mixed in some plazas and room blocks. Some researchers have argued that the differences in pottery among the room blocks support the hypothesis that social segments (such as clans or moieties) were differentiated for the purposes of regulating marriage, but this kind of interpretation has not been widely accepted in southwestern archaeology.

Different cranial modifications in the skeletal population indicate that several ethnic groups may have lived at Grasshopper. Although the ancient residents of the site were divided into groups by kin ties, wealth, and perhaps ethnicity, they also interacted across these lines. An average of three households shared a ceremonial room, while six households seem to have combined to share a kiva. The great kiva of Grasshopper is thought to have served the community as a whole. Kiva ceremonial life may have involved the members of associations not based on kinship, such as those found among the later Pueblo Indians. Reid and Whittlesey recognized several associative groups, identified by the emblems buried with deceased members, which apparently crosscut the community. A male might have belonged to one of three hypothetical groups that were mutually exclusive: at death some men were buried with *Glycymeris* shell pendants, or conus tinklers, or bone hairpins. An adult male member of any one these associations might have belonged also to a group whose symbol was a quiver of arrows.

In the interpretation of Reid and Whittlesey, women too belonged to organizations that united people outside the immediate family and beyond the domestic context. At Grasshopper, *Glycymeris* shell bracelets were worn in death by women as well as men, signaling a community association open to both sexes. Only women wore conus shell rings, an ornament that might identify an exclusively feminine organization. The participation of women in social, economic, political, and religious activity beyond the domestic context is explored in the remaining chapters of this book.

Later in the history of Grasshopper Pueblo, household size decreased. More people lived in single-room houses in the outlying room blocks, rather than in the central area, once the purview of the richer, larger families. The size of cooking hearths also decreased through time, as did the size of cooking vessels. Large households may have become strategically untenable under the circumstances of the late fourteenth century. Such a change in household size implies alterations in customary workloads, roles, and gender relations. The greater frequency of single-room households later in time may not signal a beneficial change for women, since women suffered declining health as their diets changed in the later prehistory of this site.

## Family Relations Among the Anasazi

A recent study of prehistoric funerary offerings in Arizona shows how careful observation and analysis can be used to test ideas about gender, family, and social patterns. Arelyn Simon and John Ravesloot observed patterns of vessel placement within Salado tombs of the western Anasazi or Puebloan peoples of ca. A.D. 1150–1250. By assessing the origin of vessels (including undecorated ones) based on the composition of the clays, they were able to construct hypotheses about the role of particular individuals within the community. Because different potters, coming from different families within the community, use different clay sources, the finding of vessels made from these different clays ought to point to interaction between the person who owned or was buried with the vessels and the people who made them. The vessels are evidence of individual social relationships in extinct society. Simon and Ravesloot also think that burial goods may reflect the composition of the mourning group that contributed the gifts during the funeral and that the placement of vessels with respect to the body had social significance. For example, an eighteen-year-old woman in one tomb was accompanied by vessels that fall into six of the eight recognized compositional groups of ceramics known in the cemetery. The authors argue that these vessels signal her natal house-hold and family membership (fig. 5.6).

The investigators found no simple correlation between gender and the abundance and variety of ceramic vessels. However, they did observe some relationships between the vessels and the status of individuals, prob-ably a reflection of the peoples' wealth, access to resources, and the size of their social network. In the young woman's burial, the presence of many of these compositional clusters seems to show her relationship to other individuals buried in the cemetery. Some clusters and the patterns

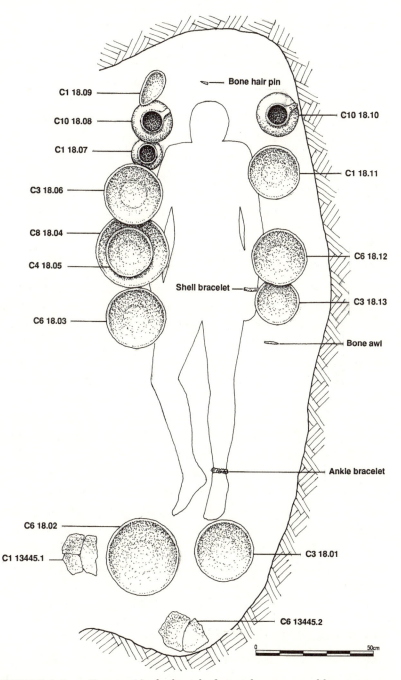

FIGURE 5.6. ■ Feature 18, the burial of an eighteen-year-old woman, was found in a Salado cemetery of the Anasazi tradition. Paste analysis demonstrates that the vessels surrounding the skeleton belong to distinct groups, suggesting that the woman was connected to various lineages within her community.

of their placement suggest gifts from natal groups, while others may be gifts from affinal groups or groups to which persons developed ceremonial ties later in life. Multiple vessels from two clusters were found on either side of her head and shoulders. The researchers concluded that the placement of the vessels reflects both the gender and the age of the person as well as familial relationships and memberships in ceremonial societies. Older individuals commonly have vessels from compositional groups other than those associated with family membership, presumably reflecting wider relationships within the community. Studies such as these are exciting and promise the possibility of tracking a person's expanding responsibilities and relationships through life.

## Family Life in Complex Societies

As some Native American societies developed a state form of government, family life changed. In states, individual families have less control over many aspects of their economic and social behavior. As some American states became more urban, elite control of the population was heightened, and women and men often suffered. It has been argued that when there are more tasks and more gendered tasks, when there is a larger material culture that also becomes gendered, and when female children are acculturated differently from male children, then women begin to lose status. In ancient American cities, family life was variable across time and space, as it was in the rest of the world. In the Maya urban centers of the Classic period, people lived in extended household units and occupied clusters of small one- or two-roomed structures. Presumably, kin lived contiguously. Excavations at Copán in Honduras have revealed large households of many families living close together. Evidently these were lineage settlements in which rich and poor relations lived close by each other. However, different kinds of households are known in other areas of ancient America, and each would have influenced the lives of women and men differently.

## Apartment Life in Early Classic Mexico

Teotihuacán was in ruins when the Aztecs entered the Valley of Mexico in late prehistory, but even covered with grass and cactus, the remains of the pyramids and palaces were so impressive that the ruins became identified with the mythological origin of humanity, and Aztec rulers made pilgrim-ages to the site. Archaeologists now know that Teotihuacán was the largest city in the Americas early in the first millennium A.D., when the Pyramids of the Sun and the Moon were erected. At its height, the city covered some 29 square kilometers of densely packed buildings aligned along the Street of the Dead. It was an immensely influential metropolis during the first 700 years of our era. Its art and architecture were emulated widely, and it had a great economic and political impact on its neighbors. The city had diplomatic relations with many Mexican and Mayan kingdoms. Teotihuacán enclaves have been identified at other sites in Mexico and Guatemala, and neighborhoods where foreigners lived have been recog-nized within Teotihuacán itself.

During the city's heyday, the vast majority of its citizens lived in apartment compounds. Within these buildings, individual residences were composed of groups of small rooms. Archaeologists have also identified at least one public area in each compound. Some of the best information on how ordinary Teotihuacanos lived comes from a compound called Tlajinga 33 (fig. 5.7). While the more elite stone and concrete apartment buildings of Teotihuacán had elaborate drainage systems, cement floors, and painted walls, Tlajinga 33 was built of adobe brick and had dirt floors and cobble paving. It had a series of irregularly interconnecting room and patio complexes associated with one group of larger, more public rooms and patios, and a shrine. The excavators of Tlajinga have inferred that the smallest units, suites of two or three rooms with a small patio, were the residences of nuclear families. Areas of contiguous apartments are associated with larger courtyards, refuse heaps, and workshop debris. The burials of the children and adults who lived in the apartments were found under the rooms and patios. These people were neither wealthy nor influential. Rather, during a period of about 500 years they engaged in craft activity, first lapidary and later ceramic manufacture, although they may have engaged in agricultural production as well.

The best-preserved apartments in the Tlajinga complex each had a main room of about 3.3 by 3.7 meters entered from a shallow, roofed porch, and a smaller room, both raised above a private, cobbled patio. These rooms are thought to have been used mainly for sleeping and storage. The Teotihuacanos had no effective artificial lighting and probably did most work and socializing outside. The common archaeological

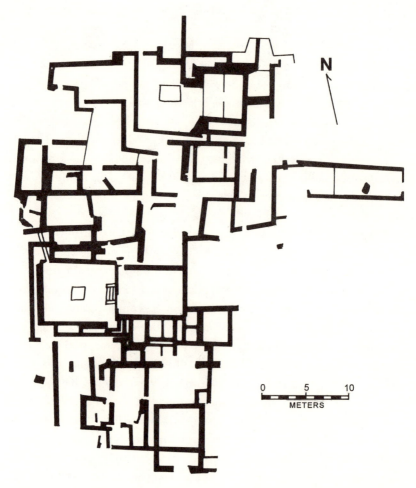

FIGURE 5.7. ■ Plan of the excavated portion of Tlajinga 33, a lower-class apartment house in Teotihuacán. The irregular forms of some rooms are the result of remodeling in response to family needs. Two large patios have shrines, and a two-room religious precinct opens into the large patio in the north part of the building.

practice of counting nuclear families by the number of fireplaces cannot be followed because the Teotihuacanos cooked on ceramic braziers, which functioned as single-burner stoves. Because broken braziers were discarded into the communal dump, there is no way to determine how many a single family had at one time.

The placement and size of the workshops within Tlajinga suggest that ceramic production was organized at the multifamily or even compound level. The workshops, drying rooms, and firing areas were located apart from the living quarters. People in other compounds in the same vicinity were also involved in pottery production, suggesting that ancient craft production was the specialty of a group of related families that were residentially localized. In contrast, the two lapidary workshops at Tlajinga were associated with a small cluster of apartments, suggesting that only limited labor was invested in this activity. Perhaps these workshops reflect the specialization of a few individuals or just two nuclear families within the large ancient household. Because both neighborhood and central city marketplaces have been identified at Teotihuacán, archaeologists think that the distribution of products was handled through markets.

Tlajinga 33 illustrates the physical and economic setting of family life at Teotihuacán. Based on this evidence, archaeologists can imagine some of the social dynamics of the ordinary inhabitants of the ancient city, and because of the custom of burying family members under the rooms and patios in which they once lived, it is possible to reconstruct some aspects of the ancient kinship organization. Skeletal analysis by Michael Spence conducted with remains from several compounds resulted in the hypothesis that the Teotihuacanos reckoned kinship in the male line. The men buried in a given compound shared skeletal traits, indicating that they were more closely related to each other than to the women buried in the same compound. This suggests strongly that each compound was the home of a patrilineage, occupied by between 60 and 200 relatives related patrilineally. The total population of a compound would have varied because of economic factors and differing reproductive histories. The size of the apartments suggests that families were monogamous, a pattern seen among later peoples of central Mexico. We do not, however, know whether groups of brothers and their families clustered together in one section of a compound.

The women who married into the patrilineages must have come from other apartments in the neighborhood, although Rebecca Storey has pointed out that ancient cities do not reproduce their population and have to recruit from without. Probably the vast majority of marriages were between people of linked lineages within the same socioeconomic group, or perhaps even between members of different segments of the same lineage. It seems likely that people sought mates in families that practiced similar economic activities. Also, it is thought that the larger, more public apartments adjacent to the shrine patio, where the more elaborate burials were found, belonged to the lineage head and his family.

Evidence from Tlajinga and some other nonelite compounds suggests that some women may have benefited from the high status of their families. This evidence comes from those women buried within the larger, more accessible patios that contained shrines. These burials seem to have more offerings, especially if they are within or near the altar itself. In this context, some tombs were found to contain women who were closely related to the males of the compound. These skeletons might be mothers of the men of the compound or they might be the remains of women who died unmarried and who were then buried with their close kin. However, in these same contexts, one finds burials of males who are evidently not related to the other males, suggesting that when nature failed to provide a male heir in those families with power and goods, a husband was married to one of the daughters of the patriline. This solution is seen in many patrilineal societies. In such cases, the patrilineage is not broken. The children of the union of the in-marrying male and the stay-at-home woman are members of the woman's patrilineage and inherit her position and goods. These daughters and wives might have had experiences different from those of other women in the compound. There is not enough skeletal evidence to indicate whether the women who brought husbands home were healthier or lived longer than the in-marrying wives of the compound.

Marriage arrangements may have meant that the young bride faced the problems of being an in-marrying women, chiefly that she might not enjoy any prestige or authority until her own sons were adults. The young wives in Teotihuacán may have been trained and supervised by their mothers-in-law, laying the young wives open to abuse from the mothers-in-law (a prevalent pattern in Asian societies); but alternatively, sons' wives may have been chosen carefully by parents, and the brides may have been highly valued for their potential contributions. The relatively short life spans of the Teotihuacanos could have ameliorated a wife's treatment by her in-laws, making her suffering short in duration. If marriages were contracted within the neighborhood or quarter, a young woman might have had her own relatives close by.

A woman's daily life in these apartments would vary with her age and status. To reconstruct daily activities, archaeologists examine the evidence and extrapolate from history and ethnography. In most traditional societies of central Mexico, married women were responsible for the daily running of the home, childbearing and care of the youngest ones, preparation of food, cleaning, and making and maintaining clothing for family members. Analysis of the domestic ceramics of Teotihuacán has shown a large number of griddles, evidence that tortillas were a basic foodstuff. This would have entailed the daily preparation of *nixtamal* (hominy, corn treated with lime water) and the laborious grinding of the dough by women and girls. Women also shouldered domestic religious duties. Judging from the numbers of figurines and incense burners in household refuse, domestic rituals were part of everyday spirituality. In most of these chores, it is likely that women worked in concert with other women.

For ordinary women, who almost certainly were involved in craft production in their compound, the workload was heavy. Moreover, it is known from skeletal evidence that adult women were malnourished and carried a heavy parasite load, exacerbated by being pregnant or lactating much of their adult lives. Discussions of the impact of poor nutrition and parasite load on labor and energy input is largely theoretical in the scientific literature, but a graphic account is found in the book *Living Poor: A Peace Corps Chronicle*, in which Moritz Thomsen describes the fatigue that sets in when your only food is low in nutritive value and how this, combined with parasites, makes even minimal activity difficult. Parasites and respiratory diseases, as well as infections, probably plagued everybody in Teotihuacán, a densely settled city where water was in limited supply part of the year and where the disposal of garbage and sewage was inadequate.

At Tlajinga women surely integrated craft tasks with domestic chores and sought labor- or time-saving behaviors to make it possible to finish their work. Perhaps those women most involved in craft production reduced their food-preparation time by acquiring either ground tortilla dough or hot tortillas. Historically, tortilla production and sale was largely in the hands of poor women. Some women likely chose to prepare certain dishes, such as stews of beans and chiles, as part of a time-saving strategy. This behavior was described among late prehistoric Aztec women studied by Elizabeth Brumfiel, who also documented archaeologically that Aztec women who committed themselves to weaving for the state chose different foods and cooking techniques from those prepared and used by women with other economic strategies. They may have made scheduling decisions similar to those of nineteenth-century women who, to free themselves for the heavy and time-consuming task of washing on Monday, saved leftovers from the festive meals they prepared for the family on Sunday. In ancient Teotihuacán, washing clothing must have meant carrying the clothing (with the older children's help) to the canalized river or, alternatively, carrying water to the compound. Perhaps both had to be done, because ceramics manufacture required quantities of water as well. The procurement and transport of water and fuel tend to be the heaviest and most time-consuming jobs in a nonmodern family, but one wonders if these tasks were specialized in ancient Teotihuacán or if the women of Teotihuacán hired help to get the washing done.

In the family residences of Tlajinga, women probably swept the house and patio, gathered trash to be carried out, and prepared food and paraphernalia for festivals, rituals, and other religious observances held in the household, compound, or another urban venue. The spinning and weaving of textiles for domestic consumption certainly were among the most labor-intensive and time-consuming tasks performed in the home, requiring the additional participation of girls and old women and men. Archaeologists have not determined whether Teotihuacanos, like many other Mexicans of the past, had to pay tribute (taxes) in cloth, but that too would have weighed on any woman's time, along with caring for children, including those who were chronically ill from respiratory diseases, malnutrition, and diarrhea. Comforting the child, trying to procure and prepare medicines, and the emotional burden of watching a child sicken and die were part of a women's burden.

It is not known whether householders went to the market for food and supplies. Some open areas in the urban core have been called marketplaces, where women, men, or both might have gone to trade their wares or acquire items for family consumption. Fuel procurement was almost certainly in the hands of specialists who gathered wood from afar and brought it into the city for exchange. The ceramics workshops would have required considerable fuel, more than the small braziers used for cooking and warming the rooms during the chilly season. Wood may have been delivered, as it is today, to the urban potters who maintained regular relationships with fuel providers.

In addition to domestic chores, it is certain that women were involved in the family or lineage craft production. Among the traditional potters of Mexico and Guatemala, production is a family endeavor. Men dig the clay; women grind and sift it, and they may be the ones who fetch the water to hydrate it. Under some conditions, both men and women form vessels. In small-scale production today, women predominate, and in larger-scale enterprises, such as the one documented by Louana Lackey at Acatlán in south central Mexico, everyone in the family is involved in all stages of production. People cooperate to prepare the clay body, form the vessels or other artifacts, dry the vessels first in the shade and then in the sun, burnish, slip, ornament, and add handles to the leather-hard vessels, dry them again, and then fire them. Even very young children make truly valuable contributions of labor because they can fetch tools, carry and rotate drying pots, and mind the fire.

Evidence suggests that the lower class women of Teotihuacán experienced very difficult lives, and, in the later years of the city, their condition seriously deteriorated. Investigations at Tlajinga 33 have shown that by the time the city was maximally nucleated, with virtually everyone living in compounds, a continuing health crisis affected women and children acutely. Infant mortality soared to 30–40 percent of all babies, and the families of Tlajinga lost perhaps 50 percent of their new members by age fifteen. Deaths were especially frequent among individuals between the ages of three and five, doubtless due to weaning stress. The bones of survivors, which often show a flattening of femur growth at this time of life, are evidence that stress affected the health of most children in the compound. A frightening aspect of neonate health was that the fetuses show no growth between the thirty-second and thirty-sixth week of gestation. The study of skeletal remains shows that ancient infants had very low birth weights and were subject to the same problems that result in high neonatal mortality rates today. This situation seems to be due to serious malnutrition of the mothers. There was chronic poor nutrition among all the residents of the Tlajinga compound, but some cultural practices associated with pregnancy may also have affected expectant mothers.

Females who experienced overwork, chronic undernourishment, and persistent infections would have experienced later menarche, earlier menopause, and a longer lactational amenorrhea after the birth of a baby that survived. These women probably had low fertility rates due to undernourishment and physical stress, but an adult woman would have been under considerable pressure to produce children that could be reared to adulthood, even though pregnancy and lactation further impaired her health and lowered the average age of death. Half of the inhabitants of Tlajinga were dead by forty, and most of the rest died within the next fifteen years. Most young adults would have lost one or both parents by the time they had begun their own families, depriving young wives of the help with child care that the older members of a household might offer. A young mother might also be expected to take up the work of her deceased mother-in-law, including raising her husband's younger siblings and other orphans from among his kin. Life was not easy for men or women in Tlajinga, but the physically burdened women had to cope with contributing to the family income by participating in craft activity and taking responsibility for so many other domestic jobs. In Teotihuacán, life was unenviable for most ordinary women.

On the other hand, women probably enjoyed the companionship of their husbands and children as they went about the important daily activities of maintaining themselves and producing an economic surplus. The work was probably shared with a wider group of kin, including cooperating sisters-in-law, a few older women of the compound, and lively unmarried girls. When there are many hands and friendly conversation, life can be good for people living in a dynamic urban community. Women born into higher-status families certainly enjoyed more freedom from work and want until the collapse of the city in the seventh century A.D.

In most archaeological narratives about the past, the emphasis falls upon religion, warfare, and elite material culture, but most human life is concerned with household and family matters such as procuring food and shelter, making marriage alliances, paying tribute, and worrying about the baby. In household contexts, women and men live together and negotiate their participation in all the spheres of activity and expertise that compose their way of life.

# CHAPTER SIX

# *Women, Production, and Specialization*

During most of human history, cultural systems were characterized solely by domestic economies. All production was household production, and households were largely independent, meaning that the members of the group made decisions based primarily upon shared values. David Cheal has suggested that in this domestic mode of production, decision making has its foundation in a moral economy. In other words, individuals are motivated by a desire to produce socially preferred, moral relationships. Thus, family members are concerned not simply with supplying their material needs, but also with reinforcing values such as sex roles and appropriate divisions of labor. In addition they seek to build and maintain a harmonious, supportive, and cooperative working environment. In domestic contexts, both women and men may negotiate positive social status for themselves. Women may occupy roles in production and reproduction that are highly valued, complementary to, and harmoniously linked with those of men and children.

In prehistory, wherever the domestic context was the principal social context, all subsystems were managed from the family center. Religious life, economic life, and political life were one fabric with many intertwined threads. Although labor may have been divided, women and men were involved in the functioning of all systems and would have been expected to participate in them all.

In many cases, gender is a key organizing principle of economic systems, and in times of change, the ability of people to alter existing gender roles and relations is part of the flexibility of economic units of all sizes and degrees of complexity. Part of this flexibility stems from women, who have always had functions beyond basic nurturing. Prehistoric women, like modern women, often were craft specialists and other kinds of professionals in addition to their roles as mothers, wives, and kinswomen. Female labor has always been pivotal, even in societies that are male dominated. States that systematically devalue females may simultaneously commit great effort to controlling female labor, which is critical to their economic systems.

In prehistory, as some societies systematically added more task domains, statuses, and roles, women and men were assigned new, diversified roles. Anthropology shows that all domains, all specializations, crafts, and statuses, can be occupied by either females or males. In many ancient societies, both women's specialized knowledge and that of men were critical and valuable for the social group. In contrast we live in a time in which critical knowledge is held by professionals, such as engineers and surgeons, whose ranks have been, until recently, dominated by men. While important functions continue to be performed by Doctor Mom and Mrs. Homemaker in domestic contexts, modern society is dominated by nondomestic contexts of production, where the most socially visible and valued activities are performed and where women's contributions are unequally valued.

Among scholars there is considerable discussion about the origins and evolution of the division of labor by sex, and much attention is focused on the process by which domestic economies are transformed and more political economies evolve. This process involves the development of a social field beyond the household and results in a situation in which the division of labor is altered, gender norms are transformed, and the interests of individuals are compromised because the locus of power lies outside the family. The valued roles that women may hold in domestic contexts may have no analogues in the larger system, resulting in what to us is the familiar system of gender asymmetry.

As economic systems evolve, the production of goods for consumption outside the household may result in craft specialization. Specialization by sex exists within almost all households, but in later prehistory some households developed specializations in addition to the existing divisions of labor by sex, age, and personal preference. Some portion of household labor was invested in production that allowed that household to be integrated into larger social, economic, and political networks. Later in prehistory, households were organized to produce for both internal consumption and external markets.

## Formative Metalworking in Argentina

Households simultaneously may be characterized by domestic labor and specialized labor. Joan Gero's work at the Yutopian site in northwest Argentina shows that production of copper artifacts was an integral part of one household's activity. Yutopian is an Early Formative site whose inhabitants made and circulated elaborate polychrome pottery, copper and gold ornaments, and bronze bracelets and bells. In Structure One, apparently the home and workshop of an extended family, archaeologists recovered the remains of communal food preparation and storage. What distinguishes this house from its neighbors is that it contained a hearth of fire-hardened clay with four stones firmly fixed in its center, as if to support a receptacle. The fireplace was associated with burned bones and beans, bits of raw copper silicates, and some scoria. It seems evident that this hearth was used both for the preparation of the family meals and for metalworking.

Copper artifacts were produced for circulation and consumption in Yutopian and beyond, but there is no evidence that any authority outside the family managed this activity. In Yutopian, where there was no market distribution and no higher political authority, copper metallurgy was carried out in the family context. Craft production for exchange probably involved a number of different family members, and it is possible that this kind of craft specialization integrated many dispersed family units into an exchange network. There is no obvious method of discerning whether women or men did the metalworking, or whether the family members scheduled the hours during which they would use the fireplace. Archaeologists are unable to say how any of the multitude of tasks involved in the production of metal artifacts were assigned. While the ethnographic literature shows us that metallurgy is often a male activity, the skilled rural bronze casters of coastal Ecuador are both female and male and may perform any task regardless of sex (fig. 6.1).

Production organized at the level of family continued to be crucial even as state societies developed. Archaeological investigations in northern Peru show us that mining and smelting originally were carried out by families, although ultimately the industry fell into the hands of the Inca state, which collected ingots as tribute.

FIGURE 6.1. ■ Adela Borbor, here seen arranging fuel in her forge, is one of
the last bronze casters of southwestern Ecuador. Formerly both women and men
learned bronze casting in family contexts.

## Metallurgy at Batán Grande, Peru

The Lambayeque or Sicán culture of the northern valleys of coastal Peru flourished in the centuries between the collapse of the Moche polity and the formation of the Conquest state of Chimor in the late thirteenth century A.D. The Lambayeque/Sicán people are best known as the producers of elaborate copper, gold, and gold alloy artifacts that have been looted in immense quantities from the royal tombs in large ceremonial centers. Based on the study of residential and manufacturing sites in and around Batán Grande, Izumi Shimada and his colleagues have demonstrated that metalworking and the large-scale manufacture of ceramics were carried out by family groups.

Excavations at the site of Cerro Huaringa revealed a major industrial smelting center, producing ingots of arsenic bronze and, perhaps, blanks that were finished into tools and ornaments in other workshops. The site was near sources of copper ore and supplies of fuel. The three major sectors of the site were connected by a banked road, and each had sets of well-built masonry and adobe room blocks adjacent to the workshops. The room groups may have been built by corporate labor to state specifications, and they appear to have been apartment houses for working families adjacent to the smelters. As in the case of the pottery workers of Tlajinga 33, the residents of the room blocks of Batán Grande worked in areas next to but separate from the living areas themselves. John Topic's excavations at the roughly contemporary site of Chan Chan show a similar pattern of metalworking near the houses but not within the formal living area. His extensive excavations in habitation areas demonstrate that materials and tools were stored in apartments and that metalworkers were concentrated in distinct neighborhoods. This may have been the case at Cerro Huaringa, where each small workshop seems to have a set of three or four linked furnaces and a set of rocker mills. These grinding implements consisted of a large flat stone slab (the *batán*) and a curved stone (the *chunga*), which was rocked back and forth across the surface of the batán, crushing its contents. These implements were used in ancient Peru for grinding grain, but here they were an essential part of the metalworking. The furnaces were preheated, charged with a mixture of lumps of charcoal, hematite and limonite, and copper ores, and then fanned by lung power. Broken tuyeres (the ceramic mouthpieces used on bamboo blow tubes) are common finds around

---

the smelters. Two or three workers with blow tubes had to force air into the furnaces to reach the temperatures necessary to fuse the contents. The end result was a block of thick slag containing copper-arsenic bronze in the form of small droplets of metal known as prills. Once the furnace had cooled, the slag was taken to the nearby rocker mills to be crushed, and the tiny prills were removed by hand. Shimada suggests that the smelters were worked by family groups. Men and adolescents would have supplied the lung power for smelting, while other members of the family could break up the ore for charging the furnace and later extract the prills, a job that requires patience but no physical strength or stamina and could easily have been done by the young and the elderly working together. That groups spent considerable time in the workshop is shown by remains of food, presumably brought to the people involved in the grueling task of smelting.

Sulfide smelting at Cerro Huaringa produced noxious fumes, explaining why the workshops were somewhat separate from living quarters. However, it is evident that entire families were involved in metal production.

When the Chimu extended political control over Batán Grande, the family-organized production of arsenical copper persisted. However, under the subsequent Inca administration, smelting was separated from the slag crushing and prill removing operations. This organization might reflect the way corvée labor was organized in the Inca state. People paying their labor tax were assigned to work a particular task, so the family organization of metallurgy was replaced by a series of discrete tasks that could be assigned to unspecialized laborers, perhaps recruited as part of the labor tax.

Although little research has been directed at discovering the division of labor within ancient Andean societies, ethnographic evidence from contemporary potters and other pyrotechnological crafts suggests that Andean kin groups commonly had craft specializations. In family-oriented workshops, skilled adult women and men labor together, and the most experienced elders do critical tasks such as firing. Children help with simple jobs, do housework, and care for younger siblings. It is tempting to project this kind of an arrangement back to Cerro Huaringa. In this scenario, young wives might crush slag and extract prills, but household tasks and child care might occupy most of their time until their children were old enough to help with domestic chores. Then, as today, the adult woman might decide to allocate more time to craft production. Working together with other family members may have been pleasurable and social, and it certainly would have involved teaching the younger people the intricacies of the family business.

One of the persistent questions in gender studies is what happens to women, men, and their labor as societies grow more complex, differentiated, specialized, and hierarchical. In the Sicán period, people far removed from the producers made decisions concerning household quarters and the disposition of much of the familial production. We see from Batán Grande that the family-organized metallurgical workshops were ultimately dismantled by the Inca state, which assigned tasks according to its own needs. Textile manufacture is another area in which we have evidence of several distinct types of labor.

## Mississippian Weaving in Eastern North America

Prehistoric textile production, which used a variety of wild and domestic plant and animal fibers, was important over much of tropical and temperate America. In many regions weaving was women's work performed in domestic contexts to satisfy the needs of the household, although under many circumstances male participation in textile production was desirable and necessary. In the Mississippian culture region, spinning yarn and producing textiles were female activities at the time the Spanish arrived. At prehistoric sites like Wycliffe in Kentucky, a great deal of time and skill was invested in fabricating textiles. The fabrics themselves are poorly preserved, but textile imprints have been identified in ancient pottery. Penelope Drooker hypothesizes that women in every household made textiles on a regular basis. Her investigations demonstrate that the majority of the textiles could have been produced by part-time artisans. However, a few twined tapestries, found in association with elite burials at ceremonial centers such as Spiro and Etowah, exhibit a variety of decorative techniques that would have required extraordinarily skilled weavers. Because there is no archaeological evidence of full-time craft specialists working in segregated spaces, it is likely that wives of chiefs produced textiles for the use of their households, as was the case in the sixteenth century. In this way women's labor supported the important political and ceremonial activity of the elite group. A woman's skill was probably part of her individual identity and an element in her prestige within the community. Some textiles functioned as clothing, but Drooker speculates that some may have served as goods for interregional exchange, an activity that created political ties among communities. The sixteenth-century chiefs stored quantities of textiles, feathers, and other valuables for elite exchange.

Some archaeological sites studied by Drooker have yielded more decorated textiles than others, but the significance of textiles in political, economic, and religious contexts is evident in all and indicative of the importance of women's productive activities in the Southeast. In many societies owning textiles demonstrates that a person or family controls both resources (fiber) and skilled labor. Moreover, the complex iconography of decorated textiles can express the family or clan identity, or the ethnic affiliation of the textile's owner. Fabrics were commonly used by elites in honoring their ancestors, they honored chiefs, and were buried with the dead. Textiles were manipulated by chiefs and warriors in connection with a falcon cult and by commoners in rituals associated with fertility. Many of the Wycliffe textiles show representations of weapons, animals and mythic beings, female and male figures, and symbols related to the community and its territory. By making textiles, individual women (and perhaps men) participated in creating social discourse, such as expressing religious ideas or reinforcing gender roles in ritual. Mississippian textiles are proof of how part-time household labor can produce extraordinary items, and it is widely recognized that some of the most beautiful products of ancient industry were made before the onset of political and economic centralization. In early Mississippian times, the production of highly prized fabrics was not subject to the centralized control of highly ranked persons, nor was access restricted to elites. Later in Mississippian history, households lost their autonomy as hierarchy developed and as high-ranking people took control of community production. Under these conditions some of the products of household labor were transferred into the hands of Mississippian elites at chiefly centers. This may have affected the quality of textiles, because the weavers of the subordinate groups lost the ability to consume the fruits of their own labor. Some craft goods were produced by artisans, including slaves, attached to elite households or temples. This facilitated the production of items for exchange and increased the quantity of artifacts that marked elite status. As more complex systems evolved, more kinds of female producers, including enslaved ones, appeared in society.

# Aztec Tribute

Household production often remained the norm even in state societies, although states create new ways to organize production. For example, there were different modes of paying tribute in the Aztec and Inca empires, and women produced goods for the state in various ways.

Spinning and weaving are key elements of the gender identity of women in many cultures. For example, on an important imperial Aztec *cuahxicalli*, a giant stone vessel designed to contain sacrificed human hearts, the artist carved into the stone a depiction of the first Moctezuma's defeat of the queen of Colhuacán. She is portrayed naked to the waist so there will be no mistaking her sex, and with a weaving sword in one hand and a handful of darts in the other, signifying that she was both a female and a leader. All women, from the most exalted to the poorest, spun and wove. Originally, women wove only for their families, but with the development of chiefdoms or small kingdoms, the local ruler exacted tribute in cloth from each household, a tax upon women. When the Aztecs of Tenochtitlán began to extend hegemony over smaller states, they too demanded tribute, which men paid by serving as warriors and as laborers in the temples and palaces, and by rendering goods they manufactured. Most women paid their tax in cloth, some of which had to be woven from agave (century plant) or other fibers produced by the farming families themselves. Some women fabricated cloth for exchange in the markets. Everyone needed the thin, crisp agave cloth because commoners were forbidden by law to wear anything but this cloth. Local rulers who acquired cotton from the warmer regions of Mexico often issued this fiber to women who spun it to satisfy their tribute obligation. Elizabeth Brumfiel argues that as the political situation grew more complex, with more layers of tribute exaction, women's tribute grew more and more burdensome, leading to changes in family structure. Polygyny became more common among the Aztec because a household with two wives could produce more cloth. Polygyny may or may not have affected women's status, although it is known to have led to an increase in disharmonious relations within the family compound. Female slavery also increased considerably. Chiefly households had always had polygyny and slaves, but with the increase in tribute demanded, even relatively humble households looked for ways to increase their labor pool.

Aztec rulers were continually at war, both to obtain sacrificial victims to feed their hungry gods and to grab land, tribute, and slaves. The women and children enslaved by the Aztecs were captured in war. City-states that would not bow down to the Aztec demand for tribute were subdued and then required to render tribute in the form of young women and men. Women slaves were put to work doing domestic chores, but, above all, they were used for spinning and weaving, freeing the wives of the household for the myriad other tasks that were woman's daily responsibility. Younger women slaves were also concubines who bore new workers. In time the exaction of tribute in cloth became so great (especially in the early Colonial period, when Spanish officials simply extended the tribute obligations of the dead onto the few survivors) that spinning, perhaps the single most female-gendered task in ancient Mexico, was also undertaken by men. In the household context, behind the walls, men would sit and spin with their relatives. Even intensive cloth production continued to be lodged in the domestic context until the Spanish introduced textile mills in which male, not female, people were forced to labor.

In an admirable archaeological study of women's production in Aztec Mexico, Elizabeth Brumfiel uses the distribution of artifacts in sites in and near the Aztec capital to illustrate how women in different geographic areas devised divergent strategies to cope with changing sociopolitical conditions in the Late Postclassic period. Brumfiel studied the changing frequency of large and small spindle whorls and showed how female productive activity, resulting in the textiles that were crucial to the functioning of the Aztec state, increased dramatically in some communities but not in others. By combining this analysis of spindle whorls with the study of artifacts used in special food processing, she generated a hypothesis that the women of the Valley of Mexico who had access to water transportation specialized in the production of food for exchange in urban markets, while women more distant from the markets produced tribute cloth for imperial authorities. Furthermore, Brumfiel's analysis of the occurrence of the remains of cooking pots and griddles resulted in the interpretation that women in the Aztec period altered their food-preparation customs in response to the demands upon their labor and to support other family members who needed portable food because increasingly under Aztec domination, they were required to work away from home. Despite the stereotype of unchanging female domestic activity, Brumfiel concludes that Aztec women adapted variably (depending upon local conditions) to changes in state political economy.

## Political Change in Peru

Christine Hastorf's study of the Inca conquest of the Wanka people in late prehispanic highland Peru describes a change in social relations that affected women's productive activities. In the Andes many social inter-actions involve the ritual consumption of food and corn beer, and the relationships between men and women are expressed in all aspects of food production, preparation, serving, and consumption.

The archaeological evidence analyzed by Hastorf shows that in the Wanka 2 period (A.D. 1300–1460) when the household was an autonomous socio-economic unit in a loosely knit polity, potatoes were the staple crop. Maize was uncommon and was processed in the patio, where women may have worked communally. Skeletal analysis shows that men and women con-sumed corn in similar percentages to other items, such as potatoes, in their diets in this period, suggesting to Hastorf their equal participation in ritual, community, and political events. This may reflect the Andean pattern of complementarity at the household level and in the cosmology, and the fact that both women and men owned resources and produced food. Traditional patterns of bilateral inheritance in the Andes often gave autonomy to women within their households because both males and females had access to the resources of the social group of their parents.

In contrast, during the Wanka 3 period (A.D. 1460–1532), after the Incas had imposed their government, potatoes disappeared, and maize was processed in increased quantities, reflecting Inca state interests. There was more restricted crop deposition in Wanka 3 patios, which led Hastorf to think that, compared to the Wanka 2 period, there was increased state control over household activity, meaning more constraints on individuals, including women. Wanka families in general, and women in particular, lost social status, and there was an increased circumscription of female activities in the Inca phase. Hastorf says that the quantity of maize and its distribution suggests intensification of female processing labor, representing an escalation of women's labor to support social-political activities, which were predominantly male concerns. In support of this, skeletons from the Wanka 3 period showed that both men and women were consuming more maize, but that half of the males were ingesting both meat and maize in greater quantities than the women. This may be due to the government's creation of work parties in which male labor was conscripted and rewarded with food and drink. This suggests a reduced social position for women: they did not participate in the important state rituals outside the house nor partake of the prestigious and symbolic corn beer. This reflects the Inca state's reconstruction of gender and its effects on production and social life.

## The Chosen Women of the Inca

The Inca government had an immense and ever-growing need for cloth and people to serve the state. To satisfy these needs, Inca administrators instituted a system wherein women labored for the state. This institution-alization of female labor avoided the interruption of women's production by childbearing and child rearing. In some societies delayed marriage, artificial birth control, and long birth intervals are used to minimize the impact of reproduction on women's productivity, but one solution adopted by the Inca state was to remove some women from participating in marriage and motherhood, a solution that has appeared at various times in history. European nunneries once served as repositories for chaste women who produced prayers, cloth, baked goods, and craft items for the male-dominated church and, in some cases, gave an opportunity to a gifted woman who wished to seek a literary or political career.

The Inca of Peru (A.D. 1438–1532) had a similar institution, the *acllahuasi*, or House of the Chosen Women. The chronicler Bernabé Cobo tells us that each major town and provincial capital had one of these houses, staffed with a number of women who remained chaste and who served the state and its religion (fig. 6.2). Every year a government official would inspect all the ten-year-old girls in each village in his charge, selecting those who were outstandingly pretty. These Chosen Women were then educated in special, guarded precincts in the provincial capital. The most handsome girls were set aside for sacrifice, assured of a life of leisure in the other world. Others learned spinning, weaving, cooking, brewing, and religious observances for about four years and then were classified again. Some were reserved to become concubines of the ruler or given as wives to men the ruler wished to honor. The ones chosen to

WOMEN IN ANCIENT AMERICA

FIGURE 6.2. ■ A sixteenth-century drawing by Guaman Poma memorializes
the *acllas*, or Maidens of the Sun, who spin under the watchful eye of the head
*mamakona*. Spinning and brewing for the Inca state were among the important
economic duties of the *acllas*.

be *mamacona* spent their lives in the *acllahuasi*, preparing the textiles, beer, and foods required for celebrations and tending the shrines.

Apparently, Chosen Women came from various strata of society, noble as well as common. It seems that the daughters of the nobility occupied more exalted positions, perhaps administrative ones, within the *acllahuasi*. In each of these houses, a woman from an exalted lineage served as the head *aclla* and as the wife of the sun deity or the *huaca* (shrine) that she served. In the main temple in Cuzco, the head *mamacona* was a sister of the ruling Inca. The headwoman, like a medieval abbess, administered the *acllahuasi* and its work, both religious and secular.

The *acllas* and the *mamaconas* were full-time professional workers, passing their lives in the confines of the *acllahuasi* and working for the state, which expended immense quantities of cloth and beer to pay administrators, facilitate ceremonies and work parties, and support the army. Women in the Cuzco *acllahuasi* wove clothing for the Sapa Inca and his family and created headdresses for the royal family and the nobility. The women also served the deity of their place with offerings of food, clothing, beer, and other objects. The Spanish chroniclers do not agree whether the *aclla* were confined perpetually to their convents or whether they sometimes left the *acllahuasi* to participate in public rituals. Draconian sanctions faced any *mamacona* who violated the no-sex rule or who became pregnant: both the woman and her lover would be buried alive.

The rewards for the Chosen Women were not insignificant in terms of their culture. In this rigidly class-structured society, the *acllahuasi* could be a means of social advancement for a pretty and intelligent girl. She might well find herself married to a man of higher class and more means than would have been available in her home village. She herself achieved higher status through education, and she was assured of respectful treatment in her new home if she was bestowed by the ruler upon a husband. The women who remained *mamaconas* were rewarded for their labor with high positions in Inca society, which in some cases compensated their families for the loss of the labor and reproductivity of their daughters.

Although we know of the Inca case from history, it is very likely that this institution had a far earlier origin. Earlier cultures in the Andes probably developed institutions that permanently added full-time female workers to the labor force.

## Gender and Work

Because of the necessary commitment of female time and energy to reproduction, woman's production for extra-domestic needs during her most active, young adult years is often interrupted and limited. Families and states frequently, today as in the past, have found it necessary to move men into what is normally defined as women's work. Men are weavers in many places. The Inca had male weaving overseers, presumably master weavers themselves, who supervised tribute weaving and may well have overseen workshops where ordinary women, not Chosen Women, paid their tribute.

Women throughout the Inca empire wove for the government. Like Aztec women, they were usually issued the fiber and expected to weave a given amount in a given style. However, recent finds at the site of Tarmatambo indicate that women may have been gathered together, much as their husbands were, to perform state service. One building at Tarmatambo has many more doors and wide widows than is normal, a design meant to let a great deal of light into the interior. Also built into the walls are stone rings at various heights, apparently corresponding to the size of looms used to produce specific fabrics. Experiments have suggested that wear marks on those rings resulted from their ancient use to affix looms, supporting the hypothesis that this was a weaving workshop. The lack of good interior lighting indicates that these women were weaving very plain cloth, probably the set-size pieces demanded by the Inca bureaucracy. The ancient women who paid taxes by weaving for the state probably received beer and meals, as did their husbands who worked on the roads and constructed government buildings.

It is not surprising that the Inca used males as supervisors in textile weaving, even though in much of the empire women alone wove. It has been documented that when domestic crafts are transformed into state-run industries, work and its supervision often pass into the hands of males, whose daily schedules are not interrupted with family care.

An illustration of this process is the history of the manufacture of ceramic figurines at Teotihuacán, where excavations have uncovered numbers of ceramic figurine workshops. Warren Barbour's analysis of figurines has resulted in a description of the evolution of their manufacture. The handmade figurines produced in the early Teotihuacán phases are overwhelmingly female (fig. 6.3). These figurines, judging by the small fingerprints

FIGURE 6.3. ■ A handmade ceramic figurine from Teotihuacán, representing a woman of high status, whose pose is associated with the performance of rituals in Mesoamerican art. These Early Classic figurines normally represent females and may have been made by women artisans.

left by their makers and fired into the clay bodies, were modeled by women. In contrast, during the later phases of occupation at Teotihuacán, mold-made figurine types proliferated, and the percentage of male figurines skyrocketed. The majority of late Teotihuacán mass-produced figurines are male. The fingerprints on the insides of these molded figures indicate that manufacture had become a male activity. Thus, at Teotihuacán production was intensified and diversified as the manufacture of figurines moved out of the hands of women and into the hands of men, who were presumably less encumbered with domestic tasks.

It is commonly argued that in the past, as in the present, a woman's household responsibilities may prevent her from entering into intensive training, engaging in full-time skilled production, or undertaking technological challenges requiring commitments of extraordinary amounts of time and labor. How women's responsibilities are defined varies, of course, from culture to culture. Some women in the past, and today, through luck or because of their special motivation, did, and do, undertake skilled production and other specialized economic activities because of a personal preference, because they have fewer children than other women, or because they live longer and find the time to pursue extraordinary goals. A woman finds it easier to cultivate her skills and talents when her society values her endeavors; when she has the support of her household, including junior wives, daughters, and/or servants; or when she can remove herself from the domestic sphere entirely.

## Female Professionals

Domestic industry is one solution to the problem of organizing production and reproduction. However, under some conditions this mode of production is not sufficient for the needs of the community or polity, at which time specializations may emerge. In the socially complex states of late prehistoric America, both men and women entered professional life. Professions are defined as positions for which the person is highly trained in technical matters not known to the general public. The material culture of the prehistoric past is strong evidence of the existence of highly trained specialists, including astronomers, architects, metallurgists, and painters. It is usually assumed, on androcentric grounds, that these specialists were male. New insights coming from Conquest-period historical sources and, especially, the writings of the ancient Maya and the now-decoded pictorial manuscripts of the Mixtec all beg for the revision of earlier interpretations concerning the gender of specialists.

The European historic literature fails to clearly identify women as professionals in America, but numbers of illustrated Colonial documents demonstrate that women occupied a variety of specialized roles among the late prehistoric Aztec. Apart from purely religious occupations, there were women merchants, members of the endogamous caste of long-distance traders. These ladies organized and administered expeditions and took the profit from them, although it is not known whether they physically accompanied their caravans to distant destinations.

Vending in the market was another common female role among the Aztecs. Father Sahagún's famous book shows women selling foodstuffs, cloth, and other things produced by women for market. Women were so important in the marketplace that there were special female administrators to oversee their dealings and resolve disputes that might arise.

There were courtesans and prostitutes both in Mexico and the Andes. Inca sex workers, according to Inca Garcilaso de la Vega, were forced to live apart from other people and have no social contact with nonprostitutes. They lived in houses under the aegis of a supervisor who was appointed and paid by the government. In the Conquest period in Mexico, there were both female and male prostitutes in the major cities. Harlots wore colorful clothing and painted their faces. Although the Aztec were as family-centered and sexually prudish as the Inca, prostitutes do not seem to have been outcasts in Aztec society.

Modern understanding of prehistoric prostitution is frustrated by the historical sources written by gynophobic clerics. Margaret Arvey has demonstrated how the *Florentine Codex*, perhaps the major document concerning the Aztecs, owes its depictions of prostitutes to pejorative European art and law. It is evident that some Aztec courtesans served young noble warriors and danced with them in various celebrations and rituals, which supports the idea that those professional ladies enjoyed a certain degree of status in their own society (fig. 6.4). Only Europeans assigned negative valuation to face paint, colored clothing, and bathing. When the Europeans disparaged prostitutes for these characteristics, they effectively tarred all native women, since these attributes of costume and hygiene were shared by prostitute and nonprostitute alike.

### Curers and Midwives

The Aztec and the Inca had women curers of various types, including trained midwives whose duties were both medical and religious. The

FIGURE 6.4. ■ An Aztec *auiani* (courtesan), as depicted by Bernardino de Sahagún. The Spaniards did not understand the role of these specialists, who were highly regarded and respected in Aztec society and served as companions to the young warriors.

Spanish remarked continually on the skill of Aztec midwives, although the Spanish religious establishment tried to suppress native medical practitioners because medicine and curing were intimately entwined with indigenous religious activities. Native curing involved, today as in the past, medicines or mechanical manipulations along with incantations, prayers, or ritual acts. Women curers were prominent in the Conquest period, if Colonial documents are to be believed, but their role was reduced gradually by Christian pressure, which defined traditional medicinal systems as witchcraft. However, traditional curing systems survive in many areas and are used alongside modern Western medicine.

The best documentation on precolumbian healing systems comes from the Aztec. Bernard Ortiz de Montellano details Aztec medical practices and notes that in many areas, such as treatment of injuries and broken bones, and especially in dealing with pregnancy and child birth, the Aztec were considerably more advanced than their conquerors. Aztec midwives as well as other medical personnel were highly trained professionals. Virtually all our knowledge concerning birthing practices and attitudes relating to birth control and abortion in ancient America comes from art or from cultural behavior noted during the historic period. Regrettably, many accounts, such as that of Bernardino Sahagún, were recorded by Spanish religious men who recorded the details of native culture described by upper-class Aztec men. Thus, much of women's knowledge has been lost. Similarly, knowledge of contraception and abortion, which was part of women's concern in premodern Europe, all but disappeared, according to John Riddle, after centuries of religious repression and witch-hunting and as medical knowledge and practice became male preserves. In Peru women who practiced medicine were denounced as witches or apostates and forced to abandon their practices on threat of terrible punishments.

Aztec medicine was (and is) known to utilize various herbal remedies to bring on menstruation or speed up labor. One contemporary remedy that has been investigated in modern clinical settings is *cihuatpatli* (*zoapatle*), "woman's medicine" (*Montanoa tormentosa*). An extract made from the leaves of this plant taken as a single oral dose can be used in the early stages of pregnancy to bring on strong uterine contractions and cervical dilation. No side effects were noted in volunteers. Another remedy used both to bring on menstruation and hasten labor is concocted from the tail of an opossum. A single laboratory study shows that a dose of opossum tail, fresh or dried, brought on contractions in rodent uterine tissue.

Among the Aztecs prenatal care began in the seventh month of pregnancy, when midwives began to visit the expectant mother. At this time the midwife palpated the fetus to check its size and position, and the mother and midwife ritually purified themselves in a sweat bath. When the mother went into labor, the midwife helped her wash in the sweat bath and massaged her, performing an external version if the infant was in breech position. If labor lasted too long, the midwife used one of several oxytocic remedies. The cleanliness considered essential for successful childbirth and the skill of the midwives in dealing with poorly positioned infants, long labor, and bleeding meant that most Aztec women were better off and safer in childbirth than their descendants.

Nevertheless, the Aztecs likened childbirth to the battlefield, and the midwife would make set speeches about delivering the infant successfully, or metaphorically taking a prisoner, which was the goal of Aztec war. Women were, in fact, given a toy shield and spears to hold while in labor, and at the moment of birth the midwife uttered a war cry. Women who died in childbirth were, in official doctrine, welcomed to the same paradise as warriors killed in battle.

Depictions of childbirth in many art styles survive from prehispanic times. Mimbres painted bowls show numerous scenes of birth, and in some the midwife is represented as well (fig. 6.5). The Mixtec codices show infants attached by umbilical cords to their nude mothers, and several Moche vessels from Peru show women seated on a stool or, perhaps, on the knees of the person who crouches and holds them from behind. In these vessels the delivery is being overseen by a female curer, often shown in supernatural guise as an owl-woman. Owls remain important supernatural helpers in modern folk religion in northern Peru. A variety of sexual practices shown in ancient Moche pots would not have resulted in conception. These vessels probably illustrate specific myths or folktales, or they may be evidence of ritual sex. It is not known if these practices were widespread, but if they were, anal intercourse, fellatio, and masturbation might have constituted contraceptive strategies. Riddle, in his study of Classical and European contraception and abortion, somewhat disingenuously claims that neither coitus interruptus nor anal intercourse were widespread among the Europeans. In contrast, Europeans noted the prevalence of certain of these practices at the time of the Conquest in Peru. One credible method of birth control is abstinence. This form of constraint upon sexual activity certainly was more effective in the past, particularly in kin-based societies, where goals and ideologies were shared by everyone. Among the Cheyenne of the northern Plains, the belief that the spiritual power of the parents was diminished by sexual activity and that this power was needed to successfully grow a child resulted in periods of abstinence lasting over a decade. Taboos on parental intercourse while a mother is lactating are widespread, and religious fasting involving abstinence from specific foodstuffs and sexual intercourse is also common. Today among the highland Maya of Mexico and

FIGURE 6.5. ■ This image of a woman giving birth and a midwife is taken from a Mimbres bowl. The vessel was ceremonially "killed" in the stippled area (see also fig. 1.1).

Guatemala, a shaman is not considered good husband material because his position demands so much purificatory abstinence.

Ethnographic evidence from South America suggests that most abortion was mechanical and dangerous, a last resort when pregnancy would bring severe penalties upon the woman. Inca midwives were said to be able to produce abortion, and modern Kallawaya herbalists have several methods for terminating a pregnancy, of which the best known is a dose of *chilca* (*Baccharis pentlandii*, a shrub of the high, cold altitudes). This herb, mentioned by early Spanish chroniclers, is also applied externally to treat inflammations, rheumatism, and bone and muscle injuries. Infanticide was, and is, a more common way of dealing with an unwanted or deformed child. Like abortion, infanticide rarely is identifiable in the archaeological record.

It is certain that herbal remedies for preventing conception and causing abortion were utilized by ancient Americans. The few remedies that have been tested clinically have poor efficacy in preventing pregnancy when judged by modern standards, but these remedies may have functioned to prevent or terminate some percentage of unwanted pregnancies in a population of women who were malnourished, carried a large parasite load, and engaged in heavy physical labor. Ancient professional herbalists and midwives had fewer weapons in their arsenals than do modern medical practitioners, but their knowledge of the medicinal properties of plants and animals was profound, and they were able to assist some women in making reproductive choices.

## Scribes in Mesoamerica

The ancient peoples of Mesoamerica devised elaborate graphic notation systems to record genealogical, historic, and economic data. The Maya developed the only true writing system ever used in prehistoric America, a visible means of reproducing exact utterances, including grammatical and phonetic elements. In contrast, the other Mesoamerican systems utilized stylized pictures plus a few more abstract notations signifying numbers, units of time, place names, movement in a given direction, warfare, and marriage—all designed to accompany memorized texts. Until recently, scholarly opinion held that literacy was not widespread in the prehistoric period and that women did not know how to read, write, or memorize these Mesoamerican texts, but this view was biased by the medieval European experience and overlooked the fact that in the classic Mediterranean world, literacy was the norm, not the exception. The analysis of hieroglyphic writing on stone monuments found in Maya archaeological sites often demonstrates that those located in more public places have more picture signs, while the monuments found in more private contexts have more syllabic signs. This might indicate widespread literacy, although more sophisticated reading and writing fell in the province of elites, as was the case in ancient (and modern) China.

Were Maya women literate? If elite Maya ladies were like those of the Mixtec royal caste, they were involved in matchmaking and power politics, and therefore they would have had as much need to consult genealogical, historic, and tribute rolls as gentlemen. The same is true of the Aztec market directors. In fact, the relatively swift transition made by nonelite Aztec people after the Conquest to writing Nahuatl and Spanish in the

Roman alphabet argues for widespread literacy among quite ordinary people, including women.

Scribes were one of the classes of prominent professionals in ancient Mesoamerica. Bookmaking must have been labor-intensive, requiring esoteric knowledge and a command of writing and graphic notation, draftsmanship, and painting. Recent studies of crafts in the central Mexican cultures and the southerly Maya ones indicate that artists and other craftspeople were recruited from among members of royal and noble lineages. Among the Maya there has been increasing evidence from studies of architecture, carving, and mural painting that high-ranking artists signed their work (through signature glyphs or a portrait or both). Some of these artists were women (fig. 6.6). Women's participation in many aspects of elite culture is now well established, and, despite scholarly androcentrism, it is now recognized that numbers of Maya figurines show women as well as men associated with codices (books). Many years ago Persis Clarkson illustrated a female scribe from a looted vessel, but at that time scholars argued that the individual had to be male, despite the female dress of the figure (fig. 6.6a). Recently, Michael Closs's translation of a Maya glyph band on a looted bowl established with certainty that women could be scribes. The inscription from the bowl first names a male as a *kahal* (a government official, probably of high rank). The second phrase names the *kahal*'s mother, "Noble Lady Scribe-Sky, Lady Jaguar Lord, the Scribe." Next, his father, also a scribe, is named. The mother has noble titles, whereas the father is not recorded as having any. The text then details the titles of the son, who evidently occupied an important political office. This inscription is unequivocal proof of a female scribe and further evidence that some noblewomen were trained as scribes, much as their male relatives were. Whether there were differentiated employment opportunities for female and male scribes is not known. Women did have inscribed possessions, including monuments and portable objects, so an equal literacy with men is plausible. It has been suggested that another Maya noblewoman was a scribe, artist/architect, and astronomer. This was Lady Xoc, one of the most prominent figures in the history of the site of Yaxchilán in southern Mexico (see fig. 1.3). Lady Xoc was apparently a sister or half-sister of Shield Jaguar I. Some have suggested that she was the wife of Bird Jaguar, although she was not the mother of his successor, Bird Jaguar IV, nor did she succeed to the throne, as seems to have been the case with Bird Jaguar's mother, Lady Ik Skull.

Although Lady Xoc's precise position in the royal hierarchy is unknown, it was evidently a high one because she appears on monuments with the ruler and then on monuments of his successor, and she is associated with blood-letting events and astronomical rituals. Her career spanned the reigns of both rulers, and she may have created a special role for a powerful woman within the government because, upon her death, Bird Jaguar appointed two younger women, Ladies Ahpo Ix and Ik, to high positions, and their ritual activity was commemorated in sculpture. Carolyn Tate has suggested that Lady Xoc was the artist who drew the text and figures on the famous Lintel 25 because the inscription contains a glyph implying authorship, followed by her name. Extrapolating from this, and from her general prominence in the relief sculpture monuments of her time (and after her time), Tate also suggests that Lady Xoc helped plan and execute Shield Jaguar's monuments. Were she not a female, in fact, archaeologists and epigraphers probably would look seriously at Lady Xoc as a likely prime minister within the governments of her close male kin.

The other direct evidence of female scribes in ancient Mesoamerica concerns an Aztec lady who was scribe for the emperor, Tlatoani Huitzili-huitl (fig. 6.6b). Identified with the Spanish gloss "La Pintora" (the painter) on an early Colonial illustrated document, this lady also bore her employer a child. The evidence suggests that elite daughters, like sons, were trained for special positions requiring skill. The system of parallel structures of administration and professions in Aztec culture makes the existence of female as well as male scribes probable. There were, after all, female medical practitioners, priests, and administrators, most of whom would have been, in the standard Aztec manner, recruited from the nobility. Ladies would have needed scribes to act as secretaries and bookkeepers, as did their male counterparts. The schools attended by the children of the nobility may have trained women in writing, learning the long narratives that recorded the history of individual polities, and keeping track of incoming tribute. It is now well established that at least some high-ranking women among the Aztecs were literate and that some functioned as scribes in elite contexts.

## Production and Reproduction

The family is a dynamic economic unit because within it a few individual women and men may decide at any time to reallocate labor and materials,

**b**

FIGURES 6.6a and 6.6b. ■ Female scribes from ancient Mesoamerica. The Maya lady (a), depicted on a painted vase, is identified in the glyphic text. The Aztec scribe (b), from an early colonial document, is glossed in Spanish as "The Painter." Both were upper-class women who painted books and did other writing tasks at royal or noble courts.

economize, or raise production by scheduling their time and increasing their labor investment. The behavior of these productive individuals is the basis of historical change. In each sociocultural system, activities are arranged in a distinctive fashion, and one of the dimensions of variation is gender. Janet Spector has shown that among the historic Hidatsa, women and men performed different and unrelated tasks in different geographical spaces and produced contrasting sets of remains of the sort that we can expect to find in the archaeological record.

Women's roles in production and in professional activity are inseparable from their efforts in reproduction. Humans, like other mammals, depend chiefly on the efforts of females for the reproduction of the species, and human societies are designed to accommodate this role, usually assigning women tasks compatible with nurturing offspring. Nevertheless, it is universal among societies that women also contribute to economic systems. Their contributions are so variable as to defy description. History and ethnography demonstrate this variability, but archaeology is hampered by the problem of attribution: the identification of the sex of the ancient performers of productive activities continues to challenge archaeologists.

Archaeologists cannot afford to ignore gender as they reconstruct ancient production because any study of historic and contemporary societies demonstrates that both sexes play key roles in any system of production, and that female-male relations are one of the crucial dynamics in the evolution of systems of production. Studies of economic change on the micro-social level demonstrate that it is initially individuals, and not whole households, who create and respond to economic opportunities. Because factors and forces affect wives and husbands differently, they will innovate distinct strategies. Economic and political changes may create opportunities that allow individual women and men to negotiate their roles in production and their control over the distribution of valued products. This may involve changes in the kind of residential group, task assignments, and gender ideology. Gender relations have always been a dynamic aspect of change in production, distribution and consumption—the constituent elements of economic systems. This has been seen dramatically in the twentieth century. During World War II, women were forced to take men's places in the workplace, and this experience, plus economic expansion after that war, opened the door for the greater participation of women in production outside the home, soon leading to their increased roles as consumers, and now to their acquisition of political power.

Historically, much of women's domestic production has been designed to satisfy the basic needs of the family, but some of the fruits of their labor helped to pay tribute, that is, to satisfy the escalating needs of elites and of the state. Women's work produced valuable goods used to create social networks, which supported the long-term well-being of their families. Women labored to provide valuable gifts used in negotiating marriage alliances, and women provided the material accouterments and food that allowed their families to succeed in competitive political and ceremonial activities. Everywhere, women's productive work involved training and knowledge, and some women organized in various ways to support their roles. Even if industry is domestic, women may be specialized, in the sense that they produce for export rather than domestic consumption. Some ancient women were professionals.

Production has a creative dimension that is very important for individual women and women in groups. Skilled women may produce ceremonial and ritual objects, as well as things labeled utilitarian that nevertheless carry social messages. Ceramic vessels or textiles may express pride, membership, or sociopolitical resistance, and this is part of the negotiation process by which some women sought to maximize their power and influence in families and communities.

# CHAPTER SEVEN

# Women and Religion

An examination of gender in ancient society must assess the concepts of female and male expressed in cosmology and attempt to understand the roles of women and men in ceremonial practice. In prehispanic America, religion permeated social behavior as people sought to communicate with the spiritual and supernatural realms. Women were prominent in the religious life of many communities. However, because of sociopolitical change and ultimately conquest and the adoption of Christian cultural patterns, many Native American women have been robbed of their traditional roles in religious ideology and ritual.

The roles taken by women in ancient religion, both in practice and in symbol, varied considerably through time and space. In many pre-Conquest societies, there were goddesses as well as gods, and both women and men served as curers, soothsayers, shamans, priests, sacrificers and sacrifices, divine ancestors, and innovators of and participants in domestic and community cults. Both women and men created ideologies and ritual practices that archeologists attempt to reconstruct with the help of ethnographic models.

## Shamans and Potters among the Canelos Quichua

The complexity and subtlety of gender relations and religious expression among contemporary South American peoples illustrate the problem of inferring past behavior. Many patterns are possible because the ritual roles of men and women are woven out of the raw materials of myths and tailored to serve ever-changing psychological and social functions.

For example, in the artistic and ceremonial life of the Canelos Quichua people of eastern Ecuador, as described by Dorothea and Norman Whitten, the apex of each segment of the social system is the shaman. He achieves his position through his knowledge of and experience in traditional and contemporary worlds. Each powerful shaman has a sister and/or a wife who is a master potter, and these knowledgeable men and women transmit the symbolism of tradition and modernity to their offspring. These men and women are as familiar with their counterparts' gender role as with their own, and each may serve as an interpreter for the other. A powerful image-making woman "clarifies" a shaman's visions while he is in seance, and a shaman himself, while chanting, may bring to consciousness symbolism deeply embedded in his wife's or sister's ceramic art. What binds these distinct yet merged male/female domains is an ancient, enduring cosmology.

Among the Canelos Quichua people, the female potters explore the actions of humans and spirits by using basic designs associated with the rain forest and the river. These designs represent life forces, living beings, and mythic spirit beings and spirit masters. Often, for a festival, the potters create vessels that represent ancient mythical and spiritual beings that remind everyone of their shared ancestral roots, extending through various layers of mythic time and space. Women making pottery link the past and present, the mysterious and the mundane. Canelos women paint their faces and adorn themselves to represent the mythic union of male and female figures, and men make music celebrating recently deceased family members, other ancestors, and ancient heroes.

Most Canelos Quichua adults are shamans or potters involved in complementary sacred and spiritual activities. Men transform part of the forest by clearing gardens, and women restore it by planting domesticated plants. The male shaman and the female potter both manipulate souls and spirits, imparting them to vessels or spirit objects. Women transfer their knowledge to the new generation through the medium of ceramic manufacture, while men do the same through shamanic performance.

Archaeologists cannot expect to reconstruct ancient religious systems in such fine detail, but the Canelos Quichua case reminds us that women and men in the past surely built complex religious systems with important roles for all adults. It seems likely that both men and women were important in ancient religious activity, both had sacred knowledge, and both had the ability to perform rituals. While some ethnographic cases show how men can dominate the public ritual life of their groups, others illustrate how women play central and even prominent roles in religious life.

## The Archaeology of Religion

Art, burial evidence, and ethnohistory all provide windows into ancient religious life. Although the painted, engraved, and sculpted representations of human beings may not be naturalistic portraits or narrations of the daily lives of people in prehistory, they do offer a direct view into ancient ideologies.

The images of women and men in ancient art were produced by the imaginations of their makers, who were intent upon expressing ideas through symbols recognizable to other members of their communities. It is likely that the ancient artists were trying to promote, recall, encourage, or emphasize ideas about manhood and womanhood, leadership, the mythical past, or some cosmic forces or relationships. Lacking the cultural gloss that could only be supplied by the ancient people themselves, researchers can only make a careful analysis of the art with the hope of discovering some details about society, ideology, and cosmology that bring us closer to understanding the experiences of ancient men and women.

Ancient figurines, which are frequently gender marked, reveal the importance of sex and gender in the worldview of ancient Americas, and the iconography is strong evidence of the gender ideologies of the past. This is supported by the fact that in the literature, poetry, myths, legends, and stories of Native Americans, female and male actors engage in gender-appropriate activity.

## Shamans

Among some Native American peoples, shamans are specialists charged with the maintenance of the well-being of the human community by controlling spiritual power. The shaman is a religious leader, female or male, who acts as an intermediary between human beings and the realm of the spirits, who is a repository of esoteric knowledge, and who may function as healer, diviner, adjudicator, agent of social control, or political leader. The practice of shamanism involves activities designed to communicate

FIGURE 7.1. ■ This West Mexican tomb figurine shows a male shaman calling up spirits while being protected from harm by a woman, a practice that continues among contemporary Huichol shamans.

directly with and control or influence spirits or the souls of animals, inanimate objects, and the dead, often by mastering ecstatic experiences, acquiring spirit helpers, and using songs.

In Late Preclassic ceramic sculptures from western Mexico, female personages carry out activities that Peter Furst has identified as shamanistic. They prepare hallucinogenic peyote buttons, hold cups containing the peyote infusion, sit in trances induced by the mescaline cactus, and hover behind male shamans, presumably protecting them from danger, as do Huichol Indian women today (fig. 7.1).

Today few Native American women are shamans, but in recent times some influential women, like María Sabina of the Alta Mixteca, who brought the sacred mushroom *teonanacatl* back to the notice of the Western world, have been recognized as shamans. Female shamans survive in South America among the Mapuche of Chile and in northern Peru, where Bonnie Glass-Coffin has documented the important role of female curers in modern culture. Although Catholicism has succeeded in transforming many women religious practitioners of all sorts into "witches," in northern Peru and Mexico alike there remains a strong tradition of women involved with supernatural curing, divination, and other non-Western religious roles. Women may well have been more prominent in shamanistic practices before the arrival of Europeans. Hans Staden remarks that among the sixteenth-century Tupinamba, virtually all women were initiated as shamans and actively sought visions to foretell the future and to cure.

## A Late Valdivia Shaman

An extraordinary Piquigua Phase (ca. 2000 B.C.) tomb found in the Jama Valley in Ecuador contained the skeleton of a woman buried in an unusual, extended position with a suite of offerings that James Zeidler and his colleagues have interpreted as evidence of a shamanic ritual (fig. 7.2). The excavators have used ethnographic analogy to reconstruct the shamanistic practice and ideology that created this pattern of remains.

The woman in the tomb died when she was between fifteen and twenty years of age. Some of the material correlates of shamanic rituals that were found in the tomb include a lime pot, associated with chewing coca leaves, still an important part of indigenous rituals; the skeleton of a bat, asso-

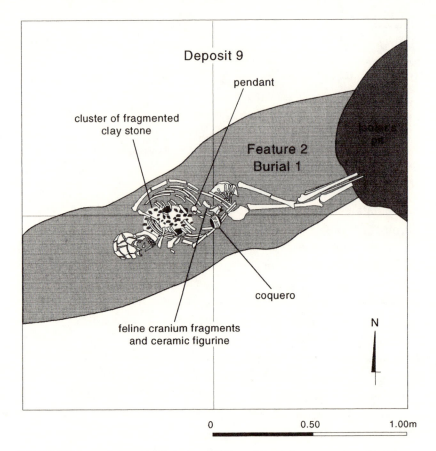

Deposit 9

pendant

cluster of fragmented
clay stone

Feature 2
Burial 1

coquero

feline cranium fragments
and ceramic figurine

N

0       0.50       1.00m

FIGURE 7.2. ■ A Late Valdivia (ca. 1500 B.C.) burial recovered in the Capa-
perro site on the central coast of Ecuador. The offerings associated suggest that
the deceased young woman was a shaman or that the burial was the focus of
shamanic rituals.

ciated with magical flight and sometimes with bloodletting; bones from
the snout of an ocelot, taken as evidence of a feline pelt cape of the sort
worn by shamans; a Valdivia-style female figurine found nestled in the
mouth of the ocelot; a polished stone pendant; over 250 unworked green
clay-stone fragments; and a milling stone, which capped the burial. This
archaeological context presents a coherent array of ancient shamanic
paraphernalia and leads to the interpretation that the Piquigua woman
was a young shaman or a shaman-in-training.

## Ancestors and Shrines

Death creates an opportunity, among people who believe in communication between the realms of the living and the dead, to transform the deceased individual into a serviceable ancestor—a supernatural intercessor or guardian. Tombs and mummy bundles in Andean culture often became shrines and the loci of ritual communication. Cieza de León remarked that in the early Colonial period, Indians took more care decorating tombs than houses because all over America, women, as well as men, were transformed into ancestors and worshipped by their descendants at death.

## Mississippian Ancestors

Large anthropomorphic sculptures and other high-status objects bearing the iconography of the Southeastern Ceremonial Complex are found near the summits of the great Mississippian earth monuments. Other figurines have been recovered from elite graves, and some were found in stone-slab tombs constructed for the figurines themselves. Between A.D. 1000 and 1500 there was growing complexity in the societies of the Southeast, each of which was dominated by an elite group that manipulated the Southeastern Cult iconography.

In one of the distinct centers of Mississippian development in Tennessee, only humans are depicted in the free-standing figurines made of stone, ceramic, and wood. While these figurines vary in style from region to region, they share standardized features and express a common meaning. Kevin Smith believes that each is a portrait of a unique individual. These icons also indicate an ideology that involved fixed roles for women and men. Male individuals were shown seated cross-legged (fig. 7.3b), but figurines showing females (identified by breasts and genitals) were always shown kneeling, with both legs folded under the body (fig. 7.3a). This male-female distinction was observed among the Indians by early visitors to the Southeast.

In the Mississippian tradition, male figures were characterized by head decorations, headdresses, helmets, or some sort of headgear, while females had little headgear and long hair hanging down their backs. In the Southeast, Indian men in historic times, especially individuals of rank, reportedly decorated their heads, especially on ceremonial occasions.

a

FIGURES 7.3a and 7.3b. ■ This pair of marble figurines, representing Mississippian ancestors or guardians, was recovered in a high-status context at Etowah, Georgia. Here, as in many New World traditions, differences in clothing, hairstyle, and sitting posture between the sexes are strongly marked.

Female figurines were characterized by packlike objects fixed to their backs. In the folklore of the historic tribes of the eastern United States, the Earth Mother carried a sacred bundle on her back containing ears of corn, representing the first seeds given to humankind.

Mississippian figurine art evokes the association of women with maize, as well as with human fertility, birth and nurturing of children, and another important social role: the modification of a child's skull. Just as scarification, tattooing, or circumcision can shape the ethnic identity of individuals in the modern world, so in ancient Mississippian society mothers literally shaped the status of their children by modifying the form of their heads.

The figurines seem to reinforce the distinct roles of men and women in reproduction. In Kevin Smith's discussion, the smaller figurines are interpreted as portraits of actual individuals who were being memorialized in local, household contexts, and the larger ones (over 30 centimeters high), which have a wider geographical distribution and were recovered at civic-ceremonial centers, are understood as paraphernalia for public agricultural rituals. These figurines occur as female-male pairs (fig. 7.3) and may represent ancestral mothers and fathers, evoked as guardians of sacred places and propitiated by elites for the welfare of the community. Historic chroniclers described guardian sculptures in native temples and sculptured memorials in the likeness of the dead, and they told how native kings manipulated female and male idols in sowing-season ceremonies.

The figurines suggest that in Mississippian ideology, gender roles were highly differentiated but that both females and males played significant parts in their cosmology. In the early historic period in southeastern society, women's and men's roles were so differentiated that, according to Smith, the two sexes were almost like different species.

Other evidence shows that women were under considerable stress in the complex societies of late prehistory in some parts of North America and that the public power in these societies rested in the hands of elite males. Nevertheless, the funerary figurines show a fundamental ideology of complementarity: the ancestral couple consisted of a male and a female, similar in size. While male posture associates them with power, the female accouterments associate women with responsibility for agricultural fertility and human increase. Religious art was designed to reinforce the identification of women with these important concerns.

## Goddesses and Priestesses

In South America the oldest pantheon of supernatural beings is known from stone sculptures and relief carvings in the Chavín style, created in Peru between 1200 and 200 B.C. This pantheon included female supernaturals who may still survive in the legends and folklore of today's Andean peoples. These early supernatural beings may occur in female-male pairs, some of which may be ancestral to the late prehistoric male-sun and female-moon deities. The iconic associations of the early female deities suggest their roles in several natural realms.

Later, female supernaturals were variously associated with the moon, earth and sea, sexuality, plants and animals, trophy heads, sacrifice, and blood. Other female nonordinary beings were associated with birds, and with fish and water creatures, one of whom may have been the ruler of the piscine realm, called by recent peoples the Mistress of Fishes. The ancient imagery of female supernaturals shows that these deities were not loving and nurturing mother goddesses, but active and often bloodthirsty characters. Chavín females prominently displayed the *vagina dentata* (fig. 7.4); other female personages wore and carried trophy heads (severed human heads strung for portability); and in historic-period descriptions, Mama Huaco, a founding mother of the Incas, waged bloody warfare. The female oracle of Apurimac was bathed in the blood of sacrifices.

Oracles were very important in ancient Andean religion. The Apurimac oracle was represented by a tree trunk with gold breasts. Dressed in the finest of women's clothing, with many golden *tupus* (decorative pins) hung with tiny silver and gold bells, and smeared with the blood of sacrifices, the oracle lived in an elaborately painted building, surrounded by smaller tree trunks similarly dressed, probably attendants. A woman named Asarpay, a sister of the Inca, spoke for the oracle and foretold the Conquest, instructing the Inca nobility to gather together and warning them to use up all their stores and goods, so that there would be nothing for the conquerors. Later, a Spaniard named Diego Nuñez Mercado, who was granted the land around Apurimac, kidnapped the oracle. Asarpay helped

FIGURE 7.4. ■ This image of the Staff Goddess of Chavín was painted on a cotton textile. Her sex is indicated by the guilloches forming her breasts and her fanged *vagina dentata*. She and her consort, the Staff God, were important deities of the later Early Horizon in Peru.

raise a tremendous ransom in gold and then threw herself into the river gorge to ensure that the idol would be returned. The political and social importance of the oracle and her priestess would be difficult to document using archaeological remains alone.

In other parts of America, anthropomorphic representations may refer to female supernaturals, but scholars cannot always distinguish goddesses and spirits from other personages in the iconography of another culture. Some images may represent deified ancestresses. Among the polytheistic Aztecs, an immense pantheon of goddesses was charged with a multitude of specific roles. They governed everything from childbirth and drunkenness to the confession of sins and the guarding of sweat baths.

Throughout the Americas, female deities are represented in prehistoric art, yet any approach that a priori identifies all female representations as goddesses is unwise. Goddess worship is the focus of new religious cults in modern times, but the reader is cautioned against projecting that faith onto prehistoric people without testing alternative hypotheses.

## The Great Goddess of Teotihuacán

While goddesses have not been prominent in standard interpretations of prehistoric America, our views are changing, and new scholarship suggests that a female supernatural was the focus of a state cult at Teotihuacán, the center of one of the earliest and most powerful polities of prehispanic Mexico. When people first began to study Teotihuacán art, they naively tried to pin Aztec deity names and functions onto the representations of supernaturals found in the ruins, which are at least 800 years older than the Aztecs. A relatively common figure in the mural paintings that decorated many of the apartment compounds and temple buildings of Teotihuacán is a male with prominent goggles around his eyes and a fanged mouth or mouth mask. On the basis of Aztec images, scholars identified these figures as Tlaloc, the Aztec rain god, or as priests or impersonators of the rain god, and then they began calling Teotihuacán the City of the Rain God.

Recently scholars have recognized feminine supernaturals in the art of Teotihuacán (fig. 7.5). Paintings of the goddess are found inside rooms and on porticoes in numbers of the residential compounds. Attempts have been made to connect this female representation with Aztec or southwestern culture heroines and deities, but she has no precise late prehistoric equivalent.

The first identification of these figures as female was based upon their clothing, especially the *quechquemitl*, a capelike blouse characteristic of central Mexican women's clothing throughout history. Once the equation between female clothing and female identity was made, other more variable characteristics associated with this important female were identified. She is usually represented with a large headdress upon which plumes, bird/animal heads, and tassels are arranged. This headdress is sometimes dominated by butterfly icons, themselves associated with military motifs such as weapons and shields. The goddess is often masked, and she wears jade ear-spools and a large nose ornament in the form of a wide bar with fangs. When the nose bar is absent, her red- or yellow-painted face exhibits a tooth-filled mouth and large oval eyes. The goddess can have prominent hands with red nails or claws. She is sometimes associated with decorated mirrors, perhaps indicating that one of her functions was prognostication. Other associations include streams of water filled with jade artifacts that gush from her hands or mouth, flowers, intertwined

FIGURE 7.5. ■ The Great Goddess of Teotihuacán in the Classic period murals of the Tetitla Palace wears a huge headdress and ear spools, indicative of her exalted state, and a woman's blouse. From her hands flows water filled with precious jade artifacts.

vines, wings decorated like a *quechquemitl*, birds, insects, water creatures, netted jaguars, and a red and yellow sawtooth design. Each of these items can stand for the goddess: sometimes the hands appear alone, or hands with water, or mirrors, or bands of eyes. These signifiers of the goddess seem to relate to specific aspects of her character or duties.

A mural at the Tepantitla palace shows her as a bust full of seeds with water and corn around her, and humans offer her gifts while the so-called

WOMEN IN ANCIENT AMERICA

Storm God is shown in the border of the mural, a subordinate of the goddess. In the Paradise of Tlaloc mural she is shown giving gifts, and in the Temple of Agriculture mural she is herself a sacred mountain giving gifts and receiving offerings. It now seems likely that the Storm Gods, or Tlalocs, represent celebrants or priests in the service of this goddess.

Of course the paintings may not always represent the goddess herself. They may be images of her priestesses or priests, idols, or humans who impersonated her during her festivals. The ancient Teotihuacanos may have conceived of her as a series of supernatural beings or as one deity with various aspects.

The preeminent deity identified in Teotihuacán is this goddess. She is intimately connected with the local landscape and the sacred geography of Teotihuacán, a place riddled with caves, entrances to the underworld and points for communication with ancestors. The goddess is depicted at least once as the sacred mountain, the source of earthly waters, suggesting her association with local abundance and the control of rain and the aquifers of the valley. She must have been responsible for the fertility of the land and the general well-being of the city and its inhabitants. It is this highly localized character of the goddess that may explain why her representation is so rare elsewhere. Her power and gifts came from the local environment, not foreign ones.

The goddess is also a lady with destructive capabilities, as indicated by representations of her with fangs, claws, and military paraphernalia. These may indicate that she also had sacrificial aspects or that blood sacrifices were made to her. Many of the deities of Mesoamerica had both beneficent and destructive characteristics and had to be appeased with sacrifices of goods and living things.

Scholarly recognition of the Teotihuacán Goddess is an exciting result of recent work on the decipherment of Classic-period religion, and it comes from looking at the religious depictions of that city in terms of themselves and their own content, rather than trying to see them as illustrations of a religion of some 800 years later. It is now evident that the Goddess of Teotihuacán is different from later female deities.

Teotihuacán was the cult center of this goddess, but depictions of her are quite uncommon except in the larger, civic-elite structures in the city center. The Teotihuacán Goddess may have been worshipped by everyone or only by elite kin groups for the benefit of the whole city. Scholars understand little about Teotihuacán religion as a whole, but it is plain that most rituals were conducted at the lineage compound level.

Did having a female paramount deity have any effect on the lives of Teotihuacán women? It may well have positively influenced the lives of elite women who, if we can judge from historic peoples in the Valley of Mexico, might have functioned as religious officials of her cults and administrators of property. If the goddess was made incarnate (a common practice in ancient America and among the Aztec), she may have had a female high priestess/impersonator. On the other hand, male actors are prominent in all murals depicting ritual activity, except for those which show the goddess or her impersonator.

There is no other evidence of who participated in the cult of the goddess. The figurines representing females were manufactured mainly by females during the early centuries of the city (judging from the fingerprints on the unfinished surfaces of the artifacts); but later these figurines, including an ever-growing number of male images, were mass-produced in molds and made by men. It has been suggested that this, along with some more bellicose themes in mural painting, is evidence of a change to a more militaristic order in the city, as well as expansion of the economic sector, which is unlikely to have enhanced the status of women. Certainly having a female paramount deity had little effect on nonelite women, whose life histories reflect poor nourishment, especially serious during pregnancy, and early death. Perhaps living near the shrine of the goddess was comforting to these women.

In societies with hierarchically arranged religious institutions, the specialized religious practitioners are called priests. Only recently in our societies have women begun to take on priestly roles, but in ancient America there are good examples of priestesses. There were priestesses among the Aztecs during their initial migration into the Valley of Mexico, and priestesses and other women played important roles in the yearly round of calendric and other festivals, especially those dedicated to female deities. For example, in the ceremony of Achpaniztli, priestesses held and sacrificed a female victim, much in the manner of male priests. In other ceremonies it is evident that women's professional participation was essential in ceremonies as well as in the everyday functioning of temples and their business.

FIGURE 7.6. ■ In this version of the Moche Sacrifice Scene, painted on a ceramic bottle, Lady C presents a goblet of blood to figure A. She wears long twisted tresses, and two plumes decorate her headdress. Excavations at Sipán and San José de Moro have shown that his sacrifice ceremony was reenacted by real people.

## *Moche Priestesses in Peru*

Study of ancient Moche art resulted in the discovery of the "Sacrifice Scene" (fig. 7.6) and the interpretation of an ancient ritual in which the key element is the presentation of a goblet of human blood to a rayed male deity (fig. 7.6-A) by a figure who is an anthropomorphized hawk or owl. Both these figures are interpreted as warriors because of their distinctive costumes. A third figure in the Sacrifice Scene is a female with long, braided tresses. She proffers a goblet and sometimes a disk as well. Other common elements in the Sacrifice Scene include subordinate human warrior figures and prisoners whose throats are cut to provide the blood that the rayed god drinks.

This scene is shown in several media, and the woman is shown consistently. Along with her tresses, which terminate in snakes' heads (a standard indication of supernatural status), she wears a calf-length tunic dress, often with an elaborately patterned belt. She may wear a mantle with polka dots, and her headdress is highly characteristic: a long head cloth and a plain headband with two large plumes or curved panaches.

Anne-Marie Hocquenghem and Patricia J. Lyon identified this woman as a supernatural as early as 1980, but other investigators working on Moche iconography were not convinced, and she was repeatedly identified as male despite her feminine tresses and dress. The problem was resolved in the late 1980s, when immensely rich tombs were discovered by looters in the Lambayeque Valley at a site called Sipán. In an unusual turn of events, the looting was stopped, and controlled excavation began under the direction of Walter Alva. The scientific results have changed many ideas concerning Moche political structure and religious ideology because the first two tombs excavated contained the bodies of people who were identified, from the offerings in their graves, as having played the roles of Figures A and B in the Sacrifice Scene. These finds showed the tremendous wealth and power of the Moche "lords" and proved that living people had enacted the Sacrifice Scene.

In 1991, Christopher Donnan and Luis Jaime Castillo began excavations at the site of San José de Moro, a large ceremonial center in the lower Jequetepeque Valley, some 65 kilometers. south of Sipán, where another elaborate Moche tomb was discovered. This time the body of an adult woman was found in a rectangular adobe chamber with niches in the walls and a roof formed of large wooden beams. Associated with the main burial were sacrificed llamas and humans, and ceramic vessels, some imported from faraway regions. The principal occupant of the tomb was interred wearing jewelry of Chilean lapis lazuli and other imported stones. She was accompanied by offerings of exotic *Spondylus* shells placed on her chest and hands, and by her right elbow was a copper chalice—a cup with a hemispherical bowl and a tall conical base. Associated with her coffin was a mask, two large plumes, arms, legs, and numbers of disks of copper-silver alloy. In one corner of the tomb, among the other offerings, was another chalice, decorated with fine-line painting showing anthropomorphized shields and clubs drinking blood from similar chalices.

The implications of the finds from this tomb are considerable. Donnan and Castillo immediately identified the woman as Figure C from the Sacrifice Scene. The plumes from the coffin were identical to those shown on Figure C, and other funerary offerings, including the chalices, were similar to artifacts depicted in the mural representation of the Sacrifice Scene at Pañamarca, some 230 kilometers away. Like the male lords of Sipán, this lady must have participated in the Sacrifice Ceremony. She has been labeled a priestess, not a ruler, in all publications. In contrast, the two male actors only occasionally are called "warrior-priests," while frequently they have been featured in discussions of Moche rulership.

Continuing excavations at San José de Moro uncovered a second tomb of a younger woman with offerings and a coffin similar to the first

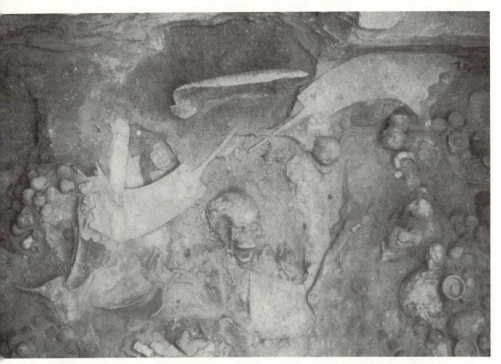

FIGURE 7.7. ■ The burial of Young Lady C at San José de Moro in northern Peru. Above her skull are two huge copper plumes like the ones often worn while performing the role of the priestess or deity impersonator in the Sacrifice Ceremony.

(fig. 7.7). In this well-preserved burial, it was possible to reconstruct a cane coffin with a mask on one end, arms and legs on the sides, plumes, and disks arranged like the dots on Figure C's mantle. The offerings with young Lady C, which may have included large quantities of textiles, were more numerous but poorer in quality than those found with the older woman.

The relationship of the two women buried at San José de Moro is not known. It is evident, however, from these two tombs that there were at least two women who sequentially, sometime in the sixth century A.D., played the part of Lady C of the Sacrifice Scene. Whether this was an inherited role or the occupant was chosen by other means, as are Tibetan reincarnated beings, is not known. It is also not known how this identification with the supernatural was conceived. Were these women reincarnates, that is, were they the deity herself? Or was dressing up as one of the players in an important myth and reenacting it part of the role of each Moche ruler? Was Lady C a ruler or member of a royal family? Certainly the offerings with neither Lady C are as lavish as those with the Sipán lords, although the now-decayed textiles hint at considerable wealth. However, the discovery of these Moche ladies demonstrates that practices in which some elite persons reenacted deity roles were widespread in ancient America.

## A Divine Mixtec Ancestress

The historical materials on the Aztecs are replete with ceremonies in which a person reenacted the role of a deity for some period of time. While the Aztec impersonators frequently were sacrificed upon the altar of the deity they served, this does not seem to have been the case with Moche or Mixtec impersonators. In one case, politically powerful Mixtec women who ruled a place called Skull (probably modern Mitlatongo) also impersonated deities in state activities. There were at least two women, both named Lady Nine Grass Death, who sequentially ruled this small principality, and both led active lives in the eternal politicking and petty warfare that characterized the Mixtec states (fig. 7.8). Although Nine Grass Death has been consistently identified as a goddess, the situation is more complicated. Joyce Marcus has cogently argued, in a discussion of the themes of anthropomorphic burial-offering vessels, that Zapotec and Mixtec religion involved the veneration of ancestors and the propitiation of the forces of nature. Because Nine Grass Death was named for a day in the Mesoamerican calendar, it is likely that she was born on that day, making her a real, historical person who became an especially venerated ancestor. Her successors, always female, apparently took their ancestor's name upon assuming rulership. Royal representations in ancient American art reinforce rulers' claims to divine ancestry by associating rulers with symbols of the supernatural and dressing them as supernatural beings.

In the early 1930s, the great Mexican archaeologist Alfonso Caso excavated the Zapotec city of Monte Albán, where his team discovered a series of tombs that had been reused by the later Mixtec as resting places for some of their own elite. The most famous of the Mixtec tombs at Monte Albán is the one that Caso called Tomb 7. The extremely rich grave furni-

FIGURE 7.8. ■ Nine Grass Death, ruler of the Mixtec state of Skull (modern Mitla-tongo), wears the mask and ritual costume of her important religious and political office.

ture included ceramic vessels, jewelry, and other objects of gold, silver, rock crystal, amber, turquoise, jade, obsidian, and pearls. Mosaics of semi-precious stones and carved bones were also found associated with the nine people who were buried in this tomb. In the east chamber, four individuals, whose bones remained in articulated position, were associated with a mosaic-covered human skull with a knife in its nasal passage, and a pile of red-painted human mandibles perforated so that they could be worn as masks by the living (a practice shown in the codices). The west chamber contained five bodies. Skeleton A, the focus of the elaborate mortuary complex, was at the far west end. This skeleton was interred as a mummy bundle, flexed, seated, wrapped in textiles, and associated with the richest offerings in the tomb. Most of these were articles of personal adornment, such as rings, earrings, pectorals, bead collars and headbands of obsidian, jade, gold, silver, shell, amber, crystal, and pearls. Jewelry among the Mixtec was not gender specific, except for pearl headbands, worn only by women.

The sex of Skeleton A has been the subject of controversy, Originally, Alfonso Caso's physical anthropologist, and later Daniel Rubín de la Borbolla, identified the remains as male. The assessment was complicated by the fact that the individual suffered from Paget's disease, a pathological condition that causes abnormal thickening of the bone. Curiously, Rubín de la Borbolla identified the mandible as female, necessitating the argument that it did not belong to Skeleton A, although it was found in anatomically appropriate position. Recent reanalysis of the physical remains and the associated offerings strongly suggest that Skeleton A is female.

Associated with Skeleton A were artifacts that reinforce the identification of this important person as female. In Mesoamerica, weaving (and public spinning and plying) were women's work, and female ancestresses and supernaturals commonly hold weaving battens and have spindles or weaving picks stuck in their headdresses. Skeleton A had with her four spindle whorls, a number of bone tools used in weaving, and a group of spinning bowls. During the Postclassic, cotton spinning was done with a supported spindle, and a special class of highly distinctive ceramic bowls used for this purpose alone are found throughout central Mexico. Skeleton A's spinning bowls, however, are made of onyx and rock crystal, as were those of the Aztec princesses. The most important offerings were the thirty-four carved eagle and jaguar bones with designs related to genealogy, history, calendrics, and animals. These carved bones are in the form of miniature weaving swords.

The physical remains of Skeleton A and the artifacts associated with the burial suggest that the primary occupant of Tomb 7 was female. The lavish personal ornaments and artifacts associated with Skeleton A, the eight people apparently sacrificed to be her companions in death, and the general richness of the other offerings tell us that the deceased was a wealthy and important lady. In their masterful reanalysis of Tomb 7, Sharisse and Geoffrey McCafferty identify her with one of the important women shown with skeletalized features in the codices. The burial corresponds well with the important Mixtec ancestress described above, Nine Grass Death. This identification is plausible given that the ladies who bore that name were rulers of a state of their own, and they wielded considerable diplomatic and religious power outside their own political unit. The calendric and personal name was originally associated with a person who became deified or who had such power that her descendants abandoned their own names and took hers as a throne name. When ruling, Nine Grass Death adopted, at least for formal occasions, a costume that included a skeletal mandible or entire skeleton mask and a black dress with bone designs (fig. 7.8). Judging by the lavish gifts made to her on state occasions, as illustrated in the painted books, Nine Grass Death had the potential of building up considerable personal wealth, which she, like the Moche ladies, took to the grave with her. The miniature battens may indicate another aspect of Nine Grass Death's ritual importance. It has been suggested that the marked miniature battens might have been used to cast fortunes. Divination, an important function of ancient Mesoamerican religious practitioners, often involved casting marked sticks, a custom that apparently came to America with the Paleoindians. Both the painted books and the investigation of the rich archaeological record in Oaxaca help scholars to feel confident about Nine Grass Death's political status. It is clear that Nine Grass Death ruled a kingdom and that her influence and access to wealth was due in part to her supernatural status and to the ritual and diplomatic duties she performed among the neighboring Mixtec kingdoms. Perhaps the Moche ladies who impersonated Lady C in ancient Peru had roles similar to those of the women who were Nine Grass Death.

## Figurines

Looters of archaeological sites in the Americas have provided the international art markets and museums with a large corpus of ceramic figurines with no archaeological context. In many of these styles, images of female human beings are predominant. Because sex is often clearly marked, the corpus of figurine images might be the basis for reconstructing change and variation in ideas about female and male in prehistory.

Today scholars are struggling to generate better interpretations of figurines and to deconstruct earlier, simplistic interpretations about fertility symbols and "Venus figurines." It is clear that anthropomorphic figures had diverse functions and that they operated in a variety of ancient contexts. Archaeologists and art historians have speculated that they were used in ceremonies of passage, marking life crises such as initiation into adulthood or transition to the next world at death; as receptacles for spirits in curing rituals and other shamanistic performances; as votive offerings; in rituals that recreated the cosmos or encouraged the increase of plants, animals, and humans; as idols in ancestor cults; as sacred icons or temple guardians; as substitutes for human beings in sacrifices; or as grave offerings. They may have functioned as focal objects to intensify participants' experiences during ritual, as power objects, or as teaching devices. Again they may have been purely decorative. In most cases we have little idea of their context and less of their meaning to the culture that made them.

Although numerous themes may be expressed by these objects, it is intriguing that female representations dominate numerically in many early styles, while in later styles, both female and male bodies are represented. The evidence indicates that in early sociocultural contexts, female bodies were important metaphors, embodying powerful and persistent religious ideas. Some data support the hypothesis that adult women were frequent actors in community rituals, but their roles and participation varied through time and across space. The increased frequency of male figurines later in history is evidence of changes in symbolism and ideology that may have accompanied transformations in gender relations that occurred as some societies became more complex.

## Pebble Imagery of the Lower Pecos

The Native North Americans described by ethnographers commonly manipulated portable objects in rituals designed to mobilize power in order to promote hunting success, cure diseases, and restore health. Some objects were said to "come alive" as they were handled by shamans as part of their rituals to control power and to heal magically. Today traditional shamans may use objects to represent ancestral spirits evoked in order to retrieve lost souls and restore a patient's health. Objects also may be employed as part of a vision quest, and still others may be used to evoke guardian spirits or channel evil.

The Archaic people who inhabited caves along the Lower Pecos River in West Texas created painted and engraved pebbles that were variously over-painted, repeatedly rubbed, ritually discarded, or wrapped and curated in preferred spots. The painted pebbles may have been part of rituals by which the people attempted to regulate their relationships in the natural, supernatural, and social worlds.

Pebble artifacts of the Lower Pecos come from rivers and are water-worn. Shirley Mock argues that water is linked to female processes in the worldview of the indigenous people of America, and water is the mythic home of ancestral spirits, game animals, and powerful and wise female deities. Thus the pebble is a natural metaphor, a form that may serve as an effective medium or repository of power in imitative or contagious magic.

Lower Pecos people selected anthropomorphic pebbles, some phallic in shape, and gave them features such as concentric circles or spiral

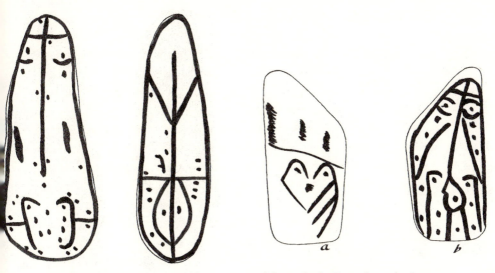

FIGURE 7.9. ■ These pebbles, recovered from Eagle Cave along the Lower Pecos River, were painted with red and black lines, which transformed them into female symbols.

patterns, which in recent times are life-producing symbols related to the cosmic order, the point from which humans emerged from the earth, and human reproduction, potent childbirth, and menstrual blood. Some of the Late Archaic pebbles seems to depict female genitals (fig. 7.9), and others show spiderwebs, which evoke the well-known Spider Grandmother of the historic Southwest, a medicine woman with supernatural powers.

Female symbols are important in many indigenous religions and art, and the creative and regenerative power associated with the vulva are important sources of shamanic power. Male shamans need female power and the power of the earth. Female deities give power to human shamans. Thus a male shaman needs female helpers. Some male shamans may themselves use female clothing, symbols, and metaphors as they pursue power. In Mock's interpretation, the Lower Pecos pebbles may have served as female icons representing spirits or spirit helpers, represented metaphorically as female genitals, which reminded people of the journey of shamans into the underworld. The painted pebbles of the Lower Pecos provide evidence from archaeological contexts that there were important sex and gender themes in the ideology of ancient people.

## Valdivia Figurines in Ancient Ecuador

In coastal Ecuador the oldest anthropomorphic figures were plain and engraved stone columnar pebbles made by the Early Valdivia people. The pebble figurines were shortly replaced by a tradition of ceramic figurine making that persisted for thousands of years.

During the middle phases of the Valdivia sequence, the figurines, often painted red, depict nude females with elaborate coiffeurs (fig. 7.10). The forms include immature and mature female bodies ranging from relatively realistic to abstract. There are pregnant figures, two-headed forms, bisexual forms, figures with babies, curious representations with elaborately cut hair or partially shaved heads, figures with a variety of arm and hand positions, and both seated and standing figures. A few figurines show individuals with a protuberance on the lower abdomen, which, according to Olaf Holm, might depict the pronounced mons pubis of a prepubescent girl, although the protuberance is sometimes interpreted as male genitalia. Valdivia figurines have been discovered mainly in domestic trash deposits, although a few are recovered in burials, and some giant ones have been found in ceremonial pits associated with public architecture.

An evolutionary interpretation developed by Jorge Marcos and Mariella Garcia suggests that the earlier Valdivia figurines were simultaneously phallic and feminine, symbolizing the duality of virility and fertility at a time in history when there was an ideology supporting reproduction and the expansion of the labor force. Later figurines seem to occur in differentiated male (extremely rare) and female forms that might correlate with differentiation of social roles in the more complex Late Valdivia communities.

In the later Valdivia phases, a number of masculine and feminine figures, some with headdresses, were designed to be seated on tiny stools, some of which have also been found. This could mean that both female and male ancestors were venerated, or perhaps that both women and men had roles as shamans. In ethnographic cases, stools are associated with shamanic power, high status, and male status and political authority. If lineage organization was important in Valdivia social and political life, as some scholars think, then the figurines may mean that the women of some lineages had access to authority and prestige in their communities.

James Zeidler's study of the distribution of the remains of ninety-four Valdivia figurines in House Structure One at the site of Real Alto demon-

FIGURE 7.10. ■ A Middle Valdivia ceramic figurine portraying an individual whose ritual status is denoted by her tonsured or depilated head.

strates a clustering of figurine fragments around a burned area where food was prepared. It has been argued that the Middle Valdivia phase households celebrated magical rites to encourage fecundity among women. One can speculate that this ideology developed to encourage population growth, which would have increased the labor available to family groups. At this time there was a change in household composition as some extended families occupied larger houses and engaged in some specialized economic activities. Under these conditions, the stylized figurines might have functioned in ceremonies designed to ensure the welfare, reproductivity, and/or productivity of households and the community as a whole.

In another interpretation, published by Costanza Di Capua, the Valdivia figurines represent various stages in the maturation of females and were made and used by women in celebrations of transitions in their lives. Such female initiation celebrations might be expected in Early Valdivia times, a time of economic expansion, when the production of children was probably highly valued, women may have controlled important agricultural resources, and people may have been organized in kin groups that were matrifocal or matrilineal.

Some of the ritual activities prominent in recent, ethnographically described, female rites of passage are suggested by the Valdivia figurines. According to Di Capua, some figurines show depilation, which may refer to the widespread haircutting ritual symbolizing a girl's death and rebirth as a woman. Body paint on the figurines may symbolize the painting of an initiate's body, or its scarification or tattooing, activities common in the initiation rituals that prepare girls for their roles in marriage, reproduction, and women's work. Similarly, ethnographically documented ceremonies of passage frequently involve ceremonial headdresses or coiffeurs, bringing the attention of everyone to the importance of the transitions from stage to stage in each individual's development. According to Di Capua, the figurines that represent prepubescent girls show evidence of their social limnality. They have partially depilated heads, indicating that they are not fully adult; their arms are stumps or absent, making them unfit for women's work; they have no breasts, showing their unreadiness for reproduction; but the pubic protuberance shows their potential to menstruate and conceive. Cult activity in ethnographic cases may involve vision quests and consuming drugs, and this is also suggested by the Valdivia figurines, which seem to depict individuals in trance states. The features of the figurines suggest that girls' puberty ceremonies, like traditional ceremonies today, emphasized the importance of women in society and ideology.

Middle Valdivia women living in large households might have created this cult, investing resources in the manufacture of paraphernalia and committing time to the ceremonial activities focused on various stages in the female life cycle. Groups of women may have invented their cult activity by creatively adapting traditional mythology, commandeering old forms (pebbles and stone figurines) for new purposes, and mobilizing new resources (ceramic pyrotechnology) in developing meaningful ceremonies. Such rites of social intensification among women are predictable if social and economic conditions favor new patterns of matrilineal descent and matrilocal residence.

Some Valdivia figurines might have functioned in rituals of shamanistic healing. Traditional Native American healing is a process that restores balance between humans and divines, between and among individuals, between humans and nature, and between men and women. Achieving balance and harmony may require that women and men act in concert, or a male healer might take on female characteristics or require a female helper to achieve balance. The preponderance of female figurines might support an argument that the shamanic healers were largely male, but this interpretation does not square well with other data, such as their distribution around cooking hearths.

Erick López has suggested that certain giant Valdivia figurines, depicting mature female bodies in a conventional style, were icons representing one of the avatars of an ancestral creator goddess who was ritually sacrificed during Valdivia rituals. The broken figurines, along with the remains of decorated Valdivia vessels, were found in a pit excavated into the yellow and white clay floor of a ceremonial precinct at a Valdivia site near Salango. This image may have been part of the dramatization of a mythic event in which participants commemorated the original sacrifice that brought the world into being.

## The Transformation of Imagery in Coastal Ecuador

After the Valdivia period, the production and use of ceramic figurines continued for many millennia, although the basic themes were transformed and elaborated by later peoples. The earlier corpuses of figurines are dominated by female images, whereas the later ones are progressively more focused on male representations. This may indicate changing ideology and concomitant changing religious ceremonialism, even, perhaps, changing gender roles.

The early, solid Valdivia figures gave rise to a series of elite styles in which hollow figurines served as mortuary offerings. As societies developed an increasing social stratification, one of the goals of the emerging elites was to create an ideology that buttressed and increased their prestige and power. Apparently they celebrated their connections to ancestors, including prominent female progenitors, and emphasized myths about female divines. In the process of creating new elite culture (including ideology and ceremonial practice), the nascent elites modified and developed the use of figurines outside the domestic context.

Tom Cummins has noted that the emphasis on female images persisted in the Chorrera period, even though a significant number of male images were made. The elite status of individuals is communicated emphatically. Chorrera artists introduced more markers of status and role on these figurines, which is consonant with the fact that people operated in larger, more complex social worlds. The social status of individuals was distinguished through visible markers (like modern uniforms), including headdresses, costumes, body paint, tattoos, necklaces, and ornaments for noses, ears, lips, arms, and legs (fig. 7.11). In Chorrera figurines both sexes wear ornaments in equal proportion, and some of the figures lack clear evidence of an intended gender. In these androgynous images, male and female roles in worship, personal sacrifice, or shamanic practice were not emphatically differentiated. Unisex in this art could mean that elite roles and statuses in that ancient society were not as gender-marked as they became in late prehistoric communities all over America. During the ceremonies in which the figurines were employed, the ranks of individuals may have been more important than their gender.

Out of the widespread Chorrera culture grew several societies of the Regional Developmental period noted for their individuality, elaboration, and distinct ceramic styles. In these daughter styles, called Guangala, Bahia, Jama-Coaque, and La Tolita, gender themes are developed, and some figurines show more diverse gestures, more elaborate costumes, and more dramatic postures than seen in the Chorrera styles. These representations

WOMEN IN ANCIENT AMERICA

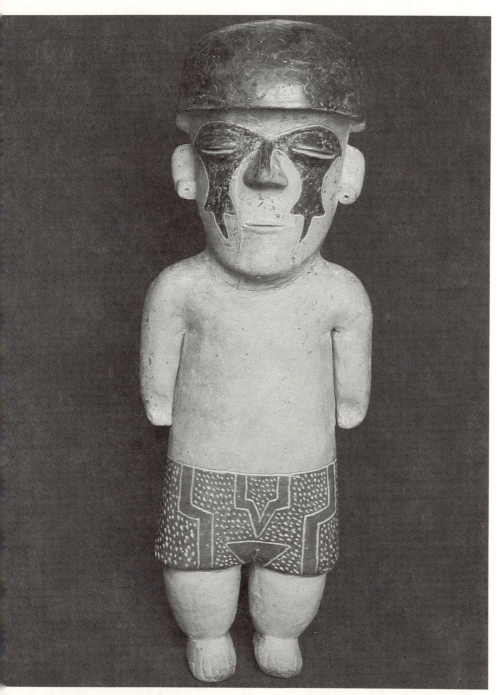

FIGURE 7.11. ■ A Chorrera ceramic figurine representing a high-status female with headdress and ear spools. The incised and painted decoration may represent body paint, tattoos, or clothing.

reveal the evolution of the ritual roles of both men and women. That female roles had to expand is shown by the association of female images with a wider variety of symbols, structures, and paraphernalia. But more dramatic development is seen in the male figurines, which demonstrate a great elaboration of costume, evidence of a proliferation of ritual activities and roles for men.

In the Regional Developmental period, as described by Betty Meggers, every aspect of the sociocultural system was subject to intensification. Agriculture was more specialized and productive, settlements were larger, burial ceremonialism was more elaborate, personal ornaments proliferated, and there was more trade than ever. Important social activities now took place beyond the household, and the figurines tell us that while more roles were available, women were not creating or filling as many of these as men. Of course it is not known whether the individuals portrayed in these figurines were humans, supernaturals, or mythic figures acting out parts of myths or legends; or if they were ancestors showing humans their assigned duties, or portraits of individuals, perhaps memorializing the recent dead, who were shown in their characteristic roles, participating in some ceremony. Nevertheless, both male and female roles in religious ritual were important enough to be portrayed frequently in clay in these regional styles. Female and male images occur in about equal numbers in these styles, but women and men are shown in distinct standardized poses, suggesting that gender roles were differentiated.

Both women and men participated in elaborate rituals and related performances, but male figures show more dynamic poses, wear more elaborate costumes, and sometimes play musical instruments. Female personages adopt hieratic poses and wear elegant costumes during worship. In the Jama-Coaque tradition, female images show the same hieratic or trance pose seen in the earlier Chorrera figurines, but with more elaborately detailed clothing and ornaments. While in Chorrera times both men and women took this pose, in Jama-Coaque it is only women, as if they were keeping that older tradition alive, while the men were participating in newly elaborated rituals. This is further evidence of the development of more differentiated roles for women and men in Jama-Coaque times.

Tom Cummins points out that in the corpus of Chorrera-style figurines, female and male personages are often distinguished by their genitalia, while in the later Jama-Coaque style, gender is marked only with cultural signifiers such as clothing and body ornaments. Similarly, women in the Jama-Coaque style are not shown pregnant but are shown in their social role as mothers. While sex and age are important social dimensions in all societies, the Jama-Coaque artists do not appear to have been as interested in sex differences as in social roles. They call attention to the distinguishing details of costume characteristic of warriors, dancers, musicians, and other persons of rank.

In the Regional Developmental period, gender roles as well as rank are spelled out in the figurines, where females and males wear very different garments and display different objects. For example, females hold pineapples and some types of manufactured objects, including metal ornaments and textiles, which apparently signal social and political rank and ceremonial roles (fig. 7.12), whereas males hold coca paraphernalia, weapons, bags, and dance staves. People apparently employed paraphernalia to signal their roles in the increasingly elaborate ceremonial life of the community. Elites invested heavily in celebrations designed to help them gain better religious and political positions. Female figures in the Jama-Coaque style are sometimes shown with roller stamps (fig. 7.13), clay seals probably used to apply complex painted designs to the human body. Body painting, a ritual activity in many societies, may have fallen into the provenance of women. Some female figurines are adorned with pairs of seals suspended around their necks, which Cummins interprets as clan symbols, indicative of the powerful social roles of some women in the kin groups of Jama-Coaque society.

In the regional styles of coastal Ecuador, women were portrayed in many roles. Nevertheless, the poses of the female figurines are often static (either seated or standing), and their dress, while elaborate, never acquires the dramatic attributes of male costume. Women, for example, never wear fantastic masks, and only male figures are shown transforming from human to animal form. Female images are often associated with plants and containers, suggesting that women were celebrated for their indispensable and valued roles as preparers of food and drink, including, perhaps, hallucinogenic brews. They may also have manufactured sacred paraphernalia, such as ritual vessels, and served as the custodians of significant symbols. Women's contributions in all these areas involve actions performed in single-sex groups before the moment of the ceremony and

FIGURE 7.12. ■ A Jama-Coaque sculpture from Ecuador portrays an elite female displaying a stack of textiles and metal artifacts, including a lunate nose ring.

ritual actions performed in public. The ancient viewer would not have seen these individuals as inactive, being aware that the food, drink, and paraphernalia were produced by female labor. Similarly, during Maya rituals in southern Mexico and Guatemala today, in fiestas in indigenous Amazon communities, or even in holiday events in the United States, the male roles are highly visible in public contexts. But if one looks more deeply into the entire celebration, one finds that many aspects of the ceremonies are orchestrated by women, whose contributions are central to the affair.

By showing females with objects the ancient artists may have created positive gender ideologies and identities, emphasizing ideal gender relationships, reinforcing desirable roles, and expressing the valuable public and nonpublic roles of women. These works of art help modern viewers to imagine that women were taking an active role in shaping their own participation in ritual, society, and economics in ancient Ecuador.

In many of the regional art styles of the Andes, the concept of symbolic symmetry and social complementarity between female and male or between women and men was expressed in the prehistoric iconography. For example, female/male couples are often depicted, and in some cultural contexts images of both sexes were employed in pairs. The social reality in the post-Chorrera period may not have been egalitarian, but the figurines reveal aspects of Andean belief: the universe is composed of complementary female and male halves, and both male and female activities are necessary for the continuance of the world. In this statuary there is no embedded message that men predominate over women.

## New Worship and New Roles

The Manteño people of southwestern Ecuador developed a stratified and more centralized political system in the last centuries before the European contact, and their material culture reflects elite activities, although in the aboriginal period, nonelite families continued to use solid female figurines in household rituals. Operating from regional centers, the Manteño elites were able to organize production of large quantities of goods and to mobilize services. They were known as great maritime traders, plying the seas from northern Peru to southern Colombia and beyond. Manteño artisans created hollow figurines in the elite style representing nude

a

FIGURES 7.13a and 7.13b. ■ A hollow ceramic sculpture in the Jama-Coaque style of the Central Coast of Ecuador depicts a high-status female seated in a ceremonial building (a). A symbolic plant adorns her head, and she holds a cylindrical ceramic seal (b).

b

males, often seated on stools, expressing their powerful ritual and political roles. In contrast, elite females are portrayed in only a few of the ancient, static poses. Manteño artists no longer represented or celebrated the myriad roles that in earlier periods elite male priests or shamanic leaders performed for the well-being of the community.

The few ceramic representations of Manteño women include standing and kneeling females with simple clothing, few accouterments, passive postures, and limited gestures. Like the male personages, they are associated with no particular activity. These female and male images are evidence that the idea of gender complementarity was important in Manteño ritual, but in the Manteño period the ceremonial expression of the complementary functions of females and males, communicated in the community rituals of the Regional Developmental period, was no longer emphasized in ceramic art. The elites may have replaced earlier rituals, which dealt with reciprocity between the sexes, families, and other social groups, with new rituals emphasizing hierarchy and elite power over complementarity and reciprocity. Perhaps the former depended upon the participation of women more directly than the latter.

This case demonstrates how in some cultures, gender roles are celebrated in art, and how that celebration changed in the art of ancient Ecuador. We do not know what roles elite Manteño women played in late prehistory, or if women's status was eroded as society became more hierarchical. However, gender stratification commonly accompanies political stratification (see chapter 8).

## Religion and Social Life

In considering alternative interpretations of figurines, it is possible to imagine scenarios in which females are framed in positive ways and in which real women are active. It would be absurd (and androcentric) to assume the biosocial passivity of women and to interpret each female representation and the remains in each tomb as evidence of victims of sacrifice, the objects of divine sexual urges, or the inactive wives and daughters of shamans, priests, and rulers. A balanced interpretation of America's past recognizes the wide range of religious and social activities performed by women and girls, and the significant portrayal in art of female goddesses, ancestors, and feminine concepts.

Figurines clearly show that in most social circumstances women's and men's religious roles were differentiated, and in societies with well-developed public religious spheres, men's roles frequently were predominant, but this does not detract from the fact that women were active, authoritative, and spiritually powerful as a group. Indeed, in some Native North American Plains groups, women traditionally lead the Sun Dance and open sacred bundles. Among some of these groups, women have been conceptualized as not only spiritually powerful, but also innately powerful, which means that they do not need to quest for spiritual power as men do.

## Music, Dance, and Sex

In the ideology and practice of Native Americans, dance and music are centrally important ritual activities performed in many contexts (fig. 7.14), although the participation of women and men differs widely across cultures. In some societies dancers of both sexes ritually mimic the activity of animal spirits, seek contact with powerful supernaturals, or transform themselves through the process of dance. Among many Native Americans, dance is widely thought to express the relationships of people to nature, to their creator, and to each other. Costumed and painted people reenact mythic moments through their musical and dance performances, in which themes of death, fertility, and regeneration are expressed. Adult women can be seen dancing in ancient ceramic sculptures, both singly and as participants in community circle and line dances.

Dancing and music are shown in many ancient art styles. Christopher Donnan has described a variety of scenes painted on Moche ritual vessels in which only males in full regalia hold hands and dance. Skeletonized women and children appear in another type of dance scene. Ancient Nazca ceramic sculptures from southern Peru depict women and men having a party with drinking and music, similar to parties of the historic Inca. Within the Andean sphere, women could be musicians, commonly drummers. From the Middle Horizon onward women are shown playing a small round drum that hangs from the wrist, while men blow animal skull or conch trumpets, shake rattles, and play other instruments. Members of both sexes danced. In the Colonial period, women became separated from their musical duties, largely because of the distaste

FIGURE 7.14. ■ A Nazca ceramic sculpture depicts a procession of people, perhaps on their way to a ceremony. The central woman holds a panpipe in each hand and bears birds on her shoulders, while the man plays a panpipe and holds a dog.

European missionaries felt for women having public roles and participating in parties in which there was drink and sexual behavior.

In ancient Mesoamerican art, there is little association between women and music. The West Mexican tomb figurines show only men with musical instruments, although women are shown participating in dances and in poses that might indicate singing or chanting. Classic Maya paintings and figurines show only male musicians. But 600 years later, among the northern Maya of the Conquest period, old women danced in the temple during the new year ceremonies. Younger women, however, did not enter the temples. Diego de Landa remarks that during religious festivals held outside the temple precincts, music and dancing were an integral part of the rituals, and both sexes participated although men and women did not dance together.

In some ancient American art styles, sexual contact between females and males is represented (fig. 7.15). This so-called erotic or pornographic

FIGURE 7.15. ■ A Recuay vessel depicts an elite couple having sexual intercourse under a blanket and surrounded by smaller, lower-status female
attendants.

art may show mythic scenes that were enacted by human impersonators
or ritual actors who performed sex acts or carried them out symbolically.
In many historic societies, rituals employed human sex metaphorically to
communicate powerful cultural meanings. In some ceremonies coitus was
performed as part of magical rituals designed to transfer power. In a study
of the function of ceremonial sexual intercourse, Alice Kehoe gives
examples from North American ethnography of how spiritual power may
be transmitted from man to man as first one, then the other has intercourse with a particular woman. High-ranking, respectable, and chaste

matrons and their husbands participated in the ritual, and the participants themselves perceived their activity as spiritual. A woman, knowing herself to be the bearer and communicator of power, might value the opportunity to exercise spiritual and political power by participating with men in rituals that expressed her status and brought prestige for herself and her family.

Native American fertility rituals may involve ritual intercourse or the symbolic reenactment of mythical intercourse. Among the nineteenth-century Arapaho, an elder man and a woman would perform the intercourse ritual by transferring a symbolic root from his mouth to hers in a ceremonial context.

Ritual sex is often a strategy developed in matrilineal societies to reinforce the role of males as "begetters" and balance the predominant role of mothers in reproduction. In performing ritual coitus, the roles of both become important. Religious interpretations of sex are likely to have been part of the ubiquitous negotiation about roles between men and women throughout human time. This negotiation resulted in the emphasis on female reproduction in some philosophical systems and an emphasis on male fertility in others. In Tom Zuidema's interpretation of the art of the late prehistoric Tairona of northern Colombia, both male and female deities are shown in "display" position, drawing attention to their roles in reproduction, and the sun is conceptualized as an impregnating male who in the course of his movement across the heavens visited "concubines."

Gender balance may be symbolized and negotiated in the ideology of people, but in some ethnographic cases ritual sex became gang rape (in the Amazon region, for instance) or some other intimidating demonstration of male power, as among the Blackfoot and some other Plains groups, where violent intimidation of "errant" females was a common practice.

## Human Sacrifice

Aside from active roles as religious specialists or believers, women could also be the victims, willing or unwilling, of their religious beliefs. Human sacrifice was widespread in the Americas. The scale as well as the ideological impetus varied with place, time, and the type of society, but certainly from the beginnings of settled life human sacrifice was an established part of many religious traditions. Although salacious Western writers emphasize the sacrifice of trembling virgins, in truth, women were too valuable in most societies to be removed from production and other social roles. Not only does Diego de Landa, the Spanish priest, chronicler (and destroyer) of Postclassic Yucatecan Maya civilization, say unequivocally that it was men who were thrown into the sacred wells as sacrifices, but analysis of human remains recovered from the legendary Cenote of Sacrifice at Chichén Itzá shows the unreliability of hearsay. Despite stories about the hurling of delicious maidens into the depths, Ernest Hooton's analysis of skeletal material shows that the people recovered from the Well were mainly men and children (thirteen males, eight females, twenty-one children). It is not surprising that children were sacrificed, since the cenotes functioned as shrines to the water spirits, and children were considered the most appropriate sacrifices to these deities. The fact that all the adults showed signs of having led hard lives suggests that they, as well as the children, were slaves.

In ancient Native American societies, human sacrifices were appropriate in the propitiation of deities and in some funerary contexts. Throughout the Americas the sacrifice of female servants or lesser wives to the burial of a ruler was relatively common. Cieza de León writes that the Quimbaya and their neighbors in central Colombia would make women drunk before burying them alive in the tomb of the ruler. The Spaniard Gaspar de Espinosa has left us a firsthand account of the burial in Panama of Chief Parita, who was wrapped in a bundle with all his jewelry and with a woman at his head and another at his feet. When Atahuallpa was murdered by the Spaniards, a number of the women attending him demanded the right to be sacrificed to accompany their ruler. Such sacrifices apparently were not always forced upon women.

Most archaeological and ethnohistoric cases of sacrifice involved small numbers of people. For example, among the historic Pawnee, one of the traditional ceremonies designed to revitalize the universe involved the commemoration of the sexual union of the Morning (male) and Evening (female) Stars, which resulted in the first girl and, later, all people. In the historic period, this involved the sacrifice of a young female captive to the Evening Star, and it is likely that earlier young men had been sacrificed to the Morning Star. From her study of an archaeological site on the Smoky Hill River in Kansas, occupied in A.D. 1300, Patricia O'Brian describes a burial mound with the remains of a number of individuals, including a twelve-year-old female. The mound of earth has been interpreted as the site of a sacrifice to the Evening Star. Among recent Pawnee people, the ceremony involved firing a number of arrows into the victim's body, which was then exposed, with the head to the east, to be consumed by animals. In the prehistoric mound, archaeologists found arrow points without their tips scattered in the fill, and disarticulated bones gnawed by rodents. The teeth of the young woman were found under the east side of the mound, as if she had been laid upon an old mound and covered with a layer of dirt.

The Aztecs, whose name is synonymous with wholesale human sacrifice, illustrate a cultural pattern in which sacrifice on a very large scale became part of the conspicuous consumption of rulers and their empire-building strategy. But many other Native American peoples from extremely early times onward practiced human sacrifice to deities and as part of funerary rituals. Human sacrifice is particularly common in Andean cultures. Sacrifices as part of the dedication of new houses may have begun in Valdivia times in the northern Andes. At the Early Horizon site of Chavín de Huántar, the main cult center of the first religious movement to spread through the central Andes, there is evidence of ritual cannibalism.

Dedicatory and retainer sacrifices continued to be made on an increasingly greater scale throughout the prehispanic period, but during the period of the Inca Empire, the number of sacrificial episodes escalated, and new concepts of human offerings developed. The Inca regulated human sacrifice in their conquered territories, directing the use of human resources to their own ends. They had various means of sacrifice, including strangling the victims and burying or cremating them, removing the heart and offering the blood and heart while burning the body, and cutting the throat and offering the blood of the victim, something seen much earlier among the Moche. The Inca also buried victims alive or made them drunk or insensible with blows to the head and left them to die of exposure on mountains, as was the case with the recently discovered frozen mummies from a number of peaks in southern Peru.

Among the Inca and their predecessors, male sacrifices often involved bloodletting, whereas female sacrifices consisted of death by a non–blood-releasing means, with subsequent interment of the entire body in the earth. Most Inca sacrificial victims were children below the age of puberty.

WOMEN IN ANCIENT AMERICA

For example, the *capa cocha* ritual was a particularly elaborate form of sacrifice in which beautiful children were brought to Cuzco to be feted in a public ceremony. Later they returned to their native provinces to be buried alive as dedicatory offerings or to propitiate female deities who received their offerings as burial sacrifices. There are historic accounts of *capa cochas*, indoctrinated children, such as a girl named Tanta Karwa, who was selected as a sacrifice by her father at birth because she was such a beautiful child. At age ten she went to Cuzco for the state ceremony, which consecrated all the *capa cocha* children. Upon her ceremonious return to her village, she willingly entered the tomb where she was to die as an offering to an irrigation ditch. Her family gained prestige within the structure of the Inca Empire, and her brother spent his life as the chief priest of the local cult, which kept alive her memory. Tanta Karwa was venerated as a minor deity at the time of the Spanish Conquest, when the tomb was opened and the offerings of precious metals were removed from her decayed body.

Children of both sexes were sacrificed like Tanta Karwa for various political and religious purposes. A few individuals seem to have been chosen by government officials and willingly offered by their parents.

In contrast, at the great shrine of Pachacamac, there is evidence of much larger-scale sacrifices involving women. Pachacamac, just south of Lima, Peru, was an important shrine for centuries before the Inca. Its apogee was in the sixth to eighth centuries, when a prestigious oracle held sway and Pachacamac became a large city prospering from the visits of pilgrims. By the time the Inca conquered the Central Coast, the shrine had fallen on hard times, but the Inca craftily embraced the oracle and assisted in its economic recovery. A huge temple to the sun and an *acllahuasi* were built at Pachacamac near the old Temple of the Oracle. On the first southeast terrace of the Sun Temple in 1896 Max Uhle found a series of burials of women. He recovered forty-six well-preserved bodies but estimated that there had originally been at least twice as many. These burials were all of adult women, mostly young, although one had long gray hair, and all had been strangled. Uhle noted that the necks of some of the mummies were less than 2 inches in diameter, and the neck vertebrae of others had been dislocated. Some still showed how the strangulation had been done: a thick, folded cloth was knotted in the middle, passed around the neck, and knotted in the back as it was pulled

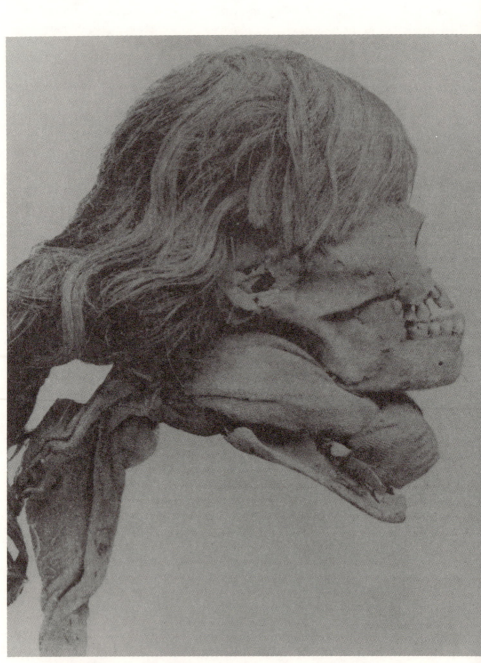

FIGURE 7.16. ■ The head of one of the women sacrificed at Pachacamac. The strangling device, a knotted cloth, is still in place under the jawbone.

in tightly (fig. 7.16). The large knot in front closed the larynx mechanically, quickening death.

Uhle speculated that these women were gathered from various locations in the highlands because the plant-food offerings associated with the burials were all of highland origin. In contrast, the ordinary burials at Pachacamac contained coastal cultigens. There was also considerable variation in the women's head shapes, the result of cranial modification, which varied by ethnic group. This suggests that the victims were assembled from various parts of the empire. Their clothing, some new and some well worn, was obviously their own. The associated pottery was both imperial Inca and local, made in the Chimu-Inca style, but the women also were buried with personal possessions such as sewing baskets and combs— some with hairs still in them. It is thought that they were brought to Pachacamac to serve the Sun, but there they were strangled and buried in temple earth. It is possible that the sacrifice was part of the rededication of the temple after its remodeling, but such mass sacrifices were common throughout ancient Peru in response to natural disasters, such as an El Niño event, or to ensure the health of an Inca ruler.

Among the Inca and some of the contemporary Andean state societies, the slaughter of women of reproductive age makes manifest an unusual ideology: women became commodities to be displayed rather than essential members of their community. Powerful religious beliefs, and perhaps religious and political fanaticism, account for these episodes of sacrifice, but one wonders if such a sacrifice would have been made had women held more power in the Inca state.

# CHAPTER EIGHT

# Women and Power

Modern people living in state-level societies usually think that hierarchy is normal and that superordination and subordination are natural or universal. Because the political domain has become preponderant in recent history and considerable asymmetry in power of women and men has developed in many societies, women's roles in political history have been neglected or suppressed, and male political leaders are the focus of archaeological interpretation.

However, it can be argued that the ranking of males and females and supposed male dominance is neither universal nor embedded in human nature. Neither sexual nor political hierarchy was invented until relatively late in human history, and even today it is poorly developed or missing in small-scale, non-Western societies in which people live in small communities organized by kinship and characterized by egalitarian relations and consensus.

It has been argued by some feminist scholars that female subordination developed in tandem with private property and the state; others have suggested that gender equality and complementarity were prevalent in America until European colonization. A careful look at the archaeological and ethnohistoric record shows that in ancient America, as in the rest of the world, there were a multitude of different means of organizing social life, that some women lived in egalitarian societies and others participated in hierarchical states. Research among Native American ethnic groups has shown that at the heart of many societies, in the family, there is often a pattern of balanced reciprocity, of collateral spheres in which "powerful" and "powerless" have no meaning and in which neither women nor men dominate the other. This is not to say that women and men did not quest for power over others, but in ancient America power was expressed in many ways and involved the interplay of politics, religion, economics, and gender.

There is no evidence of matriarchy in prehistoric American societies— or anywhere else in the world. While it is unlikely that women in any ancient society systematically dominated their community politically, it is nevertheless clear that there were some societies in which women held key leadership roles. There were many cases of matrilineal and matrifocal societies, such as the Hopi and the Iroquois, in which women exerted considerable influence within and beyond the family.

In the past, as today, women and men may predominate in distinct realms of activity, and they may develop expertise in different areas. In some tribal cases, men and women are separated, and each is autonomous and "powerful" but antagonistic to the other group. In the case of the prehistoric Inca, and in more recent Andean groups, men and women often formed parallel and distinct social groups and institutions. This arrangement confers upon both women and men leadership roles, power, and opportunities to shape their culture. Ethnographic evidence alerts us to the possibility that gender roles in the political arena were variable in the past and that our interpretations should consider how both women and men gained and used power.

In recent interpretations of the archaeological record, it has become clear how difficult it is to reconstruct the power structures of past peoples. In the Southwest region of the United States, scholars continue to argue whether the prehistoric Pueblo societies were egalitarian or hierarchical. Randall McGuire and Dean Saitta have suggested that this kind of oppositional thinking is unproductive and that a more nuanced interpretation is called for. Specifically, they argue that power should not be considered as something that is either present or absent, rather, it is always present in social life and involves the ability of individuals to alter events. They conclude that the prehistoric peoples lived in a communal society that had both consensual and hierarchical social features. People were organized in kin groups that held resources and exploited them communally. There were inequalities among these kin groups, and hierarchy existed both within these groups and between them, but without monopolies on power and wealth and without class stratification. The elites of the communal groups derived power from their own network of social, material, and ideological relationships. In this view power does not flow down a hierarchy, but exists in many forms, and is ambiguous and contradictory in the many societies where egalitarian and hierarchical features are mixed. This model is supported by the apparent stratification in burial data in many American sites, including differential distribution of trade goods and ritual paraphernalia, indicating that some individuals had extraordinary roles in clans and in sodalities.

In systems with checks and balances, power is expressed and exercised in complex ways, such that in the lived experience of the people, a variety of individuals might participate as conscious creators and negotiators of culture. This means that members of all sectors of society, including women, are expected to participate in the dialectical process of cultural change. If one is persuaded by this view of social power, it opens one's eyes to the possibility that the power to shape events, influence history, and shape one's own life might have been lodged in women's hands as well as men's.

Burial symbolism often reiterates the universal social differentiation between men and women, but the evidence from the earliest periods of American prehistory demonstrates the existence of complementarity and real measures of symmetry and equality between the sexes in those societies. In later prehistory asymmetry became more pronounced as men took opportunities to acquire power in extradomestic arenas of activity. Both women and men of the lower ranks of society suffered negative consequences as progressive social differentiation left power and authority concentrated in the hands of elites and strangers. Women's roles in families were altered when those families were integrated into hierarchical political economies. Both the division of labor and gender norms were transformed by that larger economy as men gained power bases outside the family, and women's roles, valued in the family context, had no direct significance in the public political and economic sphere. In that sphere powerful people pursued interests that were sometimes inimical to women and families.

Many tombs in later prehistory were designed to signal the power of the deceased and her or his status. Men were more successful in achieving the kind of status gained in warfare, trade, and religious practice, and subsequently they were celebrated at death. Nevertheless, one suspects that the expression of the power of particular men in art, material culture, and funerary rituals sometimes outstripped the reality of that power. Conversely, one wonders if lack of expression of women's power obscures the reality that women had more power than archaeologists guess. The nagging question is whether women publicly deferred to men while privately contesting men's public control and cultivating their own covert and indirect power, perhaps focused in the domestic context, which was centrally important in the prehistoric period.

## Changing Status among the Hohokam

By the Classic period (A.D. 1150–1400) in southern Arizona, Hohokam society grew more complex and showed increasing social differentiation along lines of wealth. Recent studies of Hohokam domestic production, architecture, ritual space, and burials have shown changing patterns of sexual stratification.

Patricia Crown and Suzanne Fish suggest that there was increasing differentiation among women in Hohokam communities in the Classic period as some women were isolated in walled compounds that limited their role in the community while promoting female integration in the family work group. The evidence summarized by Randall McGuire indicates that the labor invested in food processing and craft production increased during the Classic period. The clay griddle (*comal*) appeared, more elaborate ceramics, including highly-polished wares, were manufactured, and numerous spindle whorls demonstrated that households increased their investment in processing fiber. According to McGuire, many families abandoned the pre-Classic pit houses, and elite women became separated from the rest of the community by living in large walled compounds or residences on platform mounds. Some women in these isolated corporate groups probably enjoyed greater wealth but suffered loss of personal autonomy, although some senior women may have gained leadership roles. The grave goods indicate that female and male status was associated with different activities, represented by different sets of grave offerings. McGuire's study of the distribution of burials by sex and age at five Hohokam platform structures shows that adult females were not eligible for burial at all of these sites. Furthermore, females were underrepresented in special box burials and lined-pit burials. In terms of grave goods, the researchers made a determination of grave lot value and concluded that although the remains of adult women were buried on some platforms and did occur in special burial contexts with highly valued goods, adult males and children were buried in more valuable locations with more valuable grave goods.

In the Classic period, children, young adults, and older females tended to have more elaborate burials. An elderly adult female was the only woman buried in an adobe-lined pit. Another woman, between forty and fifty years of age, was interred atop the Las Colinas platform. She has been identified as a curer or shaman. Her pelvic area was covered with red hematite, and a leather pouch containing a large quartz crystal and asbestos was left under her head. Ethnographic analogy suggests that postmenopausal women might have participated with men in religious and political activities.

As family groups became more and more differentiated in the Classic period, women's contributions in producing goods and children must have been the very foundation of family wealth and prestige. If women were confined behind walls, their influence in the public sphere might have declined even as their prestige as members of high-ranking families increased. However, if women were autonomous and in control of the domestic sphere, they would have had significant influence over men who depended upon their labor in the areas of production and reproduction. Compared to the pre-Classic period, their grave offerings increased, but their prestige was celebrated with symbols drawn from domestic life, not with imported personal ornaments or ritual paraphernalia. It appears, then, that the female prestige hierarchy was different from that of men. Crown and Fish, who interpreted women's and men's statuses as complementary, quoted a modern Papago Indian woman: "But we have power. . . . Can any warrior make a child, no matter how brave and wonderful he is? . . . Don't you see that without us, there would be no men? Why should we envy men? We made men." If statements such as these are valid for the prehistoric past, then the complementary nature of grave goods may indeed reflect parallel statuses within the society.

Studies of southwestern indigenous groups suggest that females and males in many ethnic groups may have had parallel leadership hierarchies, but these kinds of arrangements change easily and can be affected drastically by events such as warfare or conquest.

### Kin Group Leaders of the Ancient Zuni

An archaeological study of 1,000 late prehistoric (A.D. 1350–1500) Puebloan burials at Hawikki near the modern town of Zuni, New Mexico, demonstrates that members of ancient kin groups were buried in spatially discrete cemeteries (see fig. 5.1). In this case Todd Howell and Keith Kintigh identified the burials of community leaders as those individuals with a greater number and diversity of burial goods or whose burial showed special body or other preparations. These offerings and preparations were taken to express the number of social roles that the individual performed in life. It was observed also that individuals with such offerings also were found with rare types of artifacts, which might have been reserved for high-ranking people.

Eleven leaders' burials were found. Eight were of males. Most of the male paraphernalia, including bows and arrows, war clubs, and a single human scalp, suggests the importance of their roles in warfare, but the equipment in two burials demonstrates that male leaders were active in ritual performances as well.

The three female leaders had three of the four most diverse burials in the sample. These women were associated with grave offerings of corn, squash, utilitarian vessels, decorated bowls, grinding equipment, baskets, shaped wood, paint-grinding stones, antler tools, gourds, decorated jars, feathers, human hair, and prayer sticks. The hair and a painted shrine erected in one of the tombs were unique. The grave goods are evidence of the association of women with domestic chores, food preparation, and some ritual activities.

These important people of the community were not distributed randomly among the eleven kin-based cemeteries at the site. Eight leaders were buried in Cemetery 9 and three in Cemetery 1, suggesting that leadership was determined by ascription, and not by achievement. Only members of some kin groups earned leadership roles.

Todd Howell has argued that after 1539, the encroachment of Spanish colonial forces and the migration of hostile Apaches into the Zuni region resulted in the erosion of female authority. The reasons given are the increased need for military leadership, European political practices that favored male heads of households, and the imposition of European religion and Western gender ideologies.

By the time that the Zuni came under heavy European impact and Apache attack, the most prominent male leadership roles were associated with warfare. This contrasts with the prehistoric evidence that shows men assuming both military and ritual leadership roles. In the historic period, female leaders continued to be buried with the basic suite of items attributed to matriline heads, but they lost emblems of their roles in ritual life.

The ancient societies of the Southwest were characterized by prestige leaders rather than hereditary rulers. In some cases archaeologists observe a pattern of inequality among individuals suggesting that some members of their community wielded more power than others. Nevertheless, even in the more highly ranked societies (called chiefdoms), kinship would have been the dominant organizing principal. Because kinship is reckoned in many different ways, some systems could have been more favorable to women than others. Societies that had matrilineal inheritance and matrilocal residence may have allowed women more access to political power. In matrilineal societies related women usually form the core of the social unit, and lineage headmen are the sons and brothers of highly ranked women. After marriage, women continue to live in their mother's houses, and the young woman's husband becomes part of the wife's household, although he continues to be a part of his own mother's line and participates in social, political, and ritual activities with his own matrilineage. It is thought that matrilineal societies are less prone to internal warfare as a means of social and political advancement for subgroups because matrilocal residence may diffuse the fraternal interest groups that are characteristic of patrilineal societies. In patrilineal societies groups of brothers, who continue to reside with their father, band together to pursue feuding and internal warfare against other such groups. However, when men from several villages are coresident, warfare with other households is disadvantageous because violence would be directed toward the kin of some of the men.

Women often prefer matrilocal residence so that work can be organized by groups of cooperating, related women. When external warfare is practiced, these women may take on additional productive functions, and often they assume leadership in community affairs and gain higher status because of their increased contribution to economic activities that sustain the group while the men are waging war.

## A Taino Queen

The late prehistoric chiefdoms of the Savannah River area of the United States and much of the circum-Caribbean region practiced this kind of

---

matrilineal, matrilocal pattern at the time of the Spanish invasions, and several chronicles of the sixteenth century record the names of various chiefs, some of whom were women. Because access to positions of leadership in societies organized by kinship is determined at least in part by membership in a high-ranking lineage, both sexes may enjoy such access. One instance of this is shown in accounts of the historic Taino people of Hispaniola (the island now occupied by the modern countries of Haiti and the Dominican Republic).

Samuel Wilson has presented a detailed study of Taino chiefdoms at the time of Columbus. The Taino system of kinship and politics was complex because people manipulated their relationships through both their mothers and fathers. Individuals and families, competing for social status, wealth, and political power, manipulated inheritance and succession in complex ways to gain advantage.

The Taino were characterized by matrilineal descent and inheritance. Matrilocal residence was common, and female leadership of political units was also relatively common. The Taino created very flexible political situations in which political status could be transmitted in various ways, depending upon the specific circumstances. While men were usually the political leaders, women played key roles in politics.

Wilson shows that making astute marriages was important to the success of political leaders. The negotiation of exogamous marriages crossing the boundaries between chiefdoms by high-ranking individuals, female and male, was a key mechanism of change in Taino sociopolitical structure. As high-ranking people married only each other, they formed a circumscribed and powerful elite. Particular individuals could consolidate their leadership over two or more smaller polities because of a peculiar kind of double inheritance, in which a cacique might succeed his mother's brother as well as his own father. A talented individual, capable of acquiring status through religious activities, warfare, trade, or politics, might also manipulate the rules of inheritance to build a power base.

Another route to power building was the practice of polygyny. The cacique could acquire multiple wives to gain advantage. Having many wives was a clear display of status, but more importantly, because social and political status were carried through matrilines, high-ranking caciques could use polygyny on a large scale to appropriate the products of subordinate polities and their high-ranking lineages.

Sexual negotiations were an important part of politics, but leaders also built political power through warfare, feasting, and reciprocal and competitive gift exchange. In many cases women produced the prestige goods that dazzled the guests, signaling the host's power and prestige.

The case of Anacaona, a Taino "queen," shows how an elite woman held and manipulated power. When the Spanish invaders arrived on Hispaniola, they had a high-level meeting with thirty-two chiefs in the house of Anacaona, who was both the cacique's sister and the wife of a high-ranking leader from a neighboring chiefdom. She owned several houses and controlled prestige goods, including wooden seats made by women, cotton textiles, and huge balls of cotton thread. These were stored in one of her houses in a village 5 kilometers away. She also owned a royal canoe. When her brother died, she had him buried with the most beautiful of his wives and concubines, showing her authority. She was widely respected, even by the Spaniards. They burned eighty caciques alive but chose to hang Anacaona. One hopes she appreciated the tribute.

Throughout the circum-Caribbean area in the latest prehistoric period, female leaders like Anacaona were common. The early Spanish sources mention these ladies, but the conquerors often refused to deal with them and tried to have them replaced by men.

## Female Authority in Northern Colombia

The Caribbean plain of northern Colombia is an area of swamps, seasonal flooding, and immense resources. The societies that arose and flourished from the third century onward exploited this region by intensive agriculture and fish cultivation and developed a major industry in the production of gold ornaments for use within their own group as signs of status and for trade with other Andean and Central American societies. These peoples, called Sinú after the major river system, built their habitations upon artificial earthen platforms that supported linear villages. The platforms also supported the funerary tumuluses in which women and men were buried with offerings. As delineated by the work of Juanita Saénz Samper, the Sinú tradition was one in which women had tremendous social and political importance. This is indicated by the historic accounts of the Spanish chroniclers and traceable in the archaeological record for centuries prior to the Spanish invasions.

WOMEN IN ANCIENT AMERICA

In the sixteenth century, this region was ruled by three caciques, who were all very closely related. The second most important of these three chiefs, the sister of the paramount ruler, was the Lady of Finzenú. Padre Simón, who observed this lady, says that she lived in royal state and never put her feet on the bare ground, but rather was carried in her hammock and supported by serving women who let her walk on them if she had to move about on her own. Padre Simón also comments that in the temples of the Sinú region the idols were richly covered in precious metal and that many of them were female.

Little is known about the Lady of Finzenú, but by studying the forms and contents of tumuluses in the Sinú region, Saénz has provided evidence that women were important in the prehistoric period. In the female tumuluses are found multiple burials, often with a wealth of gold, including the mammiform pectorals (fig. 8.1) for which the region is known, female figures, and other offerings. In contrast male burials are simple, gold ornaments usually are limited to lunate earrings, and multiple burials and abundant offerings are missing. In the ceramic art, male effigies are scarce. In a collection studied by Saénz, only four of more than one hundred human figures were male. The majority of these ceramic forms represent full-figure females in commanding postures, displaying their jewelry and body decorations proudly. Many figures are seated upon benches, a sign of high political and social status throughout the Andean area. The ornaments seen on the female figures are identical to those found in rich female burials.

This preponderance of women in rich burials and female images in art is echoed by related cultures of the northern Andes. The Classic Quimbaya of the third to fifth centuries commonly show women in their figurative metallurgy. Female figures sit on benches and display jewelry and ritual objects indicating their status as rulers and/or religious practitioners. The association of women and gold, a substance restricted to the highest elite, is evidence of the importance of the female chiefs.

## Olmec Elites and Rulers

Women rulers of complex chiefdoms or primitive states appeared very early in Mesoamerica. Our first view of them comes from the Preclassic period Olmec of the Gulf Coast, a people who have the best claim to being Mexico's first civilization. The Olmec ceremonial centers were

FIGURE 8.1. ■ Golden female breastplates of this kind are recovered from elite tombs in the Sinú region of northern Colombia. They apparently were worn by both female and male caciques.

adorned with monumental stone sculpture that celebrated the rulers of the sites. At the important site of La Venta, Stela 1 depicts a woman standing in the open mouth of the earth monster, a pose that everywhere in Mesoamerica was associated with the ruler of a site (fig. 8.2). Another Olmec ruler is shown in Monument 21 at the highland site of Chalcatzingo. This stone relief sculpture portrays a woman wearing the typical Olmec female dress, and, because she is shown in profile, her breasts are clearly visible (fig. 8.3). Jewelry, sandals, and an elaborately patterned cloth worn over her head are other indicators of high status. This woman stands on a stylized earth monster mask and touches or presents a large deerskin bundle, elaborately tied with bands and knots. It has been suggested that this bundle represents the marital exchange of the woman. A more parsimonious interpretation is that this is a monument celebrating an event in the reign of the female ruler of Chalcatzingo. The woman is

WOMEN IN ANCIENT AMERICA

FIGURE 8.2. ■ Stela 1 from the Olmec site of La Venta shows a female ruler standing, like other Mesoamerican rulers, in the open mouth of an earth monster.

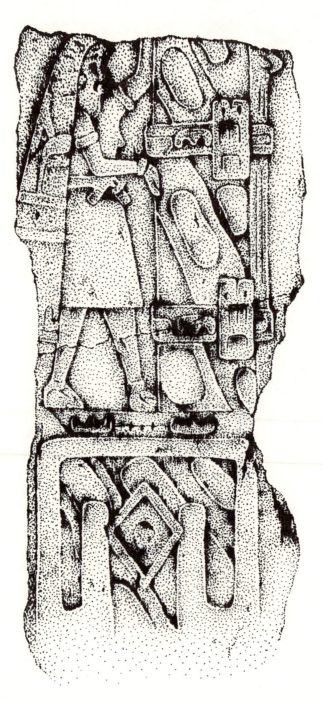

FIGURE 8.3. ■ A woman portrayed on Monument 21 from Chalcatzingo, an Olmec-related site in central Mexico, probably was a ruler. She is touching a giant deerskin bundle of the kind often associated with royal rituals.

likely to have been a ruler because nonregnant personages are rare in Mesoamerican political art. Moreover, there is reason to think that another monument at Chalcatzingo represents a female ruler or perhaps the same one. In Monument 1 a woman is depicted seated in the mouth of an earth monster cave. She holds an elaborate ceremonial bar of the sort elsewhere associated with rulers, and she is surrounded by clouds, rain, and vegetation. Although generally referred to as El Rey (The King), this figure should be called La Reina (The Queen) because she is wearing women's clothing. In the domestic refuse of the elites at Chalcatzingo, there are numerous small clay figurines showing naked females with fancy headdresses and other ornaments that have been studied by Ann Cyphers Guillen. The small figures seem to represent various stages in the life cycle of females. Although the interpretation of figurines is always speculative, it seems probable that between 700 and 500 B.C. groups of kinswomen celebrated life-crisis rituals in areas where food was processed, including ceremonial food such as dog meat. These rituals may have enhanced the social integration of the group and propagated a social ideology that facilitated women's work. However, female-directed ceremonial activity also may have allowed elite individuals to extend their social relations and engage in reciprocal and competitive exchanges that were avenues to the development of power and influence in the community. Certainly highly ranked women, as well as men, were concerned with sociopolitics at Chalcatzingo.

Numerous male rulers were celebrated in Olmec monuments, but some women also held power in other Preclassic period complex societies of Mesoamerica. During the subsequent Classic period, evidence of female rulers also is abundant. Some of the best data come from the Maya, both because of their realistic art style and because the Maya wrote their own history, which can be read, with difficulty.

## The Queens of Palenque

Female rulers are most abundantly documented at the site of Palenque in southern Mexico, where the royal line itself was descended from a mythical female ancestor ("Lady Beastie"). Among the historic rulers of the site are three queens, two of whom were definitely queens regnant. The first of these, Kanal Ikal, came to power in A.D. 583, ruling until A.D. 604.

Little is known of her reign, and her husband is not mentioned in the known inscriptions referring to the queen. The reason for this is clear. In a patrilineal system, when nature does not cooperate, a daughter succeeds, and her children belong to her patrilineage. Patrilineal systems around the world have the means built into them for managing any eventuality. In England, Elizabeth II succeeded her father in the absence of a brother, and her offspring by an in-marrying elite male bear her family name, not his. In some variations on this theme, a son-in-law might actually hold power, especially if he were closely related to his royal wife. We see this happening in, for example, Agamemnon's marriage to Clytemnestra and his assumption of the role of warrior chief. In all instances, however, the children belong to the wife's patrilineage and succeed just as if she were male. The husband of Kanal Ikal, however, did not rule and was not named as an ancestor by later rulers.

The second queen regnant of Palenque was Zak Kuk, who ruled for at least three years beginning in A.D. 612. Zak Kuk was the granddaughter of Kanal Ikal, succeeding her paternal uncle. Zak Kuk is recorded on a number of monuments, including the sarcophagus of her son Pacal II, buried in an elaborate tomb under the Temple of the Inscriptions. In 1965 a tomb was found in the adjoining pyramid. In it was a middle-aged woman in a plain stone sarcophagus covered with red pigment. It is surmised that this is Zak Kuk's tomb. Zak Kuk was an impressive woman (fig. 8.4). Her portraits show that she may have suffered from agromegaly, a condition that in its most visible characteristic leads to the enlargement of the face. Pacal recorded the name of his father on his sarcophagus, but nothing further is known of this man, who did not rule. We know that Zak Kuk associated her son Pacal with herself on the throne and that Pacal also married his full sister, a means of keeping the throne within the immediate family. We do not know if the third queen, Ahpo Hel, like England's Mary II, was titular coruler or if she was actively involved in governance. Pacal, like most Maya rulers, is concerned only with himself and his lineage on his monuments. His son, Chan Bahlum, names Ahpo Hel as his mother, but does not elaborate.

Palenque was the first site to receive intensive epigraphic attention, but the story of the queens of Palenque has suffered from the lack of understanding concerning kinship and inheritance on the part of the people who decipher ancient inscriptions and attempt to read Maya

FIGURE 8.4. ■ Zak Kuk, queen of Palenque, is shown after her death and in her grave clothes, presenting insignia of accession to the throne to her grandson Chan Bahlum.

history. In other cases, monuments and inscriptions referring to women have been ignored, such as the Altar Vase, or the figures of women have been interpreted as transvestites, as with Stela H at Copán, Honduras, a figure of a woman in elaborate netted ceremonial garments. Maya scholarship has been slow in celebrating its noblewomen and their deeds, but close scrutiny of the indigenous histories of other Mesoamerican groups reveals that there were women rulers even in the most aggressive and androcentric societies.

## Warrior Queens of Southern Mexico

The Mexican state of Oaxaca has been inhabited by the Mixtec and Zapotec peoples since at least the second millennium B.C. These closely related peoples formed (and form) a unique cultural grouping within Mesoamerica in terms of their languages, religious and political ideologies, art, and architecture. Traditionally the Zapotec were found in the large valley of Oaxaca. The Mixtec dominated western Oaxaca, where they lived in small settlements grouped into several small states, each one ruled by a supreme authority, the king or queen, who inherited her or his titles from a parent who was also a ruler.

Mixtec society was characterized by distinct social classes and highly structured social relations. Outside the family context, class status was more important than kinship in governing social interactions. In each Mixtec kingdom, descent was more important than sex in passing on the right to rule. To be a ruler, a person had to be the child of a ruler; nevertheless, the members of the ruling families and their supporters struggled constantly for power, making political life convoluted and unstable. Royal marriage was a crucial part of politics. Members of the royal caste only married other royals, Mixtec or Zapotec. In these marriages both wife and husband retained their own lands, titles, and obligations, and both wife and husband named an heir to her or his titles and kingdoms. In the naming of an heir, there was a tendency to favor male over female, yet daughters often succeeded, even when they had male siblings.

The earliest evidence we have of power politics in Oaxaca shows women as well as men occupying ruling positions. In the late centuries B.C., the rulers of Monte Albán, on a ridge above the modern capital of the state of Oaxaca, were carving a large kingdom out of their neighbors' realms. Their conquests were celebrated on a series of carved stone slabs, the Danzantes, so called because of the dancelike positions of the figures on them. Each of these monuments apparently represents a conquest and the concomitant sacrifice of the ruler of the polity. Of the 300 carved slabs at Monte Albán, at least 2 depict women (fig. 8.5). Female figures also appear on later dynastic monuments from Monte Albán. A newly discovered relief carving portrays a procession of royal women, and a stone stela celebrates Lady 12N as she passes the throne to her son. Both of these monuments were found on the North Platform, near the royal palace of the ancient city. This and other evidence from the Preclassic and Classic periods suggests that the system of inheritance and use of power known from the painted books of the late prehispanic Mixtec had deep roots in southern Mexico.

Mixtec books are another source of information about power. Although these books have been extravagantly interpreted as recording myth and arcane ritual, they appear to be the genealogies of specific families. Historical data from the Mixtec indicate that ruling and noble families kept these written records of their ancestors to support their right to position and wealth. One of these documents, the *Codex Selden*, records in its first six pages the story of a famous ruler whose ascent to power, military victories, political prowess, and final capture and sacrifice by another Mixtec ruler led to her being revered as an important ancestress.

Six Monkey Serpent Quechquemitl was the daughter of Lady Nine Wind Flint Quechquemitl, the ruler of Belching Mountain (modern Magdalena Jaltepeque). Lady Nine Wind is shown offering copal incense to a bundle (perhaps one of her ancestors) in front of the temple of Magdalena Jaltepeque. This ritual, which her two predecessors also performed, marked her ascension to the throne. After this she formally married. Since her daughter also waited to marry until she had taken possession of her inheritance, this may have been politically important in signifying sole rulership of a state. Lady Nine Wind and her husband had a daughter and three sons. The sons lived to adulthood but were all killed, sacrificed after a losing battle.

Although Alfonso Caso and others have suggested that Six Monkey was heiress by default, there is every reason to consider that she was the designated heir all along. She appears as the main protagonist in the text, and she is depicted discussing her impending inheritance with an important

FIGURE 8.5. ■ The Danzante figures, carved on stone slabs at Monte Albán, represent vanquished rulers of Preclassic Oaxaca. Although most of the figures are males, this one (D-6) represents a female ruler with long pigtails.

FIGURE 8.6. ■ Six Monkey Serpent Quechquemitl consults with another female head of state, Nine Grass Death, at the ancient Mixtec site of Skull, soliciting support for her war against two rulers who insulted her.

religious figure. She did not take the throne for some time, although she was apparently formally recognized as heiress, because eight years after her brothers were sacrificed, her father had to defend Magdalena Jaltepeque against an attack by his wife's brother. This battle was part of a larger dynastic dispute in a neighboring kingdom. In the wake of this turmoil, Six Monkey was advised by an elderly priest to undertake a round of diplomatic fence-mending. The text indicates that she first consulted with another religious potentate. The interview took place in a cave, and, as part of the discussion or ritual, Six Monkey visited the underworld (or the burial place of the ancestors). She and her fiancé also visited the ruler of Skull, Nine Grass Death, an important female religious potentate, and brought her lavish presents. This was apparently a summit meeting of some importance, because it is recorded in a number of Mixtec books, in all of which Six Monkey is clearly the protagonist, not her husband. The result of this meeting was a dance ritual in which Six Monkey took part, and finally she and her fiancé had an official wedding.

The next year Six Monkey made diplomatic visits to two neighboring lords. Not only was no agreement reached, but these two lords insulted Six Monkey. Enraged, she went to seek advice from Nine Grass Death at Skull, arranging the participation of warriors from Skull and another town in the impending conflict (fig. 8.6). She and her allies then proceeded to make war on the two lords. Six Monkey is shown in the *Codex Selden* leading the troops and making the captures herself. She is identified by name and is shown, in her woman's clothing, in the standard pose of winning the battle and taking prisoners, with spear and spear thrower at the ready, grasping the loser's forelock. Six Monkey burned the captured towns and sacrificed the insulting lords, one at Jaltepeque and the other at one of the other towns she had inherited. In celebration of her great victory she received a new name, Six Monkey Warpath Quechquemitl, and her blouse ever after is shown with a design that indicates battle.

The rest of Six Monkey's life was not as adventurous. She had a number of children and presumably carried out the normal life of a ruler, presiding over diplomatic events, ceremonies, and caring for her lands and people. Her military career continued, and in the fullness of time, Six Monkey Warpath got into a war with Eight Deer Ocelot Claw of Tilantongo. This time she lost the battle and, like the far earlier rulers shown in the Danzante bas-reliefs, ended up on the altar herself.

Six Monkey's career parallels that of other Mixtec rulers. Her story is told in detail because she was an important member of the ruling family of Jaltepeque, revered as an ancestress and a person who did mighty deeds.

In hierarchical societies, power, economic and political, is seldom restricted to members of one sex. Despite the androcentric assumption that women are mere pawns, it is evident that high-born women often achieve positions of power in both public and private spheres.


## The Aztec Queens

The Aztec of the Valley of Mexico are famous as an extremely militaristic, male-centered society. Their chief religious icon was a god of war. Histories of the kingdom of Tenochtitlán stress the succession of male rulers and the battles and victories of male warriors. Yet careful reading of historical texts, Aztec picture documents, and the archaeological record together permit a reconstruction of Aztec society that includes women. The Nahua-speaking ancestors of the Aztecs were hunter-gatherers who arrived in central Mexico from the desert north. They began their rise to power by negotiating marriage alliances between their chiefs and female scions of the civilized agricultural people of the Valley of Mexico. The Aztec dynasty was the result of the marriage of such a leader with a Colhua princess named Ilancuitl or Atotoztli. Later, Moctezuma I was succeeded by a daughter, also named Atotoztli, who may have become *tlatoani* (speaker or emperor) herself. Some Franciscan texts say she did, although her husband Tezozomoc is more commonly mentioned as having become *tlatoani* through his marriage to Atotoztli. Tezozomoc was her paternal great uncle's son and the son of a previous *tlatoani* himself. Hence, Atotoztli's marriage to a member of the Tenochtitlán ruling lineage kept power within the family, and she played a key role in dynastic politics whether she ruled alone for a time or not. It is certain that she carried the right to the throne in her person because her three sons by Tezozomoc became *tlatoanis* in turn.

Although some historians have questioned the reality of the two Atotoztlis, they have not impugned the historical validity of their fathers, brothers, husbands, and male children. In another case, there is no problem with the veracity of the story of the last Aztec queen, Tecuichpo, the legitimate offspring of Moctezuma II, later known as Doña Isabel de Moctezuma (fig. 8.7). She survived the upheavals of the Conquest, was cared for by Cortés himself, and died in 1551. Her career illustrates how a resourceful royal lady may have manipulated the system both before and after the European takeover.

Tecuichpo seems to have been more important to the Spaniards and the Aztecs than her brother, who also survived into the Colonial period. She apparently married the last real ruler of Tenochtitlán, the ill-fated Cuauhtemoc, also a distant cousin to her and a good general. She thus validated Cuauhtemoc's right to lead at a time in which the Aztecs needed a ruler who was legitimate in the eyes of all the noble factions. Cuauhtemoc, of course, did not survive his acquaintance with the Spaniards, and his widow proceeded to marry a series of Spaniards to keep the family property. These husbands aided her in lawsuits. The Spanish courts agreed that the property belonged to her and not her brother. Other noble and royal women also undertook litigation. These ladies were not passive pawns of their male relatives or the conquering Spaniards. They were reared in the full knowledge of their own superiority, and they had experience in Aztec power politics. In the Mexican Colonial period, because of the prejudices of the European system, the ancient roles of women in politics and religion were largely lost.

FIGURE 8.7. ■ The surrender of Cuauhtemoc to Cortés, recorded in this
early Colonial painted manuscript, was attended by two important women of the
Conquest period. Doña Marina (far left) served as translator for Cortés, and
Tecuichpo (top, second from right) observed from nearby. She is the only figure
in the painting identified by a name glyph (the three elements painted in front
of her face are her name, Lord's Daughter).

## Seeking Women in the Earlier Complex Societies of Peru

Given that contemporary feminist theory indicates that women lose status,
personal autonomy, and access to power in complex societies, it is worth
looking at the evidence of women's roles in the earliest complex societies
in ancient Peru, which appeared in the second millennium B.C.

Studies of religious iconography in ancient Peru indicate the importance of female deities, often paired with male ones, from the Early Horizon onward. It is less sure whether women figured among the political and religious leaders of the Early Horizon. From the site of Kuntur Wasi in northern highland Peru, there is only tantalizing evidence. Among five extraordinary tombs in the Central Platform of this site was the burial of an elite woman over sixty years of age. The other tombs contained the skeletons of middle-aged or elderly males. The woman was buried seated, with an application of cinnabar around her head. Her offerings were different from those of the males: a gold pendant, a gold necklace of twenty-five flat, bird-shaped plates, necklaces made up of hundreds of green stone, lapis lazuli, stone, and *Spondylus* beads, and a pendant of turquoise—all exotic materials. She also had a small marble vase, a ceramic stirrup bottle, and two ceramic cups. These offerings are approximately equal in value to those with two of the males buried in the same precinct. The location of the tomb and its richness suggest that this woman was of considerable importance, although her social role has not been reconstructed.

Later, in the same highland region, the ceramics of the Early Intermediate period Recuay culture reveal a world in which there were important roles for women. Joan Gero's studies of the iconography of elaborately modeled and painted Recuay mortuary ceramics demonstrate that representations of humans are strongly differentiated by gender. Only men wear ear spools, fancy headdresses, and loincloths. Women can be identified by their head cloths and dresses fastened with long pins with decorative heads, called *tupus*, which are still used by women who wear traditional garments.

Recuay ceramics depict individual women wearing rich garments, often holding cups (fig. 8.8). Less often, they are portrayed as small rigid figures surrounding a larger male figure. Other vessels show a richly attired female copulating with a similarly dressed male, which Joan Gero interprets as a representation of ritual sex (see fig. 7.15). Both kinds of vessels indicate that women of high rank had ritual roles in Recuay society, even if these vessels represent the visualization of myths or legends. Other vessels show men and women participating in feasts and other activities. In many instances, the male personage in the central position is larger than both the female and male figures surrounding him. This contrast in size is an indication of differences in social rank. There were powerful men in Recuay society, but Gero has suggested that in real life families threw

FIGURE 8.8. ■ This anthropomorphic ceramic jar in the Recuay style shows a prominent female whose dress is pinned at the shoulders by large *tupus*.

feasts as part of a strategy for building and holding power and that women were key participants in furthering the political ambitions of their families. She has interpreted archaeological remains from the elite residential site of Queyash Alto as evidence of ritual feasts in which people consumed quantities of grilled llama meat and maize beer. Presumably the event was prepared and presented by the family of a regional political leader for members of the community or some constituency. The archaeological remains in this hilltop feasting site included quantities of Recuay-style serving pottery, brewing equipment, imported obsidian artifacts, flutes and panpipes, and figurines. Because metal *tupus*, mother-of-pearl ornaments, and weaving implements, items associated with the female gender, also were present, Gero hypothesized that women collaborated with men to gain and maintain political and religious authority. Women apparently shared prestige and high status with male relatives, but they may have customarily deferred to men or were subordinate to them in public contexts. This does not obviate the possibility that Recuay women were powerful in their own realms, producing the food, beer, and craft items necessary for the success of their kin group in politics, ritual, and warfare.

## Inca Women

The most detailed information on women's place in Andean social and political structures comes from accounts written in the sixteenth century. Because of the immediate impact of the European conquest, these histories are as difficult to interpret as archaeological remains. Pre-Inca societies in Peru may have been relatively egalitarian and gender balanced, according to some scholars, but since many ancient peoples, long before the Inca, lived in complex societies, surely they were constrained by social hierarchies. The role of women, however, may have been compromised with the rise of the Inca state. In Irene Silverblatt's book on the Inca and Colonial periods, she argues that Inca hegemony meant increased suffering for women and men, and that the subordination of women that was part of the Inca state strategy was exacerbated by the ideology and legal systems imposed by the Spanish government.

Among the Inca, and many of the peoples they conquered, groups of bilaterally related kindred were organized into communities called *ayllus* that were ideally endogamous and controlled the land needed for their own support. Within the *ayllu* women and men owned their own equipment and personal effects and had usufruct over specific portions of land. Inheritance in a society in which tasks are highly gendered is, of course, from woman to daughters or other female relatives, and from man to sons or other male relatives. Inheritance of position was mildly patrilineal: sons sometimes inherited their father's position in the social and political hierarchy. However, women could and did retain land in their natal *ayllu*, even if they married outside it. Men often joined their wives in working her land if they lacked access to resources in their own *ayllu*. A woman also could ask brothers or other kin to work her land if she lived too far away to do so herself, or, if widowed, she could return to her own *ayllu* with her children.

Females had status in Andean life because of their control of land and real property and their roles in production and religion. Women took full part in religious rituals, and many of the shrines were female or associated with females. Most *ayllu* or ethnic ancestors came in female-male pairs, and gender complementarity was often expressed in social and political activities.

The chronicles record, for example, the participation of elite women in the rituals of the second month, called Camay. All the kin groups of Cuzco contributed sets of red and white clothing for a burnt sacrifice. The participants also had new black clothing for the ritual. All this clothing was made by women. Later they took a large multicolored rope from a building next to the Temple of the Sun and danced with it, women on one side of the rope and men on the other, moving around the square and executing figures as they danced in their special costumes. Women retained status under the Inca because they produced the goods necessary for rituals. In Inca culture women spun and wove the textiles that were the material expression and the tool of social life and politics. Textiles were worn as markers of ethnicity and social position, they clothed the dead, and they were a focal part of funerary ceremonies and ancestor worship. Textiles were the most prized commodities given as gifts in weddings, alliances, treaties, and initiations, and, as symbols of these events, they were sacrificed in quantities to the gods and shrines. Both ordinary and elite women spun and wove for their families and for tribute. Women also made maize beer, *chicha*, which was used in virtually every religious ritual and which formed an indispensable element in political activities at the level of family, community, and state. Elite women, religious women (*acllas*), and peasant women alike brewed *chicha* and thus made possible the celebration of rituals and the achievement of ritual intoxication—important in Inca religious and political life. In Inca contexts feeding one's kin, feeding others, and feeding the dead were valued and central activities, symbolically charged, and part of women's responsibility, identity, and status.

Women's centrality in the production of textiles, *chicha*, and food was certainly part of their identity in humble and elite contexts. We imagine that elite women also may have wielded considerable power through their wealth and kinship ties. Theresa Topic has carefully garnered information from the chronicles about the activities of elite women. Because of their mobility, she infers that they enjoyed a considerable degree of autonomy. She notes that before marriage the sisters and daughters of nobles and local-level lords traveled regularly with the Inca army. They spent the evenings singing, dancing, and in other amusements with the soldiers. Other elite women had interesting public lives, traveling to visit relatives, attend shrines and festivals, and administer their own estates.

The most powerful woman in the Inca Empire was the *coya*, or principal wife of the ruling Inca, who was often his full sister. Since the Sapa Inca was supposed to be the divine son of the sun god, only his full sisters could be as divine as himself, and, beginning with Topa Inca, the ruler married his full sister to get fully divine heirs. The sisters apparently had some choice in the matter. Huayna Capac's first *coya*, Cusi Rimay, died in childbirth, but his second sister decided to pursue a life as a *mamacona*, so the Inca married his three other full sisters. The political reason for sister-brother marriage in the ruling couple was more mundane. Although the later Inca rulers attempted to name their heirs and associate them as corulers, there was no principle of primogeniture, so circumscribing the number of people who could be legitimate heirs helped to assure a peaceful succession. This strategy for preserving the divinity of the royal line and limiting the pool of heirs is seen in many other cultures of the world.

The Inca had only one *coya*, unless the first bore no children or only daughters (except for Huayna Capac, who married a number of his sisters). In this situation a second sister or even a third would be married as co-*coya*. The Inca's daughters were also married to cement alliances.

---

When Pachacuti lay on his deathbed, he summoned all his unmarried daughters and bestowed them upon their brothers, Inca nobles in Cuzco, and upon provincial lords. Presumably he was acting upon a plan, marrying the women to men who would support his chosen heir. The Inca himself took secondary wives in abundance, many of them *acllas*, others the daughters of local lords whose lands he had conquered. These women were brought to Cuzco, but when they produced a son they often returned to their home communities to assume important positions in local government. Garcilaso mentions one of these women, a secondary wife of Topa Inca, who was living in Chachapoyas at the time of a local rebellion against the Inca. Normally the punishment for rebellion was death to all involved, but this woman was asked by the leaders of the rebellion to plead for clemency from the Inca. Accompanied by a large retinue of local women, she approached the Inca, asked his pardon, and received it.

*Coyas*, like other women, had responsibilities and public lives. The *coya* was in charge of the Cuzco *acllahuasi* and regularly made inspections. *Coyas* must have taken part in the great public ceremonies in Cuzco and at other royal residences. They were also on the road a lot, visiting their own estates and traveling with their husbands (fig. 8.9). Some sources say that the coya was the ruler of the feminine half of the empire and the regent for the Inca when he was absent from Cuzco. If so, *coyas* must have had councils of advisors and well as large retinues of servants to administer their property, including the property that they shared with their husband. However, the fact that Incas tended to leave brothers in control of the empire when they were out on the road mitigates claims of female rule. In fact, the two recorded instances of a *coya* participating in military and diplomatic activities are both tales in which she asks favors of the Inca. Both stories involve Mama Occllo, a daughter of the Sun venerated by her husband and her children, who traveled all the time with her husband as he went about establishing and consolidating the empire. In one situation the Inca wanted to march his army through the Cañete Valley, ruled by the widow of the previous (male) ruler. She demurred, knowing full well what would happen. Then Mama Occllo presented a plan, and she herself met with the ruler of Cañete and persuaded her to hold a celebration on rafts in the sea with all her people and her army. While they were so engaged, the Inca army occupied the valley. The Inca

WOMEN IN ANCIENT AMERICA

FIGURE 8.9. ■ In this sixteenth-century drawing by Guaman Poma, the Inca and the Coya are being carried in a sedan chair. Elite women accompanied their husbands, even on missions of conquest, and they traveled alone to administer their estates and take care of other important business.

praised his wife's strategy and caused the generals and officers of Cañete to surrender to the *coya* herself. This, and other stories, show the *coya*'s influence and acumen, but not her power. Even a strong *coya*, such as Mama Occllo, who was well situated because of birth and marriage and who had the ear of her powerful husband, may have had no established temporal powers. The dual organization by gender of the Inca Empire was not a political reality, despite the wishful thinking of some feminist scholars.

We know, however, that *coyas* had religious authority and were held in great respect by their kin. Huayna Capac so venerated his mother, Mama Occllo, that he dedicated to her at Tomebamba, his palace in southern Ecuador, an amazing room decorated with *Spondylus* shells, gold, and rock crystals. A gold statue of Mama Occllo, containing the afterbirth of Huayna Capac, was set up in this room and worshipped as a deity, even though the *coya* herself was still alive.

When an Inca ruler died, state ceremonies, complete with elaborate sacrifices, were carried out. Some of the Inca's concubines and even secondary wives volunteered to accompany the Inca in death, but this did not seem to be the fate of the *coya*. When she died, her body was treated in same manner as that of the Inca, wrapped in rich textiles with the face covered over, and then placed with her husband's body in the palace that they had shared in life. The bodies of the Inca, the *coya*, and other important persons were not buried but curated and taken out on occasion. Most of the embalmed corpses of the Incas and *coyas* were still extant at the time of the Conquest, kept in their palaces, moved to other houses and estates with the seasons, and cared for by their *ayllu*, which had become a *panaca*, a royal corporation charged with the care of the dead Inca and *coya* and their estates. Thus gender equality and complementarity were expressed in death.

The few glimpses we have of the *coyas* through Spanish documents indicate that they were strong women who played direct roles in government and ritual (the two were not separate in the Inca state). They also managed estates and vast retinues of servants and traveled with their husbands and alone in their managerial capacity and as a representative of the state religion in ceremonies about the empire. One can imagine the strength of character and the influence these women had on imperial policy, whether or not they always took a direct public role.

WOMEN IN ANCIENT AMERICA

## The Future of Power

There is no denying that in late prehistory, many human groups chose strategies that, while proving beneficial for the survival of their societies, resulted in the loss of ideologies and social organizations that were more favorable to women. In recent times societies characterized by hierarchical and centralized forms of organization, decision making concentrated in the hands of male political leaders and armies, and pervasive ideologies of male dominance have been successful in competing with other societies and achieving great size and political prominence. This kind of society, while common today, has not always existed and probably will be modified as circumstances change. As David Gilmore has explained, the ubiquitous phenomenon of male dominance is not predicated on male biology but is rather a practical cultural device that may have outlasted its usefulness. In the future, as sociocultural systems change, the most competitively advantaged and successful societies will be different from what we see in the world today. Although some people promote stronger male leadership and female subordination as solutions to problems in our own society, others are eager to adopt new technological, social, and ideological strategies that will in the future result in sociocultural systems that are more heterarchical and gender inclusive. The archaeological record encourages our efforts to promote female participation in social processes of change because it shows that through most of human history women were neither excluded nor subordinated. Women's authority in decision making and leadership was and still is very great in domestic and small community contexts, but in the later part of history, as some complex societies emerged, men acquired prominent roles in the political, economic, and religious institutions constituted at high levels of organization. Warfare may have been one of the causes of the worsening of women's conditions in later prehistory, although bellicose conditions also may offer some women opportunities to change their social status and acquire power and authority.

# CHAPTER NINE

# Women, War, and Conquest

Female and male individuals, as well as groups, gain power and prestige by exploiting their kin relations, manipulating ideology, and controlling natural, social, and supernatural resources. People also pursue power strategies involving physical coercion. Scholars view warfare as one of the important causes of culture change in both the short and long term. The origin of social and political hierarchy is often thought to lie in the violent extension of hegemony of one group of people over another. Viewed cross-culturally, women are supporters, perpetrators, and victims of warfare, but they only rarely take prominent roles in it.

Warfare is often related to status seeking and serves as a male rite of passage. Going to war turns boys into men even in modern societies. In many societies charismatic leaders and hereditary rulers show their fitness by their prowess in warfare. Thus among the Aztecs and Maya a new ruler was expected to instigate a raid for captives to sacrifice in celebration of his accession. When men are actively engaged in the planning and carrying out of military activities, women may adopt a variety of participatory and supportive roles, and frequently their lives are affected profoundly.

Stories of "Amazon" battalions are part of Eurasian and African folklore and history that do not appear in Native American legends. No great war chiefs such as Boudicca or Joan of Arc are revered as national folkloric or religious heroines among Native Americans, but there is considerable evidence that women took part in bellicose activities. Archaeology and art history supply some examples, but most cases are historical.

The prehistoric evidence of warfare is stronger in those periods when larger tribal groups replaced bands of foragers. Some tribal peoples developed competitive social strategies. In some groups, every male was socialized as a warrior.

Archaeologically this pattern is reflected in burial assemblages and the appearance of war gods in the iconography of ancient peoples. Sometimes archaeologists find that females are more numerous in excavated cemeteries, presumably because so many of the males of fighting age died away from home. In other cases, victorious warriors seem to have been buried in special mortuary facilities. At Sitio Conte in Panama, 75 of 100 high-status tombs dating to around A.D. 500 contained male skeletons, and all but one of the females were interred with adult men. Similarly a Mississippian elite cemetery at Moundville (A.D. 1200–1500) contained a very large number of males whose bones showed war injuries and who were accompanied by high-status goods. In historic chiefdoms, warfare was generally a pursuit of chiefs who managed several tiers of leadership and elaborate systems of insignia. In these hierarchical societies, the elite were in charge of the prewar rituals designed to buttress the authority of the chief. Chiefly warfare could be organized on a large or small scale, but it was aimed at near neighbors. Chiefly warfare often caused populations to concentrate in nucleated centers and construct defensible communities and systems of fortifications. Hostilities that provided a route for individuals to gain status and acquire victims for sacrifice also were a way for polities to expand their agricultural territory and control trade routes.

In ancient America warriors in tribal groups sought reasons to undertake raids as a principal means of acquiring high social status and magical power. A warring chief could increase and buttress his authority by displaying human trophies, and he might acquire power by consuming the flesh of dead enemies. In ancient art and in historical records, women also manipulated these symbols and feasted on human flesh (fig. 9.1). Moreover, chiefly warfare created the opportunity for warriors to accumulate and symbolize power through postwar rituals of death. Tribal warriors with great reputations as killers might deter retaliation by enemies and protect their communities by their spiritual power.

Although ancient peoples staged ritual battles and represented metaphorical warriors in art, even highly ritualized battles fought for prestige and supernatural power probably had more mundane functions. Even raiding that did *not* result in the extension of hegemony of one group over another could be part of a strategy of competition for land and hunting territory: it served to space the population and allowed some groups to

FIGURE 9.1. ■ A sixteenth-century drawing of Tupinamba women and children eating the entrails of sacrificed prisoners of war.

gain access to labor and resources. Many labor-hungry tribal and chiefly groups gained workers and maintained a positive rate of population growth by kidnapping women and children. This was not a minor part in warfare among settled groups. The Aztec enslaved or kidnapped women and children from groups who refused to send tribute, and the practice of stealing women and children from opposed groups—from indigenous peoples who refuse to admit Christian missionaries or by groups that lack women because of warfare, preferential female infanticide, or predatory neighbors—can be found until today.

## Manly Hearted Women of the Great Plains

In eighteenth- and nineteenth-century Plains Indian culture, rank and status were not hereditary but had to be achieved through participation in aggressive activities. This culture pattern developed when horses and horseback riding were introduced into North America by the early Spanish explorers and colonists of northern Mexico. The Native Americans of the Plains, who had been riverbottom farmers and foot hunters, quickly developed a nomadic hunting way of life in which prowess in the hunt and war were the main means of gaining personal status and wealth. Archaeology demonstrates that war among Plains peoples was nothing new, but the horse, and later the rifle, resulted in the escalation of earlier patterns. Raiding for slaves and horses, even outright massacres, became common as groups vied for control of hunting lands and other resources.

The ideal woman in most Plains societies was a modest, hard-working, and chaste person. Nonetheless, female participation in warfare seems to have been quite common (fig. 9.2). Documents from the mid-1700s onward record the histories of women who joined war parties as warriors. Commonly these women were motivated by desire for revenge against an enemy that had killed a husband or another male kinsman.

The most successful woman warrior known to history was Woman Chief of the Crow. Born a Gros Ventre and captured when she was about twelve, her real father and her adopted Crow father encouraged her interest in manly pursuits and trained her in male skills. Woman Chief dressed as a woman throughout her life, but she pursued the role of a male, successfully hunting large game on foot and horseback and skillfully leading war parties. Her prowess as a warrior was recognized when, later in life, she took a place in the male council and became the third ranking warrior in a band of 160 households. She had four wives whose labor, especially in processing hides for sale to the whites, made her wealthy in the mid-1800s.

Beatrice Medicine, in her 1983 study of sex-role alternatives among Plains women, noted that female warriors were described only briefly in many journals, chronicles, and ethnographies, Nevertheless, the warrior woman role was widespread in North America, found in the Southwest, California, among the northwestern coast groups, and in the Northeast. This is an interesting counterpoint to the traditional Euroamerican pre-

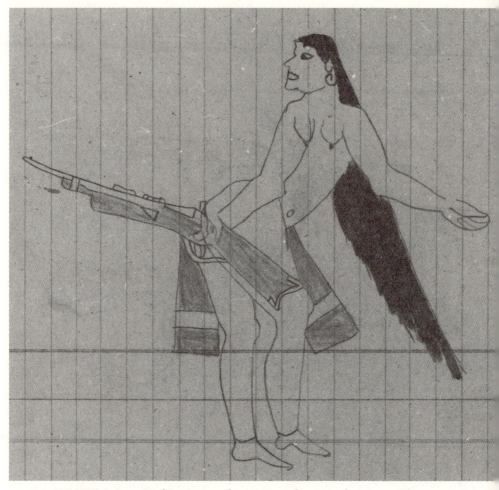

FIGURE 9.2. ■ In this nineteenth-century indigenous drawing, a Cheyenne woman warrior brandishes her rifle.

sentation of these peoples, which stresses the passivity of native women and homogenizes women's roles, emphasizing their victimization.

Although outside observers perceive the Plains Indians societies as male-dominated, Medicine points out that in many groups, Native American women traditionally could achieve prestige, power, and wealth. One of the roles open to women was that called, among the Peigan, "manly hearted woman." This was a woman who excelled in every important aspect of tribal life, including property acquisition and management,

WOMEN IN ANCIENT AMERICA

domestic life, and ceremonials. Medicine notes that manly hearted women often began their lives as favored children, as did Woman Chief, indulged and given more affection and attention than other children, so that these girls developed very high self-esteem. Their fathers encouraged these girls in dominant behavior, and they led in games, played boys' sports, and took names of famous warriors for themselves. Unlike their sisters, they also were sexually aggressive and active from an early age, and this aggressive behavior and high self-esteem led them to work to excel in female and male tasks alike. These were the women who sought wealth and prestige through military activities, gaining high status through their dominant behavior in all aspects of tribal life. The role of manly hearted woman was not, as is sometimes claimed, analogous to the role of male berdache because no gender reversal took place.

While manly hearted women and women warriors are described in historic and ethnographic documents, they have not been identified archaeologically. Archaeologists, however, should be aware that a female skeleton associated with both male and female artifacts might be evidence that a woman played a variety of roles.

On the Great Plains and elsewhere, warfare provided a route for men, and a few women, to accumulate personal prestige, magical power, social influence, knowledge about the world outside the community, and wealth. Men also acquired women, including slaves and second and third wives who presented the possibility of more offspring, another key to prosperity. Men, through wives and offspring, accumulated the labor and the social ties necessary to host feasts, bestow gifts, and build alliances and reciprocal social obligations. Warfare commonly meant social mobility for men and sometimes for women as well.

Although wives joined their husbands in enjoying elite status, wealth, and special burial, the primary routes to power were made for men and not women. Among the earlier societies of ancient America, ideologies that stressed female/male complementarity surely functioned to counterbalance ideologies that associated male gender identity with warfare, but later in prehistory, judging from precolumbian art, male-dominated ideologies of violence were most prominent in public discourse. Among the peoples who developed the first great American civilizations, elite ideologies featured male warrior deities, and the dominance of male leaders grew so that by the middle of the first millennium A.D., warrior men were being celebrated in artistic media all over America. The ideology associated with male military, political, and religious roles gained ascendancy late in prehistory, and metaphors involving creation, nurturance, motherhood, fertility, and sex were progressively deemphasized in public contexts.

## A Lone Female Warrior at Teotihuacán

The earliest tangible evidence of women's physical participation in war is the two women depicted on the Danzante slabs, Preclassic-period monuments found at the urban center of Monte Albán in Oaxaca, Mexico. They were doubtless rulers captured and sacrificed, but it is not certain if they themselves led their people into battle (see fig. 8.5). Five hundred years later, at Teotihuacán, Early Classic warriors are portrayed by artists as male, but one female was identified among the warriors interred beneath the great Temple of Quetzalcoatl. This stepped pyramid was a mortuary monument within the Ciudadela at the heart of the city, sumptuously decorated with painted sculptures of feathered serpents and other creatures. The high-status tomb found looted under the pyramid was flanked by 259 sacrificial burials interred in shallow pits before the construction of the structure. The sacrificed individuals, seated in rows with their hands tied, were young men dressed in elaborate regalia with ornaments of shell and necklaces composed of real human maxillae or shell models of these bones. Obsidian dart points were showered over the young men, who apparently were killed and interred in place. The excavators, who are in agreement concerning the military iconography, have suggested that these victims were soldiers, priestly soldiers, or men disguised as military personages whose function was to protect the sanctuary.

Among the males offered in this sacrifice ritual the investigators identified one female, barely in her teens, dressed in the same manner as the others and wearing the same jewelry. She was interred with a group of 13 young men in the center of a pit. The excavators called her a "priestess," but since the young woman wore military garb and was buried like the young men, it seems more reasonable to infer that she was the equivalent of the others. A major source of sacrificial victims in ancient Mesoamerica was prisoners of war. It seems likely that the young woman was a warrior, recognized as such by her captors, and sacrificed in the same way as her fellow prisoners of war.

Later, in the Late Classic and Postclassic periods in Mesoamerica, there is considerable evidence from artistic representations of political themes that elite women, probably rulers, took an active part in both aggression and defense of their realms.

## The Warrior Queen of Cacaxtla

One of the most amazing archaeological discoveries of the past decades is the mural paintings of Cacaxtla, a small Late Classic mountaintop site in Puebla, Mexico. The murals show a bloody battle between a group of men dressed in jaguar costumes and a group with bird costumes. The jaguar army is winning. The gore of the battle, with spilling intestines and agony on the faces of the wounded, contrasts with the well-dressed arrogance of the leaders of the jaguar men, who probably fought for the ruler of Cacaxtla. Among the warriors, in the heat of battle, stand two women wearing bird emblems, identifying them with the losing side. In addition to back ornaments in the form of wings, each lady wears a triangular *quechquemitl* and a short skirt that reaches just to the top of the knees. The textiles of these garments are richly patterned, and both ladies also wear elaborate leg ornaments, sandals, and jewelry. The importance of these women is shown by the fact that they are the central personages in the murals in which they appear and that the murals themselves stand on either side of the central stair of the building. Although the women are represented as defeated, they dominate the scenes. Sharisse and Geoffrey McCafferty, who have done the only engendered study of these murals, suggest that the two figures represent the same woman. This makes sense given the great similarity of costumes and the fact that the first scene depicts the woman in the height of combat, while the second shows her as a bound captive.

The first woman stands in the midst of the battle, grasping a spear embedded in her cheek. Blood drips from the wound, and she is crying out in anguish while making the traditional hand-to-shoulder gesture of surrender and submission (fig. 9.3a). From the pose of the jaguar warrior who stands in front of her threatening with another spear, this must represent the moment of capture. Her feminine gender is emphasized by the exaggerated curve of waist and hip as well as by her female clothing. The woman in the other mural is also threatened by a jaguar lord, again

a

FIGURES 9.3a and 9.3b. ■ The vanquished warrior queen portrayed in the murals flanking a main stairway at Cacaxtla in central Mexico. In one view (a) she is wounded by an arrow in her cheek; in the other (b) she is shown as a captive with bound hands.

b

seen with a spear in ready position. Her bare torso under the *quechquemitl* is shown, and her hands are held in front of her chest, crossed and tied at the wrist (fig. 9.3b). Clearly she has been taken prisoner and most likely will suffer the usual fate. Who is this woman? Regrettably the figures are not identified with name glyphs, and no place glyphs have been found in the murals. One can surmise that she was the ruler of one of the neighboring states. This period of prehistory was characterized by increased warfare as local groups competed with each other in the vacuum caused by the waning influence of Teotihuacán and resisted the migrations of barbarian northerners into central Mexico.

Some scholars have suggested that these women were really men dressed up to humiliate them, a custom that is not known in precolumbian societies and smacks of Euroamerican schoolboy humor. Other scholars reiterate the suggestion that women warriors are really transvestite ritual performers, analogous to the Aztec Cihuacoatl, a prime minister who took the name of the goddess of agriculture and war and functioned as the emperor's second-in-command. Alternatively, in the spirit of the *Iliad*, the Cacaxtla ladies have been interpreted as female deities represented in scenes from myth. These suggestions are representative of the inclination of many Mesoamerican archaeologists and art historians to deny women active roles in prehistoric societies. In fact, the clothing of the lady in the murals identifies her as a wealthy member of the elite. The short skirt and *quechquemitl* mark her as a central Mexican, not a Maya lady. The central position of the female figure in the battle mural and other details are strong evidence that she was the leader of the enemy bird army in this war.

Women have not yet been identified in battle scenes drawn by the ancient Maya, although sculptured representations and glyphic texts alike make it evident that women occasionally did become sole rulers of polities. Women rulers are shown standing on prisoners, but they are not yet known to appear in the scenes of capturing prisoners that are common depictions of male rulers. These ladies, like modern rulers, may have had a subordinate war chief or general, but the royal ladies took credit for his victories whether or not they actually went onto the battlefield themselves.

Maya elite women did take part in the festivities associated with warfare. The famous murals of Bonampak show the ruler's female relatives letting blood as part of the sacrifices of prisoners honoring the naming of the little heir.

WOMEN IN ANCIENT AMERICA

In the Late Postclassic in the northern Yucatán, warfare fell entirely outside women's spheres, if we can judge from Diego de Landa's description of the culture of the northern Yucatán city-states at the time of the European invasions. He says that each state was served by a hereditary war captain and one who was elected. For the three-year term of his office, this second war captain was forbidden to have anything to do with women, even his wife. He was kept in a state of ritual purity, fed only on fish and iguanas and not permitted to be served by women or mingle with ordinary people. Since warfare was a major means of elevating social and economic status among the Maya, this ideology, which assumed that women were polluting and that sexual behavior had an effect on success in warfare, would have made it more difficult for women to achieve higher position through involvement in military activity.

## Accounts of War in South America

One of the few lengthy accounts of indigenous warfare in South America prior to the major calamities wrought by the European invasion was that of Hans Staden, a German mercenary in the pay of the Portuguese, who was captured by the Tupinamba Indians of coastal Brazil and held captive for some years in the sixteenth century. He describes in great detail the care of prisoners of war by Tupinamba women. Living within a Tupinamba village until his escape, Staden was able to detail the work of women, including their crafts, their participation in ritual, and their roles as shamans. He was most personally concerned, however, with warfare and the ceremonies of sacrifice of prisoners of war. Staden says that when the prisoners were first brought home to the village, the women and children beat them. Then they painted the captives and danced around them. After this each captive was kept in the village, where a woman took on the responsibility of caring for him and having sex with him, although any children would be treated as captives and eventually eaten. Prisoners were well treated and well fed while preparations for sacrifice went on. At the time of the final rituals, the women again painted and decorated the prisoner, singing over him and drinking with him. The women also led the prisoner out for sacrifice and gave him a pile of stones to throw at them while they ran around and threatened to eat him. Despite the major presence of women in the preparation of the sacrifice, the actual killing

---

was done by a man. Once the prisoner was clubbed to death, however, the women took the body to be singed and scraped. After a man had cut it into quarters, women took the pieces, running and singing, to complete the butchering. Women and children were allotted the entrails and internal organs, which were cooked up and consumed communally (see fig. 9.1). Many tropical forest people apparently held similar feasts in the early Colonial period, although not all practiced cannibalism.

In recent times indigenous warfare has been observed among the Yanoami (Yanomamo) Indians of northern Brazil and Venezuela. Anthropologists have described patterns of intense intervillage strife, mitigated by trading between allies who are trading/feasting partners. Yanoami men are raised to be extremely bellicose and violent toward other members of the society. The paramount reason for raiding, according to the participants, is to attain women, although there are probably several practical functions. Anthropologists have observed that epochs of intense fighting interrupt the years of careful negotiations necessary for a man to arrange marriages for his brothers, sons, and himself. This interruption in marriage negotiations leaves villages with a shortage of labor, owing to the practice of a long bride service among the Yanoami.

The autobiography of Helena Valero, a woman captured by the Yanoami in the 1940s, offers a perspective on the lives of women under conditions of escalating tribal warfare, stimulated by conditions of disease and the introduction of machetes and shotguns by white traders. Like Yanoami women, Valero suffered from living in a village without her brothers to protect her. She endured the aggressive abuse of males, and she had to deal with competition among cowives for food and favor.

Valero describes the mixed reception given to captured women by Yanoami wives. On the one hand, the older women welcomed and protected captured women, who represented useful labor and wives for their sons and brothers. The younger women rightly feared loss of favor and tended to torment the prisoners, usually without hindrance from their husbands. Valero's firsthand account shows us how a war captive might acculturate into her new society, negotiating position and even happiness in this hazardous situation. In Valero's narrative, women had inconspicuous roles in war, but in the twentieth century, elaborate war rituals no longer existed among the Yanoami. In other cultures, such as among the Tupinamba, the ritual aspects of warfare must have integrated women into the largely male pursuit of battle and allowed women access to benefits and prestige gained from bellicose activities.

## Warfare in the Ancient Andes

Women warriors do not appear in representational art of the ancient Andes. The first great military-theme artwork, the relief sculptures of Cerro Sechín on the North Coast, shows only males, although it is difficult to identify dismembered body parts. War and warriors are favorite themes in the modeled and painted ceramics of coastal Peruvian cultures as well as in the painted textiles showing nude prisoners from the Late Intermediate period, but as yet, no female figures have been recognized among them.

The absence of females in this art and the magnificence of Andean fortresses, such as Chanquillo and Sacsahuaman, present the idea that ancient Peruvian societies may have been dominated by male warriors. In an alternative view, John Topic and Theresa Lange Topic have argued that the so-called fortifications and military monuments built in the Andean region since the Early Formative were ceremonial centers where ritual battles called *tinku* were staged by related communities or segments of an *ayllu*. Both ancient people and contemporary indigenous Andean people celebrated battles, considered analogous to sexual intercourse, to ensure agricultural increase. Today women join the men in ceremonial battles as part of a ritual cycle. Ritual warfare is compatible with an ideology of gender complementarity, a principle that might have been expressed socially to counterbalance hierarchical social organization and male dominance.

Moche painted ceramics sometimes show the aftermath of battle, and a very few pieces depict what may well be women taking part in the ritual manipulation of severed limbs and other trophies. This conforms to historic data from the tropical lowlands, which suggest that women had roles in the rituals following battle. In Moche art, Lady C is often illustrated in the act of presenting a goblet of blood to a deity, but on some Moche vessels, she cuts the prisoner's throat and collects the blood herself. On other vessels human and bird women feed and touch prisoners about to be sacrificed. The archaeological excavation of sacrificial bodies conducted by Steve Bourget at the Huaca de la Luna demonstrated that the ancient painted vessels accurately depicted the massive prisoner sacrifices of the ancient Moche. Only male bodies were recovered from the excavations, but in other architectural complexes in the Moche site were tombs containing the remains of elite females. The fact that women did not customarily participate in warfare in the later kingdoms of Peru must have made it difficult for them to achieve status and gain authority. Inca accounts tell us that warfare was the main means of gaining and retaining status and a major means of social advancement. Women, because they could not go to war and could not make multiple marriages, were cut off from the gifts of labor, wives, land, and other perquisites given by rulers to the victorious. It is only in exceptional cases, and in some myths, that females were involved in military action. One Inca woman who took part in battle was Chañan Kori Coca. Sarmiento recorded a Colonial-period narrative in which Chañan was the head of *ayllu* Chococchono, now Santiago Parish in Cuzco. She led a troop of *ayllu* warriors against the Chancas, who were advancing on Cuzco. There are no other details concerning her deed, save an eighteenth-century European painting showing her with the iconography of Judith carrying the head of Holofernes: she stands on the decapitated body of a victim and simpers while she holds up a head.

## Winners and Victims

The ubiquity of ancient armed conflict among later indigenous American cultures is evidence that it was positively evaluated and frequently adopted as a strategy. Apparently the people who waged war, presumably the winners, benefited. Bellicosity is known to supply winners with labor (slaves, concubines), sacrificial victims, land, and access to other commodities, but it also is a catalyst in social change that facilitates the development of leadership and other new social and political institutions that may make the system more competitive in the future. Ancient women certainly supported warfare and enjoyed its fruits, as do modern women today.

On the other hand, despite the advantages that accrue to the winners of war, prehistoric women may have been unable to participate in the important social processes initiated by male warriors, and furthermore, they were often the primary victims of war. Those few women who were war leaders or warriors suffered the same fate as their male compatriots. Wounds, death, and sacrifice to the gods of the victors awaited women such as Six Monkey and the ruler of the bird army. Ordinary women also were affected by bellicosity.

More than 200 excavated skeletons from the Norris Farm site in the Illinois River Valley indicate the scope of chronic warfare in that region around A.D. 1300. The remains of 43 women and men showed embedded projectile point fragments, massive skull injuries, penetrating skull wounds caused by ground stone axes, defensive trauma on arms and hands, and mutilations such as scalping and decapitation. Of five women who survived attacks (they had healed injuries), three had been scalped. George Milner and his colleagues reported that five tombs contained individuals of only one sex, three of which held groups of women who may have been surprised while working together away from the village. They suggest that raiding was common and that work parties were sometimes attacked at remote locations, shown by carnivore damage on some skeletons.

The Norris Farm site is not unique. A study of 751 archaeological crania of adult females and males from the Middle Missouri Valley (dating from ca. A.D. 1600 to 1832) shows that women had about as much chance of being scalped as men. Scalping was, of course, the prime means of securing war trophies among the Plains tribes. It has been noted that the incidence of scalping increased with the introduction of steel knives to the Native Americans, but evidence of scalping and the massacre of whole settlements, female, male, aged, and children alike, extends far back into the prehistoric period in North America.

Although many prehistoric groups made trophies from human bodies, only a little archaeological data can be given a gendered interpretation. In Peru in the Early Horizon, there is abundant evidence from the South Coast of head-hunting. Trophy heads appear in art imagery, and burials confirm that people buried some bodies lacking heads, other bodies with additional heads, and caches of disarticulated skulls. Some trophy heads in this area were used fresh: paintings on ceramics show heads gushing blood from the eyes, nose, mouth, and severed neck. Trophy skulls were often prepared by removing the brain and knocking a hole in the forehead so that a carrying strap could be inserted. Helaine Silverman notes that although male trophy heads are in the great majority in the Nazca Valley, female heads are occasionally found as well.

Women in the northern Andes were likewise victims of the endemic warfare and slaving that characterized late prehispanic cultures in that area. Chantal Caillevet has documented how the capture of children for food and sacrifices negatively impacted the northern Andean chiefdoms. Moreover, just as among the Tupinamba, women captured by the tribes in what is now the Department of Antioquia in northern Colombia were impregnated by their captors, and their children were reared to the age of eleven or twelve and then dispatched for meat.

At certain times and places, mortality among noncombatant women and children was very high, especially when people tried to cross frontiers and encroach upon another group's territory. There are abundant archaeological examples of changes in settlement patterns showing that in response to hostile conditions, people sought defensible locations for their villages and constructed fortified sites. Burial and osteological data dramatically illustrate the impact of violent competition. At the Heerwald site in central Oklahoma (late A.D. 1300s), the remains of a young adult female, a fetus of approximately eight months' gestation, and another child were found in an abnormal burial: apparently they had been thrown into the grave. The woman had a stone projectile point embedded in her first lumbar vertebra, and another point was found in her chest cavity. One rib had a deep cut, and another rib and the scapula were damaged from blows just before her death. Finally, the poor woman had been scalped. The child buried with her was missing some long bones and may have been mutilated.

Archaeology and history attest to the central place of warfare, from small-scale raiding to wholesale slaughter, in Plains cultures. To revenge himself a warrior might kill enemy men or women. At the Crow Creek site, where a massacre took place, 90 percent of 500 individuals had been scalped. In the historic period, large-scale slave raids and massacres became very common in the Plains. In the Southwest, massacres at Hopi and Anasazi sites such as Mancos demonstrate that women as well as men were killed and sometimes consumed. Excavations at Tikal and Uaxactún and epigraphic work on the monuments of both places have shown that on January 16, A.D. 378, Maya forces of Tikal, led by the king Great Jaguar Paw and a close associate, Smoking Frog, conquered Uaxactún. The victors chose to exterminate the enemy army instead of taking warriors prisoner for sacrifice or ransom, but the king of Uaxactún was captured, displayed as a prisoner, tortured, and eventually sacrificed. The kings' principal wives, one of whom was pregnant, and two small children were buried alive—thrown into a tomb, sealed up, and left to die.

In central Mexico there is archaeological and historical evidence concerning territorial wars in which massacres of the elite and the enslavement of many of the commoners was the rule. The Aztecs waged wars to secure tribute and gain territory. Negotiations between the Aztecs and the beleaguered might allow the civilian population to avoid violence by increasing their tribute load, but any intransigence or betrayal might provoke the Aztecs to slaughter women and children as well as noncombatant males. Many women, however, ended up as slaves, in part because the growing state had an enormous appetite for cloth, and the rapidly expanding noble class required increased services.

The forcible exploitation of women's labor and the recruitment of women into positions of sexual servitude is a widespread consequence of warfare known in modern times. Moreover, the displacement of women and families by wars also takes a substantial toll on entire communities and their way of life. When the Inca armies moved into the southern Ecuadorian highlands to consolidate their conquest of the Cañari peoples, uprisings by the indigenous folk resulted in tremendous massacres. Spanish sources estimate that a few years later, the sex ratio in this region among the Cañari was fifteen women to one man. The Inca then implemented their *mitima* policy, in which whole villages of people were moved long distances to replace bellicose peoples. Some Cañari were, in fact, forced to move to Cuzco in southern Peru, a linear distance of over 1,500 kilometers, while large numbers of Inca and non-Inca people from Peru were moved into southern Ecuador, where they still live, speaking Quechua, the language of the Inca. Unlike refugees, *mitimas* had no hope of returning to their native land.

These are the more dramatic consequences of waging war. In wartime, prehistoric women, like modern women, surely felt the increased workload. Women often have to carry out basic production while men are engaged in war. In this sense, female labor underwrites the process of arming, equipping, feeding, and deploying raiding parties and armies. Historic Iroquois women, by withholding supplies of the food that they controlled, could effectively veto plans made by men to wage war. The feminine half of the society is often called upon to fill in for missing male kinsmen and continues to shoulder the burden when they are killed. They pick up the pieces after losing, and they enjoy the benefits of winning.

## The Impact of Conquest

The European conquest of the Americas, widely recognized as having tragic consequences for native peoples and cultures, was especially disastrous for Native American women. The conquerors successfully imposed their own systems of religion, land tenure, leadership, and gender roles upon many American peoples, denying women many of the opportunities and rights that had been available to them in indigenous societies. The Conquest destroyed some of the parallel institutions controlled by women, and women lost virtually all public and remunerative roles once available to them. For example, female administrators in the Aztec markets disappeared, and feminine cults were suppressed. In Peru, Spanish officials refused to deal with women rulers, and because of disapproval by the church, female musicians disappeared from their roles in public rituals.

In the first years of the European invasions, women, in many ways more than men, bore the brunt of the Conquest. Many women were simply violated and left to die or passed on as slaves to the next man. We read uneasily the accounts of Pedro de Cieza de León, one of the major chroniclers of the Spanish conquests of Andean South America, as he classifies the women of different ethnic groups that his gang of soldiers encountered into groups, some of which are ranked as more attractive and willing than others. Women were torn from their homes and families and forced to accompany the soldiers to cook and clean for them as well as serve as their sexual partners. Accounts of the female conscripts who accompanied the invading armies emphasize that the women had bleeding hands and died quickly from overwork because the Spaniards misunderstood the amount of labor required to grind corn. When the epidemics introduced by Europeans began, pregnant women were most vulnerable, and the women who survived lost many children and other relatives. Despite the decimation of families and the loss of labor power, women often were forced by occupying forces to produce the same quantity of tribute goods as in aboriginal times.

Few detailed accounts of the sexual violation and abuse of ordinary indigenous women exist. Still, it is easy to imagine their fate based on the better-documented experiences of high-caste women.

## The Lady of Cofachiqui

In the 1590s Garcilaso de la Vega recorded interviews with survivors of the Hernando de Soto expedition in the southeastern United States. While in Florida, where he and his men unwittingly started the first of the great epidemics that eventually felled the Mississippian kingdoms, the expedition was involved in pillage, vandalism, and rape on a large scale. When De Soto heard about the teenage woman ruler of the Cofachiqui kingdom, he demanded to see her. The Spaniards had already robbed the charnel house where her relatives' bodies were stored, helping themselves to the metal, pearls, and other wealth accompanying the bodies. The Lady of Cofachiqui appeared in great state, in a large canoe attended by eight noblewomen and pulled by another canoe, which carried many rowers and six noblemen. She tried to reason with the Spaniards, telling them that the scourges of the past year had taken toll of the available food. Although the lady offered them substantial supplies and valuables, they kidnapped her. There is no record of her immediate fate, but the lady was enterprising and escaped her captors some days later, taking with her a chest of pearls. The Spaniards never could force any of her subjects to disclose her whereabouts, and she was never recaptured.

## The Maligned Doña Marina

In contrast, Doña Marina was enslaved in Mexico as a laborer and concubine by her own people and then by the Spaniards. Like the Lady of Cofachiqui, her aboriginal name has not been recorded, even though she was one of the key players in the European conquest of Mexico. The Spaniards baptized her Marina, and the indigenous people who came in contact with her called her Doña Marina or Malintzin (her name with the Aztec honorific equivalent to *doña*, "lady"). A native of Veracruz, she had been sold to the Maya, but when the Europeans arrived, she was sold or stolen again as a worker and sex object. The Spaniard who acquired her observed her linguistic genius, and Cortés himself took her as a concubine and interpreter. Marina traveled with the Spaniards, serving Cortés in both capacities, and eventually bearing him a son. When the baby was very young, Cortés passed Marina to a colleague who was going off to invade the Yucatán. In the course of this strenuous campaign, she became pregnant by her current master, bore a child, and died a month later from the childbirth. Although Doña Marina was a helpless slave, forced to sexually service each of her owners, tragically dead to her own people, and with no one to protect or help her, she has been excoriated in Mexican history. Later writers have labeled her La Chingada in an ugly attempt to transfer the guilt of the men who bought, sold, and used her to the lady herself. This is clear misogyny: a women who is defiled need not be interpreted as villainous, and Doña Marina certainly cannot be blamed for the conquest of Mexico.

The Lady of Cofachiqui was a ruler and, presumably, had the help of her subjects in escaping, since she was never found. Marina had no place to go. She was a slave, and wherever she went, she would have been in the same situation, with the added threat that slaves were usually sacrificed when they outlived their usefulness. Other women, if wealthy, were married off to Spanish soldiers as prizes. In Mexico, Tecuichpo, who was raped and impregnated by Cortés, later creatively used her marital alliances to keep control of her family estates. Ordinary women were sometimes married, more often forced to become concubines if not simply abandoned with the results of their victimization.

### Declining Status of Women in the Great Plains

When the first Europeans in North America observed indigenous women, they described miserable drudges, leading lives of unremitting toil. Kathleen Weist, who has documented the origins and nature of the European understanding of indigenous women, argues that the European vision had factual and ideological components. On the one hand, to perpetuate the myth that European control of indigenous peoples and their forced acculturation was beneficial, the conquerors developed a unfavorable concept of indigenous culture. Also, they excused their illegitimate attraction to Indian women by characterizing them as dirty and sexually promiscuous. These distorted visions were easily formed, since European observers had a poor understanding of the alien economies, social practices, and ideologies of native peoples. Nevertheless they observed correctly that Indian women were overworked, as shown in the following example, but did not recognize that this was due in large part to the impact of European economic exploitation on the native system.

By the nineteenth century, European traders in North America had created a demand for fur and hides that far outstripped the productive capabilities of traditional foraging households in the northern United States and Canada. Women's work increased tremendously as families reallocated labor in an effort to meet the demand. Women continued with the traditional tasks of child care, cooking, gathering wood, and fetching water while endeavoring to vastly increase the time they spent tanning hides. Just as among the Aztec, where tribute demands for more cloth resulted in an increase in polygyny and female slavery, the Plains peoples increased the number of women workers by acquiring secondary wives, capturing slave women from other tribes, and punishing female adulterers with hide processing. Because males were the source of hides and controlled the trade with the whites, women lost more autonomy and spent more of their lives working. When the whites finally arrived in the Plains villages, they observed that women were overworked and exploited. Because Indian men had greater access to wealth through trade, and to the prestige that accrued from warfare and ritual performance, power became ever more concentrated in male hands.

During the historic period, as traditional societies broke down under foreign attack and forced missionization, some women's roles became even less enviable. Nevertheless, other women managed to turn the introduced ideologies of oppression and pollution to their own advantage, as described in a study by Patricia Galloway, which suggests that the use of menstrual buildings was part of women's adaptive response: in some societies women successfully resisted the genocidal and ethnocidal forces of the conquerors while developing ideologies and activities that made their lives meaningful.

## Women in Inca and Colonial Peru

Irene Silverblatt has argued that a loss of autonomy and status was suffered by women within the Inca empire. As the Inca polity extended its hegemony by military force and coercion, power became associated with men, and the state became the primary locus of decision making. Even though the household continued as the basic tax paying unit, the Inca government (followed later by the Spanish government) decreed that only males could represent the household. Thus women lost their accustomed roles of self-representation as they were integrated into the hierarchical system. History records little about the regulation of Inca households, but the fact remains that the Inca bureaucracy was masculine, and, according to Silverblatt, conquered women were married to Inca men, including the Sapa Inca himself, framing the relationship between Cuzco and the conquered ethnic groups as marriage—but between a victorious and a defeated partner. Although polygyny became common among the Inca elite, women, even noble Inca ones, could not themselves have multiple spouses. Elite women were commodified as gendered possessions, owned by men for whom they labored producing cloth and food. Even though these women were amply provided for, the products of their households may not have been theirs to dispose of as they wished.

With the Spanish Conquest, women throughout the Inca Empire lost whatever autonomy they had preserved. After the horrors of the Conquest, women found themselves stripped of legal majority. In the Spanish view, it was appropriate for females to be docile, chaste, and reclusive. They should not act for themselves, but they and their goods should be administered by related males or guardians all of their lives. Irene Silverblatt has argued that the Spanish colonization was characterized by the robust European misogyny that prejudiced women of all classes. Women lost their autonomy, access to land and other resources, and dominant roles in female religious and political institutions. Only male community leaders were drawn into the Spanish colonial system, and religious persecution, called the "extirpation of idolatries," directly affected women in town and village. Guaman Poma, writing in the sixteenth century, eloquently describes the abuses of women by indigenous governmental and religious authorities (fig. 9.4).

Inca nobles and both female and male members of the aboriginal *curaca* class (of local political elites) in the Inca state responded to Spanish conquest in various ways. Some died in the several native uprisings, resisting Spanish government. Others, represented in historical accounts and Colonial paintings, developed strategies of collaboration with the Spaniards,

FIGURE 9.4. ■ The abuse of Andean women by Spanish priests is described prominently in the drawings and text of Felipe Guaman Poma's letter to the king of Spain, written in the sixteenth century. In the early Colonial period, women paid tribute by weaving, as they had under the Inca government.

thereby successfully entering the Spanish ruling class and maintaining some of their control over the native population, the source of wealth (fig. 9.5). Doña Beatriz, the last Inca's daughter, married a European, and the mother of the chronicler Garcilaso de la Vega married a Spaniard greatly her inferior in rank.

In the early Colonial period, some women were able to develop powerful positions as witches, based on the Spanish belief that women were characterized by "unbridled lust and diabolism." The healers and religious women whom the Spaniards labeled witches, idolatresses, and heretics became the foci of cultural resistance. They were sought by other members of their communities as magical curers and recognized as defenders of Andean traditions against the European onslaught. Although it was Spanish belief that created witches in the Andes where there had been no such category before, Andean women and men continued, as they do in the present, to seek traditional curers and healers. Many of these curers were women, continuing to carry out indigenous practices in the face of Christian religious and civil persecution. For example, in the region of Otuzco, many men ran away from their families and communities to escape impossible labor obligations. The women also fled, but to the high, cold *puna*, beyond the sphere of Spanish settlements, where they persisted in worshipping deities and ancestors at sacred natural places and tombs. Male leadership in local ritual became difficult under Spanish oversight, so women became the leaders of the local cults. Male indigenous leaders encouraged women to take on this role, which the Spanish stigmatized as idolatry and witchcraft.

One leader who emerged in the seventeenth century was the priestess Catalina Guacayllano, respectfully known as La Doctora, a teacher and master of ancient ceremonies who defended precolumbian customs. She instructed disciples and directed people in the worship of community deities and ancestors. According to the description of her activities left by Spanish priests, she prayed, danced, and sacrificed guinea pigs, maize, coca leaves, and fat to the idols of the local deity, who the people believed watched over their fields and irrigation canals. When the Catholic priest in charge of destroying native religion burned the idols of the cult, Catalina Guacayllano replaced them twofold and continued her leadership until she died and was buried in the traditional manner. Her tomb was discovered by priests and destroyed, but the Spanish description of its

FIGURE 9.5. ■ A Colonial portrait of an Inca noblewoman shows the combination of indigenous and European costume elements and accouterments used in the manipulation of social identity.

trappings, including the special clothing that she wore when she made offerings, showed her important religious and political position.

Although virginity was not traditionally valued by Andean peoples, the Colonial priestesses of the underground cults were virgins or widows who eschewed remarriage. These women resisted all contact with the Spanish system. By remaining celibate they separated themselves from contact with and exploitation by Spanish men. Their asexual behavior may have seemed virtuous from the Spanish perspective, but more importantly they were able to escape taxation because single women did not constitute a tribute category in Colonial censuses. Guaman Poma describes how such women lived with their children in the *puna*, working together to support themselves, afraid of the priests and civil authorities who would exile them from their native communities and compel them to forced labor in the weaving workshops and convents in which women accused of witchcraft and idolatry were confined. Living isolated in the inhospitable highlands, these women effectively vanished from the Spanish world.

The stories of La Doctora and women like her illustrate how women resisted domination and exercised a form of alternative power, serving as authorities and autonomous agents outside the reach of the early colonial government. According to Silverblatt, women temporarily reinvented the "female component" of Andean culture, some of which persisted into modern times. But by the seventeenth century, women routinely killed themselves and their children in the course of their resistance to the government. Some women also resorted to male infanticide, which Silverblatt interprets as the result of deep disillusionment due to their abuse by indigenous and colonial male authorities.

Women engaged in the religious and political struggle against the unjust colonial system and participated in several military revolutions mounted unsuccessfully against the Spaniards by indigenous groups. The wars of independence of 1820s ended the Colonial period but failed to deliver women into a just social system. Indigenous Andean women continue to suffer under the exploitation of European-dominated governments.

## Culture Wars

Miraculously, all over America today indigenous peoples resist, contest, and refuse to disappear. They are winning some battles in the culture wars as they gain recognition of their right to exist and as they develop political and economic power. In modern times, the historic pattern of devaluation and exploitation by European religious and governmental institutions has not ended, and in some places indigenous peoples have come under increased pressure to acculturate through physical attacks by violent, mestizo-led political forces and drug traffickers. Today, throughout the American continents, men, women, and children are stressed by economic conditions, weakened by alcoholism and diseases of poverty, and threatened by guerrillas, soldiers, and mercenaries from various factions. Indigenous peoples are killed and kidnapped, and men and whole families flee to the cities, where economic forces and alien cultural practices devastate families. In other instances women actively participate in political and guerrilla movements whose objectives are revolutionary change, either because they have no choice (a new twist on the capture of wives) or because they see no other way to change their lot in life. Ancient women and men confronted similar challenges and adopted similar strategies throughout history. In the process they produced the tremendous variety of cultural adaptations that characterize the prehistory of America. As American women struggle for better lives in modern societies, they can be encouraged by the history of their ancestors.

# CHAPTER TEN

# Women in Prehistory

Archaeological narratives about America's past have been, at best, gender-neutral or simply lacking in people. At worst they have been biased in favor of men's activities and have ignored the contributions of others. Historical processes have more integrity when they are viewed as the results of the activities, relationships, and ideas of everyone, including females, lower-class people, children, the elderly, and individuals who fall into other gender or social categories. Microsocial, personal, and engendered interpretations are the basis of more satisfying analyses, which can lead to a better understanding of cultural change and cultural process. In this narrative we have derived views from contemporary political and social agendas and followed other scholars in rejecting androcentric interpretations of the past while endeavoring to avoid the trap of searching for, and finding, only politically correct interpretations.

The foregoing narrative may be no more "truthful" than any other interpretation of the American past, but it has the virtue of including women as actors. Engendered archaeological research is productive for a number of reasons. For instance, we have tested the hypothesis that women were significant players in the development of prehistoric cultures from the first peopling of the Americas throughout the emergence of ancient states. We have demonstrated that women's experiences in the Americas varied dramatically across space and were subject to fundamental changes through time. By taking women and gender into account, it has been shown that women's lives were interesting and that women, as well as men, influenced the course of history.

## Imagining Alternatives

This narrative about Native American prehistory is designed to stimulate thinking about ourselves and our society. We have described and attempted to understand some aspects of prehistoric life, rejecting the androcentric bias that has been so common in archaeological research. We have discussed the risks of making engendered interpretations of house floors, figurines, and stone tools, showing how gender is an arbitrary social script, frequently and variably rewritten throughout American prehistory. The research of numerous contemporary scholars opens the door for more responsible archaeological reconstructions in the future and serves our present social purposes, not the least of which is to change the image of archaeology as a male science. Another purpose is to find women in the past, to understand their life experiences and historical contributions, and to understand how gender was an important factor in life and history. This awareness can inspire contemporary people as we make decisions about our own lives, shape our evolving social institutions, and make our own history.

There are precious few facts about the past, and, ultimately, they are not as useful or memorable as the narratives created from them. These narratives are not themselves facts but highly interpretative cultural products. In the past experts imagined men hunting; today we can confidently tell the story of ancient America with women in it.

In the twentieth century, many of us want to live in a world in which women and men, as well as other segments of society, have equal access to work, wealth, power, status, and prestige. Part of the process of reaching our goals is the deconstruction of the past and the creation of new origin myths. In many cultures people look to the past for utopian social models. Some people look back and see an Old European society focused on a great goddess, while some archaeologists think that this modern myth is built on exaggerated interpretations of scanty evidence.

Many of the archaeologists cited in our narrative looked at history and found both women and men were creative participants in ancient indigenous cultures. Working with the results of their research, we have tried to create a larger narrative that stresses the roles of real people in systems characterized by ideological, political, moral, and economic struggles.

This narrative can help students to explore both the nature of social life and the nature of female roles and has the potential to create and reinforce contemporary thinking.

Today as archaeologists reconstruct prehistory, they are providing us all with new ways to think about women and power. Matriarchy is a myth, but women have shared political power, have been involved in gender-balanced systems, managed technologies, controlled resources, created ideologies, and managed social relations. Because of the way we think about power we have diminished the roles of all but men, but there is reason to think that women in the past wielded power as well. Anne Barstow imagines ancient women and men using power cooperatively— "power with," not "power over." One can easily imagine both sexes as powerful if, as in the ideology of the modern ecology movement, people used power for "competence, not for dominance." In ancient America women as a group did not rule over men in any society, but it is clear that women created important discourse, perhaps even dominant discourse, in some contexts. They certainly manipulated ideas and material culture with competence, and, to paraphrase Anne Barstow again, women certainly had the power to express themselves autonomously in some spheres of activity and thought.

Across both time and space, female people had diverse social and cultural experiences. The variability that we perceive in the archaeological and ethnohistoric records was the result of dynamic social processes that have frequently been obfuscated by our intellectual habits. We tend to think about women and men in categorical ways, naturalizing and universalizing the two concepts, creating aesthetically pleasing dualistic and polar images that prevent us from appreciating gender as a variable social script, changing with the conditions of the moment. We tend to conceive of history as an uncomplicated evolution from simple to complex in which the normalized "rise of the state" has predictable consequences for "Woman" and "Man."

Our own research has led us to reject these formulae and views. Gender—the process by which societies conceive the fact of biological differences into social roles—is a fundamental dynamic of history and social life. As such it is worthy of study. We need to understand gender because the women and men who participate in social life have often used the fact of sexual difference to assign roles and statuses, open and close opportunities for women and men, and empower and constrain. The negotiation of gender relations can be thought of as script writing. The parties seek to gain advantage or minimize disadvantage as they invent technologies, alter economies, change social relations, develop different politics, and generate ideology. These creative activities are what humans do as they solve the organizational problems entailed in social life. The study of gender relations in the past entails the way the story of the past is told, which in turn both shapes and reflects the way we think about ourselves. The images of ancient women that are commonly shown to young girls will shape their thoughts, plans, aspirations, and life experiences. If parents have the utopian goal of giving great self-confidence and wider opportunity to both female and male children, then they are supported by a vision of the past in which both women and men participate as creative agents of change in all areas of social and economic life. Archaeological interpretation can help to achieve such a vision and erase the stereotype that women are impaired by their biology.

Ancient Native American solutions to the problems of living are relevant to all of us today. They are examples of ways of being human that move us and satisfy our curiosity. The study of ancient America has the potential to instruct us about the patterns that characterized everyone's ancestors on all continents. Half of those ancestors, everywhere, were women.

## An Archaeology of Gender

All knowledge about the prehistory of America is subject to change as the next generation of scholars uses new evidence, refined skills, and revised theories to make more plausible interpretations. Because gender is an important dynamic in social life and history, and because women's activities and gender relations need to be documented, it is important that archaeologists develop and exercise methods and theories useful in satisfying our curiosity about gender relations in the past. Today interpretations derived from ethnographic and historic analogues are the backbone of archaeology. They supply useful hypotheses that must be evaluated by thoughtful readers and tested by trained archaeologists. The business of testing hypotheses about women can be conducted by people working with burial data, DNA, and hormone residues, but other categories of evidence, such as architecture, tools, and food remains, have also been used to identify ancient gender patterns.

Archaeologists are becoming more skillful in finding gender patterns in the archaeological record, and they are mentally more inclined to do so as they increasingly recognize that women have contributed in all periods to the material base of life, the elaboration of religion and philosophy, and the functioning of society, including the reproduction of humankind, still the most costly contribution a woman can make to her society.

In the near future, the reader will see more reconstructions of history that take into consideration the contributions of women as well as men. There will be more studies in which the sexual division of labor is treated as an important variable in understanding change, and we will cease to see women omitted from narratives concerning the great episodes of change in American prehistory. The social revolutions that resulted in the emergence of states and empires had important gender dimensions. Any treatment of the development of plant cultivation and food production systems in the New World must describe the participation of women, because in ancient America women continued to have central roles in much aboriginal agriculture until European contact. Similarly, the so-called container revolution posited by Bruce Smith, which involved the development of ceramic production and the transformation of ritual practices, food storage, and food preparation, must have involved female labor and female creativity.

Today in our society, people are promoting and benefiting from alternative stories about ourselves and our past. The Goddess Movement has inspired some women and men and given them an ideological alternative to patriarchal religious institutions. Recent fiction by Elizabeth Marshall Thomas and Jean Auel entertains us with active heroines in Paleolithic contexts, where there were once just men with clubs. New archaeological narratives also serve the needs of young people who are busy constructing images of themselves and their society.

People who want to see women as more powerful or more manlike in the past may not be pleased. No examples of matriarchy are known, and prehistoric societies may not have been dominated by goddesses, although female images do predominate in the earliest religious expressions of both Europe and the Americas. Nevertheless, anthropological and archaeological research and theory has led some writers to think that in ancient

America, female personages were important deities, ancestors, rulers, priests, healers, shamans, and participants in ritual and sacrifices (both as sacrificer and sacrificed). It is now believed that social life may not have been very hierarchical in deep prehistory, where power was sometimes held by women and men together in systems characterized by ideas of complementarity. This does not mean that there was necessarily community harmony in the past. More likely, women's and men's interests came frequently into conflict, but it is also evident that women and men struggled, negotiated, contested, resisted, and finagled, working out their roles and statuses, power, and authority as they went along. It is known from ethnography that women and men negotiate in myriad ways on a daily basis and that their struggles are affected by their rank and class. Culture change happened as individuals and members of different interest groups engaged in social activities and tried new behaviors and ideas. It is happening the same way today.

## Roads to Power

Feminists have always been concerned with the autonomy, self-determination, and power of women, which arguably have been limited in many recent contexts. Fortunately it is not necessary to project scenarios derived from the organization of Colonial or nineteenth- or twentieth-century industrial societies because recent theory has made it possible to think about power in different ways. The view of power in ancient America developed in this narrative grows out of the understanding of the tremendous variation possible among cultures.

In some societies people take measures to avoid concentrating power, and by custom they eschew hierarchy. In these societies individuals find that no avenues lead to power and authority, although they may earn the admiration of their relatives for their personal qualities. In other societies people increase their productivity, manipulate kinship, and create opportunities for accumulating and wielding power. Some opportunities are designed for one sex and not the other. Trade, warfare, and religion are routes to power associated with men in recent European and Asian cultures, but these same routes offer opportunities to women in other societies in Africa and America. In some cases women have leadership roles within households, and in some societies they predominate in trade and religion.

In ancient America women's power was often related to their roles in marriage, kinship, economy, and religion, and that power was expressed and negotiated on the ideological level in ancient art. Viewed cross-culturally, where men became powerful beyond the household and occupied the obvious positions of authority, women often found ways to exercise power in spheres where they could maintain a high degree of autonomy and control. For example, women may gain prestige and control by taking on religious roles and, in some communities, men respect or are afraid of women because they believe that women are able to mobilize supernatural forces for good or evil. In some circumstances women can accumulate wealth by management of resources and labor, or they can create and promote ideologies through media such as decorated ceramics, baskets, or textiles. Women can exercise control and affect decision making by forming interest groups (like sodalities or sororities), or by managing political and social institutions parallel to those operated chiefly by men. The archaeological record might reveal patterns of female power if archaeologists were clever enough to recognize and interpret the evidence.

In some complex societies, women's social behavior is controlled and elaborate ideologies have been developed to justify the abrogation of women's self-determination. Rayna Rapp has described contexts in which women are confined, veiled, and required to conform to special standards of demeanor, expression, and movement. Their sexuality is controlled, and there are severe penalties to the woman for loss of virginity. Their relatives determine their reproductive and marriage choices, and their productive labor is managed by others. Nevertheless, ethnographic studies also inform us that even in these circumstances women can be autonomous and exercise control in certain spheres. Because their power is not flaunted does not mean it is not there, even though it might be difficult to document in the archaeological record.

These extreme cases of female restriction illustrate the tremendous variety of social arrangements possible in human culture. No pattern is biologically based or inexorable. In fact, in most societies women not only exercise control over their reproduction, contributing substantially to their families and communities by raising their offspring, but, beyond hearth and home, they contribute importantly to the wider economic and social life. The story of the many roles of Native American women, some of which have been documented in the archaeological and historical records, is relevant to us in the late twentieth century as American women begin to move back into leadership roles in religion and politics, where they have been underrepresented for a long time.

# Glossary

*agriculture*. A system for producing food and other useful materials by the cultivation of plants and tending of animals, usually involving intensified labor investment, land modification, irrigation, and animal traction or other nonhuman sources of power. Compare *horticulture*.

*analogy*. An inference based on the idea that if two or more things are similar to each other, in some respects they will probably be similar in other ways as well. Analogical reasoning is one form of interpretation in anthropology. See *ethnographic analogy*.

*androcentric*. Focused on males, their activities, and values, and favoring these above the activities and values of other social categories of people (females and other genders).

*anthropomorphic*. Having the form of a human being.

*anthropomorphized*. Adding the features of a human being to an artifact or artistic representation of an animal or plant.

*archaeological culture*. A unit of study identified by a recurring assemblage of diagnostic artifacts thought to correspond to an ancient social group distinct in time and space and having a distinct adaptive system (culture).

*archaeological record*. The totality of the remains of past activity recovered in association with each other in original position in the earth.

*archaeology of gender*. The scientific and humanistic study of the past through its material remains that seeks to reconstruct aspects of ancient gender systems and identify the activities of women and men.

*Archaic period*. Follows the Paleoindian period and is characterized by people who followed the foraging way of life. Some Archaic groups developed sedentary lifestyles, and some experimented with plant cultivation. Equivalent to the Mesolithic stage of the Old World.

*artifact*. An object that is the result of human manufacture or modification.

*berdache*. In some North American indigenous cultures, a person who cross-dresses and adopts the work of the opposite sex. This is a recognized social status and can be considered a third, or fourth, gender.

*biface*. A lithic artifact produced by reducing a core until it has a lenticular cross section caused by the removal of flakes that originate along the entire periphery and leave scars across both faces of the artifact.

*cacique / cacica*. Hereditary chief or leader.

*camelid*. One of several species of New World animals including the domesticated llama and alpaca, and the wild guanaco and vicuña.

*chiefdom*. A kind of sociopolitical organization distinguished by a permanent, hereditary, central political authority that manages the activities of several kin-based communities.

*Colonial period*. In the New World, the period before the establishment of independent states when indigenous peoples were dominated politically by Europeans, beginning in 1492 in Hispaniola, 1532 in Peru, and later elsewhere.

*context*. Spatial context refers to the relationship among archaeological remains in their original position in the ground. Temporal context refers to the location of evidence in time. Cultural context refers to the inferred social, cultural, and natural environments in which past people and things operated.

*coprolite*. Preserved feces that can be analyzed to reconstruct ancient dietary patterns.

*core*. The chunk of raw material or blank that is struck purposefully to remove flakes in the process of making stone tools.

*culture*. The central concept of anthropology referring to the complex, integrated system of learned behaviors that is the basis of the adaptation of human societies. Archaeologists reconstruct cultural systems, including technological, social, and ideological subsystems, from remains. See *archaeological culture*.

*culture area*. A geographical area identified as distinct in that the peoples who lived there shared features of culture and were more like each other than like peoples in adjacent regions. For example, the Andean culture area, Mesoamerica, the Subarctic, and (in the United States) the Southwest, the Eastern Woodlands, the Plains, and California.

*differentiated roles*. Refers to the fact that social roles (especially sex roles) are nonoverlapping: that women and men perform different activities and aim at different goals.

*direct historical approach*. A method for inferring some features of an extinct culture by analogy with historic cultures when sociocultural continuity is presumed between the two. A form of *ethnographic analogy*.

*division of labor*. The process by which tasks are assigned to individuals depending upon their sex, age, or specialization. In societies with a simple division of labor, all members classified in a particular broad category (by sex or age) perform about the same activities. In societies with a complex division of labor, there are a greater number of specialist categories beyond those of sex and age. See *specialization*.

*domestic mode of production*. The organization of labor and productive activities at the level of household.

*Early Horizon*. In Peruvian archaeology, the period of time marked by the spread of Chavín iconography and other aspects of culture, including the use of hallucinogenic drugs in ritual, the heddle loom, and gold metallurgy.

*Early Intermediate period*. In Peruvian archaeology, the time between the end of direct Chavín influence and the first appearance of Huari iconography. The major cultures at this time included Moche, Recuay, and Nazca.

*economy*. A cultural subsystem that involves the production of goods, their distribution, and consumption.

*elites.* Individuals in ranked societies who have greater access to prestige, power, and/or wealth. They may belong to an upper class or be part of a highly ranked lineage.

*endogamous.* Refers to a social system in which a person marries a member of her own kin or social group, however defined. Compare *exogamous.*

*engender* (a neologism). To introduce the dimension of gender or take real women and men into consideration in any discourse.

*epigraphy.* The study and interpretation of ancient inscriptions.

*ethnoarchaeology.* The study of contemporary cultures with the goal of understanding the relationship between behavior and material culture.

*ethnocentric.* The conscious or unconscious bias that one's own way of thinking or doing or being is natural, universal, normal, and immutable, and the tendency to judge one's own culture as inherently superior.

*ethnographic analogy.* A method for inferring certain features of an extinct culture by using ethnographic evidence from a group whose culture can be shown to be analogous to the extinct one in some ways.

*ethnography.* Within cultural anthropology, the study of living social groups and the description of their cultural patterns.

*ethnology.* The use of ethnographic evidence for the comparative study of human societies.

*ethnohistory.* A field of study related to anthropology that endeavors to reconstruct societies and their cultures from historical documents written early in the period of a people's contact with Europeans.

*exogamous.* Refers to a system in which people tend to marry outside of their own group. Compare *endogamous.*

*extended family.* A social unit composed of individuals related by blood and marriage in which several generations are represented and in which the members exhibit more degrees of relationship than do the members of a *nuclear family.*

*family.* A fundamental social group composed of people related by blood and marriage, often defined for archaeological purposes as the coresidential domestic group. See *nuclear family* and *extended family.*

*feminism.* A doctrine and movement that advocates rights for women in political and economic spheres and that encourages scholars to include women and their domains of experience in research and interpretation.

*feminist archaeology.* The scientific and humanistic study of the past through its material remains that uses contemporary feminist theory to critique androcentric research and produce prehistoric interpretations that include gender, and that redresses the balance of previous research by focusing on women.

*feminist theory.* A set of ideas that guide research and interpretation (in anthropology, sociology, history, and philosophy, for example), which is critical of ideologies that have attributed certain characteristics to women and others to men, and which seeks to include the dimension of gender in developing understanding of history and contemporary sociocultural systems.

*flakes.* The sharp-edged by-product of working stone. These pieces of material are removed when a flintknapper strikes a core of raw material with a hammerstone or applies pressure to the edge of a biface. When flakes are removed expediently, the toolmaker invests a minimum of labor and skill, and the resulting core and flakes are controlled poorly with respect to shape and size.

*fluted bifacial point.* A chipped stone artifact, used as a projectile point or knife by some Paleoindians, distinguished by one or two longitudinal, flutelike flake scars produced by a skilled flintknapper. Examples include Clovis and Folsom points.

*food production.* A kind of subsistence system involving the cultivation of domesticated plant and/or animal species. Pastoralists, agriculturists, and horticulturists all do food production.

*foraging.* An efficient mode of production under conditions of low population density involving the harvest of wild resources using low-tech strategies such as hunting and gathering. *Broad-spectrum foraging* involves strategies for utilizing a wide variety of resources. *Specialized foragers* focus their efforts on one principal resource or prey species. See *hunter-gatherers.*

*Formative.* A period in New World prehistory characterized by food production and village life. The Formative way of life is equivalent to the Neolithic of the Old World.

*gender.* A dimension of social life involving the classification of people into two (or more) categories defined loosely on the basis of sexual differences, but involving a large number of socially ascribed characteristics.

*gender attribution.* Refers to the way individuals are identified as males, females, or members of another culturally defined gender category, e.g., berdache or trans-sexual. For archaeologists, gender attribution is the process of identifying particular kinds of material remains with one sex or another.

*gender complementarity.* A cultural ideal that conceptualizes female and male as different and incomplete such that only together can they create harmony and balance.

*gender hierarchy.* A feature of social organization that involves the members of one gender group exercising power and having authority over another (frequently men over women). Also, gender stratification or sexual stratification.

*gender ideology.* The aspect of thought and worldview that expresses the meaning of male, female, masculine, feminine, sex, and reproduction in any given culture and that includes rules for appropriate male and female behavior and expectations about public and private gender relations.

*gender role.* What women and men are expected to do in a sociocultural setting: their prescribed activity patterns, social relations, and behaviors.

*gender system.* The parts of a sociocultural system that involve feminine and masculine (and sometimes other) roles and customary female-male relations.

*gynocentric.* Focused on females, their activities, and values, and favoring them above the activities and values of other social categories of people (males and other genders). See *androcentric.*

*habitation site* or *living site.* Place where ancient people resided and left the remains of their domestic activities.

*heterarchy.* A postmodern idea about an organization in which the members are unranked or have the potential for being ranked in a number of different ways (see Ehrenreich et al. 1995). Power and authority are complex in such organizations. Compare *hierarchy*.

*hierarchy*. A kind of organization in which lower-order units are subsumed under progressively fewer higher-order units. In human society it refers to the kind of organization in which rulers hold power over ranks of subordinates.

*historic period*. The span of time (which varies in length in different geographical regions) for which there are written records upon which to base scholarly study. *History* is the narrative constructed about that period. Compare *prehistoric period*.

*horticulture*. Plant cultivation using no power except human muscle and simple tools. Compare *agriculture*.

*household*. A group of people who reside together, who may or may not be kin to each other.

*household cluster*. The archaeological remains of the house and associated spaces and structures where the residents carried out activities.

*hunter-gatherers*. Human groups that subsist by exploiting wild plant and animal resources and that share a number of social and cultural features. See *foraging*.

*ideology*. The aspect of human cultural behavior that involves thought habits and includes beliefs about the nature of human beings and the structure of the world and the cosmos, including the supernatural realm. Includes gender ideology, political ideology, religious ideology, and so forth.

*kiva*. An underground ceremonial room characteristic of some prehistoric and ethnographic Pueblo peoples of the Southwest. In historic times kivas were used by men.

*Late Intermediate period*. In Peruvian archaeology the time between the cessation of direct Huari influence and the Inca conquest of the coastal cultures.

*lineage*. A corporate group of kin whose members claim descent from a common ancestor in either the female or the male line.

*masculine*. Associated with the male sex in the norms of a particular social group.

*material culture*. All the material products of a people, including artifacts and architecture.

*matriarchy*. The kind of social organization dominated by women in which female leaders have authority over men. No examples of matriarchal societies are known from history or ethnography. See *patriarchy*.

*matrifocal*. Referring to the importance of mothers or adult females in the structure and functioning of a social unit, such as a family.

*matrilineal organization*. A form of social organization in which an individual's descent is figured through his or her mother and female relatives. The social system is based on *matrilineages*. Compare *patrilineal organization*.

*matrilocal residence*. A pattern of postmarital residence in which the married couple resides with the family of the wife's mother. Compare *patrilocal residence*.

*Maya*. Contemporary indigenous people of southern Mexico and northern Central America whose ancestors, the ancient Maya of the Classic period, left impressive archaeological remains. The Maya were the only prehistoric Native American people to invent writing.

*Mesoamerica.* That portion of central and southern Mexico and northern Central America where prehistoric peoples shared certain cultural features, including hieroglyphic writing, a distinctive calendar, folding books, a religious system involving the ceremonial ball game and blood sacrifice, a three-stone hearth, and a distinctive cuisine based on maize, squash, and beans.

*metate.* Mesoamerican name for a shaped stone slab employed in combination with a shaped hand stone, called a *mano,* for grinding grain and other materials.

*microsocial perspective.* The idea that social analysis can focus on real individuals, men women and families, units which usually do not figure in interpretations generated by archaeologists. This perspective is often missing when societies are treated as systems.

*midden.* The accumulated refuse and debris resulting from human activity.

*Middle Horizon.* In Peruvian archaeology, the period when influences from the Huari culture are visible in material culture throughout much of Peru.

*Mimbres.* The archaeological culture of a group of Mogollon people who occupied sites along the Mimbres River in New Mexico and crafted ceramic vessels in a distinctive style.

*model.* A theoretical construct, designed to describe the form and function of a real set of data or phenomena, which facilitates the understanding and explanation of those data or phenomena.

*nuclear family.* A group of kin composed of an adult female, an adult male, and their biological offspring. See *extended family.*

*Paleoindian.* The earliest known inhabitants of the New World, who migrated into America from Siberia in the terminal Pleistocene.

*Paleolithic.* The long archaeological period in the Old World that ended with the Pleistocene epoch (about 12,000 years ago) and was characterized by cultures known principally from the remains of stone tools. At the end of this period, Upper Paleolithic peoples in some regions produced art work.

*paleopathology.* The study of disease patterns in ancient human remains.

*patriarchy.* The kind of social organization in which men dominate society and hold positions of authority.

*patrilineal organization.* A form of social organization in which an individual's descent is figured through his or her father and male relatives. The social system is based on *patrilineages.* Compare *matrilineal organization.*

*phytolith analysis.* A method for studying microscopic silica skeletons of plant cells found in the soil and reconstructing the inventory of plants used by ancient people.

*pollen analysis.* A method for studying the microscopic pollen grains found in archaeological soil and reconstructing the inventory of plants used by ancient people.

*polygamy.* Marriage involving multiple spouses.

*polygyny.* Marriage involving one man and several women (wives).

*polyandry.* Marriage involving one woman and several men (husbands).

*Postclassic period.* In Mesoamerica the latest prehistoric period, known as a time of major political change. The Late Postclassic was dominated by the Aztecs.

---

*postmodern theory.* An approach in anthropology in which practitioners reject the possibility of objectivity in the comparative study of peoples and cultures, are aware of their own political and social biases, and view culture as a dynamic system in which meanings and relationships are constantly negotiated and renegotiated by the interacting members of the community.

*power.* The ability of one individual or group to affect the behavior of others.

*preceramic.* A stage, or period of culture history in a particular region before the adoption of ceramic pottery.

*Preclassic period.* In Mesoamerica the time (also known as the Formative) when farming villages with ceramic industries were established, the Olmec and the Zapotec states emerged, and the great civilization of Teotihuacán began its rise.

*prehistoric period.* The span of time (which varies in length across geographical space) during which no documents were written and for which there are no written records.

*prehistory.* The narratives constructed about the prehistoric period based on the archaeological record.

*priestess or priest.* A religious specialist who operates in a bureaucratically arranged religious institution in a complex society or state and who manages the cult of a deity.

*primary burial.* The interment of a human being directly into the earth so that the skeleton is found in anatomically correct position. Compare *secondary burial.*

*projectile point.* A bifacially flaked stone artifact with a point capable of piercing the hide of an animal, sharp edges designed to cause internal hemorrhage within the prey animal, and a portion designed for hafting on a dart or arrow shaft.

*Pueblo (Puebloan).* One of the major indigenous cultural traditions of the Southwest. Modern Pueblo Indians (including Hopi and Zuni) are the descendants of the ancient Anasazi. In this tradition people reside in communal dwellings called *pueblos.*

*rank.* Differential prestige and social status. Egalitarian societies were replaced by ranked societies later in prehistory.

*Regional Developmental period.* In Ecuador the period that embraced regional cultures and ceramic styles such as Guangala, Bahia, Jama-Coaque, and La Tolita, all derivatives of the preceding Chorrera tradition.

*religion.* A subsystem of culture and aspect of human behavior that involves the spiritual and/or supernatural realms.

*rites of passage.* Ceremonial activities that mark the induction of individuals into a new social status. Commonly these celebrate birth, initiation and other forms of induction, puberty, marriage, and death.

*role.* The customary behavior expected of individuals occupying a certain status.

*secondary burial.* The interment of human bones from which the rest of the tissue has already disappeared or that have been cremated. See *primary burial.*

*sedentism.* The practice of reducing mobility and inhabiting a site on a permanent or near-permanent basis.

*sex.* The biological identification of the individual as female or male (or one of several androgynous combinations of female and male genes and genitalia).

*shaman*. A female or male intermediary between humans and the spirit world who often is responsible for spiritual healing and who may interact with the supernatural during trance. Compare *priestess*.

*site*. A discrete cluster of the remains of human behavior; the place where ancient activities took place.

*social*. Having to do with the organization of people in groups. This is distinct from *cultural*, which refers to the learned behavior of the people organized in a group.

*society*. Refers to a group of people who are organized and held together by a common set of customs and values. *Culture* refers to the system of ideas and customs that organizes social life.

*specialization*. The social processes that result in a multiplication of roles and statuses and a complex division of labor. When individuals specialize in performing a particular task, they satisfy their needs by exchanging the fruits of their labor with other specialists. See *division of labor*.

*state*. A territorial, sociopolitical organization characterized by hierarchically arranged governing institutions and distinct social strata (in which some people are separated from others by birth and privilege); kinship is not a principal organizing feature of political life.

*status*. Social standing. The relative position of an individual in society, which implies certain customary behavior (role). In some societies statuses are ranked, and status may refer to prestige or high social standing.

*stratified society*. An integrated group of human beings in which some subgroups are accorded differential treatment and in which some groups have power over others. See *gender hierarchy*.

*system*. A kind of organization in which all the constituent parts and subsystems are interdependent and interact dynamically such that alterations in any part will result in coordinated changes in other parts. See *gender system*.

*theory*. A body of ideas designed to explain phenomena and the relationships among phenomena.

*utilized flakes*. Refers to technologically simple stone flakes that show patterns of edge damage suggesting that they were employed to perform work.

*uxorilocal*. Referring to postmarital residence in the household of the wife.

# Notes on Main References

## Preface

Margaret Ehrenberg's *Women in Prehistory* (1989) was, perhaps, the first general text on the new study of gender in antiquity. Although its title is comprehensive, it mainly concerns the roles of women in Europe. Margaret Conkey and Ruth Tringham's "Archaeology and the Goddess" (1991) explores the "goddess theory" from an anthropological point of view and finds it distinctly wanting.

## Chapter 1. Women and Gender

The sources for this chapter vary from theoretical considerations and seminal papers to site reports and studies of skeletal populations. Although some of this material is not specifically about gender, it, like most other sources mentioned below, contains basic data that can be engendered, studies that are of historical interest because they initiated new lines of thought or points of view on a subject. An example is the article by Blaffer Hrdy, who in 1981 wrote a concise and pointed essay, "Lucy's Husband." She was one of the first to point out that changes in female-male interaction were crucial to the evolution of human lifeways and that changes in female patterns of choosing mates were the key, not male sexual behaviors. Berndt and Estioko-Griffin, writing in *Women the Gatherer* (1981), present revisionist thinking concerning women as hunters from ethnographic research on hunting and gathering peoples in Australia and the Philippines. Bumstead et al.'s "Recognizing Women in the Archaeological Record" (1987) is a trenchant presentation of how to identify women archaeologically. They point out that, although primary sexual characteristics are generally absent in the archaeological record and secondary sexual characteristics are often masked by traditional descriptive analyses, chemical composition of bone often can present detailed information on life experiences and differences in them between the sexes. Du Cros and Smith (1993) and Gero and Conkey (1991) are two of the earliest and most influential edited volumes concerning gender in prehistory. Articles in these volumes are referred to specifically throughout our text. Conkey and Williams, in a 1991 article, address many of the same questions that Gero and Conkey address in their introduction, but for the more general anthropological audience and in the context of political economy and the postmodern discourse, which had, at that time, taken anthropological theoreticians by storm. Prezanno (1997) evaluates studies of the Iroquois, a North American indigenous group often said to have been distinguished by its politically powerful women, considering public and private roles and women's political power and its relationship to male aggression, whereas Richards (1957) considers claims of matriarchy among the Iroquois and finds them overstated. George Peter Murdock edited the immense *Outline of Cultural Materials* (1950), a precomputer attempt to establish a data base of anthropological knowledge for use in comparative studies of humanity. It is still an invaluable resource for doing a quick survey of cultural variability. Tabitha Powledge and Mark Rose (1996) present a popularly written account of DNA studies in archaeology with specific reference to using DNA to unravel family relationships among Egyptian mummies, whereas Williams (1995) summarizes some problems in using DNA to study ethnic origins. Mark Cohen and George Armelagos's edited volume (1984b) discusses the human skeletal evidence of work patterns, morbidity, mortality at the critical point in social history in which any given society made the change from foraging to farming as their major economic endeavor. Individual papers in this compendium are referenced frequently throughout our text because, although this work does not necessarily focus on gender issues, relevant material is found throughout for she who looks. Mark Cohen and Sharon Bennett (1993) neatly summarize biological methodologies for studying sex roles and gender hierarchies in the past, and Kristin Sobolik et al. (1996) present a new method for identifying the sex of the producers of ancient fecal materiel. Norman Hammond and Theya Molleson (1994) present her analyses of Huguenot weavers' burials, which indicate the strong possibility of underaging the remains of older adults in prehistoric populations and what this may mean in terms of reevaluating Maya history. Sonia Chadwick-Hawkes and Calvin Wells (1975) discuss two anomalous Anglo-Saxon burials, suggesting that they represent women who had been forcibly raped and then buried alive for their "sin." They further suggest skeletal evidence of rape and suggest situations in which archaeologists might be alert to such evidence. Smith (1972), Adams (1971), and Saul (1972) present the site reports and skeletal analyses from the excavations at Altar de Sacrificios. Adams (1963, 1977) discusses the polychrome vase painted with an apparent scene of the Lady of Altar's funeral. Tatiana Prouskouriakoff's 1960 publication on the historical implications of the Piedras Negras dated monuments was instrumental in changing the interpretative paradigm of Maya studies, while her 1961 "Portraits of Women in Maya Art" presented incontrovertible evidence that history, even Maya history, involved both women and men. Bruhns (1988) analyzed Maya royal costume in an attempt to distinguish female and male status and role, and Benson (1988) summarized what was then thought about women in the ancient Moche culture. Anne-Marie Hocquenghem (1977a, 1977b) and again with Patricia Lyon (1980) presented data identifying important women and female supernaturals in Moche art, and Holmquist Pachas in her 1977 thesis identified women in a variety of scenes painted upon ceramic vessels. In an article on Michael Mosley and Carol Mackey's investigations at the Chimu capital of Chan Chan, published by *National Geographic* in 1973, the artist, who did a reconstruction drawing of a Chimu weaving atelier, showed the weavers as female rather than male.

## Chapter 2. The First Women in America

To date very few studies on America's earliest immigrants are engendered. As we point out, emphasis upon kill sites and hunting behaviors has dominated Paleoindian studies to the detriment of a fuller understanding of human behavior during this early epoch. Lee and Devore's 1968 volume of essays, *Man the Hunter*, demonstrated the variety of hunting behavior among contemporary people and made the point that women's gathering was crucial to foraging economies. A growing dissatisfaction with discussions about hunting behaviors later led to Frances Dahlberg's edited volume, *Woman the Gatherer* (1981), which contains important data on women hunters as well. Brumbach and Jarvenpa (1997) study Chipewayan economy in a broader sense than that presented in Dahlberg, pointing out that women's contribution to the economy is by no means as marginal as had been said and that Postcolumbian pressures probably had something to do with the worsening of women's social position among the Chipewayan as among other indigenous peoples. Osgood's 1940 study, *Ingalik Material Culture*, shows clearly how production and utilization of goods and food is engendered to promote cooperation and mutual dependence among females and males. Soffer and Praslov's 1993 edited volume on Paleoindians contains a series of useful papers on the variety of sites and adaptations of the earliest Americans. Connolly et al. (1995), Pringle (1997), and Kehoe (1987) discuss new finds and new interpretations of Paleoindian and Paleolithic tools, emphasizing the importance of textiles, netting, and basketry in ancient settings, while Jackson (1992) discusses the social consequences of dependence upon women's processing of acorns as an economic staple. Auel's fictional account of mammoth hunters (1995) places women and children into the kinds of hunting situations (mass drives of herd animals) that are widely attested to in the archaeological record. Gero (1991) talks about the importance of utilized flakes and women as stone-tool makers, emphasizing in this and her 1993 publication that the emphasis upon stone tools as a male product for male hunting has more to do with the predominance of males in Paleolithic studies than it does with any archaeological or historical reality. Furst (1972, 1976, 1986) discusses the importance of hallucinogenic substances, mainly of plant origin, to Native American religions, past and present, while Brekham (1967) details the use of similar substances in traditional Siberian cultures. Specific data regarding Paleoindian sites in South and North America comes from Dillehay (1996, Monte Verde, Chile), Chauchat (1988, Paijan, Peru), Flannery (1986), and Marcus and Flannery (1996, investigations in early sites in Oaxaca, Mexico), Davis (1993, Indian Creek and other Montana sites), McNett (1985, Shawnee-Minisink), Redder and Fox (1988, Horn's Shelter, Texas), and Correal Urrego and van der Hammen (1997, Tequendama Rock Shelter, Colombia).

## Chapter 3. Women in the Archaic

Because women have been traditionally associated with gathering, anthropological studies of Archaic, that is foraging, preagricultural or incipient agricultural societies admit to their presence. Sassaman (1992a, 1992b) discusses technology and the division of labor among North American cultures in general and then specifically at the time of the hunter-gather–Archaic transition. Flannery et al. (1981), Flannery (1986), and Marcus and Flannery (1996) discuss the Archaic and Archaic-Formative transitions in the arid valley of Oaxaca, Mexico, with reference to numbers of sites, of which Guila Naquitz provides one of the most detailed archaeological records of this important process in American prehistory. Hayden (1992) discusses European theories of matriarchy in the Archaic, bringing up the possibility of complementary opposition, and in 1996 he and his colleagues published a study on what they saw as ecological determinants of women's status in foraging societies. Joachim (1988) discussed intensive foraging behaviors and the division of labor. The Archaic Chinchorro culture of northern Chile and southernmost Peru has been the subject of numerous studies, of which the newest and best illustrated are those of Bernardo Arriaza (1995a, 1996b) and Mario Rivera (1995). Sonia Guillén (1992) has studied Chinchorro physical remains, looking for evidence of differential stresses upon females and males, while Marvin Allison (1984) has focused specifically upon Chinchorro paleopathology. The Archaic site of Paloma in coastal Peru has been studied by Robert Benfer (1984, 1990) and Jeffrey Quilter (1989), both of whom devote some time to discussing gender behaviors. Their interpretations are different, but in our opinion neither one is really supported by the evidence presented. Karen Stothert's (1985, 1988) studies of the Las Vegas culture of the arid Ecuadorian coast show changing adaptations to an unstable environment among peoples who, although successful foragers, were also in the earliest steps of farming. Douglas Ubelaker's 1980 study of the physical remains of the Las Vegas people adds physical evidence of how their changing lifeways affected females and males. Jackson (1992) is able to use historic as well as archaeological data to interpret evolving female roles in the late Archaic societies of California. Charles and Buikstra (1993) discuss Archaic mortuary behavior in the central Mississippi region, while Bird and Hyslop (1985) detail daily life and the treatment of the dead at Late Archaic–Early Formative Huaca Prieta in coastal Peru. Claassen's 1992 edited volume contains much valuable information concerning gender relations in Archaic societies in general. Many of the individual articles in this compendium are referenced separately throughout this text.

## Chapter 4. Women and Food Production

With the transition to food production, questions have been raised concerning not only the origins of agriculture and the role of gender in this revolutionary technological change, but also the effects that the "Neolithic Revolution" had socially and physically upon early farming communities, especially regarding gender behaviors and gender relations. Cohen and Armelagos's (1984) edited volume, *Paleopathology at the Origins of Agriculture*, discusses numerous cases that demonstrate health status at this crucial intersection. Flannery's 1986 study of Guila Naquitz in southern Mexico provides archaeological information concerning this change in an arid ecosystem, whereas Lee (1976) documents a living example of arid-land foragers, the !Kung "Bushmen." Cassidy (1987), Bridges (1989, 1991), Powell (1996), Perezgian et al. (1984), Pauketet (1994), Larsen

(1984), Cook (1984), and Eisenberg (1991) present data concerning changes in health among numbers of Mississippi and southeastern early cultures and changes in health and mortality related to agriculture, intensification in agriculture, specifically changes in staple crops, and the relationship between health, mortality, and status among emerging ranked societies. Buikstra et al. (1986) further discuss the relationship of female fertility and the change to an agricultural way of life, again in the eastern woodlands and mid-western river valleys. Minnis (1984) discusses early agriculture in the Desert Borderlands. Crown and Wills (1985) bring in another dimension of technological change, discussing the origins of ceramic containers in the Southwest and the changes in women's time allocation with economic intensification. Diehl (1996) adds the intensification of maize production among the Mogollon to this discussion of increasing women's tasks. McGuire (1992) discusses mortuary analysis and what it shows about society and ideology among the Hohokam, and Mitchell (1991) further elaborates upon this theme in his excavation of two Hohokam cemeteries. Berry (1985) and Ezzo (1993) discuss paleodemography and human adaptations at Grasshopper Pueblo, material that clearly shows women's changing roles. Changes in settlement, activities, and gender roles in early coastal Ecuador are presented by Karen Stothert (1988), discussing the transitional Las Vegas communities; and in the fully agricultural, ceramics-making Valdivia culture by Damp (1979, 1984) and Marcos (1988, 1990), with specific emphasis upon the changing social and ideological life at the site of Real Alto. Ubelaker (n.d.) studies the effects that economic and cultural intensification had upon the physical well being of females and males and differing stresses upon the sexes in this early community.

## Chapter 5. Women in Households

Household structures have been seen as amenable to archaeological investigation, although, all too often, ethnocentricity is applied in identifying gender-based activities and "activity areas" by using contemporary Western ideologies as a universal. Tringham (1991) writes the story of a house in an eastern European community, describing inhabitants, especially the women, their feelings, and their activities. Although this technically qualifies more as fiction than archaeology it is an interesting approach toward trying understanding the purpose of households as social constructs that leave material remains. Because plural marriage affects the form of households, Hartung (1982) has attempted to discuss polygyny and inheritance, strong social factors in household formation. Santley and Hirth's edited volume (1993) presents current research in Mesoamerica with specific reference to domestic units and their variability in time and space. Howell and Kintigh (1996) have attempted to use mortuary and biological data to identify kin groups in the American Southwest, while Hayden et al. (1996) use artifactual analysis to identify a long-lived corporate group (a family) in ancient British Colombia. Flannery and Winter (1976), in one of the earlier attempts to study prehis-toric social organization on the household and village level, discuss identifying house-holds and household activities, attempting to divide activity areas into female and male using the modern (Christian, mestizo) Oaxaca division of labor. Data are more abundant concerning ancient households and villages in coastal Ecuador, where Jonathan Damp (1979, 1984), Jorge Marcos (1988, 1990), James Zeidler (1984), and Deborah Pearsall (1988) present data concerning changes in economy, household form, and ideological activities throughout the several thousand years in which the first village, then town, then ceremonial center of Real Alto, was occupied. Susan Kent (1984), in an ethnoarchaeological study of modern Navaho, Mexican, and Anglo Americans in Arizona, presents an interesting counter to the blithe delineation of gender-related "activity areas," pointing out that these do not really exist outside of a complex society that dwells in multiroomed structures reflecting highly specialized personal, social, and economic activities. Payson Sheets (1990, 1992), working in El Salvador at Ceren, a village preserved by volcanic ash much like the Italian Pompeii, had the opportunity to reconstruct entire households and nearly the full range of activities associated with them. As a contrast, the prehistoric Tairona, much like their descendants, the Kogi of the Sierra Nevada de Santa Marta in Colombia, apparently show an interesting division of household structures and activities into male and female (Zuidema 1992; Reichel-Dolmatoff 1977, 1985). Also in Colombia, Castaño Uribe's work shows changing settlement patterns and household types, with concomitant changes in opportunities and the organization of work for both females and males in the central river valleys of Colombia. The Iroquois, owing to their matrilineal kin organization and the strong political position of mature women in their historic society, have long been a focus of feminist interest. Snow (1994, 1995) documents Iroquois history and culture as well as the forces of migrations, while Prezanno (1997) discusses the interrelationship of warfare, women, and the households they formed. Ezzo (1993), Berry (1985), and Reid and Whittlesely (1982) discuss human adaptations, paleodemography, and households at Grasshopper Pueblo and how they changed through periods of changing climate and cultural pressures upon the settlement. Simon and Ravesloot (1995) present an interesting case of social ties outside the household by analyzing trace elements in ceramics found in mortuary contexts in a Salado cemetery. Southwards, in Mesoamerica, Hendon (1997) presents elite women's work and its spatial correlates in Maya Copán, an interesting contrast to the simple villager households of Ceren. Teotihuacán, in central Mexico has, perhaps, been better studied from the household point of view than any other site or culture in Mesoamerica. Michael Spence's (1974) pioneering study of patrilineal kinship and household organization has been refined and expanded by Widmer and Storey (1993), Manzanilla (1996), and Cowgill (1992), who deal respectively with social organization and household structure, corporate groups and domestic activities, and social differentiation. Rebecca Storey has concentrated on paleodemography and paleopathology with her studies on mortality (1985), prenatal mortality (1986), and stress, nutrition, and general status as represented in the mortuary population of Teotihuacán. Ethnographic data discussing the physical and mental effects of chronic undernutrition and near starvation are provided by Mortiz Thomsen (1969), based on his experiences in the Peace Corps in Ecuador, while Louana Lackey documents a living tradition of ceramics making in Acatlán in southern Mexico, pointing out that now, as in the past, crafts such as this are family organized, not produced exclusively by one female or male members of the family.

## Chapter 6. Women, Production, and Specialization

Production, other than domestic production for the family, and professional activities by women are subjects generally ignored in archaeological interpretation, despite quantities of historic and other data suggesting that much production was done by families working together to provide for themselves and produce tribute for their chiefdom or state. Moreover, in the strongly gendered state societies of the Conquest period, there is abundant evidence of female professionals of all sorts, although these also have too often been ignored in studies of these societies. David Cheal, in the context of an edited volume on the domestic mode of production (1987), discusses differing strategies of resource management undertaken in the domestic context. These strategies, of course, involved women as well as men. Gero and Scallotini (n.d.), Shimada et al. ( 1983), and Topic (1982) discuss South American metallurgy in state societies, showing how it was organized as family production under the general oversight of the state. Penelope Drooker (1992) discusses textile production at Wycliffe, a Mississippian town, where the weaving of elaborate textiles, whether for consumption within the household or tribute, was done by women. Elizabeth Brumfiel (1991, 1996) discusses women as producers of tribute cloth and the different strategies they and their families utilized as tribute demands escalated under the Aztec domination of the Valley of Mexico and then under the Spaniards, pointing out that women might choose numbers of ways to fulfill their obligations. McCafferty and McCafferty (1988) further discuss Aztec women's varied roles, pointing out the strong androcentric bias in Aztec studies from the first records of the conquistadors and Christian priests, and the problems that unobservant or unaware anthropologists, historians, and art historians have had in taking these records at face value without taking into account the strong tradition of gender complementarity in these societies, which created parallel structures of power and domination. Anderson ( 1997) presents a detailed account of married Aztec women and what happened to them as androcentric Spanish governmental and religious structures achieved hegemony over Aztec customs. Gender complementarity is also seen in the late prehistoric Inca of western Andean South America. Major sources on the Inca include the account of "The Inca" Garcilaso de la Vega (1945 [1609]), Sarmiento de Gamboa (1043 [1572]), and Bernabé Cobo (1990 [1653]), as well as the major synthesis of John H. Rowe, written for the *Handbook of South American Indians* (1948). In 1997 Rowe also provided a caveat to overenthusiastic reconstructions of a hyperdualistic Inca society, especially regarding women, by noting that the early chronicler Martin de Marua had plagiarized most of what he called Inca history and customs from sources describing Mexico and Central America. Christine Hastorf (1990), using archaeological data, discusses how gender roles can be reconstructed from distribution of food remains and studies of individual dietary intake as recovered from skeletal material. She then pursued this line of investigating gender relations by looking at what happened when the Inca took over Sausa society and imposed their culture upon the local inhabitants of the Upper Mantaro Valley (Hastorf 1992). Anne Galloway (n.d.) provides an interesting hypothesis concerning female tribute in cloth, suggesting that they worked to produce tribute cloth communally, perhaps at the same time their husbands were paying labor tribute. Warren Barbour's (1993) studies of figurine production in Teotihuacán, Mexico, indicate that female themes and female manufacture dominated this production until mass production with molds became common, when males made the figurines and male themes dominated. Various full-time, nondomestic occupations can be associated with women throughout American prehistory. Prostitution is attested to by Father Sahagún, who discusses women of ill repute briefly in his monumental ethnography of the Aztec (1979 [1579]), although Margaret Arvey (1988) notes that both his discussion and the drawings of prostitutes are strongly colored by European prejudices and do not necessarily represent Aztec values. Likewise, Inca prostitution is described in pejorative, Europeanized terms by Garcilaso de la Vega (1609). Women as medical doctors are well attested to among the Aztec, and Ortiz de Montellano (1990) notes professional curers of various kinds in his monumental study of Aztec medicine. Sullivan (1966) discusses Aztec midwives, and Graulich (1992) documents similar professional practitioners from the time of the Aztec migrations into the Valley of Mexico. Barriga (1994) talks about the transformation of Doña Marina into various, largely negative figures in Mexican culture, something that also rose out of the suppression of female public roles and female autonomy under colonization. John Riddle's 1992 synthesis of Old World, mainly Classical birth control also documents the gradual shutting out of women from the medical profession and from control of their own fertility. Joseph Bastien (1987) documents modem Kallawaya (Bolivia) curers and their medical knowledge, including birth control and abortificants. Larco Hoyle (1965) and Kauffman Doig (1978) document sexual practices, including those that would not have led to conception, among the Peruvian Moche. Professional women scribes are now attested to in Maya society by artistic depictions (Clarkson 1978) and ancient inscriptions (Closs 1992). Carolyn Tate (1992) suggests that Lady Xoc of Yaxchilán may also have been an architect and even an astronomer. Finally, Janet Spector (1983) notes that production and tasks of all sorts among the historic Hidatsa are so strongly gendered that they must leave archaeological evidence in terms of distributions of activities.

## Chapter 7. Women and Religion

Women in ancient America played many roles in religion, from deities to priestesses to other types of religious roles, including that of being sacrificed. Much of this, except sacrifices, usually romanticized into Western terms, has been ignored in the archaeological record owing to the peripheral public roles that Western and Middle Eastern religions prescribe for females and an unwarranted assumption that the same was true throughout the world. Gross and Falk (1989) discuss women's religious lives. Whitten and Whitten (1988) provide us with the ethnographic data surrounding the production of items used in religious rituals among the Amazon Canelos Quichua. Langdon (1992) provides a useful discussion of what shamanism and shamanistic practices entail, while Peter Furst (1965, 1976, 1977, 1978) discusses evidence of shamanism in ancient Mexican art from a series of cultures. Gordon Wassen (1974), in a study of the use of hallucinogenic mushrooms among the Mazatec, provides a detailed account of the shaman María Sabina, one of the few modern Mexican female shamans to be widely known outside of her community. Tom Dillehay (1992) details female-dominated shamanism among the modern Mapuche of Chile, and Bonnie Glass-Coffin (1998) presents her fieldwork among female shamans and curers of the Peruvian North Coast. Hans Staden, during his 7 years' (1547–55) captivity among the Brazilian Tupinambá, had ample opportunity to witness women's participation in religion in a non-Western–dominated society and notes that virtually every woman undertook the training to become a shaman. That similar practices may have existed elsewhere is shown by Zeidler's (1998) publication of the burial of a young Ecuadorian female shaman of the Late Valdivia culture. Cieza de León (1984 [1533]) documents women's roles in religion among the late prehistoric Inca, especially as deified ancestors and keepers of the ancestral cults, and Smith (1991) points to similar beliefs and practices among the Mississippians of North America. Patricia Lyon's 1978 study shows the importance of female supernaturals throughout prehispanic Peru, while Bernabé Cobo's documentation of Inca religious practices (1990 [1653]) enhances our appreciation of the multiple public roles women played in local and state religion in that culture. The discovery that the Great Goddess was the major deity of the ancient city of Teotihuacán is documented by Berlo (1992) and Pasztory (1976, 1988, 1992), while Barbour (1976) deals with domestic religion as known through ceramic figurines. Women as deities, priestesses, and participants in rituals among the Aztec are documented in Jacques Soustelle's synthesis of Aztec culture (1961), Betty Ann Brown (1983) talks about women in Aztec ritual in more detail, and Ellen Baird (1993) shows how they were presented in Father Sahagún's early colonial drawings. The importance of women in the religion of the Peruvian Moche was first pointed out by Anne-Marie Hocquenghem and Patricia Lyon in 1980, although Donnan (1975) had published drawings and interpretations of the Presentation or Sacrifice Scene without recognizing that one of the major participants was female. It was not until the discovery of the unlooted tombs of the Lords of Sipán (Alva 1988, 1990; Alva and Donnan 1993) that it was known that the Sacrifice Scene was reenacted by living people who took the roles of deities and their attendants. Further investigation at San José de Moro (Donnan and Castillo 1992, 1994) showed that Lady C of the Sacrifice Scene was also a real person and that there had been several of them, suggesting a continuing religious office or a reincarnated deity. The Mixtec Lady Nine Grass Death may have been a similar reincarnate, and McCafferty and McCafferty (1994b) suggest that it may be she who is buried in the famous Tomb 7 of Monte Albán. Joyce Marcus (1983) points out that Zapotec women served as deified ancestors in that society as well. The question of the function of figurines, especially female ones, in various cultures has been discussed at length. Rice (1981) presents some interpretations of European Paleolithic "Venus" figurines, while Reichel-Dolmatoff (1961, 1988) documents an ethnographic example of the use of figurines in rituals in northern Colombia and then identifies many of the golden figures, which commonly represent women, of prehispanic Colombia as shamans. Shirley Mock (1987) and Mark Parsons (1986) discuss painted pebbles in the Lower Pecos (Texas) culture, while Anna Roosevelt (1988) attempts a synthesis of ancient American figurines from Mesoamerica and South America. More successful is Stothert's (n.d.) study of Ecuadorian Valdivia figurines, in which she sees continuities with dances and other ritual performances still found among indigenous South American peoples. Olaf Holm documents Valdivia culture and its (mainly female) figurines, while Marcos and Garcia de Manrique (1988) see phallic imagery in a sequence of figurines from Real Alto. Zeidler attempts to identify these figurines with women's rituals and contexts, as does Costanza Di Capua (1994), who compares headdresses and hairstyles and finds correlations with life passage rituals among ethnographic South American peoples. Erick López (1996) reports on some giant Valdivia female figures found as offerings in a temple platform, and Tom Cummins et al. (1996) discusses themes and possible meanings of the later Chorrera and Jama-Coaque figurines, also from coastal Ecuador. Sánchez Montañes (1981) and Váldez (1992) discuss figurines of the contemporary Tolita culture, looking at symbols and subjects in an attempt to ascertain religious beliefs, practices, and roles in that culture. Betty Meggers's general synthesis of Ecuadorian archaeology (1961), though sadly out of date, presents a general chronological framework for looking at changes in figurine themes and at evolving religious ideologies. Cummins and Holm (1991) and Cummins et al. (1996) further discuss Ecuadorian figurines of many cultures and their possible meanings. Helms (1993) presents ideas concerning the role of trade and contact in the spread of religious ideologies. Suzanne Spencer-Wood (1991) considers the construction of gender from a feminist viewpoint. Christopher Donnan (1982) documented Moche dance rituals and their participants, while John H. Rowe's (1979) translation of Cobo's account of the shrines of ancient Cuzco indicates clearly the importance of female holy places (*huacas*). Diego de Landa (1978 [1566]) presents a firsthand account of religious practices in the Yucatán at the time of the Conquest. Larco Hoyle (1965) and Kauffman Doig (1978) present artistic evidence of ritual sex in ancient Peru, while Kehoe (1970) documents ritual sex among indigenous peoples of the North American Great Plains. Earnest Hooton's 1940 analysis of the skeletons of sacrifices recovered from the Cenote of Sacrifice at Maya Chichén Itzá indicates that most were not nubile females. Cieza de León (1984 [1533]) discusses sacrifices at the burial of chiefs in northern South America while Samuel Lothrop's (1937, 1942) excavations at Coclé in Panama validate historic accounts of sacrifices made at chiefly burials and amplify these accounts. McEwan and Van de Guchte (1992) attempt to show that Inca offerings on La Plata Island in Ecuador were an Inca Capa Cocha sacrifice, and Tom Zuidema (1977–78) presents the historic data concerning these child sacrifices. Max Uhle (1903) excavated the remains of a mass Inca sacrifice of women at the Temple of the Sun at Pachacamac in Peru.

## Chapter 8. Women and Power

The idea of women wielding political power has generally been anathema to Americanist scholars, who have ignored the abundant historical and archaeological evidence of women who occupied important economic, political, or religious positions. Yet there is considerable evidence of powerful women throughout the precolumbian Americas.

Leacock's classic studies (1978, 1981, 1983) of women's status in egalitarian societies, the myth of universal male dominance, and hypotheses concerning the origins of gender inequality lay a firm foundation for considerations of inequality of various kinds. McGuire and Saitta (1996) discuss political power structures in the North American Southwest, discovering hierarchy and consensual features, while Crown and Fish (1996) consider gender and status among the Hohokam of the same region. McGuire (1992) also presents a more detailed study of a Hohokam community, considering the relationships between society, ideology, and death. Mitchell (1992) presents an interesting case from the Arikara, looking for women in ceramics production. Howell and Kentigh (1996) try to identify kin groups in a Zuni cemetery, noting some women among the high-ranking kin members, while Howell (1992) considers Zuni gender relationships and leadership from historic records of the contact period. Divale's 1974 study of the relationship between migration, warfare, and matrilocal residence has been of considerable influence in North American studies in particular. Wilson (1990) presents a detailed ethnohistory of the Taíno chiefdoms in the sixteenth century. Juanita Saénz Samper's (1993) study of figurines, gold artifacts, and archaeology in northern Colombia leads her to identify the historic tradition of powerful women chiefs having deep roots in this part of the world. The Olmec site of Chalcatzingo was studied by David Grove (1984). Here, Cyphers Guillén (1984) identified a politically important woman on a relief monument. In the same year, David Grove and Susan Gillespie wrote that the heads of figurines at Chalcatzingo represented individuals, hypothesizing that they were politically important males. In 1993 Cyphers Guillén presented evidence that virtually all the figurine bodies found at Chalcatzingo were female. She suggests that domestic rituals or rites of passage were a possible function of these figurines. Schele and Friedel's (1990) popular book *A Forest of Kings* includes discussions of women as dynastically important, although their presentation is marred by their lack of understanding of the dynamics of patrilineal inheritance and dynastic continuity. Robertson et al. (1976) discuss the important rulers of Palenque, female and male. A pyramid tomb discussed in "New Palenque Tomb Discovered" (1994) is probably that of Queen Zak Kuk or Queen Ahpo Hel. Scott (1978) illustrates all the *danzante* slabs known at Monte Albán at the time of publication. Spores (1974) discusses the role of marital alliances among the Mixtec kingdoms. In 1997 he published a historical study of the Mixtec female rulers during the Colonial period. Winter (1997) discusses a dynastic monument at Monte Albán celebrating a woman ruler passing her kingdom to her son at her death. Caso's historic study of the *Codex Selden* (1964) presents the evidence of the historic and dynastic importance of Lady Six Monkey, although he concentrates on her subordinate male relatives. *Historia de los Mexicanos por Sus Pinturas* (1988) includes the female rulers of the Aztecs, including Tecuichpo/Doña Isabel. Bell (1992) and Gillespie (1989) discuss politically important women among the Aztec and their roles in dynastic politics and succession. Kato (1993) reports upon early elite tombs at Kuntur Wasi in Peru, among them the lavish tomb of a middle-aged woman. Joan Gero (1990, 1992, n.d.) studies gender in the Recuay culture, suggesting from iconographic studies and from archaeological investigation that women were an integral part of Andean political feasting patterns. Rowe's classic study of the Inca (1948) and his uncovering of Marua's plagiarism (1987) suggest that a critical reading of Silverblatt's 1978 and 1988 studies on Inca women is necessary. In 1988 Silverblatt published "Women in States," which also relies upon Marua, although it has a wider focus than her previous works. Theresa Topic (n.d.) looks at Inca elite women and their travels to their estates, to shrines, and elsewhere. David Gilmore (1990) discusses masculinity as a variable cultural concept.

## Chapter 9. Women, War, and Conquest

Women and war is a topic generally considered from the point of view of fantasy and folktale—such as Amazon warriors or heroic maidens—or, in more modern times, as a refugee problem in general, with emphasis on the plight of children and, occasionally, the young women who are sexually mistreated by male soldiers. However, women's participation in armed combat and its aftermath is more complex. Redmond (1994) treats warfare in tribal and chiefly societies, discussing motives, organization, and participants. Lothrop (1937, 1942) presents a detailed site report of the excavation of the graves of chiefly warriors of the Panamanian Coclé culture of the late first millennium A.D. Ewers (1994) and Owsley (1994) discuss women's roles in North American plains warfare, looking, especially, at women as victims of the unending aggression of tribal groups, while Medicine (1983) and Lewis (1941) look at women as active participants in warfare, documenting historic women warriors and the "manly hearted women" seen among some of the Northern Plains peoples. Sugiyama (1989) details the excavation of mass sacrifices of young warriors to a royal interment under the Temple of Quetzalcoatl at Teotihuacán, while Mercado Rojano (1987) notes that among the sacrificed male warriors there is a young woman buried with the same regalia. McCafferty and McCafferty (1994a) discuss the murals of Cacaxtla, identifying the leader of the vanquished Bird Warriors as a warrior queen. Mary Miller, in her study of the Bonampak murals (1986), also discusses Maya warfare and sacrifice and the actions of elite women within this context. Diego de Landa (1978 [1566]) describes Maya warriors and their organization in sixteenth-century Yucatán, and Hans Staden (1963), a captive of the Tupi of eastern Brazil in the mid-sixteenth century, describes in detail warfare, sacrifice, and cannibalism in this group. Ferguson (1992, 1995) discusses warfare among the contemporary Yanoami of Venezuela and Brazil, noting the many different causes of escalation of hostilities, while Biocca (1971) recorded the experiences of a young woman who was a war captive of the Yanoami and lived for many years among them. Topic and Topic (1997) discuss Andean warfare and its symbolic as well as its more material bases. Donnan and McClelland (1979) present the burial theme in Moche art, showing that sacrifices of prisoners of war were part of the obsequies of important persons, while Bourget (1997) documents a mass sacrifice of young male prisoners of war to an El Niño event at the Huaca de la Luna at Moche. Patricia Lyon (1978) discusses Mama Huaco and Chañan Kori Coca, two mythic/folkloric female warriors of the Inca. Although Milner et al. (1991) note that women in Eastern Woodland and Plains societies were frequently killed and scalped in raids, Silverman (1993) notes that women's heads are uncommon in caches of trophy heads found in coastal Peru. Caillevet (1996) details warfare in sixteenth-century central Colombia, noting that the capture of women and children for wives and food was common throughout this region. Tim White (1992) documents prehistoric cannibalism at Mancos Pueblo in the North American Southwest. Schele and Freidel (1990) discuss warfare among the Maya and present a case at the site of Uaxactún in which the victors buried the wives and children of the losing ruler alive. Hassig's (1988) study of Aztec warfare amply documents female participation as supporting staff and victims in a situation of bellicose state expansion. Lynn Hirschkind (1995) documents Inca and Spanish genocide in highland Ecuador and how the local population was replaced in the Colonial period by indigenous peoples from many areas. Kellogg (1995) presents historical data concerning the transformation of Aztec society under Spanish law, including female participation in legal situations in the earliest Colonial period and changes in female public self-representation as Spanish law and culture increased their domination of central Mexican cultures. Trexler (1995) presents a disturbing picture of the important role of male sexual aggression in the conquest of the Americas. Numbers of the Spanish chroniclers of the conquest of South America provide further documentation of Spanish sexual abuse of indigenous women, including forced marriage of elite women to Spanish soldiers (Cieza de León 1984 [1553] especially documents Spanish reactions to local women). Kartunnen (1997) presents a revisionist reading of the sad story of Doña Marina, Cortés's translator and mistress, and Barriga (1994) documents the numerous pejorative transformations this abused woman has suffered throughout Mexican history and literature. Weist (1993) discusses the vision that nineteenth-century Europeans had of indigenous women as shamefully oppressed beasts of burden, a situation brought about by European economic pressure on North American tribal groups. Silverblatt (1980, 1987) discusses the social, economic, and legal changes that women faced under European colonization. Cummins (1991) shows the presentation of colonial Inca elite through their European style portraits.

## Chapter 10. Women in Prehistory

Barstow (1978) presents a traditional feminist view of earlier excavations at the Anatolian site of Çatal Hüyük. Smith (1987) discusses the independent domestication of plants in North America, and Thomas (1987) presents a fictionalized view of life in indigenous North America, much as Auel does for Europe. Both novels, however, present women as active agents in ancient life, a much needed change from earlier treatments of Ice Age societies. Rapp's (1977, 1987) articles are classic feminist treatments of the origin of the state and women in "archaic" civilizations.

# Bibliography

Adams, Richard E. W. 1963. A Polychrome Vessel from Altar de Sacrificios, Peten, Guatemala. *Archaeology* 16 (2): 90–92.

———. 1971. *The Ceramics of Altar de Sacrificios*. Papers of the Peabody Museum of American Archaeology and Ethnography 63 (1). Cambridge.

———. 1977. Comments on the Glyphic Texts of the "Altar Vase." In *Social Process in Maya Prehistory: Studies in Honor of Sir Eric Thompson*, ed. Norman Hammond, 409–20. New York: Academic Press.

Alaperrine-Bouyer, Monique. 1987. Des femmes dans le manuscrit de Huarochirí. *Bulletin du Institut Français d'Etudes Andines* 16 (3–4): 97–101.

Albers, Patricia C. 1989. From Illusion to Illumination: Anthropological Studies of American Indian Women. In *Gender and Anthropology: Critical Reviews for Research and Teaching*, ed. Sandra Morgen, 132–70. Washington, D.C.: American Anthropological Association.

Albers, Patricia C., and Beatrice Medicine, eds. 1983. *The Hidden Half: Studies of Plains Indian Women*. Lanham, Md.: University Press of America.

Allison, M. J. 1984. Paleopathology in Peruvian and Chilean Populations. In *Paleopathology at the Origins of Agriculture*, ed. M. N. Cohen and George J. Armelagos, 515–30. Orlando: Academic Press.

Alva, Walter. 1988. Discovering the New World's Richest Unlooted Tomb. *National Geographic* 174, no. 4 (April): 510–49.

———. 1990. New Moche Tomb: Royal Splendor in Peru. *National Geographic* 177, no. 6 (June): 2–16.

Alva, Walter, and Christopher B. Donnan. 1993. *Royal Tombs of Sipán*. Los Angeles: Fowler Museum of Culture History, University of California.

Amaroli, Paul. 1997. A Newly Discovered Potbelly Sculpture from El Salvador and a Reinterpretation of the Genre. *Mexicon* 19, no. 3 (June): 51–53.

Anderson, Arthur J. O. Aztec Wives. 1997. In *Indian Women of Early Mexico*, ed. Susan Schroeder, Stephanie Wood, and Robert Haskett, 55–86. Norman: University of Oklahoma Press.

Arriaza, Bernardo T. 1995. Chile's Chinchorro Mummies. *National Geographic* 187 (January): 75–88.

————. 1995. *Beyond Death:The Chinchorro Mummies of Ancient Chile*. Washington, D.C.: Smithsonian Institution Press.

Arriaza, Bernardo T., Marvin Allison, and E. Gerszten. 1988. Maternal Mortality in the Pre-Columbian Indians of Arica. *American Journal of Physical Anthropology* 77:35–41.

Arsenault, Daniel. 1991. The Representation of Women in Moche Iconography. In *The Archaeology of Gender: Proceedings of the 22nd Annual Chacmool Conference*, ed. Dale Walde and Noreen D. Willows, 313–26. Archaeological Association of the University of Calgary.

Arvey, Margaret Campbell. 1988. Women of Ill-Repute in the Florentine Codex. In *The Role of Gender in Precolumbian Art and Architecture*, ed. Virginia E. Miller, 179–204. Lanham, Md.: University Press of America.

Auel, Jean M. 1985. *The Mammoth Hunters*. New York: Crown Publishers.

Baird, Ellen. 1993. *Drawings of Sahagún's Primeros Memoriales: Structure and Style*. Norman: University of Oklahoma Press.

Barbour, Warren T. 1976. *The Figurines and Figurine Chronology of Ancient Teotihuacán, Mexico*. Ann Arbor: University Microfilms.

————. 1993. Interview regarding the Identification of the Makers of Teotihuacán Figurines. "Artisans and Traders," *Out of the Past*. Pittsburgh: Pennsylvania State University and Cambridge Studios, WQED.

Barriga, María Cristina. 1994. Malinalli, Malintzin, Doña Marina, y La Llorona: Una mujer y cinco mundos diferentes. *Southeastern Latin Americanist* 37 (4): 1–4.

Bastien, Joseph W. 1987. *Healers of the Andes: Kallawaya Herbalists and Their Medicinal Plants*. Salt Lake City: University of Utah Press.

Barstow, Anne. 1978. The Uses of Archaeology for Women's History: James Mellaart's Work on the Neolithic Goddess at Çatal Hüyük. *Feminist Studies* 4 (3): 7–18.

Bell, Karen. 1992. *Kingmakers:The Royal Women of Ancient Mexico*. Ann Arbor: University Microfilms.

Benfer, R. A. 1984. The Challenges and Rewards of Sedentism: The Preceramic Village of Paloma, Peru. In *Paleopathology at the Origins of Agriculture*, ed. M. N. Cohen and George J. Armelagos, 531–58. Orlando: Academic Press.

————. 1990. The Preceramic Period Site of Paloma, Peru: Bioindications of Improving Adaptation to Sedentism. *Latin American Antiquity* 1 (4): 284–318.

Benson, Elizabeth P. 1988. Women in Mochica Art. In *The Role of Gender in Precolumbian Art and Architecture*, ed. Virginia Miller, 63–71. Lanham, Md.: University Press of America.

Benzoni, Girolamo. 1962 [1565]. *La Historia del Mondo Nuovo*. Akademische Druck-u. Verlagsanstalt Graz, Austria.

Berdan, Frances F., and Patricia R. Anawalt, eds. 1992. *The Codex Mendoza*. 4 vols. Berkeley: University of California Press.

Berlo, Janet Catherine, ed. 1992. *Art, Ideology, and the Ancient City of Teotihuacán*. Washington, D.C.: Dumbarton Oaks.

————. 1992. Icons and Ideologies at Teotihuacán: The Great Goddess Reconsidered. In *Art, Ideology and the Ancient City of Teotihuacán*, ed. Janet C. Berlo, 129–68. Washington, D.C.: Dumbarton Oaks.

Berndt, Catherine H. 1981. Interpretations and "Facts" in Aboriginal Australia. In *Woman the Gatherer*, ed. Frances Dahlberg, 153–204. New Haven: Yale University Press.

Berry, David R. 1985. Aspects of Paleodemography at Grasshopper Pueblo, Arizona. In *Health and Disease in the Prehistoric Southwest*, ed. Charles F. Merbs and Robert J. Miller, 43–64. Anthropological Research Papers No. 34. Tempe: Arizona State University.

Bertelsen, Reidar, Arnvid Lillehammer, and Jenny-Rita Naess, eds. 1987. *Were They All Men? An Examination of Sex Roles in Prehistoric Society*. Acts from a Workshop Held at Utstein I, Kloster, Rogaland. Arkeologisk Museum I. Stavanger, Norway.

Binford, Louis. 1971. Mortuary Practices: Their Study and Their Potential. In *Approaches to the Social Dimensions of Mortuary Practices*, ed. James A. Brown, 6–29. Memoirs of the Society for American Archaeology No. 25.

Biocca, Ettore. 1971. *Yanoáma: The Story of a White Girl Kidnapped by Amazonian Indians*. New York: E. P. Dutton.

Bird, Junius B., and John Hyslop. 1985. *The Preceramic Excavations at the Huaca Prieta, Chicama Valley, Peru*. Anthropological Papers of the American Museum of Natural History 62 (1). New York.

Black, Francis L. 1992. Why Did They Die? *Science* 258 (December 11): 1739–40.

Blaffer-Hrdy, Sarah. 1981. Lucy's Husband: What Did He Stand For? *Harvard Magazine* (July–August): 7–9, 46.

Blakey, Michael L., and George R. Armelagos. 1985. Deciduous Enamel Defects in Prehistoric Americans from Dickson Mounds: Prenatal and Postnatal Stress. *American Journal of Physical Anthropology* 66:371–380.

Blitz, John H. 1993. *Ancient Chiefdoms of the Tombigbee*. Tuscaloosa: University of Alabama Press.

Bolen, Kathleen. 1992. Prehistoric Construction of Mothering. In *Exploring Gender through Archaeology: Selected Papers from the Boone Conference*, ed. Cheryl Claassen, 49–62. Monographs in World Archaeology No. 11. Madison, Wis.: Prehistory Press.

Boone, Elizabeth H. 1980. How Efficient Are Early Colonial Mexican Manuscripts as Iconographic Tools? *Research Center for the Arts Review* 3 (4): 1–5. San Antonio: College of Fine and Applied Arts, University of Texas.

Boulding, R. 1978. *Women, Peripheries, and Food Production*. Consortium for International Development, International Conference on Women and Food, vol. 1, 22–44. Tucson: University of Arizona Press.

Bourget, Steve. 1997. La colère des ancêctres: Découverte d'un site sacrificial à la Huaca de la Luna, Vallée de Moche. In *A l'ombre du Cerro Blanco: Nouvelles découvertes sur la culture moche, Côte Nord du Pérou*, ed. Claude Chapdelaine, 83–100. Les Cahiers d' Anthropologie No. 1. Université de Montréal.

Brekhman, I. I., and Y. A. San. 1967. Ethnopharmacological Investigation of Some Psychoactive Drugs Used by Siberian and Far-Eastern Minority Nationalities of

U.S.S.R. In *Ethnopharmacologic Search for Psychoactive Drugs*, ed. Daniel Efron et al., 415. NIMH, Workshop Series of Pharmacology No. 2. Public Health Service Publication No. 1645. Washington, D.C.

Brettell, Caroline B., and Carolyn F. Sargent. 1997. *Gender in Cross-Cultural Perspective*. 2d ed. New York: Prentice Hall.

Bridges, Patricia S. 1991. Skeletal Evidence of Changes in Subsistence Activities between the Archaic and Mississippian Time Periods in Northwestern Alabama. In *What Mean These Bones? Studies in Southeastern Bioarchaeology*, ed. Mary Lucas Powell, Patricia S. Bridges and Ana María Wagner Mires, 89–101. Tuscaloosa: University of Alabama Press.

———. 1989. Changes in Activities with the Shift to Agriculture in the Southeastern United States. *Current Anthropology* 30:385–94.

Brown, Betty Ann. 1983. Seen But Not Heard: Women in Aztec Ritual: The Sahagún Texts. In *Text and Image in Pre-Columbian Art*, ed. Janet Catherine Berlo, 119–54. BAR International Series 180. Oxford.

Brown, Judith K. 1978. The Recruitment of a Female Labor Force. *Anthropos* 73:41–47.

———. 1963. A Cross-Cultural Study of Female Initiation Rites. *American Anthropologist* 65:837–53.

Bruhns, Karen Olsen. 1984. The Ladies of Cotzumalhuapa. *Mexicon* 6 (3): 38–39.

———. 1988. Yesterday the Queen Wore . . . An Analysis of Women and Costume in the Public Art of the Late Classic Maya. In *The Role of Gender in Precolumbian Art and Architecture*, ed. Virginia E. Miller, 105–34. Lanham, Md.: University Press of America.

———. 1991. Sexual Activities: Some Thoughts on the Sexual Division of Labor and Archaeological Interpretation. In *The Archaeology of Gender: Proceedings of the 22nd Annual Chacmool Conference*, ed. Dale Walde and Noreen D. Willows, 420–29. Archaeological Association of the University of Calgary.

———. 1994. *Ancient South America*. Cambridge and New York: Cambridge University Press.

Brumbach, Hetty Jo, and Robert Jarvenpa. 1977. Woman the Hunter: Ethno-archaeological Lessons from Chipewyan Life-Cycle Dynamics. In *Women in Prehistory: North America and Mesoamerica*, ed. Cheryl Claassen and Rosemary Joyce, 17–32. Philadelphia: University of Pennsylvania Press.

Brumfiel, Elizabeth M. 1991. Weaving and Cooking: Women's Production in Aztec Mexico. In *Engendering Archaeology: Women in Prehistory*, ed. Joan M. Gero and Margaret W. Conkey, 224–51. London: Basil Blackwell.

———. 1996. The Quality of Tribute Cloth: The Place of Evidence in Archaeological Argument. *American Antiquity* 61 (3): 453–62.

Buikstra, Jane E. 1984. The Lower Illinois River Region: A Prehistoric Context for the Study of Ancient Diet and Health. In *Paleopathology at the Origins of Agriculture*, ed. Mark N. Cohen and George R. Armelagos, 215–34. Orlando: Academic Press.

Buikstra, Jane E., Lyle W. Konigsberg, and Jill Bullington. 1986. Fertility and the Development of Agriculture in the Prehistoric Midwest. *American Antiquity* 51 (3): 528–46.

Bumstead, Pamela, et al. 1987. Recognizing Women in the Archaeological Record. In *Powers of Observation: Alternative Views in Archaeology*, ed. Sarah M. Nelson and Alice B. Kehoe, 89–101. Archaeological Papers of the American Anthropological Association No. 2. Washington, D.C.

Burger, Richard L. 1992. *Chavín and the Origins of Andean Civilization*. London: Thames and Hudson.

Burkhart, Louise M. 1997. Mexica Women on the Home Front: Housework and Religion in Aztec Mexico. In *Indian Women of Early Mexico*, ed. Susan Schroeder, Stephanie Wood, and Robert Haskett, 25–54. Norman: University of Oklahoma Press.

Cabello Valvoa, Miguel. 1951. *Miscelánea antártica: Una historia del Perú antiguo*. Lima: Universidad Mayor de San Marcos, Facultad de Letras, Instituto de Entnología.

Caillavet, Chantal. 1996. Antropofagía y frontera: El caso de los Andes septentrionales. In *Frontera y poblamiento: Estudios de historia y antropología de Colombia y Ecuador*, ed. Chantal Caillavet and Ximena Pachón, 57–109. Bogotá: Instituto Français de Etudes Andines, Instituto Amazónico de Investigaciones Científicas, Departamento de Antropología, Universidad de los Andes.

Carrasco, Pedro Royal. 1984. Marriages in Ancient Mexico. In *Explorations in Ethnohistory: Indians of Central Mexico in the Sixteenth Century*, ed. H. R. Harvey and Hanns J. Prem, 41–81. Albuquerque: University of New Mexico Press.

—————. 1997. Indian-Spanish Marriages in the First Century of the Colony. In *Indian Women of Early Mexico*, ed. Susan Schroeder, Stephanie Wood, and Robert Haskett, 87–104. Norman: University of Oklahoma Press.

Caso, Alfonso. 1964. *Interpretación del Codice Seldon 3135(A.2)*. Mexico: Sociedad Mexicana de Antropología.

Cassidy, Claire. 1987. Monod Skeletal Evidence for Prehistoric Subsistence Adaptation in the Central Ohio Valley. In *Paleopathology at the Origins of Agriculture*, ed. Mark N. Cohen and George R. Armelagos, 307–45. Orlando: Academic Press.

Castaño Uribe, Carlos. 1987. La vivienda y el enterramiento como unidades de interpretación: Anatomía de dos casos de transición del modelo de cacicazgo. In *Chiefdoms in the Americas*, ed. Robert D. Drennan and Carlos Castaño Uribe, 231–48. Lanham, Md.: University Press of America.

—————. 1985. *Secuencias y correlaciones cronológicas en el Río de la Miel*. Bogotá: Fundación de Investigaciones Arqueológicas Nacionales.

Chadwick-Hawkes, Sonia, and Calvin Wells. 1975. Crime and Punishment in an Anglo-Saxon Cemetery? *Antiquity* 49:118–22.

Charles, Douglas K., and Jane E. Buikstra. 1993. Archaic Mortuary Sites in the Central Mississippi Drainage: Distribution, Structure, and Behavioral Implications. In *Archaic Hunters and Gatherers in the American Midwest*, ed. J. L. Phillips and J. A. Brown, 117–44. Orlando and New York: Academic Press.

Chauchat, Claude. 1988. Early Hunter-Gatherers on the Peruvian Coast. In *Peruvian Prehistory: An Overview of Pre-Inca and Inca Society*, ed. Richard W. Keatinge, 41–66. Cambridge and New York: Cambridge University Press.

Cheal, David. 1987. Strategies of Resource Management in Household Economies: Moral Responsibility or Political Economy. In *The Household Economy: Reconsidering the Domestic Mode of Production*, ed. Richard R. Wilk, 11–22. Boulder: Westview Press.

Cieza de León, Pedro de. 1984 [1533]. *Crónica del Perú, primera parte*. Lima: Pontificia Universidad Católica del Peru, Fondo Editorial.

Claassen, Cheryl P. 1991. Gender, Shellfishing, and the Shell Mound Archaic. In *Engendering Archaeology: Women in Prehistory*, ed. Joan M. Gero and W. Margaret Conkey, 276–300. London: Basil Blackwell.

———. 1997. Changing Venue: Women's Lives in Prehistoric North America. In *Women in Prehistory: North America and Mesoamerica*, ed. Cheryl Claassen and Rosemary A. Joyce, 65–87. Philadelphia: University of Pennsylvania Press.

Claassen, Cheryl, ed. 1992. *Exploring Gender through Archaeology: Selected Papers from the 1991 Boone Conference*. Monographs in World Archaeology No. 11. Madison, Wis.: Prehistory Press.

———. 1994. *Women in Archaeology*. Philadelphia: University of Pennsylvania Press.

Claassen, Cheryl, and Rosemary A. Joyce, eds. 1997. *Women in Prehistory: North America and Mesoamerica*. Philadelphia: University of Pennsylvania Press.

Clarkson, Persis B. 1978. Classic Maya Pictorial Ceramics: A Survey of Content and Theme. In *Papers on the Economy and Architecture of the Ancient Maya*, ed. Raymond Sidrys, 86–141. Institute of Archaeology, Monograph 7. Los Angeles: University of California.

Closs, Michael P. 1992. I Am a Kahal; My Parents Were Scribes: Soy un Kahal; Mis Padres Fueron Escribas. *Research Reports on Ancient Maya Writing* 38 (7): 7–22. Washington, D.C.

Cobo, Bernabé. 1990 [1653]. *Inca Religion and Customs*. Translated and edited by Rowland Hamilton. Austin: University of Texas Press.

Cohen, Mark Nathan, and George J. Armelagos. 1984a. Paleopathology at the Origins of Agriculture: Editors' Summation. In *Paleopathology at the Origins of Agriculture*, ed. Mark N. Cohen and George J. Armelagos, 393–424. Orlando: Academic Press.

Cohen, Mark Nathan, and George J. Armelagos, eds. 1984b. *Paleopathology at the Origins of Agriculture*. Orlando: Academic Press.

Cohen, Mark Nathan, and Sharon Bennett. 1993. Skeletal Evidence for Sex Roles and Gender Hierarchies in Prehistory. In *Sex and Gender Hierarchies*, ed. Barbara Diane Miller, 273–96. Cambridge and New York: Cambridge University Press.

Conkey, Margaret W. 1991. Contexts of Action, Contexts for Power: Material Culture and Gender in the Magdalenian. In *Engendering Archaeology: Women in Prehistory*, ed. Joan M. Gero and Margaret W. Conkey, 57–92. London: Basil Blackwell.

Conkey, Margaret W., and Joan M. Gero. 1991. Tensions, Pluralities, and Engendering Archaeology: Women in Prehistory: An Introduction to Women and Prehistory. In *Engendering Archaeology: Women in Prehistory*, ed. Joan M. Gero and Margaret W. Conkey, 3–30. London: Basil Blackwell.

Conkey, Margaret W., and Janet D. Spector. 1984. Archaeology and the Study of Gender. *Advances in Archaeological Method and Theory* 7:1–38.

Conkey, Margaret W., and Ruth E. Tringham. 1995. Archaeology and the Goddess: Exploring the Contours of Feminist Archaeology. In *Feminisms in the Academy*, ed. Donna C. Stanton and Abigail J. Stewart, 199–234. Ann Arbor: University of Michigan Press.

Conkey, Margaret W., and Sarah H. Williams. 1991. Original Narratives: The Political Economy of Gender in Archaeology. In *Gender at the Crossroads of Knowledge: Feminist Anthropology in the Postmodern Era*, ed. Micaela di Leonardo, 102–39. Berkeley and Los Angeles: University of California Press.

Connolly, Thomas J., Jon M. Erlandson, and Susan E. Norris. 1995. Early Holocene Basketry and Cordage from Daisy Cave, San Miguel Island, California. *American Antiquity* 60 (2): 309–18.

Cook, Della Collins. 1984. Subsistence and Health in the Lower Illinois Valley: Osteological Evidence. In *Paleopathology at the Origins of Agriculture*, ed. Mark N. Cohen and George R. Armelagos, 235–69. Orlando: Academic Press.

Correal Urrego, Gonzalo, and Thomas van der Hammen. 1977. *Investigaciones arqueológicas en los abrigos rocosos del Tequendama: 12.000 años de historia del hombre y su medio ambiente en la Altiplanacie de Bogotá*. Bogotá: Fondo de Promoción de la Cultura del Banco Popular.

Cowgill, George L. 1992. Social Differentiation at Teotihuacán. In *Mesoamerican Elites: An Archaeological Assessment*, ed. Diane Z. Chase and Arlen F. Chase, 206–20. Norman: University of Oklahoma Press.

Crown, Patricia L., and Suzanne K. Fish. 1996. Hohokam Gender and Status. *American Anthropologist* 98 (4): 803–17.

Crown, Patricia L., and W. H. Wills. 1995. The Origins of Southwestern Ceramic Containers: Women's Time Allocation and Economic Intensification. *Journal of Anthropological Research* 51:173–86.

Cummins, Thomas. 1992. Tradition in Ecuadorian Pre-Hispanic Art: The Ceramics of Chorrera and Jama-Coaque. In *Amerindian Signs: 5000 Years of Precolumbian Art in Ecuador*, ed. Francisco Váldez and Diego Veintimilla, 63–82. Quito: Dinediciones.

————. 1991. We Are the Other: Peruvian Portraits of Colonial Curakuna. In *Transatlantic Encounters: Europeans and Andeans in the Sixteenth Century*, ed. Rolena Adorno and Kenneth Adrien, 203–31. Berkeley and Los Angeles: University of California Press.

Cummins, Thomas, and Olaf Holm. 1991. The Pre-Hispanic Art of Ecuador. In *Ancient Art of the Ancient World*, ed. Shozo Matsuda and Izumi Shimada, 167–84. Tokyo: Iwanami Shoten.

Cummins, Thomas, Julio Burgos Cabrera, and Carlos Mora Hoyos. 1996. *Arte prehispánico del Ecuador: Huellas del pasado: Los sellos de Jama-Coaque*. Miscelanea Antropológica Ecuatoriana, Series Monográfica 11. Guayaquil: Banco Central del Ecuador.

Cyphers Guillén, Ann. 1984. The Possible Role of a Woman in Formative Exchange. In *Trade and Exchange in Early Mesoamerica*, ed. Kenneth Hirth, 115–23. Albuquerque: University of New Mexico Press.

————. 1993. Women, Rituals, and Social Dynamics at Ancient Chalcatzingo. *Latin American Antiquity* 4 (3): 209–24.

————. 1994. Las mujeres de Chalcatzingo. *Arqueología Mexicana* 2, no. 7 (April–May): 70–73.

Dahlberg. Frances, ed. 1981. *Woman the Gatherer*. New Haven: Yale University Press.

Damp, Jonathan E. 1979. *Better Homes and Gardens: The Life and Death of the Early Valdivia Community*. Ann Arbor: University Microfilms.

————. 1984. Architecture of the Early Valdivia Village. *American Antiquity* 49 (3): 573–85.

Danforth, Marie Elaine, Keith P. Jacobi, and Mark Nathan Cohen. 1997. Gender and Health among the Colonial Maya of Tipu, Belize. *Ancient Mesoamerica* 8 (1): 13–22.

Davenport, J. Walker, and Carl Chelf. 1941. Painted Pebbles from the Lower Pecos and Big Bend Regions of Texas. Bulletin 5. San Antonio: Witte Memorial Museum.

Davis, Leslie B. 1993. Paleo-Indian Archaeology in the High Plains and Rocky Mountains of Montana. In *From Kostenki to Clovis: Upper Paleolithic-Paleoindian Adaptations*, ed. Olga Soffer and N. D. Praslov, 263–77. New York: Plenem Press.

Denver Art Museum. 1995. Female Ballplayer. *News from the Center* 3 (1): 8. Denver Art Museum, Center for Latin American Art and Archaeology.

Di Capua, Costanza. 1994. Valdivia Figurines and Puberty Rituals. *Andean Past* 4:229–79.

Dickel, David N., P. D. Schulz, and H. M. McHenry. 1984. Central California: Prehistoric Subsistence and Health. In *Paleopathology at the Origins of Agriculture*, ed. Mark N. Cohen and George R. Armelagos, 439–62. Orlando: Academic Press.

Diehl, Michael W. 1996. The Intensity of Maize Processing and Production in Upland Mogollon Pithouse Villages, AD 200–1000. *American Antiquity* 61 (1): 102–15.

Dillehay, Tom D. 1992. Keeping Outsiders Out: Public Ceremony, Resource Rights, and Hierarchy in Historic and Contemporary Mapuche Society. In *Wealth and Hierarchy in the Intermediate Area*, ed. Frederick W. Lange, 379–422. Washington, D.C.: Dumbarton Oaks.

————. 1996. *Monte Verde: A Late Pleistocene Settlement in Chile*. Vol. 2, *The Archaeological Context and Interpretation*. Washington, D.C.: Smithsonian Institution Press.

Dillehay, Tom D., ed. 1995. *Tombs for the Living: Andean Mortuary Practices*. Washington, D.C.: Dumbarton Oaks.

Dincauze, Dena F. 1993. Fluted Points in the Eastern Forests. In *From Kostenki to Clovis: Upper Paleolithic-Paleoindian Adaptations*, ed. Olga Soffer and N. D. Praslov, 279–92. New York: Plenum Press.

Divale, William T. 1974. Migration, External Warfare, and Matrilocal Residence. *Behavioral Science Research* 9 (2): 75–133.

Divale, William T., and Marvin Harris. 1976. Population, Warfare, and the Male Supremist Complex. *American Anthropologist* 78:521–38.

Donnan, Christopher B. 1975. The Thematic Approach to Moche Iconography. *Journal of Latin American Lore* 1 (2): 147–62.

————. 1982. Dance in Moche Art. *Ñawpa Pacha* 20:97–120.

————. 1995. Moche Funerary Practice. In *Tombs for the Living: Andean Mortuary Practices*, ed. Tom D. Dillehay, 111–60. Washington, D.C.: Dumbarton Oaks.

Donnan, Christopher B., and Luis Jaime Castillo. 1992. B. Finding the Tomb of a Moche Priestess. *Archaeology* 45 (6): 38–42.

————. 1994. Excavaciones de tumbas de sacerdotisas moche en San José de Moro, Jequetepeque. In *Moche: Propuestas y perspectivas*, ed. Santiago Uceda and Elías Mujica, 415–24. Travaux de L'Institut Français d'Etudes Andines, Vol. 79. Lima.

Donnan, Christopher B., and Donna McClelland. 1979. *The Burial Theme in Moche Iconography*. Studies in Pre-Columbian Art and Archaeology No. 21. Washington, D.C.: Dumbarton Oaks.

Dransart, Penny. 1992. Pachamama: The Inka Earth Mother of the Long Sweeping Garment. In *Dress and Gender: Making and Meaning in Cultural Contexts*, ed. Ruth Barnes and Joanne B. Eicher, 145–63. New York: Berg.

Drooker, Penelope Ballard. 1992. *Mississippian Village Textiles at Wickliffe*. Tuscaloosa: University of Alabama Press.

Du Cros, Hilary, and Laurajane Smith. 1993. *Women in Archaeology*. Research School of Pacific Publication Series. Canberra: Australian National University.

Ehrenberg, Margaret. 1989. *Women in Prehistory*. Norman: University of Oklahoma Press.

Ehrenreich, Robert M., Carole L. Crumley, and Janet E. Levy. 1995. *Heterarchy and the Analysis of Complex Societies*. Archaeological Papers of the American Anthropological Association, No. 6.

Eisenberg, Leslie E. 1988. Mississippian Cultural Terminations in Middle Tennessee: What the Bioarchaeological Evidence Can Tell Us. In *What Mean These Bones? Studies in Southeastern Bioarchaeology*, ed. Mary Lucas Powell, Patricia S. Bridges, and Ana María Wagner Mires, 70–88. Tuscaloosa: University of Alabama Press.

Englestad, Erika. 1991. Images of Power and Contradiction: Feminist Theory and Post-Processual Archaeology. *Antiquity* 65:502–14.

Espenshade, Christoper B. 1997. Mimbres Pottery, Births, and Gender: A Reconsideration. *American Antiquity* 62 (4): 733–36.

Espinosa Soriano, Waldemar. 1976. Las mujeres secundarias de Huayna Capac: Dos casos de señorialismo feudal en el Imperio Inca. *Revista del Museo Nacional* 42:248–96. Lima.

Estioko-Griffin, Agnes, and P. Bion Griffin. 1981. Woman the Hunter: The Agta. In *Woman the Gatherer*, ed. Frances Dahlberg, 121–52. New Haven: Yale University Press.

Etienne, Mona, and Eleanor Leacock. 1980. *Women in Colonization: Anthropological Perspectives*. New York: Praeger.

Ewers, John C. 1994. Women's Roles in Plains Indian Warfare. In *Skeletal Biology of the Great Plains: Migration, Warfare, Health, Subsistence*, ed. Douglas W. Owsley and Richard L. Janz, 325–32. Washington, D.C.: Smithsonian Institution Press.

Ezzo, Joseph A. 1993. *Human Adaptation at Grasshopper Pueblo, Arizona: Social and Ecological Perspectives*. International Monographs in Prehistory, Archaeological Series 4. Ann Arbor.

Ferguson, R. Brian. 1995. *Yanomami Warfare: A Political History*. Santa Fe: School of American Research.

—————. 1992. A Savage Encounter: Western Contact and the Yanomami War Complex. In R. Brian Ferguson and Neil L. Whitehead, *War in the Tribal Zone: Expanding States and Indigenous Warfare*, 199–298. School of American Research Advanced Seminar Series. Seattle: University of Washington Press.

Finerma, Ruthbeth. 1989. The Forgotten Healers: Women as Family Healers in an Andean Indian Community. In *Women as Healers: Cross-Cultural Perspectives*, ed. Carol Shepherd McClain, 24–41. New Brunswick: Rutgers University Press.

Flannery, Kent V. 1976. Interregional Exchange Networks. In *The Early Mesoamerican Village*, ed. Kent V. Flannery, 283–86. Orlando: Academic Press.

Flannery, Kent V., ed. 1986. *Guila Naquitz: Archaic Foraging and Early Agriculture in Oaxaca, Mexico*. Orlando: Academic Press.

Flannery, Kent V., Joyce Marcus, and Stephen A. Kowalewski. 1981. The Preceramic and Formative of the Valley of Oaxaca. In *Handbook of Middle American Indians, Supplement 1: Archaeology*, ed. Jeremy A. Sabloff, 48–93. Austin: University of Texas Press.

Flannery, Kent V., and Marcus C. Winter. 1976. Analyzing Household Activities. In *The Early Mesoamerican Village*, ed. Kent V. Flannery, 34–48. Orlando: Academic Press.

Freidel, David, and Linda Schele. 1993. Maya Royal Women: A Lesson in Precolumbian History. In *Gender in Cross-Cultural Perspective*, ed. Caroline B. Brettell and Carolyn F. Sargent, 59–63. Prentice Hall.

Frisbie, Charlotte Johnson. 1967. *Kinaalda: A Study of the Navaho Girl's Puberty Ceremony*. Middletown: Wesleyan University Press.

Frison, George C. 1993. North American High Plains Paleo-Indian Hunting Strategies and Weaponry Assemblages. In *From Kostenki to Clovis: Upper Paleolithic-Paleoindian Adaptations*, ed. Olga Soffer and N. D. Praslov, 237–49. New York: Plenum Press.

Furst, Peter T. 1965. West Mexican Tomb Sculpture as Evidence for Shamanism in Prehispanic Mesoamerica. *Antropologica* 15 (Diciembre): 29–60. Caracas.

—————. 1974. Morning Glory and Mother Goddess at Tepantitla: Iconography and Analogy in Pre-Columbian Art. In *Mesoamerican Archaeology*, ed. Norman Hammond, 187–217. Austin: University of Texas Press.

—————. 1976. *Hallucinogens and Culture*. San Francisco: Chandler and Sharp.

—————. 1978. *The Ninth Level: Funerary Art from Ancient Mesoamerica*. Iowa City: University of Iowa Museum of Art.

—————. 1986. Shamanism, the Ecstatic Experience, and Lower Pecos Art: Reflections on Some Transcultural Phenomena in Ancient Texans. In *Rock Art and Lifeways along the Lower Pecos*, ed. Harry J. Schafer, 210–25. Dallas: Texas Monthly Press.

Gailey, C. W. 1987. Evolutionary Perspectives on Gender Hierarchy. In *Analyzing Gender*, ed. Beth B. Hess and Myra Marx Ferree, 32–37. Newbury Park, Calif.: Sage Publications.

Galloway, Anne. N.d. Archaeological Evidence for Textile Production at Tarmatambo, an Inca Administrative Center in the Peruvian Central Highlands. Manuscript in the possession of the author.

Galloway, Patricia. 1997. Where Have All the Menstrual Huts Gone? The Invisibility of Menstrual Seclusion in the Late Prehistoric Southwest. In *Women in Prehistory: North America and Mesoamerica*, ed. Cheryl Claassen and Rosemary A. Joyce, 47–64. Philadelphia: University of Pennsylvania Press.

Garcilaso de la Vega, "El Inca." 1945 [1609]. *Comentarios reales de los Incas*. Buenos Aires: Emecé Editores.

————. 1951. *The Florida of the Inca*. Translated and edited by John G. and Jeannette J. Varner. Austin: University of Texas Press.

Garza Tarazona de González, Silvia. 1991. *La mujer mesoamericana*. Mexico: Editorial Planeta Mexicana.

Gero, Joan M. 1990. Pottery, Power and Parties! At Queyash Alto. *Archaeology* 43 (2): 52–56.

————. 1991. Genderlithics: Women's Roles in Stone Tool Production. In *Engendering Archaeology: Women in Prehistory*, ed. Joan M. Gero and Margaret W. Conkey, 163–93. London: Basil Blackwell.

————. 1992. Feasts and Females: Gender Ideology and Political Meals in the Andes. *Norwegian Archaeological Review* 25 (1): 15–30.

————. 1993. The Social World of Prehistoric Facts: Gender and Power in Paleoindian Research. In *Women in Archaeology*, ed. Hilary du Cros and Laurajane Smith, 31–40. Research School of the Pacific Publication Series. Canberra: Australian National University.

————. N.d. La iconografía recuay y el estudio de género. *Gaceta Arqueológica Andina* 25–26.

Gero, Joan M., and Margaret W. Conkey. 1991. *Engendering Archaeology: Women in Prehistory*. London: Basil Blackwell.

Gero, Joan M., and M. María Scattolini. N.d. Household Production as Glue: Insights from the Early Formative of Northwest Argentina. Paper in the possession of the author.

Gifford-Gonzales, Diane. 1995. The Drudge on the Hide. *Archaeology* 48, no. 2 (May–June): 84.

Gillespie, Susan D. 1989. *The Aztec Kings: The Construction of Rulership in Mexica History*. Tucson: University of Arizona Press.

Gillespie, Susan D., and Rosemary A. Joyce. 1997. Gendered Goods: The Symbolism of Maya Hierarchical Exchange Relations. In *Women in Prehistory: North America and Mesoamerica*, ed. Cheryl Claassen and Rosemary A. Joyce, 189–210. Philadelphia: University of Pennsylvania Press.

Gilmore, David D. 1990. *Manhood in the Making: Cultural Concepts of Masculinity*. New Haven: Yale University Press.

Gimbutas, Marija. 1991. *The Civilization of the Goddess: The World of Old Europe*. San Francisco: Harper Collins.

Glass-Coffin, Bonnie. 1998. *The Gift of Life: Female Spirituality and Healing in Northern Peru*. Albuquerque: University of New Mexico Press.

Goldstein, Marilyn. 1988. Gesture, Role, and Gender in West Mexican Sculpture. In *The Role of Gender in Precolumbian Art and Architecture*, ed. Virginia E. Miller, 53–62. Lanham, Md.: University Press of America.

Graham, Elizabeth. 1991. Women and Gender in Maya Prehistory. In *The Archaeology of Gender: Proceedings of the 22nd Annual Chacmool Conference*, ed. Dale Walde and Noreen D. Willows, 470–78. Archaeological Association of the University of Calgary.

Gramby, Richard Michael. 1982. *The Vail Site: A Paleo-Indian Encampment in Maine*. Bulletin of the Buffalo Museum of Natural Sciences 30. Buffalo.

————. 1988. *The Adkins Site: A Paleo-Indian Habitation and Associated Stone Structure*. Buffalo Society of Natural Sciences, Occasional Paper No. 3. Buffalo: Persimmon Press Monographs in Archaeology.

Grange, Roger T., Jr. 1979. An Archaeological View of Pawnee Origins. *Nebraska History* 60:134–60.

Graulich, Michel. 1992. Las brujas de las peregrinaciones aztecas. *Estudios de Cultura Nahuatl* 22:87–98.

Gross, Rita, and Nancy Falk. 1989. *Unspoken Worlds: Women's Religious Lives*. 2d ed. Belmont, Calif.: Wadsworth Press.

Grove, Davis C. 1984. *Chalcatzingo: Excavations on the Olmec Frontier*. London: Thames and Hudson.

Grove, David C., and Susan D. Gillespie. 1984. Chalcatzingo's Portrait Figurines and the Cult of the Ruler. *Archaeology* 37 (4): 20–26.

Guaman Poma de Ayala, Felipe de. 1936 [1615]. *Nueva corónica y buen gobierno: Codex peruvien ilustre*. Université de Paris, Traveaux et Memoires de l'Institut d'Ethnologie 23. Paris: Institut d'Ethnologie.

Guillén, Sonia Elizabeth. 1992. *The Chinchorro Culture: Mummies and Crania in the Reconstruction of Preceramic Coastal Adaptation in the South Central Andes*. Ann Arbor: University Microfilms.

Hammond, Norman, and Theya Molleson. 1994. Huegnot Weavers and Maya Kings: Anthropological Assessment versus Documentary Record of Age at Death. *Mexicon* 16 (4): 75–77.

Hanmann, Bryon. 1997. Weaving and the Iconography of Prestige: Lord 5 Flower's/Lady 4 Rabbit's Family. In *Women in Prehistory: North America and Mesoamerica*, ed. Cheryl Claassen and Rosemary A. Joyce, 153–72. Philadelphia: University of Pennsylvania Press.

Harris, Olivia. 1978. Complementarity and Conflict: An Andean View of Women and Men. In *Sex and Age as Principles of Social Differentiation*, ed. J. S. La Fontaine, 21–41. Orlando: Academic Press.

Hartmann, Roswith. 1994. Achikee, Chificha, y Mama Huaca en la tradición oral andina. *Revista del Instituto Azuayo de Folklor* 12:180–97. Cuenca, Ecuador.

Harvey, Herbert R. 1986. Household and Family Structure in Early Colonial Tepetlaoztoc. *Estudios de Cultural Nahuatl* 18:275–94.

Hassig, Ross. 1988. *Aztec Warfare: Imperial Expansion and Legal Control*. Norman: University of Oklahoma Press.

Hastorf, Christine. 1990. The Effect of the Inka State on Sausa Agricultural Production and Crop Consumption. *American Antiquity* 55 (2): 262–90.

———. 1991. Gender, Space, and Food in Prehistory. In *Engendering Archaeology:Women in Prehistory*, ed. Joan M. Gero and Margaret W. Conkey, 132–59. London: Basil Blackwell.

———. 1993. *Agriculture and the Onset of Political Inequality before the Inca*. Cambridge and New York: Cambridge University Press.

Hartung, J. 1982. Polygyny and the Inheritance of Wealth. *Current Anthropology* 23:1–12.

Haury, Emil W. 1976. *The Hohokam: Desert Farmers and Craftsmen: Excavations at Snaketown, 1964–1965*. Tucson: University of Arizona Press.

Haviland, William A. 1997. The Rise and Fall of Sexual Inequality: Death and Gender at Tikal, Guatemala. *Ancient Mesoamerica* 8 (1): 1–12.

Hayden, Brian A. 1986. Old Europe: Sacred Matriarchy or Complementary Opposition. In *Archaeology and Fertility Cult in the Ancient Mediterranean*, ed. Antonio Bonnano, 17–30. Amsterdam: Gruner Publishing.

———. 1992. Contrasting Expectations in Theories of Domestication: Models of Domestication. In *The Transition to Agriculture in Prehistory*, ed. A. B. Gebauer and T. D. Price, 11–20. Madison, Wis.: Prehistory Press.

Hayden, Brian A., Edward Bakewell, and Rob Gargett. 1996. The World's Longest-Lived Corporate Group: Lithic Analysis Reveals Prehistoric Social Organization near Lilooet, British Columbia. *American Antiquity* 61 (2): 341–56.

Hayden, Brian A., Cannon Deal, and J. Casey. 1986. Ecological Determinants of Women's Status among Hunter/Gatherers. *Human Evolution* 1 (5): 449–74.

Hegmon, Michelle, and Wenda R. Trevathan. 1996. Gender, Anatomical Knowledge, and Pottery Production: Implications of an Anatomically Unusual Birth Depicted on Mimbres Pottery from Southwestern New Mexico. *American Antiquity* 61 (4): 747–54.

———. 1997. Response to Comments by LeBlanc, by Espenshade, and by Shaffer et al. *American Antiquity* 62 (4): 737–39.

Helms, Mary. 1980. Succession to High Office in Pre-Columbian Circum-Carribbean Chiefdoms. *Man* 15:718–31.

———. 1993. *Craft and the Kingly Ideal: Art, Trade, and Power*. Austin: University of Texas Press.

Hendon, Julia A. 1997. Women's Work, Women's Space, and Women's Status among the Classic-Period Maya Elite of the Copan Valley. In *Women in Prehistory: North America and Mesoamerica*, ed. Cheryl Claassen and Rosemary A. Joyce, 33–46. Philadelphia: University of Pennsylvania Press.

Herr, Rebecca Lynn. 1987. Women of Yaxchilán and Naranjo: A Study of Classic Maya Texts and Contexts. M.A. thesis, University of Texas, Austin.

Heth, Charlotte, ed. 1992. *Native American Dance: Ceremonies and Social Traditions*. Washington, D.C.: National Museum of the American Indian, Smithsonian Institution, and Starwood Publishing.

Hickmann, Ellen. 1986. Instrumentos musicales del Museo Antropológico del Banco Central del Ecuador, Guayaquil: Ocarinas. *Miscelanea Antropológica Ecuatoriana* 6:117–41.

———. 1987. Instrumentos musicales del Museo Antropológico del Banco Central del Ecuador, Guayaquil II. *Miscelanea Antropológica Ecuatoriana* 7:7–30.

Hirschkind, Lynn. 1995. History of the Indian Population of Cañar. *Colonial Latin American Historical Review* 4:311–42.

*Historia de los Mexicanos por sus pinturas.* 1988. Paris: Associación Oxomoco y Cipactamal.

Hocquenghem, Anne Marie. 1977a. Un "vase portrait" de femme mochica. *Ñawpa Pacha* 15:117–22.

———. 1977b. Les représentations de chamans dans líiconographie mochica. *Ñawpa Pacha* 15:123–30.

Hoquenghem, Anne Marie, and Patricia J. Lyon. 1980. A Class of Anthropomorphic Supernatural Females in Moche Iconography. *Ñawpa Pacha* 18:27–48.

Hollimon, Sandra E. 1991. Health Consequences of Divisions of Labor among the Chumash Indians of Southern California. In *The Archaeology of Gender: Proceedings of the 22nd Annual Chacmool Conference*, ed. Dale Walde and Noreen Willows, 462–69. Archaeological Association of the University of Calgary.

———. 1992. Health Consequences of Sexual Division of Labor among Prehistoric Native Americans: The Chumash of California and the Arikara of the North Plains. In *Exploring Gender through Archaeology: Selected Papers from the 1991 Boone Conference*, ed. Cheryl Claassen, 81–88. Madison, Wis.: Prehistory Press.

Holm, Olaf. 1987. *Valdivia: Una cultura formativa del Ecuador.* Lima: Museo del Arte.

Holmquist Pachas, Ulla Sarela. 1992. *El personaje mítico feminino de la iconografía mochica.* Memoria para Obtener de Grado de Bachiller en Humanidades con Mención en Arqueología, Pontificia Universidad. Lima: Católica del Perú, Facultad de Letras y Ciencias Humanas.

Hooton, Earnest A. 1940. Skeletons from the Cenote of Sacrifice at Chichén Itzá. In *The Maya and Their Neighbors*, ed. Clarence L. Hay et al., 272–80. New York: Appleton-Century.

Hosler, Dorothy. 1996. Technical Choices, Social Categories, and Meaning among the Andean Potters of Las Animas. *Journal of Material Culture* 1 (1): 63–92.

Howell, Todd L. 1995. Tracking Zuni Gender and Leadership Roles across the Contact Period. *Journal of Anthropological Research* 51 (2): 125–47.

Howell, Todd L., and Keith W. Kentigh. 1996. Archaeological Identification of Kin Groups Using Mortuary and Biological Data: An Example from the American Southwest. *American Antiquity* 61 (3): 537–54.

Hoyt, Margaret A. 1977 (issued 1980). *Archaeology in Literature: A Semi-Annotated Bibliography.* Bulletin of the Philadelphia Anthropological Society 29.

Idrovo Urigüen, Jaime. 1995. La tumba de una yana aclla en Pumapungo, Tomebamba. *Caspicara* III, 8 (5): 3–5.

Jackson, Thomas L. 1991. Pounding Acorn: Women's Production as Social and Economic Focus. In *Engendering Archaeology: Women in Prehistory*, ed. Joan M. Gero and Margaret W. Conkey, 301–25. London: Basil Blackwell.

Jansen, Maarten. 1990. The Search for History in the Mixtec Codices. *Ancient Mesoamerica* 1 (1): 99–112.

Jills, Barbara. 1995. Gender and the Reorganization of Historic Zuni Craft Production: Implications for Archaeological Interpretation. *Journal of Anthropological Research* 51:149–71.

Joachim, Michael J. 1988. Optimal Foraging and the Division of Labor. *American Anthropologist* 90 (1): 130–36.

Johnson, Eileen. 1991. Late Pleistocene Cultural Occupation on the Southern Plains. In *Clovis: Origins and Adaptations*, ed. Robson Bonnichson and Karen L. Turnmire, 215–36. Corvallis: Center for the Study of the First Americans, Oregon State University.

Joyce, Rosemary A. 1992. Images of Gender and Labor Organization in Classic Maya Society. In *Exploring Gender through Archaeology: Selected Papers from the 1991 Boone Conference*, ed. Cheryl Claassen, 63–70. Madison, Wis.: Prehistory Press.

———. 1993. Women's Work: Images of Production and Reproduction in Pre-Hispanic Southern Central America. *Current Anthropology* 34 (3): 255–73.

Kartunnen, Frances. 1997. Rethinking Malinche. In *Indian Women of Early Mexico*, ed. Susan Shcroeder, Stephanie Wood, and Robert Haskett, 291–12. Norman: University of Oklahoma Press.

Kato, Yasutake. 1993. Resultados de las excavaciones en Kuntur Wasi, Cajamarca. In *El mundo ceremonial andino*, ed. Luis Millones and Yoshio Onuki, 203–28. Senri Ethnological Studies No. 37. Osaka: National Museum of Anthropology.

Kauffman Doig, Frederico. 1978. *Comportamiento sexual en el antiguo Peru*. Lima: Kompactos.

Kehoe, Alice B. 1970. The Function of Ceremonial Sexual Intercourse among the Northern Plains Indians. *Plains Anthropologist* 15:99–103.

———. 1987. Points and Lines. In *Powers of Observation: Alternative Views in Archaeology*, ed. Sarah M. Nelson and Alice B. Kehoe, 23–37. Washington, D.C.: American Anthropological Association.

Kellogg, Susan. 1984. Aztec Women in Early Colonial Courts: Structure and Strategy in a Legal Context. In *Five Centuries of Law and Politics in Central Mexico*, ed. Ronald Spores and Ross Hassig, 25–38. Publications in Anthropology No. 30. Nashville: Vanderbilt University.

———. 1988. Cognatic Kinship and Religion: Women in Aztec Society. In *Smoke and Mist: Mesoamerican Studies in Memory of Thelma D. Sullivan*, ed. J. Kathryn Josserand and Karen Dakin, 666–81. BAR International Series 402. Oxford.

———. 1993. The Social Organization of Households among the Tenochca Mexica before and after Conquest. In *Prehispanic Domestic Units in Western Mesoamerica*, ed. Robert Santley and Kenneth Hirth, 207–24. Boca Raton, Fla.: CRC Press.

———. 1995. *Law and the Transformation of Aztec Culture, 1500–1700*. Norman: University of Oklahoma Press.

———. 1997. From Parallel and Equivalent to Separate but Unequal: Tenochca Mexica Women, 1500–1700. In *Indian Women of Early Mexico*, ed. Susan Schroeder, Stephanie Wood, and Robert Haskett, 105–22. Norman: University of Oklahoma Press.

Kent, Susan. 1984. *Analyzing Activity Areas: An Ethnoarchaeological Study of the Use of Space.* Albuquerque: University of New Mexico Press.

Klein, Laura F. 1980. Contending with Colonization: Tlingit Men and Women in Change. In *Women in Colonization*, ed. M. Etienne and Eleanor Leacock, 80–108. New York: Praeger.

Klein, Laura F., and Lillian A. Ackerman. 1995. *Women and Power in Native North America.* Norman: University of Oklahoma Press.

Kloos, Peter. 1969. Female Initiation among the Maroni River Caribs. *American Anthropologist* 71 (4): 898–905.

Koehler, Lyle. 1997. Earth Mothers, Warriors, Horticulturalists, Artists, and Chiefs: Women among the Mississippian and Mississippian-Oneota Peoples, A.D. 1211 to 1750. In *Women in Prehistory: North America and Mesoamerica*, ed. Cheryl Claassen and Rosemary A. Joyce, 211–26. Philadelphia: University of Pennsylvania Press.

Kojo, Yashushi. 1996. Production of Prehistoric Southwestern Ceramics: A Low Technology Approach. *American Antiquity* 61 (2): 325–39.

Lackey, Louana M. 1982. *The Pottery of Acatlán: A Changing Mexican Tradition.* Norman: University of Oklahoma Press.

Landa, Diego de. 1978 [1566]. *Yucatan before and after the Conquest.* Translated by William Gates. New York: Dover Publications.

Langdon, Jean Matteson. 1992. Introduction: Shamanism and Anthropology. In *Portals of Power: Shamanism in South America*, ed. E. J. M. Langdon and Gerhard Baer, 1–24. Albuquerque: University of New Mexico Press.

Larco Hoyle, Rafael. 1965. *Checan: Essay on Erotic Elements in Peruvian Art.* Geneva: Nagel Publishers.

Larsen, Clark Spencer. 1984. Health and Disease in Prehistoric Georgia: The Transition to Agriculture. In *Paleopathology at the Origins of Agriculture*, ed. Mark N. Cohen and George R. Armelagos, 367–92. Orlando: Academic Press.

Larsen, Clark S., and C. B. Ruff. 1991. Biomechanical Adaptation and Behavior on the Prehistoric Georgia Coast. In *What Mean These Bones? Studies in Southeastern Bioarchaeology*, ed. Mary Lucas Powell, Patricia S. Bridges, and Anna María Wagner Mires, 102–13. Tuscaloosa: University of Alabama Press.

Leacock, Eleanor. 1978. Women's Status in Egalitarian Society: Implications for Social Evolution. *Current Anthropology* 19 (2): 247–75.

———. 1981. *Myths of Male Dominance.* New York: Monthly Review Press.

———. 1983. Interpreting the Origins of Gender Inequality: Conceptual and Historical Problems. *Dialectical Anthropology* 7 (4): 263–84.

LeBlanc, Stephen A. 1997. A Comment on Hegmon and Trevathan's "Gender, Anatomical Knowledge, and Pottery Production." *American Antiquity* 62 (4): 723–26.

Lee, Richard B. 1976. *Kalahari Hunter-Gatherers: Studies of the !Kung San and Their Neighbors.* Cambridge: Harvard University Press.

Lee, Richard B., and Irven Devore. 1968. *Man the Hunter.* Chicago: Aldine.

Lepper, Bradley T., and David J. Meltzer. 1991. Late Pleistocene Human Occupation of the Eastern United States. In *Clovis: Origins and Adaptations*, ed. Robson Bonnichson and Karen L. Turnmire, 175–84. Corvallis: Center for the Study of the First Americans, Oregon State University.

Lesure, Richard G. 1997. Figurines and Social Identities in Early Sedentary Societies of Coastal Chiapas, Mexico, 1550–800 B.C. In *Women in Prehistory: North America and Mesoamerica*, ed. Cheryl Claassen and Rosemary A. Joyce, 227–48. Philadelphia: University of Pennsylvania Press.

Levy, Janet, and Cheryl Claassen. 1992. Workshop I: Engendering the Contact Period. In *Exploring Gender through Archaeology: Selected Papers from the Boone Conference*, ed. Cheryl Claassen, 111–27. Monographs in World Archaeology No. 11. Madison, Wis.: Prehistory Press.

Lewis, Oscar. 1941. Manly-Hearted Women among the Northern Peigan. *American Anthropologist* 39 (2): 173–87.

López Reyes, Erick. 1996. *Las Venus valdivia gigantes de Río Chico (OMJPLP-170A): Costa Sur de la provincia de Manabí, Ecuador*. Boletín Arqueológico No. 5: 157–74. ARAS (y Avances de Investigación No. 6). Guayaquil, Ecuador: Centro de Estudios Arqueológicos y Antropológicos de la ESPOL.

Lothrop, Samuel Kirkland. 1937. *Coclé: An Archaeological Study of Central Panama*, pt. 1. Memoirs of the Peabody Museum of Archaeology and Ethnology 7. Cambridge: Harvard University.

———. 1942. *Coclé: An Archaeological Study of Central Panama*, pt. 2. Memoirs of the Peabody Museum of Archaeology and Ethnology. Cambridge: Harvard University.

Lothrop, S. K., W. F. Foshag, and Joy Mahler. 1959. *Pre-Columbian Art: The Robert Woods Bliss Collection*. New York: Phaidon Press.

Lyon, Patricia J. 1978. Female Supernaturals in Ancient Peru. *Ñawpa Pacha* 16:94–140.

Manzanilla, Linda. 1996. Corporate Groups and Domestic Activities at Teotihuacán. *Latin American Antiquity* 7 (3): 228–46.

Marcos, Jorge R. 1988. *Real Alto: La historia de un centro ceremonial valdivia*. Biblioteca Ecuatoriana de Arqueología, Tomos 4 y 5. Quito: Corporación Editora Nacional.

———. 1990. Economía e ideología en Andinoamerica septentrional. In *Nueva historia del Ecuador*, vol. 2, *Epoca aborigen II*, ed. Enrique Ayala, 167–88. Quito: Corporación Editorial Nacional and Editorial Grijalbo Ecuatoriano.

Marcos, Jorge R., and Mariella Garcia de Manrique. 1988. De la dualidad fertilidad-virilidad a lo explictamente feminino o masculino: La relación de las figurinas con los cambios en la organización social valdivia, Real Alto, Ecuador. In *The Role of Gender in Precolumbian Art and Architecture*, ed. Virginia E. Miller, 35–52. Lanham, Md.: University Press of America.

Marcus, Joyce. 1983. Rethinking the Zapotec Urn. In *The Cloud People*, ed. Kent V. Flannery and Joyce Marcus, 144–48, Orlando: Academic Press.

Marcus, Joyce, and Kent V. Flannery. 1996. *Zapotec Civilization: How Urban Society Evolved in Mexico's Oaxaca Valley*. London: Thames and Hudson.

Mazel, Aron David. 1989. People Making History: The Last Ten Thousand Years of Hunter-Gatherer Communities in the Thukela Basin. *Natal Museum Journal of Humanities* 1:1–158. Pietermaritzburg, South Africa.

McCafferty, Sharisse D., and Geoffrey G. McCafferty. 1988. Powerful Women and the Myth of Male Dominance in Aztec Society. *Archaeological Review from Cambridge* 7 (1): 45–59.

——. 1991. Spinning and Weaving as Female Gender Identity in Post-Classic Mexico. In *Textile Traditions of Mesoamerica and the Andes: An Anthropology*, ed. Margot Blum Schevill et al., 19–44. New York: Garland Press.

——. 1994a. The Conquered Women of Cacaxtla: Gender Identity or Gender Ideology? *Ancient Mesoamerica* 5:159–72.

——. 1994b. Engendering Tomb 7 at Monte Albán: Respinning an Old Yarn. *Current Anthropology* 35 (2): 143–66.

McClain, Carol S. 1989. *Women as Healers: Cross Cultural Perspectives*. New Brunswick: Rutgers University Press.

McEwan, Bonnie G. 1991. The Archaeology of Women in the Spanish New World. *Historical Archaeology* 25:33–41.

McEwan, Colin, and Maarten Van de Guchte. 1992. Ancestral Time and Sacred Space in Inca State Ritual. In *The Ancient Americas: Art from Sacred Landscapes*, ed. Richard F. Townsend, 359–71. Art Institute of Chicago.

McGaw, Judith A. 1989. No Passive Victims, No Separate Spheres: A Feminist Perspective on Technology's History. In *Context: History and Technology*, ed. Stephen H. Cutliffe and R. C. Post, 172–91. Bethlehem: Lehigh University Press.

McGuire, Randall H. 1992. *Death, Society, and Ideology in a Hohokam Community*. Boulder: Westview Press.

McGuire, Randall, and Dean J. Saitta. 1996. Although They Have Petty Captains, They Obey Them Badly: The Dialectics of Prehispanic Western Pueblo Social Organization. *American Antiquity* 61 (2): 197–216.

McNett, Charles W., Jr. 1985. *Shawnee Minisink: A Stratified Paleoindian-Archaic Site in the Upper Delaware Valley of Pennsylvania*. Orlando: Academic Press.

Medicine, Beatrice. 1983. "Warrior Women": Sex Role Alternatives for Plains Indian Women. In *The Hidden Half: Studies of Plains Indian Women*, ed. Patricia C. Albers and Beatrice Medicine, 267–80. Lanham, Md.: University Press of America.

Meggers, Betty J. 1966. *Ecuador*. London: Thames and Hudson.

Meltzer, David J. 1988. Late Pleistocene Human Adaptations in Eastern North America. *Journal of World Prehistory* 2 (1): 1–52.

Mercado Rojano, Antonio. 1987. ¿Una sacerdotisa en Teotihuacán? *México Desconocido* 121 (March): 6–9.

Milbrath, Susan. 1988. Birth Images in Mixteca-Puebla Art. In *The Role of Gender in Precolumbian Art and Architecture*, ed. Virginia E. Miller, 153–78. Lanham, Md.: University Press of America.

Miller, Mary Ellen. 1986. *The Murals of Bonampak*. Princeton: Princeton University Press.

Miller, Virginia E., ed. 1988. *The Role of Gender in Precolumbian Art and Architecture*. Lanham, Md.: University Press of America.

Milner, George R., Eve Anderson, and Virginia G. Smith. 1991. Warfare in Late Prehistoric West Central Illinois. *American Antiquity* 56 (4): 581–603.

---

Minnis, Paul E. 1984. Earliest Plant Cultivation in the Desert Borderlands of North America. In *The Origins of Agriculture: An Evolutionary Perspective*, ed. David Rindos, 121–42. Orlando: Academic Press.

————. 1985. Domesticating People and Plants in the Greater Southwest. In *Prehistoric Food Production in North America*, ed. Richard Ford, 309–39. Anthropological Papers No. 75. Ann Arbor: Museum of Anthropology, University of Michigan.

Mitchell, Christi. 1992. Activating Women in Arikara Ceramic Production. In *Exploring Gender through Archaeology: Selected Papers from the 1991 Boone Conference*, ed. Cheryl Claassen, 89–94. Monographs in World Archaeology No. 11. Madison, Wis.: Prehistory Press.

Mitchell, Douglas R. 1991. An Investigation of Two Classic Period Hohokam Cemeteries. *North American Archaeologist* 12 (2): 109–27.

Mock, Shirley Boteler. 1987. *The Painted Pebbles of the Lower Pecos: A Study of Medium, Form, and Content*. M.A. thesis, Graduate Faculty, University of Texas, San Antonio.

Molloy, John P., and William L. Rathje. 1974. Sexploitation among the Late Classic Maya. In *Mesoamerican Archaeology: New Approaches*, ed. Norman Hammond, 431–44. Austin: University of Texas Press.

Moogk, Susan. 1991. The Construction of "Woman" in the Nuu-chah-nulth Girl's Puberty Ceremony in 1910. In *The Archaeology of Gender: Proceedings of the 22nd Annual Chacmool Conference*, ed. Dale Walde and Noreen D. Willows, 103–7. Archaeological Association of the University of Calgary.

Moseley, Michael E., Carol J. Mackey, and David Brill. 1973. Peru's Ancient City of Kings. *National Geographic* 143, no. 3 (March): 318–45.

Murdock, George P., et al. 1950. *Outline of Cultural Materials*. New Haven: Human Relations Area Files Press.

Nelson, Sarah Milledge. 1987. Diversity of the Upper Paleolithic "Venus" Figurines and Archaeological Mythology. In *Powers of Observation: Alternative Views in Archaeology*, ed. Sarah M. Nelson and Alice B. Kehoe, 11–22. Archaeological Papers of the American Anthropological Association No. 2. Washington, D.C.

————. 1997. *Gender in Archaeology: Analyzing Power and Prestige*. Walnut Creek, Calif.: Altamira Press.

Nelson, Sarah M., and Alice B. Kehoe. 1987. *Powers of Observation: Alternative Views in Archaeology*. Archaeological Papers of the American Anthropological Association No. 2. Washington, D.C.

Netting, Robert McC. 1987. Small Holders, Householders, Freeholders: Why the Family Farm Works Well Worldwide. In *The Household Economy: Reconsidering the Domestic Mode of Production*, ed. Richard R. Wilk, 221–44. Boulder: Westview Press.

New Palenque Tomb Discovered. 1994. *Mexicon* 16, no. 4 (August): 71–72.

Niles, Susan. 1988. Pachamama, Pachatata: Gender and Sacred Space on Amantani. In *The Role of Gender in Precolumbian Art and Architecture*, ed. Virginia E. Miller, 135–51. Lanham, Md.: University Press of America.

Nimis, Marion Marshall. 1982. The Contemporary Role of Women in Lowland Maya Stock Production. In *Maya Subsistence: Studies in Memory of Dennis E. Puleston*, ed. Kent V. Flannery, 313–25. Orlando: Academic Press.

O'Brian, Patricia J. 1990. Evidence for the Antiquity of Gender Roles in the Central Plains Tradition. In *Powers of Observation: Alternative Views in Archaeology*, ed. Sarah M. Nelson and Alice B. Kehoe, 61–72. Archaeological Papers of the American Anthropological Association No. 2. Washington, D.C.

Ortner, Sherry B. 1978. The Virgin and the State. *Feminist Studies* 4 (3): 19–36.

Ortiz de Montellano, Bernard R. 1990. *Aztec Medicine, Health, and Nutrition*. New Brunswick: Rutgers University Press.

Osgood, Cornelius. 1940. *Ingalik Material Culture*. Yale University Publications in Anthropology No. 22. New Haven.

Owsley, Douglas W. 1994. Warfare in Coalescent Tradition Populations of the Northern Plains. In *Skeletal Biology in the Great Plains: Migration, Warfare, Health, and Subsistence*, ed. Douglas W. Owsley and Richard R. Janz, 333–43. Washington, D.C.: Smithsonian Institution Press.

Owsley, Douglas W., and Richard L. Janz. 1994. *Skeletal Biology in the Great Plains: Migration, Warfare, Health, and Subsistence*. Washington, D.C.: Smithsonian Institution Press.

Parsons, Mark L. 1986. Painted Pebbles: Style and Chronology. In *Ancient Texans: Rock Art and Lifeways along the Lower Pecos*, ed. Harry Schafer, 180–85. San Antonio: Witte Museum and Texas Monthly Press.

Pasztory, Esther. 1976. *The Murals of Tepantitla, Teotihuacán*. Garland Press.

———. 1988. A Reinterpretation of Teotihuacán and Its Mural Painting Tradition. In *Feathered Serpents and Flowering Trees: Reconstructing the Murals of Teotihuacán*, ed. Kathleen Berrin, 45–77. Fine Arts Museums of San Francisco.

———. 1992. Abstraction and the Rise of a Utopian State at Teotihuacán. In *Art, Ideology and the Ancient City of Teotihuacán*, ed. Janet Catherine Berlo, 281–320. Washington, D.C.: Dumbarton Oaks.

Pauketat, Timothy R. 1994. *The Ascent of Chiefs: Cahokia and Mississippian Politics in Native North America*. Tuscaloosa: University of Alabama Press.

Paul, Lois, and Benjamin D. Paul. 1975. The Maya Midwife as Sacred Specialist: A Guatemala Case. *American Ethnologist* 2 (4): 707–26.

Pearsall, Deborah Marie. 1988. *La producción de alimentos en Real Alto*. Guayaquil, Ecuador: Biblioteca Ecuatoriana de Arqueología, Corporación Editora Nacional.

Peebles, Christopher S., and Susan M. Kus. 1977. Some Archaeological Correlates of Ranked Societies. *American Antiquity* 42 (2): 421–48.

Perzigian, Anthony J., Patricia A. Tench, and Donna J. Braun. 1984. Prehistoric Health in the Ohio River Valley. In *Paleopathology at the Origins of Agriculture*, Mark N. Cohen and George R. Armelagos, 347–66. Orlando: Academic Press.

Pohl, John M. D., and Bruce E. Byland. 1990. Mixtec Landscape Perception and Archaeological Settlement Patterns, *Ancient Mesoamerica* 1 (1): 113–31.

Pohl, Mary Leland, and Lawrence Feldman. 1982. The Traditional Role of Women and Animals in Lowland Maya Economy. In *Maya Subsistence: Studies in Memory of Dennis E. Puleston*, ed. Kent V. Flannery, 295–311. Orlando: Academic Press.

Powell, Mary Lucas. 1988. *Status and Health in Prehistory: A Case Study of the Moundville Chiefdom*. Washington, D.C.: Smithsonian Institution Press.

Powledge, Tabitha M., and Mark Rose. 1996. The Great DNA Hunt. *Archaeology* 49 (5): 36–44.

Pozorski, Thomas G. 1979. The Las Avispas Burial Platform at Chan Chan, Peru. *Annals of the Carnegie Museum* 48 (8). Pittsburgh: Carnegie Museum of Natural History.

Prezzano, Susan. 1997. Warfare, Women, and Households: The Development of Iroquois Culture. In *Women in Prehistory: North America and Mesoamerica*, ed. Cheryl Claassen and Rosemary A. Joyce, 88–99. Philadelphia: University of Pennsylvania Press.

Pringle, Heather. 1997. Ice Age Communities May Be Earliest Known Net Hunters. *Science* 277 (August 29): 1203–4.

———. 1998. New Women of the Ice Age. *Discover* 19, no. 4 (April): 62–69.

Proskouriakoff, Tatiana. 1960. Historical Implications of a Pattern of Dates at Piedras Negras, Guatemala. *American Antiquity* 25 (4): 454–75.

———. 1961. Portraits of Women in Maya Art. In *Essays in Pre-Columbian Art and Archaeology*, ed. S. K. Lothrop et al., 81–99. Cambridge: Harvard University Press.

Quilter, Jeffrey. 1989. *Life and Death at La Paloma*. Iowa City: University of Iowa Press.

Rapp, Rayna. 1977. Gender and Class: An Archaeology of Knowledge concerning the Origin of the State. *Dialectical Anthropology* 2:309–16.

———. 1987. Women, Religion, and Archaic Civilizations: An Introduction. *Feminist Studies* 4 (3): 1–6.

Redder, Albert J., and John W. Fox. 1988. Excavation and Positioning of the Horn Shelter's Burial and Grave Goods. *Central Texas Archeologist* 11:1–10.

Redmond, Elsa M. 1994. *Tribal and Chiefly Warfare in South America*. Studies in Latin American Ethnohistory and Archaeology No. 5, Memoirs of the Museum of Anthropology, University of Michigan 28. Ann Arbor.

Reichel-Dolmatoff, Gerardo. 1961. Anthropomorphic Figurines from Colombia: Their Magic and Art. In *Essays in Pre-Columbian Art and Archaeology*, ed. Samuel K. Lothrop et al., 229–41. Cambridge: Harvard University Press.

———. 1977. La conquista de los Tairona. *Estudios Antropológicos* 29:49–77.

———. 1985. *Los Kogi*. Bogotá.

———. 1988. *Goldwork and Shamanism: An Iconographic Study of the Gold Museum*. Medellín, Colombia: Editorial Colina.

Reid, J. J., and S. M. Whittlesey. 1982. Households at Grasshopper Pueblo. *American Behavioral Scientist* 25 (6): 687–703.

Reina, Ruben E., and Robert M. Hill II. 1978. *The Traditional Pottery of Guatemala*. Austin: University of Texas Press.

Rice, Prudence. 1981. Prehistoric Venuses: Symbols of Motherhood or Womanhood? *Journal of Anthropological Research* 37 (4): 402–16.

Richards, Cara B. 1957. Matriarchy or Mistake: The Role of Iroquois Women through Time. In *Cultural Stability and Cultural Change*, ed. Verne F. Ray, 36–45. Seattle: American Ethnological Society, University of Washington Press.

Riddle, John M. 1992. *Contraception and Abortion from the Ancient World to the Renaissance*. Cambridge: Harvard University Press.

Rivera, Mario A. 1995. The Preceramic Chinchorro Mummy Complex of Northern Chile: Context, Style, and Purpose. In *Tombs for the Living: Andean Mortuary Practices*, ed. Tom D. Dillehay, 43–78. Washington, D.C.: Dumbarton Oaks.

Robertson, Merle Greene, Marjorie S. Rosenblum Scandizzo, and John R. Scandizzo. 1976. Physical Deformities in the Ruling Lineage of Palenque and the Dynastic Implications. In *The Art, Iconography and Dynastic History of Palenque*, pt. 3, ed. Merle Greene Robertson, 59–86. Pebble Beach, Calif.: Pre-Columbian Art Research, Robert Louis Stevenson School.

Rogers, Susan Carol. 1974. Female Forms of Power and the Myth of Male Dominance: A Model of Female/Male Interaction in Peasant Society. *American Ethnologist* 2 (4): 727–56.

Roosevelt, Anna C. 1988. Interpreting Certain Female Images in Prehistoric Art. In *The Role of Gender in Precolumbian Art and Architecture*, ed. Virginia E. Miller, 1–34. Lanham, Md.: University Press of America.

Rowe, Ann Pollard. 1979. Textile Evidence for Huari Music. *Textile Museum Journal* 18:5–18.

———. 1997. Inca Weaving and Costume. *Journal of the Textile Museum* 34–35:5–153.

Rowe, John Howland. 1948. Inca Culture at the Time of the Conquest. *Handbook of South American Indians*, vol. 2, 183–330. Bureau of American Ethnology Bulletin 148. Washington, D.C.: Smithsonian Institution.

———. 1979. An Account of the Shrines of Ancient Cuzco. *Ñawpa Pacha* 17:1–81.

———. 1987. La mentira literaria en la obra de Martín de Marua. In *El libro de homenaje a Aurelio Miro Quesada Sosa*, vol. 2, 753–61. Lima.

Russell, Pamela. 1991. Men Only? The Myths about European Paleolithic Artists. In *The Archaeology of Gender: Proceedings of the 22nd Annual Chacmool Conference*, ed. Dale Walde and Noreen D. Willows, 346–51. Archaeological Association of the University of Calgary.

Sacks, Karen. 1982. *Sisters and Wives: The Past and Future of Sexual Equality*. Urbana: University of Illinois Press.

Saénz Samper, Juanita. 1993. Mujeres de barro: Estudio de las figurinas cerámicas de Montelíbano. *Boletín de Museo del Oro* 34–35:77–110. Bogotá.

Sahagún, Bernadino de. 1979 [1579?]. *General History of the Things of New Spain: Florentine Codex*. 13 vols. Translated by Arthur J. O. Anderson and Charles E. Dibble. Santa Fe: School of American Research.

Salomon, Frank. 1988. Indian Women of Early Colonial Quito as Seen through Their Testaments. *The Americas* 44 (3): 325–41.

———. 1991. *The Huarochirí Manuscript: A Testament of Ancient and Colonial Andean Religion*. Austin: University of Texas Press.

———. 1995. "The Beautiful Grandparents": Andean Ancestor Shrines and Mortuary Practices as Seen through Colonial Records. In *Tombs for the Living: Andean Mortuary Practices*, ed. Tom D. Dillehay, 315–54. Washington, D.C.: Dumbarton Oaks.

Sánchez Montañés, Emma. 1981. *Las "figurillas" de Esmeraldas: Tipología y función*. Memorias de la Misión Arqueológica Española en el Ecuador 7. Madrid: Ministerio de Asuntos Exteriores, Dirección General de Relaciones Culturales.

Santley, Robert S., and Kenneth G. Hirth. 1993. *Prehispanic Domestic Units in Western Mesoamerica*. Boca Raton, Fla.: CRC Press.

Sarmiento de Gamboa, Pedro. 1943 [1572]. *Historia de los Incas*. 2d ed. Buenos Aires: Emecé Editores.

Sassaman, Kenneth E. 1992a. Lithic Technology and the Hunter-Gatherer Sexual Division of Labor. *North American Archaeologist* 13 (3): 249–62.

———. 1992b. Gender and Technology at the Archaic-Woodland Transition. In *Exploring Gender through Archaeology: Selected Papers from the 1991 Boone Conference*, ed. Cheryl Claassen, 71–80. Madison, Wis.: Prehistory Press.

———. 1993. *Early Pottery in the Southeast: Tradition and Innovation in Cooking Technology*. Tuscaloosa: University of Alabama Press.

Saul, Frank P. 1972. *The Human Skeletal Remains of Altar de Sacrificios: An Osteobiographic Analysis*. Papers of the Peabody Museum of American Archaeology and Ethnography 63 (2).

Scarry, C. Margaret. 1993. *Foraging and Farming in the Eastern Woodlands*. Gainesville: University Press of Florida.

Schele, Linda, and David Freidel. 1990. *A Forest of Kings: The Untold Story of the Ancient Maya*. New York: William Morrow.

Schlegel, Alice. 1972. *Male Dominance and Female Autonomy: Domestic Authority in Matrilineal Societies*. New Haven: Human Relations Area Files Press.

Schroeder, Susan. 1992. The Noblewomen of Chalco. *Estudios de Cultural Nahuatl* 22:45–86.

Schroeder, Susan, Stephanie Wood, and Robert Haskett. 1997. *Indian Women of Early Mexico*. Norman: University of Oklahoma Press.

Scott, John F. 1978. *The Danzantes of Monte Albán*. 2 vols. Studies in Pre-Columbian Art and Archaeology No. 19. Washington, D.C.: Dumbarton Oaks.

Seeman, Mark F. 1979. Feasting with the Dead: Ohio Hopewell Charnel House Ritual as a Context for Redistribution. In *Hopewell Archaeology: The Chillicothe Conference*, ed. David S. Brose and Níomi Greber, 39–46. Kent: Kent State University Press.

Sempowski, Martha L., and Michael W. Spence. 1994. *Mortuary Practices and Skeletal Remains at Teotihuacán*. Salt Lake City: University of Utah Press.

Shaffer, Brian S., Karen M. Gardner, and Harry J. Shafer. 1997. An Unusual Birth Depicted in Mimbres Pottery: Not Cracked Up to What It Is Supposed to Be. *American Antiquity* 62 (4): 727–32.

Sharp, Harry S. 1981. The Null Case: The Chipewyan. In *Woman the Gatherer*, ed. Frances Dahlberg, 221–44. New Haven: Yale University Press.

Sheets, Payson D., et al. 1990. Household Archaeology at Ceren, El Salvador. *Ancient Mesoamerica* 1:81–90.

———. 1992. *The Ceren Site: A Prehistoric Village Buried by Volcanic Ash in Central America*. New York: Harcourt Brace Jovanovich.

Shimada, Izumi, Stephen Epstein, and Alan K. Craig. 1983. The Metallurgical Process in Ancient North Peru. *Archaeology* 36 (5): 38–45.

Sieff, Daniela F. 1990. Explaining Biased Sex Ratios in Human Populations: A Critique of Recent Studies. *Current Anthropology* 31:25–48.

Silverblatt, Irene M. 1978. Andean Women in Inca Society. *Feminist Studies* 4 (3): 37–61.

———. 1980. "The Universe Has Turned Inside Out . . . There Is No Justice for Us Here": Andean Women under Spanish Rule. In *Women and Colonization: Anthropological Perspectives*, ed. Mona Etienne and Eleanor Leacock, 149–95. New York: Praeger.

———. 1987. *Moon, Sun, and Witches: Gender Ideologies and Class in Inca and Colonial Peru*. Princeton: Princeton University Press.

———. 1988. Women in States. *Annual Review of Anthropology* 17:427–60.

Simon, Arleyn W., and John C. Ravesloot. 1995. Salado Ceramic Burial Offerings: A Consideration of Gender and Social Organization. *Journal of Anthropological Research* 51:103–23.

Smith, Augustus Ledyard. 1972. *Excavations at Altar de Sacrificios: Architecture, Settlement, Burials, and Caches*. Papers of the Peabody Museum of American Archaeology and Ethnography 62 (2).

Smith, Bruce D. 1987. The Independent Domestication of the Indigenous Seed Bearing Plants in Eastern North America. In *Emergent Horticultural Economies of the Eastern Woodlands*, ed. William Keegan, 3–47. Occasional Paper of the Center for Archaeological Investigations of Southern Illinois University No. 7. Carbondale.

———. 1989. Origins of Agriculture in Eastern North America. *Science* 246:1566–71.

———. 1992. *Rivers of Change: Essays on Early Agriculture in Eastern North America*. Washington, D.C.: Smithsonian Institution Press.

———. 1995. *The Emergence of Agriculture*. New York: Scientific American Library, a Division of HPHLP.

Smith, Kevin E. 1991. The Mississippian Figurine Complex and Symbolic Systems of the Southeastern United States. In *The New World Figurine Project*, vol. 1, ed. Terry Stocker, 125–26. Provo: Research Press.

Smith, Mary Elizabeth. 1983. Regional Points of View in the Mixtec Codices. In *The Cloud People*, ed. Kent V. Flannery and Joyce Marcus, 260–66. Orlando: Academic Press.

Snow, Dean R. 1995. *The Iroquois*. London: Basil Blackwell.

———. 1994. Migration in Prehistory: The Northern Iroquoian Case. *American Antiquity* 60 (1): 59–79.

Sobolik, Kristin D., Kristin J. Gremillion, Patricia L. Whitten, and Patty Jo Watson. 1996. Technical Note: Sex Determination of Prehistoric Human Paleofeces. *American Journal of Physical Anthropology* 101:283–90.

Soffer, Olga, and N. D. Praslov. 1993. *From Kostenki to Clovis: Upper Paleolithic-Paleo-Indian Adaptations*. New York: Plenum Press.

Soustelle, Jacques. 1961. *Daily Life of the Aztecs on the Eve of the Spanish Conquest*. Stanford: Stanford University Press.

Spector, Janet D. 1983. Male/Female Task Differentiation among the Hidatsa: Toward the Development of an Archaeological Approach to the Study of Gender. In *The Hidden Half: Studies of Plains Indian Women*, ed. Patricia Albers and Beatrice Medicine, 77–100. Lanham, Md.: University Press of America.

———. 1992. What This Awl Means. In *Engendering Archaeology: Women in Prehistory*, ed. Joan M. Gero and Margaret W. Conkey, 388–406. London: Basil Blackwell.

———. 1993. *What This Awl Means: Feminist Archaeology at a Wahpeton Dakota Village*. St. Paul: Minnesota Historical Society Press.

Spence, Michael W. 1974. Residential Practices and the Distribution of Skeletal Traits in Teotihuacán, Mexico. *Man* 9:262–73.

Spencer-Wood, Suzanne. 1991. Toward a Feminist Historical Archaeology of the Construction of Gender. In *The Archaeology of Gender: Proceedings of the 22nd Annual Chacmool Conference*, ed. Dale Walde and Noreen Willows, 234–44. Archaeological Association, University of Calgary.

Spielmann, Katherine A. 1995. Glimpses of Gender in the Prehistoric Southwest. *Journal of Anthropological Research* 51 (2): 91–102.

Spores, Ronald. 1974. Marital Alliance in the Political Integration of Mixtec Kingdoms. *American Anthropologist* 76 (2): 297–311.

———. 1997. Mixteca Cacicas: Status, Wealth, and the Political Accommodation of Native Elite Women in Early Colonial Oaxaca. In *Indian Women of Early Mexico*, ed. Susan Schroeder, Stephanie Wood, and Robert Haskett, 185–98. Norman: University of Oklahoma Press.

Staden, Hans. 1963. *The Captivity of Hans Staden of Hesse in A.D. 1547–1555 among the Wild Tribes of Eastern Brazil*. Translated by Albert Tootal. New York: Burt Franklin.

Stephens, Lynn. 1991. *Zapotec Women*. Austin: University of Texas Press.

Stocker, Terry. 1991. *The New World Figurine Project*. Vol. 1. Provo: Research Press.

Stone, Andrea. 1988. Sacrifice and Sexuality: Some Structural Relationships in Classic Maya Art. In *The Role of Gender in Precolumbian Art and Architecture*, ed. Virginia E. Miller, 63–74. Lanham, Md.: University Press of America.

———. 1991. Aspects of Impersonation in Classic Maya Art. In *The Sixth Palenque Round Table, 1986*, ed. Merle G. Robertson and Virginia M. Fields, 194–202. Austin: University of Texas Press.

Storck, Peter L. 1991. Imperialists without a State: The Cultural Dynamics of Early Paleoindian Colonization as Seen from the Great Lakes Region. In *Clovis: Origins and Adaptations*, ed. Robson Bonnichson and Karen L. Turnmire, 153–62. Corvallis: Center for the Study of the First Americans, Oregon State University.

Storey, Rebecca. 1985. An Estimate of Mortality in a Pre-Columbian Urban Population. *American Anthropologist* 87:519–35.

———. 1986. Prenatal Mortality at Pre-Columbian Teotihuacán. *American Journal of Physical Anthropology* 69:541–48.

———. 1992. *Life and Death in the Ancient City of Teotihuacán: A Modern Paleodemographic Synthesis*. Tuscaloosa: University of Alabama Press.

―――. 1992. The Children of Copan. Issues in Paleopathology and Paleodemography. *Ancient Mesoamerica* 3:161–67.

Stothert, Karen E. 1985. The Preceramic Las Vegas Culture of Coastal Ecuador *American Antiquity* 50 (3): 613–37.

―――. 1988. *La prehistoria temprana de la península de Santa Elena: Cultura Las Vegas*. Miscelánea Antropológica Ecuatoriana, Serie Monográfica, No. 10. Quito and Guayaquil: Museo del Banco Central del Ecuador.

―――. N.d. Expression of Ideology in the Ecuadorian Formative. In *The Formative of Ecuador*, ed. Richard Burger and J. Scott Raymond. Washington, D.C.: Dumbarton Oaks.

Sugiyama, Saburo. 1989. Burials Dedicated to the Old Temple of Quetzalcoatl, Teotihuacán, Mexico. *American Antiquity* 54 (1): 85–106.

Sullivan, Norman C. 1990. The Biological Consequences of the Mississippian Expansion into the Western Great Lakes Region: A Study of Prehistoric Culture Contact. In *Powers of Observation: Alternative Views in Archaeology*, ed. Sarah M. Nelson and Alice B. Kehoe, 73–87. Archaeological Papers of the American Anthropological Association No. 2.

Sullivan, Thelma D. 1966. Pregnancy, Childbirth, and the Deification of the Women Who Died in Childbirth. *Estudios de Cultura Nahuatl* 6:63–95.

Tate, Carolyn E. 1992. *Yaxchilán: The Design of a Maya Ceremonial City*. Austin: University of Texas Press.

Thomas, Elizabeth Marshall. 1987. *Reindeer Moon*. Boston: Houghton Mifflin.

Thomsen, Moritz. 1969. *Living Poor: A Peace Corps Chronicle*. Seattle: University of Washington Press.

Topic, John R., Jr. 1982. Lower-Class Social and Economic Organization at Chan Chan. In *Chan Chan: Andean Desert City*, ed. Michael E. Moseley and Kent C. Day, 145–76. Albuquerque: University of New Mexico Press.

Topic, John R., and Theresa Lange Topic. 1997. Hacia una comprensión conceptual de la guerra andina. In *Arqueología, antropología, e historia: Homenaje a María Rostworoski*, ed. Rafael Varón Gabai and Javier Flores Espinoza, 567–90. Lima: Instituto de Estudios Peruanos / Banco Central de la Reserva del Perú.

Topic, Theresa Lange. N.d. The Mobility of Women in the Inca Empire and in the Spanish Colony of Peru. *The Archaeology of Contact: Processes and Consequences*. Proceedings of the 25th Annual Conference of the Archaeological Association of the University of Calgary. Calgary.

Trexler, Richard C. 1995. *Sex and Conquest: Gendered Violence, Political Order, and the European Conquest of the Americas*. Ithaca: Cornell University Press.

Tringham, Ruth E. 1991. Households with Faces: The Challenge of Gender in Prehistoric Architectural Remains. In *Engendering Archaeology: Women in Prehistory*, ed. Joan M. Gero and Margaret W. Conkey, 93–131. London: Basil Blackwell.

Trocolli, Ruth. 1992. Colonization and Women's Production: The Timacua of Florida. In *Exploring Gender through Archaeology: Selected Papers from the 1991 Boone Conference*, ed. Cheryl Claassen, 95–102. Madison, Wis.: Prehistory Press.

Ubelaker, Douglas H. 1980. Human Skeletal Remains from Site OGSE-80, a Preceramic Site on the Santa Elena Peninsula, Coastal Ecuador. *Journal of the Washington Academy of Science* 70 (1): 3–24.

————. N.d. Health Issues in the Early Formative of Ecuador: Skeletal Biology of Real Alto. In *The Formative of Ecuador*, ed. Richard Burger and Scott Raymond. Washington, D.C.: Dumbarton Oaks.

Uhle, Max. 1903. *Pachacamac*. Philadelphia: Dept. of Archaeology, University of Pennsylvania.

Váldez, Francisco. 1992. Symbols, Ideology, and the Expression of Power in La Tolita, Ecuador. In *The Ancient Americas: Art from Sacred Landscapes*, ed. Richard Townsend, 229–43. Art Institute of Chicago.

Verano, John W. 1994. Características físicas y biología osteológica de los Moche. In *Moche: Propuestas y perspectivas*, ed. Santiago Uceda and Elías Mujica, 307–26. Travaux de l'Institut Français d'Etudes Andines, Vol. 79. Lima.

Walde, Dale, and Noreen D. Willows. 1991. *The Archaeology of Gender: Proceedings of the 22nd Annual Chacmool Conference*. Archaeological Association of the University of Calgary.

Walker, Phillip L. 1989. Cranial Injuries as an Index for Violence among Southern California Indians. *American Journal of Physical Anthropology* 80:313–23.

Wasson, Gordon. 1974. *María Sabina and Her Mazatec Mushroom Velada*. New York: Harcourt, Brace, Jovanovich.

Watson, Patty Jo, and Mary C. Kennedy. 1991. The Development of Horticulture in the Eastern Woodlands of North America: Women's Role. In *Engendering Archaeology: Women in Prehistory*, ed. Joan M. Gero and Margaret W. Conkey, 255–75. London: Basil Blackwell.

Weist, Katherine. 1983. Beasts of Burden and Menial Slaves: Nineteenth Century Observations of Northern Plains Indian Women. In *The Hidden Half: Studies of Plains Indian Women*, ed. Patricia C. Albers and Beatrice Medicine, 29–52. Lanham, Md.: University Press of America.

Welch, Paul D., and C. Margaret Scarry. 1995. Status-related Variations in Foodways in the Moundville Chiefdom. *American Antiquity* 60 (3): 397–419.

White, D. R., and M. L. Burton. 1988. The Causes of Polygyny: Ecology, Economy, Kinship, and Warfare. *American Anthropologist* 90 (4): 871–87.

White, Tim D. 1992. *Prehistoric Cannibalism at Mancos, 5MTUMR-2346*. Princeton: Princeton University Press.

Whiting, Beatrice B. 1993. *Six Cultures: Studies of Child Rearing*. New York: Wiley.

Whitten, Dorothea S., and Norman E. Whitten, Jr. 1988. *From Myth to Creation: Art from Amazonian Ecuador*. Urbana: University of Illinois Press.

Widmer, Randolph J., and Rebecca Storey. 1993. Social Organization and Household Structure of a Teotihuacán Apartment Compound: S3W1:33 of the Tlajinga Barrio. In *Prehispanic Domestic Units in Ancient Mesoamerica*, ed. Robert S. Santley and Kenneth G. Hirth, 47–104. Boca Raton, Fla.: CRC Press.

Williams, Mary Beth, and Jeffrey Bendremer. 1997. The Archaeology of Maize, Pots, and Seashells: Gender Dynamics in Late Woodland and Contact-Period New England. In

*Women in Prehistory: North America and Mesoamerica*, ed. Cheryl Claassen and Rosemary A. Joyce, 136–54. Philadelphia: University of Pennsylvania Press.

Williams, Nigel. 1995. Ancient DNA: The Trials and Tribulations of Cracking the Prehistoric Code. *Science* 269 (August 18): 923–24.

Willig, Judith A. 1991. Clovis Technology and Adaptation in Far Western North America: Regional Patterns and Environmental Context. In *Clovis: Origins and Adaptations*, ed. Robson Bonnichson and Karen L. Turnmire, 91–118. Corvallis: Center for the Study of the First Americans, Oregon State University.

Wilson, Diane. 1997. Gender, Diet, Health, and Social Status in the Mississippian Powers Phase Turner Cemetery Population. In *Women in Prehistory: North America and Mesoamerica*, ed. Cheryl Claassen and Rosemary A. Joyce, 119–35. Philadelphia: University of Pennsylvania Press.

Wilson, Samuel. 1990. *Hispaniola: Caribbean Chiefdoms in the Age of Columbus*. Tuscaloosa: University of Alabama Press.

Winter, Marcus. 1997. Who Was Lady 12N? *News from the Center* 5 (1): 1–3. Center for Latin American Art and Archaeology, Denver Art Museum.

Wylie, Alison. 1991a. Gender Theory and the Archaeological Record: Why Is There No Archaeology of Gender? In *Engendering Archaeology: Women in Prehistory*, ed. Joan M. Gero and Margaret W. Conkey, 31–54. London: Basil Blackwell.

———. 1991b. Feminist Critiques and Archaeological Challenges. In *The Archaeology of Gender: Proceedings of the 22nd Annual Chacmool Conference*, ed. Dale Walde and Noreen D. Willows, 17–23. Archaeological Association of the University of Calgary.

———. 1992. The Interplay of Evidential Constraints and Political Interests: Recent Archaeological Research on Gender. *American Antiquity* 57 (1): 15–35.

———. 1994. On "Capturing Facts Alive in the Past" (Or Present): Response to Fotiadis and to Little. *American Antiquity* 59 (3): 556–60.

Zeidler, James A. 1984. *Social Space in Valdivia Society: Community Patterning and Domestic Structure at Real Alto, 3000–2000 B.C.* Ann Arbor: University Microfilms.

Zeidler, James A., Peter W. Stahl, and Marie J. Sutliff. 1998. Shamanistic Elements in a Terminal Valdivia Burial, Northern Manabí, Ecuador: Implications for Mortuary Symbols and Social Ranking. In *Recent Advances in the Archaeology of the Northern Andes: Essays in Honor of Gerardo Reichel-Dolmatoff*, ed. Augusto Oyuela Caycedo and J. Scott Raymond, 109–120. Los Angeles: Institute of Archaeology, University of California.

Zilhman, Adrienne. 1981. Women as Shapers of the Human Adaptation. In *Woman the Gatherer*, ed. Frances Dahlberg, 74–102. New Haven: Yale University Press.

Zuidema, R. Tom. 1977–78. Shaft Tombs and the Inca Empire. In *Prehistoric Contact between Mesoamerica and South America: New Data and Interpretations. Journal of the Steward Anthropological Society* 9. Urbana.

———. 1992. The Tairona of Ancient Colombia. In *The Ancient Americans: Art from Sacred Landscapes*, ed. Richard Townsend, 245–57. Art Institute of Chicago.

# Sources of Figures

Fig. 1.1. Mimbres bowl courtesy of the Museum of Western Colorado. Cat. # G 495.

Fig. 1.2. Sacrifice of Altar woman, drawn by Tom Weller after Adams 1963, color plate 1.

Fig. 1.3. Lady Xoc, drawn by Wes Christensen after Lintel 26, Yaxchilán, Chiapas, Mexico.

Fig. 1.4. Moche figurine. Height 15.5 cm. Cat. # 1909.12-18.4. Photograph © The British Museum.

Figs. 1.5a–b. New World sites and cultures mentioned in the text, drawn by Tom Weller.

Fig. 1.6. List of named periods commonly recognized in American archaeology. Analysis by Karen E. Stothert.

Fig. 2.1. Mammoth kill at the La Brea Tar Pits, painted by John C. Dawson. Courtesy of the George C. Page Museum.

Fig. 2.2. Ingalik material culture. Analysis by Karen E. Stothert from descriptions in Osgood 1940.

Fig. 2.3. Reconstruction of Monte Verde site. Courtesy of Tom Dillehay, from Monte Verde: A Late Pleistocene Settlement in Chile. Vol. 2: The Archeological Context and Interpretation (Washington, D.C.: Smithsonian Institution Press), p. 216.

Fig. 2.4. Floor plan of the Tequendama Rock Shelter. Redrawn after Correal and van der Hammen 1977, fig. 101.

Fig. 3.1. Chinchorro female mummy, Burial I-4, Morro I, Chile, now in the Museo de Tarapacá. Photograph courtesy of Mario Rivera.

Fig. 3.2. Los Amantes de Sumpa, Santa Elena Peninsula, Guayas Province, Ecuador. Photograph by Neil Maurer.

Fig. 3.3. Bedrock mortars and petroglyphs at Volcano, Calif. (1955). Photograph by Adan Treganza, courtesy of the Treganza Anthropology Museum, San Francisco State University. Slide #11369.

Fig. 4.1. Moche figurine showing a woman carrying a burden. Cat. # 1909.12-18-28. Photograph © The British Museum.

Fig. 4.2. Drawing after Girolamo Benzoni, *La historia del Mondo Nuovo, Libro Primo*, "Modo di fare il pane," 1962 [1565].

Fig. 4.3. Floor plan of the Charnel House at Real Alto. Redrawn with modifications from Marcos 1988, Mapa 16C.

Fig. 5.1. Cemetery plan at Hawikki, after Howell and Kintigh 1996, fig. 2.

Fig. 5.2. Early Valdivia house, Structure 4 at Loma Alta. Redrawn from Damp 1984, fig. 5.

Fig. 5.3. Middle Valdivia house, redrawn after Zeidler 1984, Map 90.

Fig. 5.4. Reconstruction drawing by Andrea Gerstle of Household One, Joya de Ceren, El Salvador. Courtesy of Payson D. Sheets.

Fig. 5.5. Reconstruction of an Iroquois longhouse. Drawing by Richard McReynolds.

Fig. 5.6. Feature 18, burial of an eighteen-year-old woman, found in Salado cemetery of Anasazi tradition. Drawing from Arelyn Simon and J. Ravesloot, "Salado Ceramic Burial Offerings, *Journal of Anthropological Research* 51 (1995): 103–25. Courtesy of Arelyn Simon.

Fig. 5.7. Tlajinga 33, redrawn with modifications by Tom Weller after Storey 1992, fig. 3.2.

Fig. 6.1. Bronze caster of coastal Ecuador. Photograph by Neil Maurer.

Fig. 6.2. Maidens of the Sun spinning after Guaman Poma de Ayala 1936 [1615], illustration # 298 [300].

Fig. 6.3. Teotihuacán figurine. Height 6.3 cm. Cat. #95. Treganza Museum of Anthropology, San Francisco State University. Photograph by Yoshiko Yamamoto.

Fig. 6.4. Aztec courtesan, redrawn by Tom Weller from Sahagún 1979 3.42.

Fig. 6.5. Mimbres painted scene of midwife and woman giving birth, redrawn by Tom Weller after Shaffer et al. 1997, fig. 3.

Fig. 6.6a. Maya woman scribe, redrawn by Tom Weller after Clarkson 1978, fig. 5.

Fig. 6.6b. "La Pintora," Aztec scribe. Redrawn by Tom Weller from the *Codex Telleriano-Remensis*.

Fig. 7.1. Jalisco-style figurine group. Height 49.5 cm. Cat. # M86.296.84. Photograph, "Joined Couple," courtesy of the Los Angeles County Museum of Art, The Proctor Stafford Collection, museum purchase with funds provided by Mr. and Mrs. Allan C. Balch.

Fig. 7.2. Drawing of a Late Valdivia burial by Mary Jo Sutliffe, courtesy of James Zeidler.

Fig. 7.3a – 7.3b. Pair of marble figurines from Etowah. Parks and Historic Sites Division, Georgia Department of Natural Resources, Atlanta. Photographs courtesy of Lewis Larson.

Fig. 7.4. Staff goddess, painted textile from Carhua, Peru. Drawing courtesy of Dwight Wallace.

Fig. 7.5. Teotihuacán goddess, Tetitla Palace fresco. Photograph courtesy of David Starbuck.

Fig. 7.6. Sacrifice Scene, drawing by Donna McClelland, from Donnan 1978, fig. 4.

Fig. 7.7. Burial of young Lady C, San José de Moro, Peru. Photograph by Christopher B. Donnan.

Fig. 7.8. Nine Grass Death, drawn by Wes Christensen after the *Codex Nuttall*, p. 44.

Fig. 7.9. Painted pebbles from Eagle Cave, Lower Pecos River, Texas. The largest is 12 cm long. Drawing by J. Walker Davenport. Courtesy of the Witte Museum, San Antonio, Texas.

Fig. 7.10. Middle Valdivia figurine. Height 12 cm. Cat. # GA-4-851-78. Photograph courtesy of the Museo Antropológico, Banco Central del Ecuador, Guayaquil.

Fig. 7.11. Hollow Chorrera figurine. Height 27.7 cm. Cat. # GA-1-12-1289-79, Museo Antropológico, Banco Central del Ecuador, Guayaquil. Photograph courtesy of Tom Cummins.

Fig. 7.12. Jama-Coaque figurine of a female with textiles. Height 21 cm. Cat. # GA-1-2503-83, courtesy of the Museo Antropológico, Banco Central del Ecuador, Guayaquil.

Fig. 7.13a–b. Jama-Coaque female in building. Height 18.7 cm. Cat. # GA-1-149-177, Museo Antropológico, Banco Central del Ecuador, Guayaquil. Photograph courtesy of Tom Cummins.

Fig. 7.14. Nazca processional figurative ceramic. Photograph courtesy of Helaine Silverman.

Fig. 7.15. Recuay vessel showing ritual intercourse. Hersey Collection, New York, #PCP30 P700 3 W-10. Photograph by Raphael X. Reichert.

Fig. 7.16. "Head of a sacrificed woman from the cemetery of the sacrificed women, Sun temple." From Max Uhle, Pachacamac, Plate #18, #13. Courtesy of the University of Pennsylvania Museum, Philadephia.

Fig. 8.1. Gold Sinú breastplate. Field Museum of Natural History, Chicago. Photograph by Karen Olsen Bruhns.

Fig. 8.2. La Venta Stela 1, Museo Parque La Venta, Villahermosa, Tabasco, Mexico. Photograph by Karen Olsen Bruhns.

Fig. 8.3. Monument 21, Chalcatzingo, Puebla, Mexico. Drawing by Barbara Fash, courtesy of David Grove.

Fig. 8.4. Queen Zak Kuk, drawing by Wes Christiansen after the Tablet of the Slaves, Palenque.

Fig. 8.5. Danzante D-6, Mound L, Monte Albán, Mexico, photograph by Karen Olsen Bruhns.

Fig. 8.6. Six Monkey Serpent Quechquemitl consults with Nine Grass Death at Skull. Drawing by Tom Weller after Codex Selden, p. 6.

Fig. 8.7. Tecuichpo, Doña Marina, Cortés, Cuauhtemoc, drawing by Tom Weller after the Lienzo de Tlaxcala, Lámina 43.

Fig. 8.8. Recuay female, Museo Nacional de Arqueología y Antropología, Lima # C.C. P 32 R. A. B. Photograph by Raphael X. Reichert.

Fig. 8.9. The Inca and the Coya traveling. After Guaman Poma de Ayala 1936 [1615], illustration # 331 [333].

Fig. 9.1. Tupinamba women and children eating prisoners' entrails, after Staden 1963 (1557).

Fig. 9.2. Cheyenne warrior woman. P. 78 of ledger with drawings in colored pencil, watercolor and ink by Yellow Nose (Hehúwesse) and others, before 1889. Cat. #

166,032, Neg. # 89-4691. Courtesy of the National Museum of Natural History, Smithsonian Institution.

Fig. 9.3a–b. Warrior queen, Cacaxtla, Puebla, Mexico. Drawings by Sherisse McCafferty, courtesy of Sherisse and Geoffrey McCafferty.

Fig. 9.4. Priest abusing woman, Guaman Poma 1936 [1615], illustration # 645 [659].

Fig. 9.5. High-ranking Inca lady. Oil on canvas, Collections of the Museo de Arqueología, Cuzco, Peru. Photograph courtesy of Tom Cummins.

# Index

Abortion, 125, 158–60
Abstinence, 159–60
Acatlán, 137
Achpaniztli (Aztec ceremony), 182
*Acllahuasi* ("House of the Chosen
    Women"), 150–52, 211, 242
*Acllas* ("Chosen Women"), 152, 241, 242
Acorn-eating people, 69–70
Adams, Richard, 14, 16
Adena, 82–84
Aging of skeletal remains, 11–13
Agriculture, 76–79, 90–94, 98–102
Ahpo Hel, Lady, 228
Ahpo Ik, Lady, 163
Ahpo Ix, Lady, 163
Algonquians, 123–24
Allison, Marvin, 53
Alta Mixteca, 171
Alva, Walter, 184
Amaranth, 40–41, 79
"Amazons," 246
Amenorrhea, 137
Anacaona (Taino "queen"), 221–22
Anasazi, 128–29, 262
Anemia, 12, 77, 88, 100
Apaches, 91, 219
Apurimac, 177
Arapaho, 207
Archaeology, 10–16
Arthritis, 13, 53, 86, 90
Arvey, Margaret, 156

Asarpay (Inca priestess), 177
Atahuallpa, 209
Atotoztli (Aztec ruler), 235
Auditory exostoses, 53
Auel, Jean, 34, 278
Autosacrifice, 15
Averbuch site, 88
*Ayllus* (Inca communities), 239–40, 244,
    259, 260
Aztecs, 147–49, 156–59, 163, 178, 179,
    182, 186–88, 210, 234–35, 246,
    248, 263, 265–67

Bakewell, Edward, 107
Barbour, Warren, 153
Barstow, Anne, 276
Barton Gulch, 41
Baskets and basketry, 43, 47, 53, 60, 92,
    280
Batán Grande, 143–45
Beatriz, Doña (Inca princess), 270
Beer, 6, 99, 119, 149–52, 240–41
Benfer, Robert, 59
Berdaches, 251
Bering Land Bridge, 27, 43
Bird Jaguar IV, 162–63
Birthing and babies, 137, 150, 158–60,
    176
Birth rate, 66–68, 81, 85–88, 92, 100
Blackfoot, 207
Borbolla, Daniel Rubín de la, 187

Cummins, Tom, 196–99
*Curaca* class, 268
Curers, 156–58, 167, 171–72, 270
Cusi Rimay, 241
Cuzco, 152, 211, 240–42, 260, 263, 268

Damp, Jonathan, 109
Danzantes, 231, 234, 252
Deg Hit'an (Yupik) people, 31
Deities, 177–82, 237
De la Vega, Garcilaso, 156
De Soto, Hernando, 265
Di Capua, Costanza, 194
Dickel, David, 66, 67
Diehl, Michael, 93
Disease, 12–13, 53–54, 67–68, 76–78, 86–90, 93–94, 97–98, 100, 102, 135–36, 187
DNA, 6, 11, 105, 277
Dolni Vestonice, 43
Domestication, 78–79, 81–82, 88
Donnan, Christopher, 184, 204
Drooker, Penelope, 145, 146

Eight Deer Ocelot Claw, 234
Elizabeth I (English queen), 228
El Niño, 212
Enamel hypoplasia, 12, 59, 100, 102
Epidemics, 86–87, 264
Eskimos, 28
Espinosa, Gaspar de, 209
Etowah, 145
Ezzo, Joseph, 97

Fellatio, 159
Feminism, 4, 7–8, 24, 29–30, 79–80, 236, 244, 279
Fertility. *See* Birth rate
Figurines, 153–55, 189–90, 192–205
Fish, Suzanne, 217–18
Flannery, Kent, 107
Florentine Codex, 156

Food and food production, 27–30, 39–41, 47–50, 67–70, 76–102, 148–50
Frison, George C., 34
Furst, Peter, 44, 171

Galloway, Patricia, 267
Garcia, Mariella, 192
Garcilaso de la Vega, Inca, 156, 242, 265, 270
Gargett, Rob, 107
Gathering, 29, 78–79, 88–90, 101–102
Gero, Joan, 36–37, 48, 141, 237–39
Gilmore, David, 245
Goddesses, 177–83
"Goddess Movement," 278
Grand Canal site, 95
Grasshopper Pueblo, 96–98, 126–28
Great Goddess of Teotihuacán, 179–82
Great Jaguar Paw (Maya ruler), 262
Gros Ventre people, 249
Guacayllano, Catalina ("La Doctora"), 270–72
Guaman Poma, Felipe, 268, 272
Guangala, 196
Guillen, Ann Cyphers, 227
Guillén, Sonia, 53–56

Hallucinogens, 44–45, 171, 199
Hardin Village, 88
Harris lines, 12, 53–54, 59, 102
Hastorf, Christine, 149
Hawikki (Pueblo site), 105, 218
Hayden, Brian, 51–52, 107
Health. *See* Disease
Heerwald site, 262
Hidatsa, 165
Hocquenghem, Anne-Marie, 183
Hohokam, 94, 95, 96, 216
Holm, Olaf, 192
Hooton, Earnest, 209
Hopewell culture, 82–84
Hopi, 214, 262

Maya, 13–20, 116–20, 130–31, 155, 159–62, 201, 206, 209, 227–30, 246, 256–57, 262, 265
Medicine, Beatrice, 249
Meggers, Betty, 198
Mercado, Diego Nuñez, 177
Metallurgy, 141–44
Midwives, 156–61
Milner, George, 261
Mimbres culture, 4, 159
Minnis, Paul, 90, 93
Mississippian phase, 86–90, 145–46, 173–76, 247, 265
Mitchell, Douglas, 95–96
*Mitimas*, 263
Mitlatongo (Skull), 186
Mixtec, 155, 159, 161, 186–89, 230–34
Moche, 17, 20–24, 159, 183–86, 189, 205, 210, 259–60
Mock, Shirley, 190–91
Moctezuma I (Aztec ruler), 147
Moctezuma II (Aztec ruler), 147, 235
Mogollon Tradition, 92–93, 96, 126
Monogamy, 104, 118, 133
Mono people, 35, 69
Monte Albán, 186, 230–231, 252
Montellano, Bernard Ortiz de, 158
Monte Verde, 37–39, 42–43
Morro de Arica, 54–56
Mortality, 11, 59, 66–68, 88–90, 97–98, 100, 102, 137
Moundville, 247
Mummies, 54, 55, 56, 187, 210–13
Music, 205–206, 264

Nahua, 234
Nahuatl, 161
*National Geographic*, 23
Navaho, 114
Nazca, 205, 261
Nine Grass Death, Lady, 186–89, 233
Nine Wind Flint Quechquemitl, Lady, 231
Norris Farm site, 261

Oaxaca, 39–40, 42, 189, 230–31, 252
O'Brian, Patricia, 209
Olmec, 223–27
Oracles, 177–78, 211
Osgood, Cornelius, 32
Osteoarthritis, 58, 90
Osteoporosis, 53, 88
Otuzco, 270
*Outline of Cultural Materials*, 5
Owasco, 123–24

Pacal (Palenque ruler), 228
Pachacamac, 211–13
Pachacuti (Inca emperor), 242
Paiján-style points, 35
Palenque, 227–30
Paloma, 57–61
Pañamarca, 184
Papago, 218
Parita, Chief, 208
Patrilineage, 104, 118, 123–24, 133–34, 220, 228, 240
Pawnee, 209–10
Pearsall, Deborah, 114
Peigan, 250
Piedras Negras site, 18
Piquigua phase, 172
Polyandry, 59, 104
Polygamy, 3
Polygyny, 3, 104, 122, 147, 221, 267, 268
Porotic hyperostosis, 12
Pottery-making. *See* Ceramics
Primogeniture, 241
Proskouriakoff, Tatiana, 18–20
Prostitution, 156
Puebla, 253
Puebloan people, 128, 214, 217

*Quechquemitl*, 179, 180, 253, 256
Quechua, 263
Queens, 147, 220–22, 227–35, 253–57
Quetzalcoatl, 252